D0724403

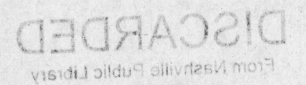

THE MASKS OF CHRIST

BEHIND THE LIES AND COVER-UPS ABOUT THE LIFE OF JESUS

LYNN PICKNETT and CLIVE PRINCE

A TOUCHSTONE BOOK
PUBLISHED BY SIMON & SCHUSTER
NEW YORK   LONDON   TORONTO   SYDNEY

Touchstone
A Division of Simon & Schuster, Inc.
1230 Avenue of the Americas
New York, NY 10020

First Touchstone trade paperback edition November 2008

TOUCHSTONE and colophon are registered trademarks of Simon & Schuster, Inc.

For information about special discounts for bulk purchases, please contact Simon & Schuster
Special Sales at 1-800-456-6798 or business@simonandschuster.com.

Manufactured in the United States of America

1   3   5   7   9   10   8   6   4   2

Library of Congress Cataloging-in-Publication Data
Picknett, Lynn.
Masks of Christ : behind the lies and cover-ups about the life of
Jesus / by Lynn Picknett and Clive Prince.
p.   cm.
"A Touchstone book."
1. Jesus Christ—Historicity.   I. Prince, Clive.   II. Title.
BT303.2.P53 2008
232.9'08—dc22
2008013650

ISBN-13: 978-1-4165-3166-1
ISBN-10:   1-4165-3166-1

In memory of Eric Taylor (1922–2007)
A true gentleman and a true friend

With love

ACKNOWLEDGMENTS

Keith Prince, as always, for his unstinting and enthusiastic help with our research, especially his insight into the parallels between the stories of Jesus and Nero.

Jeffrey Simmons, our agent and friend, who is always there for us.

The team at Simon & Schuster: our editor, Meghan Stevenson; Mark Gompertz; Chris Lloreda; Trish Todd; Ellen Silberman; Martha Schwartz; Rebecca Cox; Cherlynne Li; Alison Brennan; Kevin McCahill; Julie Adams; Michael Kwan; Megan Clancy, and Rachel Bostic.

For their unswerving help, encouragement, and friendship: Vida Adamoli; David Bell; Ashley Brown; Jenny Boll; Robert and Lyndsey Brydon; Deborah and Yvan Cartwright; Michele Cascarano; Bert de Wit; Carina Fearnley; Dr. Robert Feather; Stewart and Katia Ferris; Andrew Gough; William Kirchen; Vera Koutou; Sarah Litvinoff; Jane Lyle; Lisa Mead; John and Joy Millar; Charmaine Misson; Sally Morgan; Paul Nemeth; Craig and Rachel Oakley; Graham Phillips; Phyllis Pointer; Trevor Poots; Lily and David Prince; Francesca Prior; Nathan Renard; Rat Scabies; Javier Sierra; Mick Staley; Sheila and Eric Taylor; Mike Wallington; and Caroline Wise.

Thanks, too, to the staff of the British Library.

CONTENTS

INTRODUCTION

Incredible though it may seem today, in early nineteenth-century Britain it was illegal not to believe that Jesus Christ was the Son of God. Christianity was mandatory: not to believe, at least in a way that was suitably visible to your servants, your peers, and—most of all—your elders and betters, was not an option. Everyone, in any walk of life, was expected not only to believe privately but also to pray publicly: the morning's work in hospital wards, for example, did not begin without doctors and nurses joining in prayer. The legacy of this religious imposition could be seen well into the twentieth century, when to declare oneself a nonbeliever was to provoke horror, certainly from the older generation, to whom being a Christian was synonymous with being both a decent person and a good citizen.

However, things are very different now. In the early twenty-first century, when Britain is notoriously one of the most secular nations in the developed world, one might be forgiven for thinking, in this country at least, that Christianity is largely irrelevant. Yet the roots of ancient Christianity still run deep, and new life is being breathed into the Anglican community by a charismatic and energetic Ugandan archbishop of York and an army of dedicated and courageous women in dog collars. However, it may well be too late for the established churches: to the vast majority of people in Britain they are increasingly irrelevant, while television drama routinely presents devout Christians as slightly sinister, as on the brink of a nervous breakdown, or even as comic weirdos.

However, the failure of the churches to inspire and exalt the masses has not, it seems, led to total apathy toward Christianity in general. A completely unexpected resurgence of interest in the religion on an unprecedented scale erupted, ironically, not from some evangelical crusade or mystical revelation, but from an airport thriller. This was of course the phenomenon of Dan Brown's *The Da Vinci Code*, a book which has swept the globe in the past few years, inspiring a new and urgent desire to see behind the lies, obfuscations, and manifest cover-ups that have largely made Christianity what it is today.

Nevertheless, as we are the first to admit, the furor did not begin and end with *The Da Vinci Code*. In recent years there has been a feeding frenzy among the world's media as certain discoveries have been presented as challenges to the conventional view of Jesus. The major examples were Hollywood film director James Cameron's apparent revelation of the "Jesus family tomb," and the publicity surrounding the discovery of the long-lost Gospel of Judas. Yet what strikes us as most important about these two media "revelations" is the hype and near hysteria that greeted them, the debates among hastily convened talking heads, and the fluttering hearts of Christians everywhere. Obviously Jesus is still a hot topic, but it must be remembered that the media hype only tapped into the great groundswell of interest; it did not create it. Passions will continue to be aroused.

As we rarely pass up an opportunity to point out, our book *The Templar Revelation: Secret Guardians of the True Identity of Christ* (1997) was acknowledged by Brown as a major inspiration for his novel. Our book is unashamedly part of a subset of the "alternative history" genre that is regarded by academia as largely beyond the pale: those who—after attempting to strip away the many layers of ecclesiastical propaganda and canonical editing and revision—ask fundamental questions about Christianity and try to provide some answers, especially about its true origins.

Two sets of reactions to *The Templar Revelation* made us realize that a book such as *The Masks of Christ* was needed. The first came from within the Christian community. Many took the line—as they did with other books proposing alternative views of the origins of Christianity—that if they could show our hypothesis to be wrong, then they would have proved that the conventional idea of Jesus, the one that underpinned the four Gospels of the New Testament and was imposed on its flock by the Church for two thousand years, remains unassailable.

This claim doesn't stand up for a minute. The one thing beyond any doubt is that, from a historical perspective, the conventional view of Jesus is wrong. A succession of discoveries in the past two centuries has shown that many of the Gospel stories are mistaken or distorted—which is why researchers such as ourselves feel the need to try to discover what really happened and to offer alternatives, simply because there are so many embarrassing holes and inconsistencies in the conventional narratives.

One of the most unsettling discoveries of all was that the vast majority of this new knowledge is readily acknowledged by New Testament scholars and theologians, but only within the safety of academe's high, cloistered walls. It is rarely even discussed outside—except in our sort of book. And the last people who will ever hear about it are the devout who frequent church groups and Bible study classes. There is obviously something wrong with the state of affairs if the only way they get to hear about this new knowledge is through the inevitable furors that surround despised and derided alternative nonfiction works such as, classically, *The Holy Blood and the Holy Grail* (1982) by Michael Baigent, Richard Leigh, and Henry Lincoln; our own books; and, of course, imaginative treatments like Brown's thriller. The rank-and-file Christians are the ones who have been betrayed over the years and are still being kept in near-complete ignorance about the often cataclysmic flaws in the Gospel stories, treated condescendingly by the scholars and priests as if they were children unable to cope with the revelation that Santa does not exist. (Pope John Paul II's pronouncement that Christ was not actually born on December 25 upset a great many of his flock, and even greater revelations about the man believed to be God would have a traumatic effect on millions—but then whose fault is that? Who lied to them in the first place?)

Some conventionalists argue that the very fact that so many different—and contradictory—theories have been proposed somehow proves that the traditional view of Jesus is more or less correct. An advocate of this view is British author Geoffrey Ashe, writing in *The Virgin* (1988):

> He [Jesus] is made out to have been a moralist, or an exorcist, or a healer, or a prophet of doomsday, or a socialist, or a pacifist, or a lunatic, or a Jewish nationalist, or an Essene Teacher of Righteous-

ness. He is made out to have been a sun-myth or a vegetation-myth . . . or a sacred mushroom. The only plain deduction from this critical chaos is that the reality was richer than the critics care to admit.[1]

In his statement Ashe manages to miss two important points. The first is that the reason so many researchers, both inside and outside academia, feel a need to try to identify the historical Jesus but find him behind so many masks is precisely that the traditional view has so many flaws. The fact that they come up with different solutions may be owing to the limitations of the available data and their own intellectual biases, but that does not mean that one of them hasn't managed to hit on the correct solution. They don't necessarily cancel each other out.

The second overlooked point is that the list of the "critical chaos" theories should also include the notion that Jesus was the Son of God sent to save humanity from its sins. Just because that was the concept seized on and perpetuated, often aided by fire and sword, by the Church, it is not set in stone. In fact, seen objectively—as it should be—it is just another theory and has no inherently greater claim to be true than any other.

One of the most unsettling aspects of Jesus' masks is how contradictory they are. As long ago as 1908 one prominent German Protestant theologian noted that, working with the same data, scholars could come up with images as divergent as "King and beggar . . . revolutionary and sage, fighter and prince of peace, ruler and servant, man of action and poet."[2]

More encouragingly, the Christian establishment's response to our book was to a large extent balanced by the reactions that came loud and strong from many of our readers. In presenting our alternative picture of the Jesus story in *The Templar Revelation*, naturally we had to attempt to explain the shortcomings of the conventional view—the discoveries that have challenged certain long-cherished ideas and in many cases shown them to be false. However, simple lack of space meant that although we had to summarize some of the latest findings, inevitably we had to concentrate on the aspects most relevant to the main themes of our book, particularly the relationship between Jesus and John the Baptist, and Mary Magdalene.

Talking to our readers made us realize that they longed to know more about the problems with and challenges to the conventional picture—especially as it was still being taught in schools and churches as if nothing had changed.

For both these reasons we felt there was a need for a book that concentrated on those aspects, summarizing the current state of New Testament discoveries and setting out what is now known to be accurate, what has been proven to be false, and what is still uncertain about Jesus' life and mission.

In the last ten years, naturally, we have continued to delve into the subject of Christianity and attempted to resolve the questions we had left unanswered. *The Masks of Christ* not only carries the story forward but also took us into unexpected new territory, which in some cases meant that we had to revise our views, shifting the emphasis here and there. Gratifyingly, however, the main conclusions of *The Templar Revelation* have not only stood up to the scrutiny of a further decade, but have been vindicated by new research and discoveries—both our own and others' in the field. Now we can present a much clearer and more three-dimensional picture: certain matters we could only speculate about ten years ago have now hardened, becoming surer and more exciting. Of course we can never pretend to have all the answers—on this subject the information simply isn't complete—but we consider we have gone more than the extra mile.

One thing that has become startlingly clear, however, is the extent of the Church's cover-up of certain matters that are absolutely fundamental to the understanding of Christianity and Christ himself. And make no mistake, it continues to this day.

The Jesus of History and the Christ of Faith

Books such as this, which seek to find the historical Jesus, usually begin with a disclaimer drawing a distinction between the "Jesus of history" and the "Christ of faith." The former is an individual—maybe man, maybe God, perhaps a bit of both—who lived out his strangely significant life in a specific geographical location in a certain period of history, and because he did, he is open to the same methods of historical inquiry as any other individual from the past. On the other hand, the Jesus Christ of pure faith is beyond the reach of historians, since they have no means of dealing with the transcendental and ineffable, and what people claim to "know" in their hearts and souls can never be weighed, measured, or assessed by any of the usual academic methods.

However, this distinction is in many ways an evasion. Christianity, more than any other religion, demands that certain events really happened, in real locations and on specific dates. In most religions it is the revelation, not the circumstances in which it is given, that is important. Christianity, by contrast, is based on an *event*, or sequence of events, through which salvation was made available to all: the crucifixion and resurrection of Jesus Christ. This opens up the "revelation" of Christianity to historical inquiry and poses a risk for the religion: if it could be shown, for example, that these events never happened, or happened in a way fundamentally different from the Gospels' description, then Christianity has a major problem.

This makes it a top priority to establish the reliability of the writers who recorded the alleged revelation. Our major source of information about Jesus is a set of texts—the four New Testament Gospels—which can be examined according to the same criteria that may be applied to any historical document. And once their narrative is seen in the cold light of day, it becomes apparent that not only have the writers rewritten the story to suit their own personal agendas, but what they produced was subsequently edited and changed, sometimes long after the event. It is a grave error to take anything the Gospels say about Jesus as fact simply because it is in the Gospels.

To many, particularly modern evangelical and born-again Christians, Christianity is an experience, not an argument. The presence of Christ is something that is *felt*, creating an inner certainty beyond any logical analysis or criticism. And it is true that it is impossible for an outsider to argue with this kind of experience, to prove that it doesn't mean what the individual who has lived through the experience believes it means. But even given such subjectively shifting sand, there is an important point to be made.

In discussions with evangelical Christians—particularly during public debates generated by *The Da Vinci Code*—we have found a certain doublethink concerning a historical approach to Jesus. Many simply dismiss the discussion of historical and linguistic details as irrelevant compared with their inner experience. This is fine—except that the same people then turn to the Gospels to try to explain their faith to others, or to persuade others that they too should become Christians. They want it both ways.

The Jewish Jesus versus the Pagan Jesus

Another major reason we had for writing this book was that the debate surrounding one of the most important themes of *The Templar Revelation* has intensified. As we argued, Jesus owed at least as much to religious and spiritual ideas drawn from the non-Jewish—i.e., pagan—world as to the Jewish milieu. Since 1997 this split has become even more polarized in the world of New Testament scholarship.

One school—it must be said, the majority—has seen Jesus in ever more Jewish terms, arguing that his mission was aimed solely at Jews and expressed solely in Jewish terms, so that the creation of a separate religion in his name was a huge mistake. For this group—including James D. Tabor and Robert Eisenman—all the passages that distinguish Christianity from Judaism, in terms both of Jesus' significance and of subsequent religious practices, were later inventions, tacked on by the Gentile world. By contrast, a very influential faction, personified by Burton L. Mack, sees it the other way round: Jesus is perceived in an ever *less* Jewish context and as more influenced by ideas from the Greek world around him. For this school, it was the *Jewish* elements in Jesus' story that were later inventions.

It is revealing that two sets of equally eminent scholars, working with exactly the same source material, can arrive at two such diametrically opposed positions. But in the hothouse world of biblical scholarship this is the norm, not the exception.

Of all the masks given to Christ, these two are the most critical. Whether he was essentially Jewish or pagan is the single most important question that can ever be asked about Christ, since we can never begin to understand him without answering it. Trying to resolve it—by finding either conclusive evidence for one or the other or a way of reconciling the contradictory evidence—is the very backbone of this book.

Lynn Picknett
Clive Prince
London, 2008

1

BETWEEN THE LINES

For one of the most beloved and influential characters in history, Jesus Christ is curiously elusive. Our mission to discover the truth about the teacher from first-century Palestine who is still believed by millions the world over to be nothing less than God incarnate is seriously hindered by the paucity of reliable writings about him. Jesus himself left no written testimony, nor indeed did any of the primary eyewitnesses to his life and pivotal death. For such a uniquely significant individual, his life is strangely unrecorded.

There *are* writings that purport to be accurate accounts of Jesus' life—the most familiar being the four New Testament (or "canonical") Gospels of Matthew, Mark, Luke, and John. But as they stand, they are a cacophony of different voices, as well as the result of later editing and accretions over the centuries. And although it is very likely that parts of contemporary records are embedded in those early texts, even beginning to peel off the layers of myth and sometimes—it must be said—outright propaganda that have accrued over two millennia is by no means a straightforward task.

Delving and Digging

There are not even any archaeological remains to compensate for the relative lack of written records. Unsurprisingly, modern Israel is a magnet for Christian tourism. What devotee of Christ would not want to walk in his footsteps by the Sea of Galilee or retrace the terrible journey through Jerusalem to Golgotha, the Place of the Skull, where he died on the cross? Yet of the many individual sites on the Christian tourist map—such as the Church of the Nativity in Bethlehem and the Church of the Holy Sepulchre in Jerusalem—in all cases the link is merely traditional. Sadly—and to many Christians no doubt astonishingly—there is no hard evidence that any of these particular places was actually associated with Jesus. Every one of them is dubious, and most are provably bogus.

The problem with accepting any of these sites as genuine is that there was a huge displacement and discontinuity of population in that area between Jesus' lifetime and the arrival of the first pilgrims in the fourth century, after Christianity became the official religion of the Roman Empire. When the Romans suppressed two great uprisings by the Jews, in 66–70 CE and 132–35 CE, whole towns and cities were depopulated either by massacres or enslavement. So did anyone really remember, three hundred years later, where these events had happened—or were the locals just trying to make a quick shekel out of the first Christian tourists?

Besides these dubious traditional sites, certain archaeological discoveries may relate directly to Jesus' life, but none is proven beyond doubt and, even if they were, few would add substantially to the sum of our knowledge. For example, in the 1960s there were excavations in the area around the ancient synagogue in the town of Capernaum (modern Kefar Nahum) on the shore of the Sea of Galilee, where, according to three of the Gospels, Jesus first began preaching and where he recruited his first disciples. The archaeologists uncovered the foundations of several nearby houses from the same period that belonged to fishermen (hardly a revelation in a lakeside town). A Christian church had been built over one of them in the fifth century CE—some four hundred years after Jesus' time. Graffiti scratched into plaster indicated that the worshippers believed that the church stood on the site of the house of Peter, the disciple who, according to the New Testament, was closest to Jesus.

However, all this tells us is that four centuries after Peter lived, local Christians *believed* the house was his. Why they did so is unknown, so it is impossible to judge whether they were right. Capernaum had been utterly destroyed during the two Jewish revolts and since repopulated. The fifth-century Christians may have simply picked one house on the basis of accounts in the Gospels, which imply that Peter's house was close to the synagogue.

Some of the most dramatic claims based on archaeological finds relate to ossuaries, the stone or clay boxes used by first-century Jews for the bones of their dead. Because of a shortage of space, they would place the shrouded corpses in a tomb for a year, until the flesh had rotted away, then store the bones in an ossuary laid in a family vault, usually a cave.

The late twentieth century saw several media sensations over claims that certain ossuaries had some direct or indirect connection with Jesus. Some were found by archaeologists; others surfaced in the antiquities trade. The latter are always treated with caution; solid evidence of their provenance is essential before they can be accepted as genuine.

Unsurprisingly, the most dramatic discoveries are those claimed to contain the bones of Jesus himself, since if genuine, they would not only provide hard evidence for his existence but also undermine the very reason he took such a hold on history. As he is supposed to have triumphed over death by rising from his tomb and, after making several appearances to his followers, to have been taken up bodily into heaven, the discovery of his entombed body would utterly destroy the religion founded in his name.

Several ossuaries have been discovered over the years that bear the inscribed name of Jesus (or Yeshua), and even of Jesus, son of Joseph. This is hardly surprising: depending on the survey, Jesus was either the third or sixth commonest male name,[1] and as Joseph was the second most popular, to find a Joseph who named one of his sons Jesus is not very remarkable.

In 2002 another stir was caused by an ossuary that came into the possession of an Israeli antiquities dealer; it was inscribed "James, son of Joseph, brother of Jesus." Although it was of uncertain provenance, various clues—the style of writing and laboratory tests—pointed to the ossuary's having originated in the sixties CE, when Jesus' brother James is believed to have died. However, the dealer, Oded Golan, and three others were charged in December 2004 with being members of a ring that had forged antiquities for twenty years, and the ossuary was said to be part of their scam. At the time of writing the case continues.

As James, Joseph, and Jesus were all common names, we can never be sure that the inscription refers to the biblical characters. And even if it did, it would merely confirm what we already know from written sources: that Jesus existed and had a brother named James.

But in February 2007 another discovery of a "Jesus" ossuary caused an almost seismic sensation across the globe, not only because it was championed by Oscar-winning film director James Cameron, but also because, at last, it seemed that there was solid evidence that it really did contain the bones of Jesus Christ. But could it be true? For a start, despite the sudden clamor of banner headlines, the discovery had actually been made back in 1980 and had been the subject of a BBC documentary in 1996. But further analysis since then had, it was claimed, uncovered new evidence of a connection with Jesus. We will discuss the Talpiot ossuary more fully when we come to Jesus' resurrection, so here let us note simply that there are some serious—even embarrassing—flaws in the argument for its authenticity.

Throughout Christian history there have been claims that certain artifacts connected with Jesus or others in the Gospel stories—holy relics—have survived, such as fragments of the cross on which Jesus was crucified, the nails and pieces of the crown of thorns, and so on. However, it can be said with confidence that all these alleged relics were fakes, circulating among gullible pilgrims with more money than sense. At the height of the medieval and early Renaissance relics industry in Europe, there were dozens of Our Lady's chemises on the circuit, at least half a dozen of the baby Jesus' foreskin, and a timber yard full of splinters from the True Cross. As the craze for relics escalated, monasteries and cathedrals vied with one another to possess the most impressive artifact.

Even genuine relics, however, would be of limited use to our quest. Even if one tiny bit of the cross, or a nail, could be dated to the first century, there could be no guarantee that it had really been used at Jesus' execution. And it certainly would provide no confirmation that any of the events recounted in the Gospels really happened, or much useful information about them if they did.

Some would say that the Turin Shroud is the one tangible piece of evidence to link us with Jesus and his era. However, as we show in our book *The Turin Shroud: How da Vinci Fooled History* (1994, revised 2006), the evidence is overwhelming that the cloth is a forgery—if not the most remarkable fake ever!

Paul the Godmaker

Jesus himself apparently wrote nothing. Not only do we not have anything even purporting to be from him, but no early Christian commentator—gospel writer or Church Father—makes any reference to him setting down his thoughts. He is only ever described as giving his teachings orally, either in private sessions with his inner circle of disciples or in public.

It gets worse. Neither are there any writings dating from Jesus' actual lifetime or the years immediately afterward, although his closest followers and those who joined the movement in the years after the crucifixion would undoubtedly have told or set down stories about him in their efforts to expound his teachings. Those oral and written memories were later brought together in the four Gospels and other early Christian writings. But we no longer have the original sources, and what we do have has clearly been changed over the intervening period, so it would be a mistake to take any of these texts at face value. It is possible, however, with dedicated detective work to determine what the originals may have been like, and to assess the value of the material we do have.

Incredibly, the first known Christian writings are by someone who knew nothing about Jesus and indeed had no wish to know. Saint Paul, the persecutor turned zealot, created a new and potent religion in the name of a man he never knew by interpreting his life and mission in his own vivid and mystical way, remaking Christ in his own image. But although today Paul's is almost the only version of Christianity practiced the world over, in his own day it was by no means the sole interpretation of Christ's message.

Paul's fourteen Letters, or Epistles, date from roughly between the late forties and early sixties CE. His Letter to the Galatians, written between 48 and 54, is generally accepted as the oldest known Christian writing. The Letters are clearly only a fraction of Paul's output, and—to modern readers especially—they are extremely frustrating, making no attempt to describe Jesus the man or the background of his life.

Paul was a fanatical preacher and missionary of the new spiritual movement or sect (it was not yet a religion proper) which called itself simply "the Way" (*odos*)—a common description of religious movements at the time, with no exceptional significance. (The term "Christian" had yet to be coined. According to the Acts of the Apostles, it was first used of believers in Antioch in Syria, and probably intended as an insult.)

As he journeyed around the Roman Empire—mainly the eastern Mediterranean—preaching the Way, Paul won new converts and organized networks of local groups, *ecclesia*. With one exception, which addresses a personal issue, Paul's Epistles deal with matters of organization, administration, and discipline—encouraging, exhorting, censuring, and reproaching—besides addressing vexing questions about the new faith.

He wrote in Greek, the common language of the eastern half of the Roman Empire after the Romans essentially took over the nations conquered by the Greek Alexander the Great. More specifically, Paul used the vernacular Greek dialect Koine, spoken by virtually everybody as a second language; when the Gospels appeared, they too were written in Koine.

Too fragile on their scrolls of papyrus to survive, none of Paul's original writings has come down to us, but his letters were collected and copied at an early date. However, authorship was regarded in a different light in the first century, and those who came after Paul—much as they respected his memory—had no qualms about inserting their own contributions into his writings, or even completely changing them. Nor did Paul's near contemporaries see anything wrong with putting his name to entirely new texts. As the French theologian and philosopher Jean-Yves Leloup notes, "In the ancient world, the concept of literary property was radically different from what it is now. An author who wrote under the name of an apostle was considered to be performing an act of homage, not an act of forgery." [2] Even in the early days the authenticity of some of Paul's Letters was disputed. For example, even though it was and still is included in the New Testament, the Letter to the Hebrews was recognized at least as early as the fourth century to be by another author.[3]

But what do Paul's Letters tell us about Jesus and the early days of the Way? And where did he get his information about his Lord? Immediately we find ourselves plunged into the problem of the Jesus of history versus the Christ of faith. Paul never knew Jesus. His entire belief that Jesus was divine came not from anything the real man said or did but from the visions and voices he experienced after Jesus' death. With what might well be considered objectively as staggering chutzpah or just plain insensitive arrogance, Paul believed that those who *had* known and followed Jesus, even members of his own family and closest disciples—most significantly Peter—had got it all wrong. Only he knew the truth. Unsurprisingly, his lofty and elitist attitude was to cause major ructions within the Christian communities.

Even though Christianity as we know it is, unquestionably, based on Paul's interpretation of Jesus' mission, right from the outset this basis required belief—faith—in his mystical experiences, and not just his famous conversion on the road to Damascus but also the voices and visions he claimed continued to guide his missionary activities. This conviction is echoed by today's evangelical Christians, who regard attempts to set Jesus in the context of historical fact as irrelevant when compared with their own powerful and intimate inner experience.

It is only possible to piece together the bare bones of Paul's life story from scattered references in his Letters and the Acts of the Apostles, the continuation of Luke's Gospel that is essentially Paul's biography. However, Acts was compiled probably two or three decades after his death, and therefore has to be treated with caution. Indeed, there are contradictions between the biographical information in Acts and Paul's own writings that show, unsurprisingly, that the author of Acts has at least embellished, if not actively mythologized, his tale.

However, it is just about possible to piece together Paul's story as follows: no one knows when he was born or precisely how old he was when he undertook his self-imposed mission. Acts describes him as a "young man" (*neanias*, an adolescent) at the time of the first persecutions of Jesus' followers in Jerusalem, within at most five years of the crucifixion (but as we will see, almost certainly considerably less). But this account is immediately contradicted by Acts having him take the lead in the persecutions, which he could do only as a grown man. However, Paul's greatest period of missionary activity, during which the Epistles were written, did not begin until the late forties CE, and he disappears from history in the early sixties, by which time he was writing of the travails of old age. A reasonable guess is that he was between fifty and sixty when he wrote his last letters, which puts the year of his birth between 1 and 10 CE.

Paul was Jewish by birth and religion—from the tribe of Benjamin, he writes—and trained in the schools of the Pharisees. He was also, according to Acts, proud of his Roman citizenship, which bestowed privileges he often exploited. Acts tells that he was born at Tarsus, a prosperous seaport in Cilicia (today's southern Turkey), and was by profession a tent maker, an important and respectable trade. He had settled in Jerusalem by the time his story really starts.

From Acts we learn that he was known by two names, Saul (which is Jewish) and Paul (which is Roman), although it seems that he favored the second during his missionary days, probably because "Paul" identified him with his Gentile flock. Roman citizens customarily took three names, the last being a cognomen, a nickname based on their appearance or something else distinctive about them. "Paul" makes sense only as a cognomen, since it means "small." We never learn Paul's full name.

Paul acknowledged that he was a zealous Jew, and presumably he moved from Tarsus to Jerusalem to be close to the Temple, the heart of the Jewish faith. But like most fanatics, he was paradoxically easy to convert. And that is exactly what happened. Once an extremist, always an extremist, but not always on the same side.

Paul's fanaticism for Judaism made him virulently opposed to the new sect begun by Jesus' followers, which had attracted the disapproval of the Jewish authorities in Jerusalem. Acts states—this incident is conspicuous by its absence from the Letters—that Paul was involved in the killing of the first Christian martyr, Stephen, though only to the extent that he looked after the cloaks of those doing the stoning. Later Paul volunteered his services to suppress the new sect, eventually asking for letters of authority from the Temple leaders to go to Damascus in Syria and bring back to Jerusalem the Christians who had moved there. It was either on that road or in Damascus itself that Paul had his famous and dramatic revelation (in Greek an apocalypse)—a vision of Jesus that turned him from Jesus' most vehement enemy to his greatest champion.

Curiously, Paul himself gives no details of his conversion in the Letters, just stating that God chose "to reveal his son in [not 'to'] me" and that it happened in or near Damascus.[4] Acts tells the dramatic story of a dazzling light accompanying Jesus' voice and Paul being struck blind and subsequently miraculously cured by a Christian named Ananias.

The revelation could not have happened before 33 or after 37 CE. Paul himself says that afterwards he did not return to Jerusalem for three years, during which he traveled between Arabia and Damascus. He describes how, on his return visit to Damascus, he was lowered from the town's walls in a basket to flee from the officials of the king, the Nabataean Arab ruler Aretas IV. This king had captured Syria from Roman-controlled Palestine in 36 CE and died four years later. We are not told if Aretas ruled Damascus at the time of Paul's first visit, but he certainly did at the end of the three-year period, which therefore must have started some time between 33 and 37 CE.

Paul believed he had been chosen by Jesus not merely on the road to Damascus but even before his birth, to bring God's true message not just to the Jews but to all mankind. Even Paul's persecution of Jesus' followers was part of God's plan, since his volte-face would give his preaching on his Lord's behalf more impact. He believed not only that he himself received instruction directly from Jesus, but, most important, that he alone had a full and true understanding of Christ's message, more so than even those who had been close to him. Paul saw it as his mission to take the "gospel"—the "good news"—to as many people as possible and characteristically threw himself into his new role with zeal at least equal to that of his persecuting days.

The core of Paul's message was that the end was nigh. For him, God's purpose in sending Jesus to the earth was to set in train events that would lead to the end of the world and the final judgment—

which Paul clearly thought would happen within his own lifetime. He invested his preaching, that salvation came through Jesus' death and resurrection, with such passion and urgency because he believed that only true followers of the Way like himself would pass God's judgment and be saved. Paul was in a race to proclaim the "good news" to as many people as he could before time literally ran out. As Ed Parish Sanders, the eminent American New Testament scholar and author of several studies of Paul, notes:

> No two elements of Paul's thought are more certain, or more consistently expressed, than his conviction that the full salvation of believers and the destruction of unbelievers lay in the near future, and his related conviction that Christians possessed the Spirit as the present guarantee of future salvation.[5]

So, although Paul was the founder of Christianity as a religion, such a founding was emphatically not his intention. Had he known that a global church based on his ideas would exist two thousand years in the future, he would have been appalled, disillusioned, and utterly crushed, since it would have destroyed the very basis of his belief. What excited and motivated him was that there would be no future. So we have a great irony: *the very existence of today's Christian churches invalidates the basis on which the religion was founded.*

Nevertheless, can Paul enlighten us about Jesus? In fact, we learn almost nothing about Jesus from Paul, who was blithely unconcerned with his Lord's earthly life. As he had his own direct line to Jesus and God, he had no need for biography, declaring with supreme confidence: "the gospel I preached is not of human origin. I did not receive it from any human source, nor was I taught it; rather I received it by revelation from Jesus Christ."[6] For Paul, Jesus' story started with his death on the cross; everything before that was irrelevant.

Far from seeking out those who had known Jesus to absorb their memories, as would today's hagiographers, Paul went out of his way to avoid all eyewitnesses, also evincing no interest in stories or writings being circulated by Jesus' companions. Virtually the sum of what Paul knows—or deems important—about Jesus' life is contained in a single paragraph in his First Letter to the Corinthians:

That Christ died for our sins according to the Scriptures, that he was buried, that he was raised on the third day according to the Scriptures, and that he appeared to Cephas [Peter], and then to the Twelve. After that, he appeared to more than five hundred of the brothers and sisters at the same time, most of whom are still living, though some have fallen asleep. Then he appeared to James, then to all the Apostles, and last of all he appeared to me also, as to one abnormally born [meaning "runt of the litter"].[7]

Earlier in the same Letter he refers to Jesus as being "betrayed"—without elaborating—on the night that he initiated the ritual of the Eucharist, the mystical partaking of bread and wine. In others he speaks of Jesus' being crucified, and in the First Letter to Timothy he refers to his being tried by Pontius Pilate, the Roman governor of Judea (although this is one of the Epistles of uncertain authenticity).

There are certain fundamental—and remarkably significant—omissions. For example, Paul never refers to the *physical* resurrection of Jesus that today's Christians believe in as the bedrock of the faith. Although he "is risen" on the third day, he appeared to Paul only in the spirit. Similarly he never refers to Jesus' being born of a virgin.

Through Paul's Eyes

Although Paul was never slow to imply that his was the most important mission, his Letters make it obvious that he was competing with several other forms of the new movement, mentioning other apostles working throughout the Empire and stating that the Way had even been established in Rome itself, and not by him. The most serious competition to Paul's movement came from Jesus' former disciples—who, according to later Christian writings, had been personally instructed by Jesus to carry on his work and word—and his own family. This other version of Christianity, which was radically different from Paul's, was based in Jerusalem and led by Jesus' brother James "the Just" and the leading disciple, Peter. But that version, too, was already spreading beyond the borders of Palestine.

The fundamental split between "Pauline" and Jerusalem Christianity is well known today, but incredibly it was only as recently as

1831 that the German scholar Ferdinand Christian Baur first suggested that even the earliest Christians suffered schisms and major disagreement. Until then, despite the evidence in the New Testament itself, the accepted idea was that there had only ever been one form of Christianity, taught by Jesus and continued by his Apostles, Paul included.

With amazing gall, Paul even calls the preachers of "the other Jesus" "false brothers"[8]—quite astonishing given their closeness to Jesus—but, no doubt tellingly, he never tried to compete. He specifically avoided evangelizing in places where other Apostles had already established their missions, declaring with perhaps a hint of bravado, "It has always been my ambition to preach the gospel where Christ was not known, so that I would not be building on someone else's foundation."[9]

From what little we know of the Jerusalem group (almost entirely from the unreliable Acts, with a few scraps from Paul's Epistles), its members lived communally, pooling property and money. They saw themselves as a sect within Judaism, not a breakaway movement, observing the Jewish Law and worshipping at the Jerusalem Temple. Even so, the Jewish authorities looked upon these dissidents with suspicion, at times taking draconian action and even executing the group's leaders—which was where Paul came in. Exactly why they disliked the Jerusalem Christians is unclear.

As the early records are so heavily Pauline in attitude, there is no way we can be absolutely sure exactly how the Jewish believers viewed Jesus, but evidently they saw him as the Messiah prophesied in the Jewish scriptures, the divine king who would deliver his people from oppression. But Paul preached a radically different idea, in which Jesus' death became the whole point: he acknowledged that Jesus fulfilled the criteria laid down by the great Jewish prophets by which the Messiah would be recognized but argued that God had changed his mind about the nature of the role. He was no longer sent to physically deliver the Jewish people but sent to usher in the Day of Judgment—the end of the world. It was Paul who created the concept of Jesus as redeemer.

Paul proclaimed that Jesus voluntarily took on human form and sacrificed himself on the cross to redeem not only humankind but even the cosmos itself, his death becoming the pivotal point of history and creation. And it was this idea that became the fundamental doctrine of the Christian church.

Paul also introduced an important change to Jesus' title of Christ (*Christos*). The Gospels tell us that his immediate followers called him "the Christ" ("*ho Christos*"), showing they regarded him as the prophesied Messiah. Paul dropped the definite article, calling Jesus simply *Christos*, turning it into a name—Jesus Christ—probably to emphasize his uniqueness and distance him further from the Jewish interpretation of his mission.

Another vital difference was that Paul believed that the "good news" and the possibility of salvation offered by Jesus' sacrifice were not reserved exclusively for Jews but available to any man or woman who accepts its truth. This fundamental difference between Paul's vision of the religion and that of the Jerusalem community accounts for the discussion in the Letters of issues such as the relevance of the Laws of Moses and whether, for example, male Christians should be circumcised. For Paul, faith in Jesus Christ had replaced acceptance of the Law as the "qualification" to become one of God's chosen.

The essence of being one of that Elect was a mystical union between the believer and Jesus. Many authorities argue that in this Paul was influenced by the pagan mystery cults of the Roman and Greek world, with which he would have been familiar, and that he freely borrowed concepts from them.

Paul's reinterpretation of Jesus and redefining of the message for the Empire's Gentile population mean that right at the beginning of the Christian religion there was a fundamental split between a Jewish form of "Jesus-ism" based in Jerusalem and a Hellenistic or pagan form. The often tangled relationship between the two is one of the recurring problems in identifying the historical Jesus behind them. Michael Goulder, professor of biblical studies at the University of Birmingham, sums up in *A Tale of Two Missions* (1994) (his emphasis):

> From as far back as we can trace (to the 40s [CE]) there never was a single, united church. There were (in fact from the 30s) two missions: one run from Jerusalem, with Peter and the sons of Zebedee in charge, and later James, Jesus' brother, and other members of his

family; the other run by Paul, from various centres. The two missions were agreed about the supreme significance of Jesus, but they disagreed about almost everything else—the validity of the Bible, whether the Kingdom of God had arrived or not, sex, money, work, tongues, visions, healings, Jesus' divinity, and the resurrection of the dead, for example. The New Testament gives the impression of a united, developing body of belief because it is a *selection* of writings; naturally it was selected by the winning mission, that is the Paulines, and that is why it consists of the Epistles of Paul (and his followers), and four Gospels, two of them ultra-Pauline and two building bridges to Jerusalem.[10]

Today's prevailing view is that the movement founded by Jesus was entirely Jewish, and that Paul "paganized" it, creating a religion that was totally different from what his Savior intended. According to this view, through an accident of history the Jerusalem version was wiped out by the Romans at the end of the Jewish Revolt in 70 CE, when the population was either slaughtered or carried off into slavery. However, the story is much more complicated than that.

For a start, the Jewish Christians appear to have survived the fall of Jerusalem. In the second century the Church Fathers condemned as heretical a Christian sect known as the Ebionites (from the Aramaic *ebionim*, "the poor"), who interpreted Jesus' life and mission purely in terms of his being the Jewish Messiah. The Ebionites—who were still being condemned two centuries after that—were possibly remnants of the Jerusalem church. (Paul once describes the group led by James the Just as "the poor.")

And the idea that Christianity was entirely Jewish until Paul came along and paganized it—generating an entirely new religion out of what had been just another Jewish sect—is certainly an oversimplification. So too is the concept that embryonic Christianity was split into just two branches: there were in fact several other forms, all competing on the same territory. Paul himself warned against those who preached "other Jesuses."[11]

Paul was not alone in "Hellenizing" the Jesus movement—interpreting it in terms of pagan concepts of divinity. There appears to have been a very early flourishing Hellenistic-Christian community in Antioch (the third-largest city in the Roman Empire after Rome and Alexandria), which Paul joined but did not found. This community chose not to observe the Jewish Law, especially the dietary rules, leading to great tension between the two, a departure from the Law that was *not* due to Paul but was already a feature of the community.[12]

The other apostles against whom Paul warns were preaching both the Jewish version and the other Hellenized versions, but we also learn from Acts that there were "apostles" spreading the word not of Jesus but of John the Baptist. So there were four categories of missionary proselytizing the Empire: the Jewish version, Paul and those following his "revealed" form, others who also added a Hellenistic twist, and John the Baptist's followers. It was a busy, chaotic, and heady mix, all inspired by those events that had taken place in a few short years in a far-flung corner of the Empire.

The fact that the movement founded by Jesus split so early into Jewish and Hellenistic groups suggests an important ambiguity. If Jesus had been, as many argue, entirely Jewish, preaching purely for Jews, why should the markedly un-Jewish Antioch community have sprung up so early? On the other hand, if Jesus had not specifically targeted Jews or was even (as many maintain) explicitly critical of their religion, why should others of that first generation have built their worship around the Jerusalem Temple?

Matthew, Mark, Luke, and John

Although Paul seemed to care nothing about Jesus the man, stories about Jesus' deeds and words circulated among his followers, certainly orally and perhaps in writing. That much we can be sure about—but not much more than that. Those stories about him eventually coalesced into written texts, and from this pool a few were selected as the most authentic, in time being sanctioned by the Church as the four Gospels of the Christian New Testament. Many of the rest were banned, some just dropped out of favor, and a few were tolerated alongside the officially endorsed accounts. No one knows how many other gospels were circulating in the early years, although Luke's begins with the statement that "many" before him had set down accounts of Jesus' deeds.

The Gospels attributed to Matthew, Mark, Luke, and John respectively are the main sources of information about Jesus' life known to most practicing Christians today. But they were put together several decades after he lived by men who had not been there at the time. And while the authors used material that had been handed down from those days, it reached them mixed with other, less reliable information. The main problem facing any biblical detective is to strip away the fantasy to reach the anecdotes from people who had actually known Jesus and seen him in action.

The process of selection that created the New Testament meant that a great deal of material has been lost to us. And there is no way we can be sure that the people who selected its constituent books—a process finalized three centuries after Jesus lived, when Christianity became the official religion of the Roman Empire—made the right choices.

Apart from a few works that deviated not too far from the version authorized by the Church and were tolerated as "apocryphal," for most of Christian history the fact that any sources about Jesus outside the New Testament even existed was known to very few. The four New Testament Gospels were the preeminent and unquestioned source of information, and it is only over the past two hundred years or so that scholars have come to recognize that sources of equal weight exist apart from them. And, more scandalously, it is only in recent decades that this fact has filtered through to a wider public—largely through popular but derided books such as *The Holy Blood and the Holy Grail* and *The Da Vinci Code*.

Despite attempts to say otherwise by the clergy and certain academics, the fact remains that at least some of these other sources have as strong a claim to validity as the gospels chosen for inclusion in the New Testament. But first let us take a look at the famous four, and the Acts of the Apostles, which deals with events after Jesus' resurrection, as it was written by the same author as Luke's Gospel, being basically a sequel.

To understand the shaping of the Gospels, we need first to consider two crucial and traumatic events of the late first century CE. Paul disappears, rather mysteriously, from history at the beginning of the sixties, and Acts ends with him in Rome awaiting an audience with the Emperor Nero in order to appeal against charges brought against him in Judea. Tradition says he (and Peter) were martyred in

64, during the first trauma, the first persecutions of Christians in Rome, ordered by Nero.

The second trauma was the Jewish Revolt of 66–70. An uprising by nationalist Jews had managed to drive the Romans out of a substantial part of Palestine. Naturally the Empire dispatched an army to retake the province, and although the Jews held on to Jerusalem for four years, after a bitter siege Roman troops ruthlessly sacked the city. The Temple, the center of the Jewish religion, was utterly destroyed.

The fall of Jerusalem and the destruction of its Temple was a watershed for both Jews and Christians. Many believe it marked the end of the Jerusalem Church and the triumph, by default, of Paul's Christianity. Even though the Jerusalem Church probably survived as the Ebionites, its authority lay in tatters.

Also changed was the way the Christians perceived themselves and their public image. In order to survive, they realized, they had to distance themselves from the rebellious Jews who were now the focus of Rome's enmity. And it was against this background that the Gospels took shape.

The four books add some flesh to the scant details of Jesus' life given in Paul's Letters. They tell the familiar story of the man born of a virgin who traveled around Roman Palestine performing miracles, healing the sick, and preaching, and who was finally arrested in Jerusalem and executed by crucifixion, but who was believed to have risen from the dead and, after appearing to his disciples, ascended into heaven.

It is important, at the outset, to dispense with the idea that the Gospels are the "word of God"—that the authors were divinely inspired and their writings little less than the unvarnished truth. There are so many blatant contradictions among the Gospels that at least one of them must be wrong. Not all of them can be infallible.

The Gospels disagree on whether Jesus' parents were married at the time of his birth (as in Matthew) or merely betrothed (as in Luke). Although they agree he was born in Bethlehem, in Luke it is because his parents lived there, in Matthew because they were visiting for a census; John, ever the outsider, reports the claim that Jesus doesn't come from Bethlehem at all and fails to challenge it. The accounts of events surrounding what is, for Christians, the most important aspect of Jesus' life and meaning, his resurrection, are among the most contradictory. The details of the discovery of the empty tomb are not only different but irreconcilable. And as for Jesus' appearances to his disciples after he has risen from the dead, the Gospels are plainly incompatible. Moreover, as we will see, the first Gospel to be written included no postresurrection appearances at all. As S. G. F. Brandon, eminent professor of comparative religion, understated, "Such a divergence of tradition on a matter of such basic importance as the place where the Risen Lord had appeared to the disciples and ascended into heaven is very revealing."[13]

There are even contradictions in the reports of Jesus' teaching. A simple example is that while in one passage he tells his disciples that "whoever is not against us is for us," elsewhere he declares "whoever is not with me is against me."[14] Did he really mean everyone is simultaneously for and against him and his followers?

The Gospels themselves disprove their own infallibility, but some Christians claim, like David Marshall in his *The Battle for the Book* (1991), that "supernatural guidance" was responsible for all the decisions that produced the New Testament, just as the four Gospels were the only "God-inspired" ones and all those rejected were rightfully so. It is difficult to argue logically with this position because it isn't a logical position. For the moment, suffice it to say that the historical evidence is against it. Briefly, many of those choices—from the original writing through to the compilation of the "official" New Testament—were clearly made out of expediency and in response to specific circumstances. Very human motives lay behind the composition of the Gospels.

However, there are objective reasons to regard the Gospels as special. They represented an innovative genre of religious writing never really seen before. Normally books about a religious teacher or philosopher concentrated on his sayings; where and when he said them was usually of no concern. But in the Gospels Jesus' teaching is embedded in what purports to be an account of his life. There is a parallel with a Greek literary genre in which a collection of anecdotes about an individual was presented in a semibiographical narrative intended to defend the subject against critics—Xenophon's *Memorabilia* (fourth century BCE) does this with Socrates—but the Gospels have certain differences that make them unique in their time.

However, they are emphatically not biographies in today's sense. The message came first, for the Gospels were written above all to make a point. As one scholar wrote of John, the gospel writer felt it his prerogative "to modify the factual record in order to bring out the meaning." [15]

The Gospels display the workings of four different minds, choosing to emphasize independent points for their own particular purpose. Clearly they were written to be circulated within certain communities, only later reaching a much wider audience. (The exception was Luke, written to explain the new religion to an individual.) Naturally there are common motivations—most obviously the desire to spread the "good news" and present Jesus in as positive a light as possible. But there are others, and one with especially far-reaching consequences was the writers' desire to portray the new religion in as Roman-friendly a light as possible. This desire led them to put a certain spin on the story, and in particular to misrepresent the events surrounding Jesus' crucifixion.

All four Gospels place the blame for Jesus' arrest, condemnation, and execution squarely on the Jewish leaders in Jerusalem, regarding the Roman authorities, in the person of Pilate, as at worst acting out of expediency. However, as modern historians are very well informed about the laws and customs in Roman-occupied Palestine, it is now obvious that the New Testament version is by no means the whole truth. Crucifixion was a Roman penalty specifically reserved for rebels against Rome's authority, and it punished political, not religious, transgressions.

Trying to establish their religion in the Roman Empire—and especially against the backdrop of Nero's first persecution and the Jewish Revolt—the gospel writers had to allay any official suspicions, and admitting that the religion's founder had been sentenced to death by those same authorities was hardly calculated to win them over. So the burden of blame was shifted onto the Jewish leaders (who were not exactly popular with Rome) and by extension all Jews—a charge that is particularly glaring in John.

These subtexts become increasingly important when we turn our attention to the question of who wrote the canonical Gospels, and when—and their comparative reliability.

Incredibly, having studied the origins of the Gospels for over two centuries, historians and other experts have been unable to agree on when they were written—or even by whom. Quite simply, there is nowhere near enough information. Initially New Testament scholars had only the Gospels themselves as sources, but from the late nineteenth century and throughout the twentieth new discoveries were made: ancient fragments of the canonical Gospels, copies of long-lost alternative gospels, and other Christian and non-Christian documents providing valuable background, the most significant being the Dead Sea Scrolls. Although these were eagerly added to the body of information and pored over by scholars for clues about the origins of the four Gospels, there is still too little to settle the question decisively, and barring a completely new discovery of the magnitude of the Dead Sea Scrolls, it is unlikely that there will ever be complete agreement on even the most basic questions.

However, there is a natural assumption that the closer a Gospel's origin is to Jesus' lifetime, the more accurate it must be, but as the song says, it ain't necessarily so. What is important is the accuracy and reliability of the author's sources. An account written ten years after an event can be less accurate than one composed fifty years later. Information could be, and often was, passed down perfectly accurately by word of mouth for several generations before someone wrote it down, whereas a chronicler who based his account on information from a prejudiced informant could produce a badly garbled story just a few months after the event. Thus it is not essential to know the exact dates of the Gospels. What matters is the writers' *sources* and the extent to which the text was subsequently amended.

Before we turn to the question of reliability, we need to examine the basic information about the canonical Gospels. Like nearly everything at that time they were written in Greek (specifically Koine). Mark, Matthew, and John are written in a very rough-and-ready style, with frequent changes of tense within a single sentence. For example, where they speak of the visit of the wise men to the newborn Jesus, the literal translation is "When they had gone back, one night a messenger of the Lord appears and says . . ." All translations smooth out the grammar, making the Gospels appear more polished than they are. Luke, by contrast, is written in an educated

Greek style.[16] The language spoken in Palestine in Jesus' time was Aramaic, the main tongue of the region, not exclusive to Jews and still spoken in a handful of villages in Syria. And, as we will see, it was the language of some of the sources used by the gospel writers, suggesting that they come from very close to Jesus' own time.

The fact that we read the Gospels in translation—from not just a foreign language but a dialect of an ancient one, in turn a translation from Aramaic—creates its own problems. As will become apparent, some of the crucial questions about Jesus turn on how certain words were understood at the time, which modern translators are often unsure about. As even scholars who have devoted their lives to the study of ancient Greek have been known to disagree on the precise meaning of some key terms, no English translation can be considered definitive. (Although we have chosen as our standard the most recent, Today's New International Version [TNIV]—which unlike many acknowledges the alternative readings in early manuscripts—we have used others when they appear to be more accurate, a particularly useful source being Andy Gaus' *The Unvarnished New Testament* [1991], which gives a literal translation of the Greek.)

The oldest complete copy of the New Testament, the British Museum's *Codex Sinaiticus*, dates from around 330–50 CE (a codex being a document in the form of a bound book, as distinct from a scroll). A roughly contemporary copy is a treasure of the Vatican Library, known as the *Codex Vaticanus*. Most scholars regard the *Sinaiticus* as the oldest complete manuscript of the New Testament but agree that it is a close-run thing.

These are the earliest full versions of the Gospels—some three centuries after the events they are supposed to describe—although there are a couple of incomplete copies that might push the date back another century or so. The collection in the Bodmer Library of World Literature in Geneva contains papyrus codices of the Gospels of Luke and John that are substantially complete and have been dated to between 175 and 225. This shows that those two Gospels, at least, had essentially reached their current form by about 200. Before 200 there are only more fragments, the earliest from John's Gospel. This is the "Rylands Fragment," discovered in Egypt and now owned by Manchester University, a tiny scrap of papyrus dated to between 85 and 125. A fragment of Mark dates from about 150, the earliest of Matthew from the late second century.

All these fragments were identified as pieces of the canonical Gospels because they contain recognizable passages. However, as the Gospels were clearly put together from several separate sources, logically the fragments could have come from one of them, and they are by no means proof that the rest existed at that time. The Rylands Fragment, for example, contains barely a dozen words, identifiable as being from John's account of Jesus' interrogation by Pilate. But to conclude from this, as one scholar did, that this "proves the existence and use of the Fourth Gospel in a little provincial town along the Nile . . . during the first half of the Second Century"[17]—i.e., that the *whole* of that Gospel must also have existed then—is to grossly exceed the evidence.

The total of physical evidence for the origins of the Gospels may not seem much to go on, but it needs to be compared with other ancient works. The earliest known manuscript of Julius Caesar's *The Gallic War*, written in the fifties BCE, dates from the eighth century CE—about seven hundred years after the book was first written. With Josephus' *The Jewish War*, an important chronicle of events in first-century Palestine, the earliest complete manuscripts come from the tenth century, though there is also a fragmentary third-century papyrus copy. In the case of both works, all the intervening handwritten copies have been lost. Nothing like a first edition survives.

These books were the best sellers of their day—one by an emperor, no less. The Gospels were produced by a minority cult with very few resources, who for much of their early days suffered persecution that involved their books being burnt. The fact that there is only a 250-year gap between the Gospels' composition and the earliest surviving complete manuscripts, and that there are many fragments bridging the gaps, is actually very impressive. Even so, what we have is frustratingly little. As one New Testament scholar complained, "Why, if God took such pains to preserve an inerrant text for posterity, did the spirit not provide for the preservation of original copies of the Gospels? It seems little enough to ask of a God who creates absolutely reliable reporters."[18]

Only fundamentalists indulge in the luxury of believing that the Gospels were fixed from the beginning and never changed. The texts have manifestly been amended many, many times by a host of hands, bent on tweaking the message and re-creating Jesus in their own image. The classic example is the story of the adulterous woman ("Let any one of you who is without sin be the first to throw a stone at her"), which many regard as Jesus' finest hour. In modern Bibles this episode is found in John, in chapters 7–8, and is often quoted as an example of Christ's wisdom and compassion. However, the incident was conspicuous by its absence in Bibles before the *twelfth century*. And it was first added to Luke, only later being transferred to John.[19] Many argue that it was a genuine story about Jesus that had been passed down through the generations, and therefore deserves a place in the Gospels. Perhaps so, but there is no proof, and the fact remains that some eight hundred years after the earliest known copies of the New Testament, the text was still being changed.

It was not until the Council of Trent in 1545 that the Roman Catholic Church decreed that no more alterations or additions could be made to the Bible. (Even so, the editing process continues. For example, because the passage known as the "longer text of the Eucharist" in Luke [22:19–20] is now believed not to have been part of the original text, it is left out of some modern translations, among them the New English Bible.) And if the four Gospels have changed since the earliest surviving copies, there is every likelihood they also changed *before* they were made.

The Borrowers

The consensus is that Mark's is the earliest of the four New Testament Gospels. Everything in it is also in Matthew and Luke, and in almost exactly the same order, whereas certain passages appear in Matthew and Luke but not in Mark. Matthew reproduces 51 percent of Mark's actual words, Luke 53 percent.[20] The logical conclusion, first suggested in the 1830s by Ferdinand Christian Baur, was that Matthew and Luke both based their accounts partly on Mark. So Mark came first: QED.[21]

This discovery had some very profound implications. Mark had *never* been regarded as an eyewitness account: from the earliest days, it was ascribed to a companion of Peter's in Rome who recorded his recollections but never himself met Jesus. (The connection with Peter has been generally discounted, although it is largely accepted that this Gospel was written in Rome.) The earliest reference to Mark's Gospel came from Papias, Bishop of Hierapolis in Asia Minor, in around 120 or 130 CE:

> Mark, who had been Peter's interpreter, wrote down carefully, but not in order, all that he remembered of the Lord's sayings and doings. For he had not heard the Lord or been one of His followers, but later . . . one of Peter's. Peter used to adapt his teachings to the occasion, without making a systematic arrangement of the Lord's sayings, so Mark was quite justified in writing down some things as he remembered them.[22]

On the other hand, Matthew's Gospel *had* always been believed to be a firsthand account by one of Jesus' followers, but if Mark came first, that must be wrong.

Mark is also conspicuous for certain highly significant omissions—such as the virgin birth and, in the earliest manuscripts, Jesus' postresurrection appearances. When Mark was grouped together with the other three Gospels, these lacunae were relatively inconsequential. But when it was realized that Mark came first, serious questions had to be asked about why these episodes, so fundamental to Christian belief, were not there and why they only appeared in the Gospels that came after his.

Matthew and Luke have added entirely different and irreconcilable accounts of Jesus' birth. Mark's story begins with Jesus being baptized, with not so much as a hint about his earlier life. Matthew and Luke also have accounts—again completely different from each other—of Jesus' postresurrection appearances. They also evince a greater desire to tie up otherwise dangerously thought-provoking loose ends, for example by offering yet again different accounts of what happened to Judas Iscariot, on which Mark is silent. (Luke's version is in Acts.)

Conversely Mark includes a few incidents that are dropped by Matthew and Luke, and it is not difficult to see why, being inconvenient or embarrassing for the Christian story and its image of Jesus. While Mark relates that Jesus' family tried to have him "taken away" as a madman, clearly neither Matthew nor Luke felt comfortable with this and left it out.

It is uncertain whether it was Matthew or Luke that came next, as there are no similar signs of borrowing between them, nor indeed any indication at all that they even knew about each other's existence.

These two Gospels shared another source apart from Mark, which no longer exists as an independent entity, although its basic form can be reconstructed. Scholars designate it "Q," from the German *Quelle*, meaning "source" (Q's existence being first determined by German scholars).

The onetime existence of Q was deduced from the observation that Matthew and Luke have about 250 verses in common (some in almost identical words) that are *not* from Mark. Moreover, Mark contains very few direct sayings of Jesus, whereas the "non-Mark" material in the other two synoptic Gospels is almost entirely made up of sayings and teaching. From this, in 1838 the German religious philosopher Christian Weisse proposed that the writers of Matthew and Luke both had access to a compilation of Jesus' sayings that Mark did not.

The original Q consisted solely of teachings allegedly delivered by Jesus, including many familiar sayings, some of which, because of the way Matthew inserted them into his narrative as a single peroration, are now known as the Sermon on the Mount. The obvious conclusion is that Q was a "teaching book"—a handbook of Jesus' aphorisms, injunctions, and ethical code—used by the first Christians.

Linguistic detective work has shown that Q was written in Aramaic, which of course makes perfect sense. For example, when parts of the Sermon on the Mount are translated into Aramaic, they naturally fall into verse, revealing that it must have been composed in that language and translated into Greek. Some clues suggest Q was written before the watershed of the Jewish Revolt: both Luke and Matthew, drawing on a Q saying, refer to God withdrawing from the Temple but returning under "one who comes in the Lord." Obviously this suggests that Q was written when the Temple had not yet been destroyed, therefore before 70 CE.

John's Gospel, or the Fourth Gospel as it is sometimes known, appears to have little or no relationship to the other three. This fundamental split has always been recognized, but in the eighteenth century the term "synoptic," from the Greek for "seen as one," was coined to describe Mark, Matthew, and Luke. Notoriously, John's Gospel relates the events of Jesus' mission in a completely different sequence, missing out incidents that are crucial turning points in the other books and including equally key episodes that are absent from the synoptic Gospels, as well as presenting an entirely different view of Jesus' mission. In fact John is so different that we wonder that if by some chance it had been lost to history and was only discovered now, it would be rejected as too late and inauthentic, as happened recently with the Gospel of Judas.

Because of these differences, and the fact that John obviously comes from a different strand of Christian thought from the synoptics, the consensus is that it was written much later than the other three. But, as we will see, recent scholarship has presented compelling reasons for believing that at least one of John's sources predated those of the others.

Having examined the relationships among the Gospels, it is time to consider them individually.

The Gospel According to Mark

As we know, Papias attributes Mark's Gospel to a Mark who was with Peter in Rome and who penned his account after Peter's death. Scholars doubt the connection with the "Big Fisherman," and although the author does seem have been named Mark, unfortunately Mark happened to be the commonest name in the Roman world, so it tells us nothing about him. It is also fairly well accepted that Mark's Gospel was a product of the Christian community in Rome (which is probably how the connection with Peter crept in, since he is said to have ended his days in the Eternal City).

Papias and others believe Mark was cobbled together from Peter's random recollections. And, perhaps surprisingly, modern scholarship actually agrees with the views of the earliest commentators. In 1919 German theologian Karl Ludwig Schmidt published a landmark study in which he showed that Mark had been constructed from many individual stories and recollections, assembled into a single narrative with short connecting passages. In other words, Mark had basically written the Gospel's "plot" by connecting up individual stories about Jesus—exactly as Papias said. However, Mark is not without a plan, organizing his narrative thematically. For example, an episode in which Jesus addresses the spiritual blindness of those around him is followed by his curing a blind man.

But if Mark did invent the narrative as a device for putting his collection of eyewitnesses' recollections in order—a story line subsequently followed by Matthew and Luke—then his sequence of events can never be totally trusted, apart from the obvious flow from baptism to crucifixion and resurrection.

Startlingly, in Mark there are no postresurrection appearances: the last passages tell of Mary Magdalene and two other women finding Jesus' tomb open, his body gone, and a man dressed in white who informs them he has risen from the dead. The story ends with the women running off. Beyond the mysterious man's word, there is no attempt to convince the reader that Jesus really had risen (although clearly Mark himself believed in the resurrection).

Turn to the last verses of Mark today and there are indeed the stories of the risen Christ's appearances, but sadly they were added much later, simply because their absence was so glaring—not to mention embarrassing. (Whoever took it upon himself to add them based his version on Luke's Gospel.) Neither of the two earliest complete versions of the New Testament, the *Codex Sinaiticus* and *Codex Vaticanus*, included any postresurrection episodes. But was Mark truly unaware of these momentous happenings, or was what he wrote about Jesus after the resurrection deemed unacceptable later and hastily removed? Or was his original ending somehow lost?

Without knowing the exact circumstances in which Mark's Gospel was composed and handed down, nobody can answer these questions conclusively. But it is very odd that what is for Christians the single most important event in Jesus' life is missing.

But are there any clues about when the Gospel was written? The majority view among New Testament scholars is that it dates from the seventies CE (i.e., some forty years after Jesus' life). However, what is really important is the relative reliability of Mark's sources, and there is persuasive evidence that they retained some very early material indeed.

Gerd Theissen, professor of New Testament theology at Heidelberg, in *The Gospels in Context* (1992), demonstrated that many stories in Mark reveal a genuine familiarity with social, economic, and political conditions in Palestine that can be dated quite narrowly—to the situation as it was *before* the Jewish Revolt of 66–70, which obviously caused massive upheavals at both regional and local levels. This familiarity is sometimes reflected in very specific situations within a small geographical area, such as Jesus' intriguing encounter with the Syro-Phoenician woman, which we will discuss later.

For example, Mark often refers to toll stations on the northern side of the Lake of Galilee, positioned on the border, which in Jesus' day ran between the territories of Galilee (controlled by Herod Antipas) and Gaulanitis (controlled by his brother Philip). But the frontier was there only between 4 BCE (when Herod the Great's territories were divided) and 39 CE (the year of the accession of Agrippa I, who again ruled both territories), and it had certainly ceased to have any relevance after the Revolt. All of this makes it highly likely that Mark's source recalled the area as it was before 39.[23] None of this necessarily means that the whole of Mark's Gospel in the form we know it today was actually written then—anachronisms elsewhere indicate a later date—but at least it establishes that *some* of his sources were very early. So the challenge is to isolate the earliest passages.

Another impressive detail is that Mark includes certain Aramaic phrases (for example, "*Talitha koum*" ["Girl, arise!"] when raising Jairus' daughter from the dead), which shows that some of his sources originated in Palestine and suggests that he considered these too special to change radically. (And, as he had to explain such phrases, he must have been writing for a community unfamiliar with Aramaic.)

One of Mark's sources can even be plausibly traced back to an actual eyewitness of at least part of Jesus' crucifixion. Simon of Cyrene makes a brief and almost irrelevant appearance as the poor wretch the Romans force to carry Jesus' cross as he labors toward Golgotha. Mark also tells us, even more casually and without further explanation, that Simon was the father of Alexander and Rufus, implying that his readers must know who they were. But the Simon of Cyrene connection, tangential though it may seem as far as the New Testament is concerned, has resurfaced in recent times—with extraordinary implications.

In 1941 a set of eleven ossuaries from the same family tomb were found near the village of Silwan in Israel, although their significance was not appreciated until the mid-1990s. Two inscriptions mentioned a Simon: one contained the bones of "Sarah, daughter of Simon of Ptolemais" (a city in Cyrene, a part of modern Libya), and the other those of Simon's son Alexander, but in this one the father is explicitly called "Simon of Cyrene."

While Simon was a very common Jewish name at that time, Alexander certainly wasn't, and to find two Simons who came from Cyrene living in Jerusalem who gave that name to their son is stretching coincidence rather far. Most archaeologists and New Testament historians agree that the Simon of Cyrene named on the ossuaries is the same as the man mentioned in Mark.[24]

Although at first glance this may not seem remotely as exciting as finding an artifact connected with Jesus, John the Baptist, or any of the major disciples—after all, Simon of Cyrene is a very minor character in the Gospel stories, making just one brief appearance—in fact this discovery is, in its own quiet way, potentially dramatic.

From Paul's Letter to the Romans, written in the late fifties, we know that a Rufus was a leading member of the Christian community in Rome, singled out by Paul as being "chosen in the Lord"—a unique compliment used only about this man. And clearly Paul, who had never visited Rome at that time, knows Rufus, as he also commends Rufus' mother, "who has been a mother to me, too," which suggests their paths had crossed somewhere else before.[25]

As Rufus, like Alexander, was an uncommon name, it is widely accepted that the one in Rome was Simon of Cyrene's son.[26] The ossuary shows that there did exist *a* Simon of Cyrene, the father at least of an Alexander. Presumably, given that Mark was almost certainly written for Roman Christians, this explains why there was no need to say who Alexander and Rufus were. His readers already knew. But more important, it strongly suggests that Mark got his information from Simon of Cyrene's son, who must have heard it from his father. In other words, at least part of the crucifixion story is based on eyewitness testimony, and from a man who actually played a part in the event.

Now we turn to a potentially much more sensational angle on this Gospel. In the late 1960s the academic world was seriously rattled when it was claimed that there had once been a second, but secret, version of Mark. Soon it was the center of a storm, including allegations that the whole thing was a hoax. But the secret gospel has surprises—not to say shocks—that cast doubt on many of Christians' most cherished certainties about their Lord.

The Secret Gospel

But first, the curious prequel to this story. In 1940 a novel, somewhat in the genre of The Da Vinci Code, by James Hogg Hunter called The Mystery of Mar Saba was published, which described a plot by the Nazis to undermine Christianity—and thereby the free world—by creating a forged document that disproved Jesus' resurrection. This forgery was planted in the library of the fifth-century Mar Saba monastery in the Judean desert a few miles southeast of Jerusalem, so it could be found by an unsuspecting British scholar. In real life, perhaps owing to the machinations of the ever-vigilant and ultramischievous Cosmic Joker (who seems to be especially tempted by the most earnest and reputable scholars), the very next year a young American academic, stranded in Palestine by the Second World War, visited that same library. As a result, right on cue, some years later he discovered a document with far-reaching implications for our understanding of Jesus.

Morton Smith, a research fellow at Harvard Divinity School, when stranded in Jerusalem enrolled in a doctoral course at the Hebrew University, during which he was invited to visit Mar Saba. No doubt suitably wide-eyed, he saw the monastery's library with its centuries of books and documents and wondered what treasures it might contain. Smith returned to the United States in 1944, eventually becoming a professor of ancient history at Columbia University, New York. In 1958 the Greek Orthodox patriarch of Jerusalem gave him special permission to return to the monastery to study its treasures in gratitude for his charity work, and it was then that he made a discovery that was to change his life.

What Smith found was a copy of a letter written by one of the most eminent of the Church Fathers, Clement of Alexandria (Titus Flavius Clemens, ca. 150–ca. 215). It was a *much* later copy, dating from the seventeenth century, although it was standard practice to copy valuable documents when they began to deteriorate with age. The document was the property of the Patriarchate, which refused Smith permission to remove the original, although he was allowed to take photographs. (He has since been criticized for "preventing" other scholars' having access to the original documents, but that is unfair: the Patriarchate was responsible.)

Clement's letter was a reply in Greek to one Theodore, concerning their joint opposition to a gnostic sect called the Carpocratians (after its founder, Carpocrates). Known from other early Christian writings, they were enthusiastic devotees of a libertine form of gnosticism, employing sexual practices as sacramental rites. According to Clement's letter, they had managed to get hold of a copy of an alternative version of Mark's Gospel that belonged to the Church in Alexandria, and added bits to justify their debauchery by appealing to Jesus' own teaching, suggesting that he himself had indulged in such practices, particularly homosexual rites. Like a modern spin doctor, Clement advised Theodore to deny everything, on the grounds that "not all true things are the truth, nor should that truth which merely seems true according to human opinions be preferred to the true truth, that according to the faith."[27]

This is Clement's explanation of how the alternative version came to be written:

As for Mark, then, during Peter's stay in Rome he wrote an account of the Lord's doings, not, however, declaring all of them, not yet hinting at the mystic ones, but selecting what he thought most useful for increasing the faith of those who were being instructed. But when Peter died a martyr, Mark came to Alexandria, bringing both his own notes and those of Peter, from which he transferred to his former book the things suitable for those studies which make for progress toward knowledge. Thus he composed a more spiritual Gospel for the use of those who were being perfected. Nevertheless, he yet did not divulge the things not to be uttered, nor did he write down the hierophantic teaching of the Lord, but to the stories already written he added yet others and, moreover, brought in certain traditions of which he knew the interpretation would, as a mystagogue, lead the hearers into the innermost sanctuary of the truth hidden by seven veils. Thus, in sum, he prepared matters, neither grudgingly nor incautiously, in my opinion, and, dying, he left his composition to the church in Alexandria, where it even yet is very securely kept, being read only to those who are being initiated into the great mysteries.[28]

In other words, according to Clement there were effectively *three* levels to Jesus' teaching: one for public consumption—in the canonical Mark; a more spiritual set for "initiates only"; and a third grade so exalted that it was beyond the capabilities of human expression and could never be written down at all, presumably reserved for highest graduates and passed on orally.

After telling Theodore how the Carpocratians had managed to steal a copy of the "mystic gospel" which they adulterated, Clement quotes a couple of extracts as examples, which comprise one long and one short episode, not found in the canonical Mark. Of the two the first, longer one is more significant, telling of Jesus' raising an unnamed young man from the grave in what is clearly an alternative version of the famous raising of Lazarus (now only found in John's Gospel).

Smith dubbed the text from which Clement quoted "the Secret Gospel of Mark," his translation of Clement's "*mystikon evangelion.*" However, as one critic comments, this was "not only incorrect but misleading."[29] It is "secret" in the sense that it has hidden meanings, not because it had to be *kept* secret (though reserved for initiates only). It really means, as Clement calls it, a "more spiritual Gospel." Some prefer to refer to it as the "Longer Gospel of Mark," abbreviated to LGM, or simply "Longer Mark," but for us "Secret Mark" says it all.

So we have two questions: was the letter really by Clement, and if so, were the extracts he quoted genuinely from an alternative version of Mark?

Smith made an in-depth comparison of the style and vocabulary of the letter to Clement's other writings, concluding that it did indeed reproduce many of his characteristics of vocabulary, style, and use of scripture. He submitted his research to eighteen leading scholars, all but three of whom agreed with his findings. At least it seems the letter itself was genuine.

After two years of meticulous work it was time for Smith to announce he had discovered a new letter by Clement of Alexandria. This in itself was enough to generate a sensation among historians of the early Church even though at that stage he said nothing about the contents and its alleged extracts from an alternative version of Mark. He devoted another six years of research to the contents and the question of the extracts' authenticity.

This proved more difficult. However, although the extracts from the secret gospel are short, for many reasons it was clear that, as Canadian religious historian Scott G. Brown, who reviewed Smith's work, concluded, "the consistency of literary technique and theology between these two versions of the Gospel of Mark strongly suggests common authorship."[30]

However, from the beginning, experts were distinctly reluctant to take Smith's discovery seriously, as it would risk setting a flagrantly heretical cat among the theological pigeons. First, there was the notion that the canonical Gospels might have been edited to remove "initiates only" material, which introduced further complications into what was already a vexed subject. Then there was the content of Secret Mark, which indicated that Jesus had reserved special rituals—with uncomfortable echoes of pagan mysteries—for his closest disciples. Although virtually everybody agreed that the letter itself was genuine, most took the line that the extracts from the "other Mark" were a mid-second-century creation—a reworking of Mark's Gospel that Clement incorrectly believed to be authentic.

This was the line taken by the leading names in the field, although few bothered to spend much time on the subject. But, as Brown notes scathingly, "Their reputations supplied the footnote documentation that other scholars would use for the next thirty years to excuse themselves from the task of analyzing this evidence and familiarizing themselves with the secondary literature."[31] He points out that by the same logic the Sermon on the Mount (as a separate tradition about Jesus inserted into Mark's narrative by Matthew and Luke) should be rejected. Outside academia, for Christians, who basically ignored Smith's work, the whole notion that Jesus had delivered secret teachings, and that the Gospels had been censored, was even worse.

However, in the mid-1970s two scholars went much further, suggesting that the letter was a modern forgery, pointing out that an ancient hoaxer would not have been capable of reproducing the stylistic quirks of both Clement's writing and the canonical Mark that had enabled it to pass the scholarly tests of authenticity. If it is a fake, then it must be a modern one. Of course—although it would be many years before anyone would say so openly, and only since Smith's death in 1991 has it become widely discussed—this was basically to accuse Smith himself of perpetrating a hoax. (One of the two scholars, Quentin Quesnell, admitted privately that he thought Smith invented it, but as some kind of experiment.) [32]

This theory was based not on any problems with the text itself or with Smith's work, but on the basic premise that since the Secret Gospel *can't* be genuine, and only a modern scholar could have fabricated it, a modern scholar *must* have done so. As Brown puts it, for those who wanted to dismiss Secret Mark, the hoax explanation was "too good not to be true." [33]

Although the hoax theory failed to gain much ground at first, it really took off in the 1990s, when it supplied the only way out of what had become a deepening dilemma. (It was also, conveniently, after Smith was no longer around to defend himself—or sue.) Gradually scholars had been drawn into examining Smith's work more seriously, and many of the arguments for a second-century hoax had been eroded away, strengthening the evidence for its being written by the same author as the familiar version of Mark. Worse, it became increasingly apparent that (contrary even to Clement's belief) Secret Mark must have been the *original* form of the Gospel and the New Testament book merely an edited version. Some of the most eminent names in the field threw their weight behind this theory, and it was accepted by, for example, Ron Cameron, author of *The Other Gospels: Non-Canonical Gospel Texts* (1983). [34] Now the only way out for supporters of the status quo was to brand the whole thing a hoax. Secret Mark was either genuine or a hoax by Smith: there was no middle way and no other explanation.

The year 2005 saw not only the hoax theory championed by the lawyer Stephen C. Carlson in *The Gospel Hoax: Morton Smith's Invention of Secret Mark* but also a major defense of Smith's work by the specialist in Christian origins at the University of Toronto, Scott G. Brown, in his *Mark's Other Gospel: Rethinking Morton Smith's Controversial Discovery*. Brown is by far the more persuasive—and better qualified to judge. His meticulously argued book presents many reasons why the hoax theory fails to stand up. For example, many of the literary characteristics used to identify the letter as Clement's and the Gospel extracts as being from the same hand as Mark have been recognized only *since* Smith made his discovery public: neither he nor any other forger could have known about them when creating their hoax. Also, some of Smith's original translation is now recognized as wrong (even the term "secret gospel" itself), which would be very odd for a forger.

The evidence is very much in favor of Clement's letter being genuine. But much more significantly, it seems that the extracts of Mark he quotes are not just authentic but actually come from the *original* gospel. *It is the New Testament Gospel that was adulterated.*

Unlike today, when even a suggestion of clandestine doings rouses suspicions of sleazy or sinister cover-ups, the ancient world *expected* a religion to have secrets. In Jesus' day all religions routinely kept information back from their rank-and-file membership, drawing a distinction between public rites and the inner ceremonies in which only the priesthood participated.

All the pagan religions in the Roman and Greek world had their inner mysteries. In Judaism, only priests were allowed into the inner sanctum of the Temple, where their activities were strictly guarded from ordinary people. (Ironically, for this reason, Judaism was categorized by Greeks and Romans as a mystery religion.) Those Jewish sects that had rejected Temple worship, such as the Qumran community responsible for the Dead Sea Scrolls, threatened severe penalties for revealing their doctrines to outsiders, even refusing new members knowledge of them until they had passed a period of probation.

So, although the concept that there was a secret version of

Christianity might seem odd, even off-putting, in the context of the time it was not only unsurprising but actually expected. It would have surprised people then if Jesus *hadn't* had secret teachings. In any case even the Gospels make it clear that his words operated on two levels: one for the public and one for his disciples.

Secret Mark has many serious implications about the origins of the Gospels. First, it confirms the reasonable assumption that they went through a process of editing between their composition and the creation of the New Testament. Second, it casts an important light on the relationship between the first of the synoptic Gospels and John's Gospel. As we have seen, Mark—the source of the synoptics—and John seem to represent entirely different and independently transmitted traditions about Jesus.

However, the Secret Gospel shows that one of the most significant episodes that is unique to John among the New Testament books, the raising of Lazarus, *was* originally in Mark but was deliberately omitted from the version copied by Matthew and Luke. This entirely changes our view of the relationship between the synoptics and John. There was a connection of some kind between Mark and John: at the very least they both used the same source material. Ron Cameron comments:

> The close similarity between the stories of the raisings of the dead in the *Secret Gospel of Mark* and in the Gospel of John suggests that Mark and John may have drawn upon a shared tradition, and raises the question whether this story came from a common collection, perhaps written in Aramaic, from which Mark and John have also taken their other miracle stories. Moreover, since this story occurs in the same sequence in the structural outline of both the *Secret Gospel of Mark* and the Gospel of John, it is possible that this story is part of a more comprehensive source used independently by both evangelists.[35]

We believe the weight of evidence to be firmly on the side of Secret Mark being both genuine and earlier than the canonical version. But this makes it even more frustrating that all we have are the two small extracts quoted by Clement of Alexandria. What we really want to know is how much else of the New Testament version has been changed.

The Gospel According to Matthew

In the Church's formative years—the second and third centuries— Matthew was by far the favorite Gospel, and the most often quoted, which is probably why it comes first in the New Testament.

The internal evidence suggests that Matthew was written after the Jewish Revolt, its basic theme being, in the words of S. G. F. Brandon, that "the failure of the Jews to recognise the true nature of Jesus was the cause of their downfall,"[36] which indicates that it was written after the "downfall" in 70 CE, although the Gospel never explicitly mentions it.

Early Christian writers all ascribed the Gospel to Jesus' disciple Matthew, the tax collector who joined him in the early days. But since it was recognized that Matthew draws upon Mark's Gospel (among other sources), this has been impossible to sustain. (And as this Matthew appears in the Gospel, why doesn't the writer use the first person?)

Matthew's Gospel is the most Jewish-oriented of the four as it assumes more familiarity with Jewish customs and appeals far more to the scriptures. It is also more specific than any other of the Gospels about Jesus' alleged fulfillment of Old Testament messianic prophecies. Although on a few occasions Mark points out that an event in Jesus' life had been prophesied, Matthew does so much more often and more emphatically. Clearly his intention was to persuade Jews, or affirm the belief of a Jewish-Christian community, that Jesus was their Messiah according to the criteria laid down in their own scriptures.

After explaining his understanding of the origins of Mark's Gospel, Papias goes on: "Matthew compiled the *Sayings* [literally "oracles"] in the Hebrew language, and everyone translated them as well as he could."[37] (Although normally translated as "sayings," implying it was just a collection of Jesus' words, Papias' "oracles" (logia) could technically cover both words and deeds.)[38] It had always been assumed that when Papias said Hebrew he really meant

Aramaic, but once again it seems he was right all along, as apparently Matthew's Gospel *was* originally written in Hebrew—and that version still exists. This is of more than just academic interest, since a comparison between the Hebrew and the Greek with which Christians have always been familiar reveals some significant—even startling—differences.

In the late fourteenth century a Spanish Jew named Shem-Tob ben-Shaprut wrote an anti-Christian treatise in which he incorporated the whole of Matthew's Gospel (in order to familiarize his readers with the Christian position so that they could follow his arguments against it). As the treatise is in Hebrew, it has always been assumed, quite naturally, that Shem-Tob had either translated Matthew himself from the Latin or Greek or had used a convenient translation. Either way, it was long thought that since the Gospel was originally written in Greek, the Hebrew version in Shem-Tob's treatise had nothing of significance to tell us.

However, in the 1980s the American professor of religion George Howard revisited this work and concluded that Shem-Tob had used an *original* version of Matthew that had been passed down within the Jewish community. Howard showed that Jewish writers who quoted from Matthew as far back as the sixth century had used the same version as Shem-Tob, at least establishing that the Hebrew version had been around that long. But comparison of the "Hebrew Matthew" revealed that while at least 95 percent of it is the same as the familiar version, the different passages are hard to explain if the Hebrew edition was a later development—but much easier if it was the other way round.

Tellingly there is, for example, a line in the canonical Matthew in which Jesus says of John the Baptist, "among those born of women there has not risen anyone greater than John the Baptist; yet whoever is least in the kingdom of heaven is greater than he."[39] Scholars have long realized that the second part of this sentence was a later addition (and was, as we will show in due course, added for seismically significant reasons). But in the Hebrew Matthew that part is conspicuously absent. Several similar episodes also can be explained only if the standard version is a translation of the Hebrew version, not vice versa.

Howard summarizes the differences, including some that are

hard, if not impossible, to explain as amendments, especially as the Jewish writers used them to illustrate what they saw as the errors of Christianity:

> It never identifies Jesus with the Messiah. John the Baptist is given an exalted role (even takes on messianic traits) similar to the one polemicized against in the Gospel of John and the Pseudo-Clementine Writings. Shem-Tob's text envisions the salvation of the Gentiles only in the Messianic era. It reflects a lesser disparity between Judaism and Christianity than the Greek or Latin canonical texts. Finally Shem-Tob's text employs the Hebrew Divine Name where the canonical version simply uses the word "Lord." [40]

(The crucial significance of the Pseudo-Clementine texts will become apparent later.)

The Gospel and Acts According to Luke

Both Luke's Gospel and his Acts of the Apostles were written to and for one Theophilus (presumably a high-ranking Roman official as he is addressed as *kratistos*, meaning roughly "Your Excellency"), apparently in response to his request for a briefing on the emergent religion, but the writer's underlying agenda was, as Burton L. Mack of the Claremont School of Theology writes, "to claim for the church its rightful place in the Roman world, demonstrate that it was no threat to the Roman order, and make a case for its positive contributions to society." [41] Theologian Alfred Leaney says, "Luke was influenced, among other considerations, by the desirability of showing that Christianity was politically innocent." [42]

To suit his aim of persuading Theophilus that Christians were beyond suspicion, Luke plays down the ambiguous passages that might clash with the Roman way—sometimes so transparently as to verge on the comic. For example, both Mark and Matthew describe a scene where Herod Antipas, the Roman-appointed ruler of Galilee, hears rumors that Jesus is John the Baptist risen again, and is afraid. In Luke this becomes "and was anxious to meet him." [43]

Tradition attributes Luke and Acts to a companion of Paul's on his missionary journeys, on the basis of the occasional (and inconsistent) use of "we" in describing the journeys in Acts. Early Christian writings, from about a century after the books were written, describe Luke as a physician from Antioch, and the doctor named Luke mentioned in three of Paul's Epistles was assumed to be the same one. However, it is more likely that Acts was written some time after Paul's Epistles, although prossibly using material written by one of his traveling companions, and the Gospel must date from around the same time.

As usual, the date of composition is uncertain and depends on what date is accepted for Mark, since Luke must come afterwards. Like Matthew, most scholars would place it in the eighties or nineties CE. From references put into Jesus' mouth found in no other source, clearly Luke was written after the calamitous events that befell Jerusalem in 70 CE.[44]

Although Luke's Gospel follows almost exactly the same story line as Mark and Matthew, it relates certain events and sayings of Jesus that appear in neither. Indeed, academic detective work has established that Luke incorporated material from some earlier sources not available to either of them.

This Gospel, alone of the synoptics (and not including Secret Mark), shows signs of overlapping with John's Gospel; for example, the presence among the Twelve of a second disciple called Judas (not Iscariot) is mentioned only in Luke and John. However, most of their common ground is less specific, such as their treatment of certain characters—for example, Martha and Mary, the sisters of Bethany—even though the stories they tell about them are completely different. The combination of similarities and differences indicates that Luke and John were ultimately drawing on the same tradition, but that it reached them through entirely different routes, rather than one taking it directly from the other.

The Gospel According to John

Despite all the reservations, understanding the origins, orientation, and purpose of the other three Gospels is relatively easy, but in John nothing is quite as it seems.

Where Mark is straightforward, even simple, storytelling,

Matthew and Luke put their own spin on the material, but their agenda is still transparent. John, by contrast, is a complex piece of writing, weaving together many themes and layers of symbolism, besides drawing on several literary genres, not just Jewish traditions. With the synoptics, basically what you see is what you get, but with John's Gospel everything is shrouded in layers of paradox and mystery. In the writer of John we have an author whose mind is recognizably similar to a modern novelist's—seeking to tell a well-rounded, multilayered story without any loose ends.

This is the only one of the New Testament Gospels that explicitly claims to be derived from the eyewitness account of one of Jesus' followers, the mysterious "beloved disciple." It ends with the bald statement—after Jesus has said farewell—that "This is the disciple who testifies to these things and who wrote them down. We know that his testimony is true."[45] However, the use of the third person makes it clear it was not actually set down by the disciple but based on his written memoirs.

It is not even certain that the testimonial was supposed to apply to the whole book rather than, as the eminent specialist in John's Gospel C. H. Dodd, argued, only the immediately preceding verses, concerning Jesus' words to the disciple before leaving him.[46] Reinforcing this idea, the beloved disciple appears in the story only toward the end, making his first entrance during the Last Supper.

The man is never named, being referred to only as "the disciple whom Jesus loved," but early traditions identified him as young John, one of the two sons of Zebedee, who were among the first to join Jesus' band of disciples. However, this identification is undoubtedly wrong. Early Christian commentators on the Gospels, such as Papias, make no mention at all of a gospel by John, and Justin Martyr, writing around 150 CE, omitted such a book from his list of those with apostolic authority. The first known references to a text "according to St. John" were in works by Irenaeus of Lyon and Theophilus of Antioch, both dating from around 180 CE. In fact even prominent Catholic scholars now acknowledge that the weight of evidence is against it having been written by John the apostle.[47] (Because of this, and the potential for confusion between the other Johns in the Jesus story, most academics prefer the neutral term "Fourth Gospel.")

So who was the disciple? Did he really exist—and if so which one was he? Or was he, as some maintain, purely a literary device, created as "proof" that the author's version of events was the most credible? As usual, there is evidence both ways.

Suggestions about the identity of the beloved disciple have included Thomas or Nathaniel, Lazarus, Jesus' brother James the Just, Judas Iscariot—and even Mary Magdalene (who was certainly a beloved disciple, but may not have been honored with the definite article). But as British professor of New Testament studies Andrew Lincoln points out succinctly, "If readers were meant to discover his identity, the evangelist would have provided far clearer clues."[48] Why was his identity supposed to be a secret?

Undoubtedly the author does exploit the beloved disciple to add an authoritative gloss, especially in emphasizing that he was closer to Jesus even than Peter, enjoying more of his master's trust and with a greater understanding of his purpose. On the other hand, a fabricated character hardly gels with the ending:

> Peter turned and saw that the disciple whom Jesus loved was following them. (This was the one who had leaned back against Jesus at the supper and had said, "Lord, who is going to betray you?") When Peter saw him, he asked, "Lord, what about him?"
>
> Jesus answered, "If I want him to remain alive until I return, what is that to you? You must follow me." Because of this the rumor spread among the believers that this disciple would not die. But Jesus did not say that he would not die; he only said, "If I want him to remain alive until I return, what is that to you?"
>
> This is the disciple who testifies to these things and who wrote them down. We know that his testimony is true.[49]

Obviously this is intended to counter a rumor that Jesus said the disciple would never die. As Andrew Lincoln observes, "It would be very strange and highly contrived to attempt to expose a rumor about a purely fictional character."[50] Moreover, in order for the rumor to circulate, at least the audience for whom this Gospel was written must have known the identity of the disciple. It would be a pretty pointless rumor otherwise.

It seems that the beloved disciple may well have been a real person, although the gospel writer was clearly not above exploiting him to add authority to his own theological perspective. But, in the end, it is just another of the Fourth Gospel's many mysteries.

In fact John's Gospel possesses so many mysteries, paradoxes, and puzzles that we might be forgiven for thinking that the author deliberately set out to mystify us. For example, in the synoptics most of Jesus' activity takes place in Galilee and other places outside Judea and it is only at the end that he makes his fateful journey to Jerusalem, where he causes a major upset in the Temple by attacking the traders. But in John's Gospel he makes several visits to Jerusalem, initially right at the beginning of his ministry—and it is then that he causes mayhem in the Temple. Which are we to believe? It is not just a question of John's Gospel being outvoted by the other three, since Matthew and Luke are based on Mark, so if he got something wrong, they would too.

As we have seen, there is evidence, from both early traditions and modern academic analysis, that Mark created his story line when putting together isolated stories about Jesus, so his plot is not to be taken too literally. But does that mean we should totally accept John's Gospel? Unfortunately no. Seemingly the author of John tweaked his chronology to fit the cycle of Jewish festivals.[51] As Dodd wrote, "the arrangement of the narrative in the Fourth Gospel is now widely recognised as dictated by the order of thought much more than the order of events."[52] So sometimes John's Gospel is more credible than Mark's, sometimes vice versa.

Much more important, the Fourth Gospel presents Jesus in a fundamentally different way. Although to Mark, Matthew, and Luke he is the Son of God, he is also essentially a mortal man in the mold of the prophets, becoming something more transcendental only when he resurrects. But right from the beginning John unequivocally has Jesus as the "word made flesh" and "the Logos . . . preexistent and one with God."[53] This is similar to the way Paul talks about Jesus, and how later gnostics regarded him.

His character is different too. In Mark, Matthew, and Luke, Jesus talks directly about himself (using "I") just nine, seventeen, and ten times respectively, but in John he does so *118* times. In the Fourth Gospel Jesus speaks much more about his own importance and uniqueness: clearly the writer saw him not merely as God's messenger but actually as the message.

There is more. In the synoptics he characteristically speaks in short, pithy aphorisms; in John he delivers lengthy speeches in the manner of Greek discourse and engages in long, erudite disputes—and never presents his teaching in the form of parables, for which he is so famous in the other three Gospels. There are fewer miracles than in the synoptics—and no exorcisms at all. The miracles and healings in John serve to illustrate a point much more than they do in the other Gospels, suggesting that the writer is consciously shaping his story, his message taking priority over the biographical facts. As early as the opening words it is obvious that the author has devoted considerable thought to Jesus' meaning and purpose, producing a much more metaphysical work than the synoptics, even to the point of rewriting his character to fit the theological profile rather than the other way round.

One of John's most noticeable characteristics compared with the synoptics is the focus on incidental and circumstantial detail, giving it a more authentic feel. For example, in all four Gospels, when Jesus is arrested in the garden, a disciple lops the ear off one of the high priest's men. Only in John are we told the servant's name, Malchus, such attention to detail being typical of the writer (making it even odder that he never mentions the identity of the beloved disciple). Impressive though this may seem, it may not be evidence of inside information; after all, liars tend to overload their tales with elaborate detail.

There are other paradoxes in the way the Fourth Gospel treats Jesus' opposition or rivals. It is the most virulently anti-Jewish of all the Gospels, being more insistent that culpability for Jesus' death belongs collectively to all the Jews (rather than just their corrupt and spiritually blind leaders). The writer shows little interest in the distinctions between Pharisees, Sadducees, and so on; to him they are just "the Jews." Yet he is demonstrably conversant with Jewish customs and even seems to contrive his story to fit into the annual cycle of Jewish holy days. And paradoxically, given its anti-Semitic agenda, this Gospel provides the best evidence that it was the Romans, not the Jewish leadership, who condemned Jesus. There is a similar contradiction in John's depiction of the relationship between Jesus and the Baptist, presenting the clearest evidence that the latter was a much greater influence on Jesus than the first Christians cared to admit—yet being the most emphatic that the Baptist was inferior to Jesus.

Even dating this quirky, infuriating, and tantalizing book is by no means straightforward. Church tradition has always held it to be the last to be written, and modern scholarship concurs, albeit on different grounds. Although John's Gospel is generally thought to be the last—dated between 85 and 120 CE, with the academic consensus going for the later limit—this conclusion depends on certain assumptions, which are considered below. As it is by no means dependent on Mark in the same way as Matthew and Luke, it could come anywhere in the sequence. Since the 1960s scholars have generally become more open to the idea that at least parts of John might preserve material that is even earlier than Mark.

One of the major reasons why scholars originally considered John to be relatively late is that it was seen as too Hellenistic, in that it incorporates ideas and language derived more from the Greek world than the Jewish, suggesting a later development of the Jesus story in a Greek-style community. But this does not necessarily follow: Israel had been under Greek influence for centuries before Jesus came along, so the ideas could have crept in at any time.

Aside from theological considerations, another way of dating John's Gospel is by its content. And here we hit another wall of contradiction: some passages seem to reveal more authentic information about Jesus' time even than Mark, while the glaring anachronisms in other parts mean it must have been written quite late. In fact such apparent anomalies are not quite so hard to reconcile, since linguistic and stylistic evidence shows that the work was put together from several sources and in at least two stages. John originally began, like Mark, with the appearance of John the Baptist, and the "In the beginning was the Word" prologue was added later. Similarly it initially ended at chapter 20; the final chapter, including the beloved disciple's testimonial, was also a finishing touch.[54] So it is quite possible it was written in its final form comparatively late while containing some of the earliest, possibly eyewitness, information.

Another characteristic of John may not be so well recognized but was teased out by Andrew Lincoln in his 2005 commentary on the Gospel: it frequently features themes and motifs from Greek literature—including the myths of various pagan gods—showing that

the writer was familiar with them himself and suggesting that he expected his audience to be, too.[55] Lincoln shows that John was very
fond of drawing subtle comparisons between Jesus and pagan gods,
but was he trying to suggest that Jesus was superior or that essentially he resembled them?

Perfect Partners

Despite the long-maintained consensus that John's Gospel owed
nothing to the synoptics, since the 1990s opinion has split on the
question. It has been suggested that clues in John show that the
writer was at least aware of Mark, even though he may have simply
chosen to ignore most of his Gospel.

For a start, the very fact that John is a Gospel implies some
awareness of the others: after all, this was a brand-new genre, Mark
being the first of its kind. For an early Christian chronicler to write
in the same style, he must at least have heard about the others.
Mark and John also share certain literary idiosyncrasies, the classic
example being the delightfully named "Markan sandwich," where
Mark weaves two thematically connected stories together by starting to tell one, interrupting himself to tell the whole of another,
then returning to finish the first, as in the twinning of the healing of
Jairus' daughter and the woman with the issue of blood, and Peter's
denials of Jesus while Jesus is being tried. This is obviously a particular quirk of the author, but then John does the same, and with
some of the same stories, such as Peter's denials, which is surely
stretching coincidence too far.

Then there is the fact that John's Gospel is so different—almost
perversely so—from the synoptics. Before the climax in Jerusalem
beginning with Jesus' triumphal entry, when the two Gospel traditions, synoptic and "Johannine," fall into step, they share only two
events: Jesus' baptism and the feeding of the five thousand. (Even
the baptism is different, as the Fourth Gospel never actually describes Jesus being baptized by John the Baptist at all.) Apart from
that, everything diverges during the Galilee mission.

It is curious that the pivotal moments in the synoptic version are
absent from John, and vice versa. A major event at the start of Jesus'

ministry as related by Matthew, Mark, and Luke is his temptation by Satan in the wilderness, but this story is simply absent from John. The start of the mission in the Fourth Gospel, the first miracle and the sign by which Jesus reveals himself, is the turning of the water into wine at the wedding in Cana, which is not in the synoptics. And so it goes on. The two traditions are like two pieces of a jigsaw puzzle—or perhaps the yin and yang symbol. What is missing from each is provided by the other.

The avoidance of reprising the synoptics and featuring what they lack is so consistent it must be deliberate; the author must have known what was in Mark to be able to avoid it. This has long been recognized by Christian tradition, which came up with unconvincing explanations. The early idea was that the elderly apostle John wanted to set down his memories but, being familiar with the other Gospels, had no wish to duplicate them, so wrote down only what they left out. Apart from the fact that the traditional attribution to John is wrong, can we really imagine anyone working in that way? More metaphysically, perhaps it was deliberate on God's part: maybe the synoptic and Johannine traditions are supposed to work together like a lock and key in order to illuminate each other and reveal the truth about Jesus. One part alone doesn't work. But then neither does this explanation, because, as we will see, there are many incompatibilities between the two traditions that cancel each other out.

At least the early Church recognized that there was a link of some strange kind between the synoptics and John. Academia has only recently begun to properly recognize that the two gospel traditions should not be regarded as completely isolated. But how can we explain the "jigsaw fit"? Why should material have been taken out of Mark? And why should that same material (and broadly speaking that alone) end up in John?

A clue comes from the discovery that one part of the story that had always been seen as part of the jigsaw was originally in both Gospels. This is the raising of Lazarus, which is absolutely pivotal in John but entirely absent from the synoptic Gospels. Not only is it one of Jesus' most sensational miracles—bringing a young man back from the dead after four days in the tomb—but it is also a turning point in the story, since it is this that brings down the wrath of the Jewish leaders in Jerusalem on his head and inspires their plot to have him killed. Why would the other gospel writers want to keep quiet about such dramatic evidence of their hero's divine power?

But thanks to Morton Smith's discovery of the "Secret Gospel" of Mark, we now know that this event *was* in one of the other Gospels. And we also know it was taken out because it represented an "inner doctrine" meant not for all the faithful but only for certain higher initiates. And there is an intriguing sequel to the story, omitted by John, in which the youth Jesus raised from the tomb subsequently joins him in a nocturnal initiatory rite. The way John's Gospel presents this episode changes the meaning entirely, making it serve his own theological ideas and his obsession with the antagonism between the Jews and Jesus.

What if the Fourth Gospel was based on the parts of the original Mark that were removed because they were for initiates only? Precisely because they *were* secret, John obscured their real meaning, couching them in terms borrowed from other traditions and genres, while at the same time shaping them to fit his overall message. This would explain the strange "jigsaw fit" between Mark and John—John literally filling in the gaps created by removing the secret material from Mark, because it was *based* on the removed material in the first place. This would explain also the paradox of a clear literary connection between the two texts without any obvious borrowings between them. Indeed some researchers have already proposed, on other grounds, that the Fourth Gospel was based on certain "special teachings" that Jesus reserved for his inner circle of disciples.[56]

The Gospel of the Samaritans

Another aspect of the origins of John's Gospel that, in our view, has never received nearly enough attention is its connection with Samaria. We would go so far as to say that it is effectively the "Gospel of the Samaritans." Back in 1967 New Testament scholar Wayne A. Meeks demonstrated in *The Prophet-King* that its portrayal of Jesus was tailored to a specifically Samaritan audience.

An essential difference between Jews and Samaritans was that the latter accepted only the first five books of the Old Testament— the Pentateuch—which were attributed to Moses, and rejected the other books, particularly the prophets. To the Samaritans, Moses was the only prophet. They, like the Jews, had their own distinct beliefs about the imminent end of days and a messiah-like figure who would come to restore God's rule on earth. But none of their expectations focused on a messiah of the line of David—the royal line of the detested Jews—but on the return of either Moses himself or the advent of the Taheb ("the Returner" or "Restorer"), a kind of second Moses.

Meeks demonstrated that John's Gospel, while never making it explicit, constantly draws parallels between Jesus and Moses. This was done with subtle, underlying references and allusions that would inspire automatic, even subconscious associations in the minds of readers familiar with the greatest of the Old Testament prophets. So, Meeks concluded, it must have been written for a community in which Moses was not only held in especially high regard but also seen in terms of feverish "end-times" expectations. The best candidate, he argued, was a Samaritan community.

In addition, Samaria and the Samaritans feature in John as they never do in the synoptics, which saw them as very much to be avoided. The most obvious Johannine reference is Jesus' encounter with the Samaritan woman, to whom he is the first person to publicly declare his messiahship. Clearly, as American Catholic priest and theologian Raymond E. Brown observed, the Fourth Gospel "betrays a knowledge of local color and Samaritan beliefs that is impressive."[57]

A point not stressed by Meeks is that the Samaritans also regarded the Taheb as a kind of second Joshua, the ancestor who conquered the Promised Land, and Jesus' name—Yeshua—was actually a contraction of Yehoshua or Joshua.[58] The Samaritans could have easily been persuaded that he was the long-awaited Taheb.

Although Meeks' case for a Samaritan connection is convincing, New Testament experts as a whole have tended to disagree. Some commentators, however, are less critical. For example, the German-born theologian Oscar Cullmann wrote (his emphasis): "insufficient use has been made of more recent studies of *Samaritan* religion in seeking to understand certain Johannine conceptions, although this religion is in some respects especially close to the Gospel of John and heterodox Judaism."[59]

As we will see, the Samaritan subtext recurs again and again, even becoming the key to resolving the essential mysteries of Jesus.

Lost and Found

From the writings of the Church Fathers we know of at least the onetime existence of about forty noncanonical gospels. Today we have the more or less complete texts of a dozen, such as the recently discovered Gospel of Judas.

There are also a large number of fragments of lost works, sometimes referring to sayings or deeds of Jesus that are not in the New Testament but of roughly the same age. In fact one of the fragments—actually four small scraps of papyrus—in the British Museum known by the riveting title of "Egerton Papyrus 2" is possibly the oldest surviving document about Jesus in existence. Dated to between 90 and 150 CE, it is approximately the same age as the Rylands Fragment of John's Gospel; nobody can say for sure which came first. The Egerton fragments are all that is left of a book about Jesus that has otherwise gone for ever, but even those tiny bits contain stories—the healing of a leper and Jesus' escaping from a stoning "because the time of his betrayal had not yet come"—which are similar to the canonical Gospels but far from identical, besides an episode that is unlike any known gospel. In it Jesus stands on the bank of the River Jordan and seems to perform some miracle—perhaps producing fruit from trees by sprinkling river water on them, but because of the fragmentary nature of the text it is hard to be sure.[60]

There is one candidate for the title of "Fifth Gospel," since unquestionably it is at least the equal in age and authenticity to the canonical books. It is the Gospel of Thomas, attributed to the disciple of that name. A collection of Jesus' sayings, this book has been known in full for only sixty years. The first hints of its existence came from a number of papyrus fragments found between

1897 and 1903 in the major early Christian center of Oxyrhynchus (modern El Bahnasa) in Egypt. What startled scholars was that not only did the fragments contain several sayings attributed to Jesus not found in the Gospels, but they could be dated to between 150 and 200 CE, making them the oldest writings known about him at that time. However, it was another fifty years before a full copy of this lost work was found among the collection of documents discovered at Nag Hammadi in Egypt in 1945.

The Gospel of Thomas is something of a thorn in the flesh for those who believe the current New Testament is nothing less than God's own word. An analysis of its language reveals that it was composed between 75 and 100 CE, therefore at about the same time as the canonical Gospels were taking shape. But there are clues that point to it *predating* them.

The book is a collection of 114 sayings described, in the opening lines, as "the hidden words that the living Jesus spoke," written down by "Didymus Judas Thomas." Thomas is Aramaic for "twin," and Didymus also means "twin" in Greek, so it is really just a translation of his name, or rather nickname. Some of the sayings are presented as statements by Jesus, others in the form of a question-and-answer session with the disciples, as in other gnostic books. About a third echo or parallel sayings in the New Testament, but many are completely new.

Some of the sayings are simpler forms of parables that occur in the synoptic Gospels, suggesting that the writers of Mark, Matthew, and Luke elaborated—and, even more significantly, in some cases misunderstood—the original lesson. For example, in the "Consider the lilies" passage, Luke and Matthew have "They do not labor or spin," but in Thomas it is "They do not card or spin," carding being the preparation of wool for spinning.[61] Therefore Thomas seems to have a more accurate version of the original saying, which became slightly muddled by the time it reached Luke and Matthew, arriving there, like all the common sayings material in those Gospels, via Q. In other words, Thomas gives a purer, and therefore earlier, version, showing that it must have predated even Q. The fact that the Gospel of Thomas appeals to the authority of two apostles, James the Just and Thomas himself, whose roles were soon eclipsed by those associated with Rome, Peter and Paul, also points to an early date.

The implications are truly far-reaching. At the very least we should take the Gospel of Thomas as seriously as the canonical Gospels, as indeed do New Testament scholars and non-Catholic theologians. The Catholic Church, however, has condemned it as heretical. To them, had God meant Christians to read it, it would have been in the New Testament.

One of this gospel's most interesting features is how it portrays Jesus' disciples. First, and most strikingly, they included women, two in particular, Mary (almost certainly the Magdalene, although not explicitly stated) and Salome, among his questioners. Secondly, while Thomas, Mary, and Salome ask intelligent, searching questions that show they understand Jesus' teaching, those posed by Peter and Matthew (besides various unnamed disciples) reveal they have little idea of his mind-set, giving Jesus the chance to correct them. There is a distinct impression that a few favored disciples constituted an inner circle—and while this includes the only two named women, it emphatically does not include Peter. This is strikingly different from the way the disciples are portrayed in the New Testament.

This theme recurs in another important "lost and found" gospel. Often mistakenly lumped together with the Nag Hammadi collection (because it was included in the first major translation of all the texts), the Gospel of Mary is known from a single fifth-century papyrus copy. Frustratingly missing some key pages, including the opening ones, it was found in an antique shop in Cairo in 1896 and ended up in the Berlin Museum, its existence remaining unknown outside specialist circles. It was not until 1955 that a full translation was published. A fragment found at Oxyrhynchus has been dated to the early 200s. Some scholars place its original writing as 150 or even earlier—making it possibly contemporary with the canonical Gospels.[62]

The Gospel of Mary is short and rather sweet, opening with "the Teacher" or "the Blessed One" giving a last lesson to his disciples, including Mary Magdalene, the only woman mentioned, before he finally leaves them. Although it seems to describe Jesus' valedictory postresurrection appearance before ascending bodily into heaven, without the opening pages it is impossible to be sure. It is Mary who rallies the bereft and despairing male disciples: it seems that without her articulate and vigorous intervention they would have sunk into a depressed apathy. She tells them of a vision she had of Jesus, who gave her more teaching, which divides the disciples, particularly Peter (never her friend nor inclined to be sympathetic to women), over whether they should accept what she has said, with some suggestion she invented the whole thing. Levi then steps in and effects a reconciliation—which one suspects was reluctant and only temporary, at least on Peter's side. At that point the Gospel ends.

There are in fact good reasons for believing that the work was based on an original that really had been passed down from Jesus' day. It is apparent that the Gospel of Mary as we have it was produced by combining two separate sources.[63] The original core seems to have been very early. In particular the relationship between Jesus and Mary Magdalene—and her problems with Peter—chime with other suppressed texts. Although we will be returning to this issue, at this stage we can conclude that the Gospel of Mary, like the other gnostic texts, should not be rejected out of hand, but perhaps not credulously believed in its entirety either.

The Gnostic Gospels

Significantly, most of the recently discovered texts are gnostic works. Even the Gospel of Thomas is basically gnostic in spirit, which is probably partly why it fell out of favor.

The formative period of Christianity, the first and second centuries, was characterized by a great conflict between two opposing fundamental approaches: *pistis* (faith) and *gnosis* (knowing). Faith—Paul's approach—tacitly admits that mere humans find it impossible to comprehend God's will, seeing the way to salvation in trusting in Jesus. Gnosis, on the other hand, sees salvation as achieved through a direct, personal experience and understanding of Jesus. (In that sense, modern evangelical Christians, in their insistence on the primacy of their inner experience of Jesus Christ, are more gnostic than they would care to admit. However, as we are about to see, there is considerably more to the definition of a gnostic.)

The difference between the two approaches has obvious implications for the concept of authority. In the "faith" system, an organized church, sanctioned by God and with a distinct hierarchy, is needed to guide the believer and help with any crisis of faith. Gnosis requires no such organization: since salvation is in one's own hands, gnostic teachers are more like gurus, guiding individuals along the path but unable to lead them. Small wonder, then, that gnosis lost the battle.

Faith's victory means that history has been biased in its favor: not unnaturally, the Church portrayed its approach to Christianity as the authentic version taught by Jesus himself, while gnosticism was condemned as a contamination of the religion that bore little or no relation to his true meaning. This was the prevailing view for centuries: by definition gnosticism was just plain wrong. However, modern scholarship has shown that this is a gross oversimplification.

It is not often appreciated that the struggle between faith and gnosis shaped conventional Christian doctrine and theology just as much as it did gnostic Christianity. Gnosticism helped orthodox Christianity define itself. As Yale professor and specialist in gnosticism Bentley Layton puts it, "to some degree proto-orthodox theology was conceived of as being what gnostic theology was *not*."[64]

But what exactly is gnosticism? The Greek *gnostikos* referred to the ability to acquire knowledge, but an early Christian sect adapted the term, calling itself *gnostikoi*, "the Knowers." The earliest reference to this sect is in a condemnation by Irenaeus, Bishop of Lugdunum (modern Lyon), written about 180 CE. This "knowing" relates to *personal understanding* rather than intellectual cognition—analogous to the French *connaître* as opposed to *savoir*. Gnostics often claimed a secret revelation as the source of their information and authority—but then again, so did Paul.

However, there is considerably more to gnosticism than just the attitude that salvation is essentially in one's own hands and requires the building of a direct personal communion with the divine. It also encompasses a specific set of beliefs about the nature of the material world. To gnostics, the world is inherently flawed, having become separated from its creator, causing an antipathy between the divine and matter, a view known as dualism. Since gnostics regarded creation itself as intrinsically evil, they had a radically different view of the nature of sin: rather than it being solely the province of individual ethics, to them it was nothing less than a cosmological problem. (At the start of the gnostic Gospel of Mary, Jesus himself talks in these terms.) And it was this idea that led them to a concept of salvation entirely different from that of conventional Christianity.

To heal the rift and build a bridge between the worlds of matter and the divine, the creator sends a redeemer—who had coexisted with God since the beginning of time—who either takes on the appearance of human form or enters into a human being. To gnostic Christians, this redeemer was Jesus: a semidivine entity who had always existed and whose incarnation brings the possibility of redemption to the material world, starting the process of reversing the original fall. (In that sense, gnostic thinking is reminiscent of Paul's teachings, but the expression of their ideas was very different.)

Gnostic Christianity took one of two views about Jesus, representing different attempts to explain the same basic concept of him as redeemer. Some held that he was a mortal man into whom the semidivine entity, Christ, entered. Others believed that Jesus was only ever that entity and had merely appeared to take on a material form, a kind of walking hologram—a belief known as docetism.

Gnostics developed the basic two-way split between spirit and matter into increasingly complex—and often unintentionally ludicrous—cosmologies, of multileveled planes of existence inhabited by spirit entities and angels, through which the individual soul had to ascend in order to reunite with God.

Their view of the material world as inherently evil inspired them to choose one of two paradoxically opposite lifestyles: either extreme asceticism, in which the things of the world are shunned, or, less commonly, extreme libertinism. The latter was adopted—presumably enthusiastically—by the colourful Carpocratians, whom we met earlier.

Despite the Church's later identification of gnosticism as the antithesis of "true" Christianity, many of its ideas lurk between the lines of the New Testament. Paul viewed Jesus as a preexistent being who had been sent by God to redeem humankind. And most strikingly, the opening of John's Gospel, describing Jesus as the Word that had existed alongside God from the beginning being made flesh, encapsulates perfectly the gnostic conception of the redeemer.

The Church Fathers unhesitatingly identified gnosticism as heretical, therefore by definition occurring after Jesus. Until the twentieth century, historians tended to subscribe to the idea it was a "parasite" on the body of the Church (and a few still do). But it became increasingly apparent that the relationship was by no means so simple and that gnostic Christianity drew on schools of thought that predated Jesus: "We now know that Gnosticism was not simply a Christian heresy of the second century."[65]

The big question is, if gnosticism existed before Christianity, where did it come from?

The question has been hotly debated for decades but never conclusively answered. There are essentially three views: in a Jewish, Greek, or Persian milieu. Or perhaps it was some permutation of all three: contact between cultures under the Greeks and Romans meant many philosophies intermingled and even fused, particularly in Alexandria.

Most commentators assume that wherever it came from, gnosticism was essentially grafted onto Christianity, having no connection with what Jesus himself taught. If so, fascinating though it might be for our understanding of theological development, it is not strictly relevant to our quest to find the historical Jesus. On the other hand, if, as many are beginning to believe, the gnostics' texts *are* based on Jesus' own teachings, this fact would provide valuable clues. If, for example, we could confirm that he himself was a devotee of, say, Egyptian gnosticism, then we would be much nearer to identifying the real Jesus.

Scholarly study of gnostic Christianity and its relationship to what Jesus himself was about was hampered by the fact that all the available information was in the form of summaries and quotations embedded in deeply hostile works. However, a discovery some sixty years ago finally allowed us to hear the voice of the gnostics themselves.

Under the Sands of Egypt

Discovered in Nag Hammadi, near the small town of Chenoboskion in Upper Egypt, in 1945, this momentous find consisted of thirteen codices, written in Coptic (the Egyptian language written in the Greek alphabet) on papyrus and bound in leather, containing forty-six separate texts (six of which are duplicated). Twelve of the books are complete, one is fragmentary, but all have suffered serious damage, with parts difficult to read or completely missing.

Not all of them are Christian. Some of the texts are pagan gnostic, some Jewish gnostic commentaries on Old Testament books such as Genesis, some Hermetic treatises, and there is even a fragment of a translation of Plato's *Republic*. Of the works in which Jesus appears, most are markedly gnostic, leading to the slightly inaccurate collective term "gnostic gospels." Clearly the collection was from a library owned either by an individual or a sect, and presumably the books were hidden during the persecution of heretical Christian groups (along with pagan religions) by the new mainstream, Roman form of the religion that took control in Egypt toward the end of the fourth century.

Although the books were easily dated to around 350 CE, as with the canonical Gospels, the crucial question is, how old was the source material? (After all, nobody would claim on the basis of this discovery that the *Republic* was written in 350 CE.) There is in fact no doubt that they are copies of older books, since all these Coptic works have obviously been translated from Greek originals. What is unclear is just how much earlier they were. Sometimes clues appear in other sources: for example, since one of the books, *The Secret Book According to John*, was condemned in the writings of Irenaeus around 180 CE, it must have existed about two centuries before the Nag Hammadi copy.

Argument about the dating of the gnostic gospels tends to be circular: since they disagree with the canonical Gospels, they must be later, apocryphal writings, and therefore have nothing useful to offer about Jesus and his time. They are often airily dismissed purely on the grounds that they have such a different flavor from the canonical Gospels. British historian Ian Wilson writes that they are "typical of the apocryphal flights of fancy concocted by the gnostic sects of Christianity's early years." [66] And Bishop John A. T. Robinson says uncompromisingly, "these myths are speculative and mystical versions, and perversions of the Christian preaching." [67]

However, such arguments rest on the assumption that the canonical Gospels are the most authentic accounts of Jesus and his teaching, and the only reason for making that assumption is that they were selected by the early Church as authentic. But how did the selection committee know what was authentic and what was not? And, as we have seen, the formulation of the Christian canon took place against a struggle between *pistis* and *gnosis*, and those who made the decisions were always going to favor the nongnostic works. What if the gnostics are closer to Jesus' message and the New Testament books are wrong?

There is a certain double standard in the bias toward the canonical Gospels and against the gnostic works. For example, discussing the story of the woman taken in adultery—inserted into John's Gospel in the twelfth century but first recorded in the third— Andrew Lincoln writes that "the lateness of a tradition does not rule out its basic historicity."[68] It certainly doesn't, so why does "lateness" undermine the gnostic gospels?

This said, however, undoubtedly most of the gnostic works in the collection have little or no connection with Jesus: they were written in the second or third centuries by people with no real interest in the historical facts (any more than Paul had). Some seem to have been based on what they think Jesus should have said rather than confining themselves to what he actually said (again, like Paul).

But does this mean the gnostic gospels are entirely without value? Could they perhaps retain a genuine memory of, for example, the relationship between Jesus and his disciples—particularly Mary Magdalene? After all, the creators of these documents had decided to become Christians, so they must have known something about the religion. True, they may have recast parts of it to suit their worldview, but their core beliefs must have been basically the same as those of the Christians who read and accepted the canonical Gospels. (After all, as we will see, even the writers and editors of the New Testament books were not above reinventing passages when it suited them theologically or even politically.) But on the other hand, although both their supporters and their detractors tend to lump the books together, as they are a collection of disparate texts, each one needs to be assessed on its merits. The gnostic gospels can be used to help us in our search for the real Jesus, although we have to tread carefully and with discernment.

2

THE MAN WHO NEVER WAS AND THE CHRIST WHO SHOULDN'T HAVE BEEN

Before embarking on our quest for the historical Jesus, there is one question we must address, or all our work—not to mention the purchase of this book—will have been in vain: did he actually exist?

As the Internet demonstrates, there is a rapidly growing group who believe that any quest to identify the real Jesus is doomed from the start. To them he was either a mythical or fictional character, at best only loosely based on a flesh-and-blood man or a composite of several people, both actual and legendary.

The idea has been around ever since scholars started—or were allowed—to study Jesus from a historical perspective. They soon recognized the unsound historicity of much of the New Testament Gospels and the many glaring parallels between their depiction of Jesus and pagan gods and heroes. The earliest advocates of this theory included Scottish writer and MP J. M. Robertson (*Christianity and Mythology*, 1900, and *Pagan Christs*, 1903). More recent exponents are the British-based Egyptian researcher Ahmed Osman (*The House of the Messiah*, 1992); the British philosopher/historian team of Timothy Freke and Peter Gandy (*The Jesus Mysteries*, 1999, and other books); "Acharya S.," or Dorothy M. Murdock (*The Christ Conspiracy*, 1999); and philosopher and filmmaker Jay Raskin (*The Evolution of Christs and Christianities*, 2006).

We can also include such theories as the famous proposal by Dead Sea Scroll scholar John M. Allegro in the 1970s that early Christianity was a cult based on the altered state of consciousness created by a type of hallucinogenic mushroom, "Jesus" being code for the phenomenon. It is quite a demotion—from God incarnate to an edible fungus, albeit a foodstuff with wildly interesting side effects.

Although we believe there was a real Jesus, we do agree that the Christ created by the Church when it established itself as the official religion of the Roman Empire in the fourth century—the supreme and omniscient Son of God, the second person of the Trinity, which took him way beyond even the reinventions of Paul—is only loosely related to the man in the Gospels. However, it is not impossible, even now, to catch vivid glimpses of the historical Jesus behind the fabricated halo of the mythical Christ.

Most of the "mythical Jesus" theories are based on the absence of contemporary references to him outside the Gospels and the similarity between his story and those of pagan gods, heroes, or sometimes historical characters from the Gentile world. Neither proves Jesus never existed. His nonappearance in secular sources was probably simply because he was nowhere near as famous in his lifetime as later Christians believe. In any case there is enough evidence outside the Gospels to establish that Jesus really did live and breathe.

First, there are Paul's Letters. Although he never met Jesus, Paul did write (to fellow believers, not propagandizing like the Gospels) of his meetings with Jesus' brother James and chief disciple Peter. How could a nonexistent character boast a brother and a right-hand man?

And there *is* one—albeit controversial—source that mentions Jesus, which, while not precisely contemporary, dates from about the same time the Gospels were taking shape: the works of the Romanized Jew Flavius Josephus (37–ca. 100 CE). At the outbreak of the first Jewish Revolt in 66 CE he became commander of the Jewish defense in Galilee. Captured by the Romans, he acted as interpreter and negotiator for their commander, Vespasian, who was proclaimed emperor and handed over command to his son Titus—another subsequent emperor—for whom Josephus continued to work and even befriended. At the end of the campaign Josephus accompanied him to Rome, even taking his family name of Flavius. Titus gave him a villa and a pension that kept him as he penned his books.

Josephus wrote two great books, *The Jewish War*, in the late seventies CE and *Antiquities of the Jews* in the early nineties. Although he was a generation younger than Jesus, these works—researched from Roman archives and interviews with eyewitnesses—cover the period in which we are interested. They provide valuable context to Jesus' life, including appearances of several leading Gospel characters such as Pontius Pilate, the high priest Caiaphas, and, most significantly, John the Baptist. And *Antiquities of the Jews* includes two controversial references, one direct and the other indirect, to Jesus. If these anecdotes are genuine, they are among the earliest—perhaps *the* earliest—memories to be immortalized. This is the first reference:

> Now, there was about this time Jesus, a wise man, if it be lawful to call him a man, for he was a doer of wonderful works, a teacher of such men as receive the truth with pleasure. He drew over to him both many of the Jews, and many of the Gentiles. He was [the] Christ. And when Pilate, at the suggestion of the principal men amongst us, had condemned him to the cross, those that loved him at the first did not forsake him; for he appeared to them alive again at the third day; as the divine prophets had foretold these and ten thousand other wonderful things concerning him.[1]

The second reference appears in a passage about the persecution in 62 CE:

> So he [Annas the high priest] assembled the sanhedrin of judges, and brought before them the brother of Jesus, who was called *Christ*, whose name was *James*, and some others. And when he had formed an accusation against them as breakers of the law, he delivered them to be stoned . . .[2]

Sadly the first reference could never be genuine Josephus, reading far too blatantly like second- or third-century Christians' enthusiasm about Jesus. It also jars with "called the Christ" in the second reference, which implies some skepticism.

Eusebius, bishop of Caesarea, in the fourth century quotes the first passage as we know it, so it was certainly in the book by then. But a century before him, Origen of Alexandria wrote that Josephus, in *Antiquities*, explicitly *rejected* Jesus as Messiah. This suggests that an original uncomplimentary comment had been changed some time between Origen and Eusebius. Of course, in Eusebius' time the Church was in a position of power and could doctor chronicles such as Josephus', whereas in Origen's day it was relatively inconsequential and lacked editorial muscle.

For these reasons the first reference has long been recognized as a later addition, while the second is considered more likely to be authentic. (Origen does refer to the second, which is less likely to have been invented by later Christians.) But was the reference to Jesus just invented to cover up the embarrassing fact that the major Jewish chronicler of the time thought he was only important because of his brother? Or did it replace a slighting comment about Jesus? The evidence points to the latter (a conclusion which incidentally marks a change in our own thinking over the past ten years).

The leading New Testament scholars Geza Vermes and Fergus Millar have suggested that certain parts of the passage are originally by Josephus: he calls Jesus a "wise man"—odd for a Christian to write but one of his favorite phrases—and refers to his "wonderful works" (*paradoxon*, literally "paradoxical works," but usually meaning miracles), which is also characteristic. Apparently this passage was adapted by Christians, not completely invented.[3]

Even though Josephus is disappointing as a source of information about Jesus, the reference does at least show that to the chronicler he was a real person.[4] There is also a brief mention in the works of the Roman writer Tacitus of the (unnamed) founder of the Christian sect having been crucified by Pilate—written ca. 115 CE, long after the event but at least revealing that Tacitus, too, believed him to have been a flesh-and-blood man.

Other arguments also seriously undermine the "nonexistent Jesus" theory. The concept of inventing purely fictional characters was unknown at that time: even completely imaginary stories were peopled either with figures from myth or, as in Plato's dialogues, real historical characters. Even fabricated tales about Jesus would have been based on a real man, who must have made some sort of impression.

Then there is the "irrefutability principle," which, as applied to this issue, is explained by Geoffrey Ashe: "if Jesus had not been a real person, somebody would have said so."[5] From the very beginning Christianity had its opponents in both the Jewish and pagan worlds, but even they took Jesus' existence as read. Finally, why should such time and energy have been devoted to convincing people about the reality of a nonexistent man? Why did so many people invest so much effort in perpetuating a completely false memory?

Inside Q

Another influential group, while not denying that Jesus existed, believe that the New Testament Gospels were so heavily fictionalized as to be useless as information about Jesus. This is the "Q school," promoted most prominently by Burton L. Mack in a series of books.

As we saw in the previous chapter, the origin of the text designated Q was deduced from the fact that Matthew and Luke share certain of Jesus' sayings taken from a common source—but one which certainly wasn't Mark. This school argues that Q was the earliest Christian text, a collection of Jesus' sayings. Mack concludes that Jesus was revered solely as a great and profound teacher, *everything else* being later invention and mythmaking. In other words, we should recognize only Q as authentic, and not any other parts of the Gospels. According to Mack, Mark consciously invented most of his Jesus story, including such pivotal moments as his baptism by John the Baptist (Mack arguing that the two never actually met) and even the great climax where Jesus was betrayed, condemned to death, and crucified. But is Mack correct?

Reconstructing Q was easy enough: all scholars had to do was pull out the sayings shared by Matthew and Luke. But by analyzing the language, style, and content, the current Q scholars claim to be able to distinguish two distinct strands within the original text, representing Q as it was first written and a substantial later revision. The earlier version, being closest in time to Jesus' life, is considered to be the most faithful to his message.

The scholars argue that the original Q reveals Jesus as at best a kind of generic wisdom teacher, without any hellfire-and-damnation end-times message (or even any affiliation to Judaism). But a first-generation group of followers in Judea, living through the horrors of the Roman suppression of the Jewish Revolt, adopted a more apocalyptic vision and reinvented Jesus as an end-time visionary. Mack claims it was at that time that the revision happened. The original book of sayings was left intact, but extra passages developed his words in terms of the revisionists' new, extreme message. After that another group rewrote Jesus even further, creating the tale of his crucifixion and resurrection—a new myth encapsulated in Mark's Gospel. Both versions were put together when Matthew and Luke used Mark and the revised Q for their own Gospels. So to the Q school, although Jesus was real, all the alleged biographical information, from birth to crucifixion, is fiction or myth. Only the original Q represents the true man: simply a wisdom teacher.

The notion of collecting the teachings of a holy man in a "wisdom book" was not unknown in the Jewish world, but these academics discern a significant difference between them and the style of Q and a much closer parallel with the Greek school of Cynic philosophers, which originated in the fourth century BCE but was very much in vogue in the Roman Empire of Jesus' day. Cynics practised *parresia*, "boldness of speech," intended to startle or shock the hearer into thinking about a familiar concept in a novel way. In fact the similarity of certain sayings of Jesus to aspects of Cynic philosophy has long been recognized by New Testament scholars, who, however, have largely dismissed its importance. But Mack and his colleagues have now decided that Jesus was literally a Cynic teacher, no more and no less. (This is by no means as out of place as it seems: there was a celebrated Cynic school in Gadara, a city only about a day's travel from Lake Galilee.)[6]

The material in Q concerned with matching Jesus to scriptural prophecies, and also preaching a coming day of judgment when he will return in triumph, does not fit the Cynic style. These parts have no connection with the historical Jesus, Mack responds robustly, writing, "The recent studies of Q suggested . . . that Jesus was first remembered as a Cynic sage and only later imagined as a prophet who uttered apocalyptic warnings."[7] He entirely dismisses any notion that Jesus might have been thought of as the Messiah by his followers, declaring this to be a part of the revision or even added later.

However, as we will see, we believe the evidence does not support Mack's argument: Jesus did preach an end-times message and there is no doubt that he was crucified, even if parts of the story are essentially fantasy. There are other possible scenarios to explain why the original Q should have been revised—perhaps to create a more complete story of Jesus by incorporating other sources.

The major problem for Mack's reconstruction is the need to justify the claim that only Q retains anything genuine about Jesus. He himself identifies several different groups of early traditions about Jesus that coalesced in the Gospels. Besides those who collected Jesus' sayings to produce Q, Mack identifies a further group that created other "pronouncement stories"—from which came the parts of Jesus' teachings in the Gospels that did not come from Q— and another that invented "miracle stories" about Jesus. But because they make no appearance in Q, Mack rejects them as later folklore. But why would anyone who didn't *already* believe Jesus did these things revere him highly enough to invent the stories?

Neither does Mack satisfactorily explain why, if Jesus was merely a Cynic-style itinerant teacher, with no religious or political ambitions whatsoever, different groups of his followers should have wanted to reinvent him in so many ways after his death. One turned him into the Jewish Messiah by linking his teachings to Jewish scriptures. Another made him a divine hero who died a noble death to bring us salvation. And so on. Mack explains these reinventions as side effects of the social, religious, and psychological turmoil that exploded in the wake of the Roman suppression of the Jewish Revolt. Their reinvented Jesus met an inner need to reassure an uncertain world.

But as the very core of Mack's conclusion that Jesus was a Cynic comes from a comparison with the many similar figures at that time, *by definition* there was nothing particularly special about Jesus. Why then should the first generation of his followers have felt so compelled to reinvent this particular teacher? Why didn't it happen to the others? After all, there were many to choose from—would-be messiahs and strange, ranting, apocalyptic figures with the fires of hell in their eyes. Why not find solace with them, instead of somebody with (to Mack) no hint of messiahship or the characteristics of an archetypal sacrificial dying-and-rising god? Why invent stories to force him into the role, like Cinderella's stepsisters painfully and pointlessly trying to cram their feet into the glass slipper? None of this account explains why this particular man inspired so many different reinventions.

However, there *is* a genuine paradox when the Q sayings are compared with the other passages of the Gospels: they are indeed reminiscent of Cynic aphorisms, containing nothing specific about the religious or political side of Jesus that runs through the rest of the gospel story. The basis of the Q scholars' reconstruction is that it is far easier to imagine the followers of a Cynic-style teacher recreating him as the Messiah or the Son of God than it is to imagine followers of someone they believed to be the Messiah or the Son of God reducing him to a Cynic-style philosopher. To that extent they have a point.

Could both texts be essentially correct? Could Jesus have taught like a Cynic, while also harboring a revolutionary religious and political ambition? Even in ancient times surely no one was quite as single-minded and uncomplicated as the Q school would have us believe, particularly those who were exceptional enough to leave their mark on history.

To take a more recent example, consider Mahatma Gandhi, a devout Hindu holy man and spiritual teacher, but nevertheless a political activist and campaigner for Indian independence from the British Empire. He was also known for his sharp wit and aphorisms, some of which were rather similar to the Cynics' *parresia*. ("What do I think of Western civilization? I think it would be a very good idea," and, perhaps more relevantly, "I like your Christ, I do not like your Christians; your Christians are so unlike your Christ.") On Mack's logic, Gandhi could not have been all these things, so some of them—presumably anything that didn't appear in his followers' collections of his sayings—must have been myths invented by his later followers. This example highlights the limitations of Mack's black-and-white reasoning: if Q represents the genuine sayings of Jesus, then *no other source* is genuine; if Jesus used Cynic-style aphorisms, then he was a Cynic teacher *and nothing else*.

However, while the Q school's conclusions may be overstated, they have made two valuable contributions. The first is to recognize that many of Q's sayings came from a Greek, not a Judaic, worldview. The second is to stress that the story of Jesus must be set against the context of his time and place, particularly in presenting Galilee as a cosmopolitan place in which the religious and philosophical ideas of many cultures were often interwoven, rather than confined to the Gospels' limited picture. Jesus could have been— and probably was—open to influences other than a narrow schooling in Judaism.

The Emperor's Rival

None of this is to say that the Gospels' description of Jesus' life and mission is to be taken at face value: far from it. Nobody would (or rather should—the Church would) deny that Jesus has been mythologized. All major figures are mythologized to some degree—just look what happened to Princess Diana—but in Jesus' case there is even more incentive for invention, as his followers justified him by reference to Old Testament prophecies. And, as we will see, they were not above bending his biography to fit the prophecies. Factor in the genuinely blank spots in his life story and there is more than enough scope for invention and imagination. But Jesus must have been a remarkable man to begin with; nobodies are not turned into gods.

Another layer of reinterpretation comes from the fact that by the time they came to write the Gospels, Christians—usually referred to as "post-Easter" Christians, but perhaps "postcrucifixion" or "postresurrection" Christians is better—were living in different circumstances from Jesus and his disciples. Inevitably this difference influenced the way the writers chose to tell their story, so that they emphasized what was relevant to the new situation, while minimizing or leaving out altogether what was no longer relevant. Sometimes, because of his different environment, one of the authors would completely miss the point about a particular episode— incidentally revealing that he was reporting Jesus' real words or deeds (hard to explain if he was entirely fictional). And sometimes an event has been reinterpreted: what Jesus said has been amended to fit the current situation.

As none of the Gospels is very long, clearly the writers were highly selective about the information they included. After all, obviously not every conversation, healing, or journey is included, so we are presented from the start with a somewhat restricted picture. But detective work can still effectively strip away the accretions to lay bare the historical person.

Some layers of symbolism are no longer immediately obvious. Mark's Gospel opens with the words "The beginning of the good news about Jesus the Messiah, the Son of God."[8] "Good news" is *evangelia*, but at that time the word had no immediate association with an itinerant miracle worker from a distant part of the Roman Empire. At that time it specifically referred to the emperor's birthday, which had to be celebrated throughout the Empire by order. An inscription to Augustus in Priene in Asia Minor, dating from 9 BCE, makes the parallel clear:

> That Providence which guides all things in our life . . . conferred on our life the most perfect ornament by granting to us Augustus, and for the well-being of mankind filled him with virtue and sent him to us and to our offspring to be a savior, destined to make every war to cease . . . the birthday of this god is become the beginning of glad tidings [*evangelia*] regarding him for the world.[9]

Reading back then about the "good news" of a "Son of God," most people would naturally assume it was the beginning of an emperor's life story. But as it became obvious this was rather different, as New Testament historian Carsten Peter Thiede points out (our emphasis), "those readers of Mark's Gospel would have understood that the dramatic beginning, the hitherto unheard-of good news . . . concern[ed] a *rival* to the emperor."[10] Without inviting disaster by spelling it out, Mark is telling his audience that Jesus, despite his humble origins—and the fact that he was, as far as the Romans were concerned, very dead—was superior to the great emperor in Rome, the man who ruled the world.

In fact parallels with the emperors consistently bubble along under the surface of the story, especially when Jesus returns from the dead, a phenomenon claimed for even the most dissolute emperor, such as Nero.[11] And as he was the first and most notorious of the imperial Christian persecutors, there was a blatant motive for implicitly portraying Jesus as not merely his equal but his superior. But how far did this agenda shape the Gospels? Were certain passages shamelessly invented simply to make the analogy work?

A perfect example of the conscious drawing of parallels with Roman emperors comes right at the start of Jesus' ministry. In the synoptic Gospels, after his baptism he undergoes a major trial in the wilderness, where he is tested by Satan. As the story comes from two root sources, Mark's Gospel and Q, it must represent a very early tradition, and seemingly it was a real experience marking some kind of turning point or personal epiphany. Perhaps it was a similar type of experience to that of St. Anthony the Hermit in the desert, where it is hard to tell whether the temptations were visions generated in his head as a result of fasting and other privations or some objectively real experience.

Mark tells us virtually nothing other than that it happened. Jesus is "driven out" into the wilderness by the Spirit that descended on him at his baptism. He spends "forty days"—an umbrella term for a long time—in the wilderness, where he is tempted by Satan and taken care of by angels. Matthew and Luke elaborate, however (with shared details from Q), describing how Jesus rejects the Devil's three requests: to turn stones into bread to feed himself; cast himself from the highest tower of the Temple as proof of his faith that God will save him; and become king of the world in return for paying homage to Satan.[12]

But did Q describe what really happened to Jesus, or was the story more or less invented to point a moral? Obviously it was intended to set an example to Christians not to compromise their beliefs for sustenance, security, or power, but the tests also link Jesus to Old Testament tales about Moses and the founding of Israel. In fact Jesus' responses are taken directly from Deuteronomy and are the correct responses according to the earliest Israelite tradition, creating inescapable parallels between him and Moses.

Appropriately enough, two relate to the Israelites' time in the wilderness under Moses. The "stones" temptation relates to the episode in Deuteronomy when the people of Israel craved bread and were told by God that bread alone was not enough to save them. The "tower" test urges trust in Yahweh in the trials to come, which the Israelites failed while Jesus is triumphant.[13]

It has been pointed out that these abilities were exactly what was expected of the Messiah—"material welfare, stunt-type wonder-working, Jewish world power."[14] Some have suggested that this represented Jesus' *rejection* of the role, or at least its conventional interpretation.[15] Others have even seen it as a rejection of Yahweh himself, and therefore Judaism as a whole.[16] But the apparent rejection of these messianic expectations is only superficial: doing any of these things is not wrong in itself: they should be done for the right reason, to further God's plan, not Satan's (or one's own personal ambitions). Indeed, as Gerd Theissen argues, the whole episode is actually about *defining* the Messiah's role, being

> a struggle over the correct understanding of the Messiah, either as determined by faith in miracles (as in the first two temptations) or by hope in a political messiah who will assume power over the world (as in the last temptation). If the emphasis lies on the third temptation, we would have to agree in principle with a "political" interpretation, except to say that here it is no Zealot ideal of the messiah that is being rejected, but a religiously inflated absolutist claim to power (a point on which those behind this text would have agreed with the Zealots).[17]

In other words, Jesus is not rejecting world power as such, but a specific type of global domination, which Theissen believes is hinted at in Luke and involves another layer of symbolism that can only have been added after Jesus' time. To Theissen the "kingdoms of the world" temptation was a veiled attack on the Roman emperor of the day. In the apparently innocent language of the Gospels we detect a simmering cauldron of political unrest just under the surface, which their first readers would have understood immediately.[18]

Satan takes Jesus to a high place and shows him all the kingdoms of the world, saying, "I will give you all their authority and splendor, for it has been given to me, and I can give it to anyone I want to. So if you worship me, it will all be yours." Jesus rejects the offer, again quoting from Deuteronomy that one should serve only God.[19] Theissen observes that this test consists of prostration before a world ruler who has the power to bestow kingdoms and whose worship is a direct offense against God. All these elements were features of the reign of Caligula—but no emperor before him.

The incompatibility of Jewish monotheism with the imperial cult—worshipping the emperor as a living god was mandatory throughout the Empire—created an obvious dilemma for Jews under the Romans. However, their leaders agreed to a compromise in which Temple sacrifices were offered up *for* the emperors but not *to* them. This satisfied most of the rulers, to whom such a subtle distinction was hardly worth a draconian reaction. It was only the most megalomaniac emperors, the most insistent on their own divinity, who tried to force the Jews into recognizing the imperial cult. The first to make an issue of it was the monstrous but—from the safe vantage point of the twenty-first century—highly entertaining Caligula.

Matthew describes the world over which Satan offers total power as *kosmos*, "all creation," whereas Luke employs *ecumene*, "the known world," a synonym for the Roman Empire. Luke also spells out that Satan can create kings, consciously emphasizing the common ground between Satan and the Roman emperor: Caligula, for example, created six monarchs in the East, starting with Herod Agrippa I in 39 CE. (The Herodian rulers of Jesus' day were tetrarchs, not kings.)

A further clue lies in the word translated as "worship," *proskynesis*, more accurately "prostrate yourself before." This refers to the practice of making a full-length obeisance before the emperor, which the Roman Republic and early Empire found repugnantly redolent of the monarchy it had rejected. Under Augustus and Tiberius it was tolerated from visiting foreigners from the East, accustomed to prostrating themselves before a totalitarian ruler, but the idea that a proud Roman citizen should do so was repellent. The spectacularly insane Caligula, however, who ruled between 37 and 41 CE, shocked Rome by instituting the practice for everyone: senators were even required to grovel on the ground before his empty throne in the Capitol. His successor Claudius (41–54) forbade the practice, but unsurprisingly it was reintroduced by Nero

(54–68). Luke was deliberately pointing up the similarities between Satan and an emperor, but which one? Theissen argues that Caligula fits best, so this part of the temptation scene must come from the time of his rule, but admits it could possibly be Nero.

However, Theissen seems not to have noticed that there is also a strongly implicit contrast between Jesus and Herod Agrippa I. This grandson of Herod the Great, who became king of parts of Roman Palestine in 39 CE and king of the Jews in 41, was loathed because of his allegiance to Rome. And persecution of the Christians of Jerusalem by the Jewish authorities he backed reached its zenith under his reign. If Satan represented the emperor, a parallel was also being drawn with a ruler who had effectively failed the test passed by Jesus and had accepted the throne in return for acknowledging Satan/Caligula's authority—Agrippa I. This form of the temptation story must therefore date from his rule, which lasted until his death in 44 CE, or at least from a time when he was still fresh in the memory.[20]

A Man of His Time

Although to Christian mystics and evangelicals the historical background to Christ's story is totally irrelevant to their personal relationship with him, to anyone trying to locate the historical Jesus without fear or favor, it is crucial to understand the political reality of the time. Jesus Christ was first and foremost a creation of his place and time, with a mind-set that was the result of centuries of Jewish history.

The origins of Judaism are at least as mysterious and controversial as those of Christianity, but fortunately need only be summarized here. The sacred texts of the people of Israel—to Christians, the Old Testament—were put together in the sixth century BCE and, though obviously based on more ancient sources, were heavily edited and adapted, making it impossible to judge their accuracy (and representing a kind of magnified version of the difficulties of assessing the Gospels as history).

The legendary history—undoubtedly containing nuggets of truth, although opinions differ as to just how much—goes back to the time when Yahweh made a covenant with the patriarch Abraham that if he and his descendants worshipped him as the one true God, he would make them into a mighty people and present them with Canaan as their homeland. Abraham's grandson Jacob—whom God renamed Israel—was, through his sons, the legendary progenitor of the twelve tribes of the nation.

According to the story, the sons settled in Egypt, where their descendants were enslaved. Generations later Moses led the Israelites out of Egypt to the promised land of Canaan, which was divided among the twelve tribes, around the thirteenth century BCE. However, many historians and archaeologists, including Jewish ones, now believe that the Israelites were a mix of immigrants from Egypt and already established Canaanites. One school holds that only three tribes—Ephraim, Manesseh, and Benjamin—made the Exodus out of Egypt and the other nine derived from the Canaanites.[21] Some even believe that none of the tribes was ever in Egypt.

Similarly the evidence reveals that the Jews' early religion was by no means as uncompromisingly monotheistic as the sixth-century BCE reformers pretended. Although Yahweh reigned supreme, other deities, particularly his spouse the Canaanite goddess Asherah, sat with him in the pantheon.[22] (The first commandment, "You shall have no other gods before [or "besides"] me,"[23] implies that other gods existed.)

It should be stressed, however, that this depends on one's definition of "monotheistic." Although today we take the word to mean a belief in one God and one only, in the ancient world many— probably most—religions that we see as "polytheistic" believed in a single supreme creator-god who existed before, and created, all the other gods and goddesses. The individual gods depended on the creator for their existence and were regarded as aspects of him or her, as exemplified by the Heliopolitan religion of Egypt, which inspired the Giza pyramids. This is probably how the early Israelites saw it, and only later were the lesser gods written out of the script. (And even then not entirely, as the very first sentence of the Bible reveals: the "God" who created the heavens and the earth is described by the Hebrew *elohim*—which is *plural*.)

For about three hundred years the Israelites were a loose confederacy of tribes under the dominant Ephraim, which produced

Moses' successor Joshua, conqueror of the promised land, and also had the honor of protecting the Hebrews' most sacred object, the Ark of the Covenant. It was only in ca. 1000 BCE that the Israelites were unified into the kingdom of Israel under the iconic King David, who moved the Ark to Jerusalem, triggering the age-old rivalry between the tribes of Judah and Ephraim that endured until Jesus' day in the form of antagonism between Jews and Samaritans. (Previously Jerusalem was sacred to the Canaanite god Shalim, from which the name is derived—and not, as is often claimed, from the Hebrew *shalom*, peace—as can be seen in an Egyptian text of the nineteenth century BCE in which the city appears as Urusalim, "the foundation of Shalim.") [24] David's son and successor Solomon, famed for his wisdom, had the great Temple built in Jerusalem as the focus for the worship of Yahweh.

However, after Solomon the kingdom split into two. Ten tribes in the north, led by Ephraim, formed the Kingdom of Israel, while the two in the south—centered on Jerusalem—became the Kingdom of Judah (after the largest of the two tribes, the other being Benjamin, although the two became virtually indistinguishable because of intermarriage). Two centuries afterwards the northern kingdom was invaded by the Assyrian Empire, leaving Judah predominant. As a result, Judah gave its name to the religion and the people itself (although they would always think of their land and religious community as "Israel").

But in 607 BCE it was Judah's turn to be invaded, by the Babylonians under Nebuchadnezzar. Solomon's Temple was utterly destroyed and the people carried off into captivity in several traumatic waves of deportation. Seventy years later the Babylonians were defeated by the Persians, and the exiled Hebrews—almost all of whom, having been born in captivity, had never seen Jerusalem—returned to their homeland, where, although it remained under Persian control, they were permitted to practice their religion. Eagerly they repaired the Temple as best they could. It was at this time that the religion was "codified," the prime mover being the scribe Ezra, who ironically introduced elements from the Babylonian religion of Zoroastrianism.

A significant result of these events—which will become unexpectedly relevant to our quest for the historical Jesus—was the division between Jews and Samaritans, widening the post-Solomonic rift. Both peoples emerged from that chaotic period claiming that they preserved the original religion and that the other possessed a bastardized version. The Jews claimed that the long association with the Assyrians and other cultures had corrupted the Samaritans' religion, while the Samaritans accused the Jews of being too influenced by their time in Babylon and of reinventing the religion in the guise of reform, exacerbating the deep-rooted friction between them.

The catalogue of conquest continued. In 331 BCE Alexander the Great drove the Persians out and Israel was absorbed into the Hellenistic world, and after his death it fell under the control of the Seleucids, a dynasty of Hellenized Syrians. In 167 BCE the Seleucid king Antiochus Epiphanes, concerned by the number of his subjects converting to Judaism, began a concerted pogrom. The religion was banned, women and their circumcised male babies executed, the Temple was plundered, and—an act of deliberate blasphemy—a statue of Zeus was set up over the high altar. It was this that sparked off the Maccabean Revolt, led by Judas Maccabaeus ("the Hammer"), son of the high priest. After a lengthy struggle the Maccabees drove out the Seleucids and established themselves as both secular and spiritual rulers of Jerusalem, founding the Hasmonean dynasty (after Hasmon, a venerable Maccabean ancestor).

Now it was the Jews' turn to be conquerors. Under the Hasmoneans there was a forty-year period of expansion and conquest of neighboring regions: Samaria, Idumea (the biblical Edom) to the south, and later Galilee to the far north, beyond Samaria. One result was the destruction of the Samaritans' own Temple on the sacred mountain of Gerizim—a rival to the one in Jerusalem—which did nothing to endear the Jews to them.

In 63 BCE the Roman general Pompey was invited to intervene in an internal power struggle: an unwise move as, somewhat predictably, he claimed the land for Rome instead. After various struggles a distinguished Idumean general named Herod—"the Great"—was appointed king of the Jews; he ruled from 37 to 4 BCE. Despite frequent claims to the contrary, Herod was Jewish by religion (but only because the Hasmoneans had forcibly converted the Idumeans to Judaism a couple of generations earlier).

Although reviled by his people, Herod was a major patron of

building programs, even ordering the reconstruction of the Temple in 19 BCE, the work continuing long after his death. (Hence Jesus is said to have lived in the "Second Temple period.") Pliny the Elder described Herod's Jerusalem as the most famous of the great cities of the East.

When Herod died in 4 BCE, his lands were divided among his three sons. The eldest, Herod Archelaus, received half the kingdom, Judea (Latinized Judah), Idumea, and Samaria; Herod Antipas was granted Galilee and Perea; and Philip received Gaulanitis and Iturea in the northeast. Archelaus was such an incompetent ruler that ten years into his reign, after a deputation of Jews and Samaritans went to Rome to complain about him, the Emperor Augustus banished him to Gaul, giving over his lands to a Roman prefect, or governor. The third and most (in)famous prefect, Pontius Pilate, was appointed in 26 CE. Although the prefect had overall control, in Judea the council of the Sanhedrin had authority over certain civil matters—mainly the practice of the religion, subject to oversight by the Romans.

So the Palestine into which Jesus emerged was complicated and fraught with division and tension, most obviously between the people and their Roman overlords, although the degree to which the Jews actively opposed their rule varied. There were militant nationalist groups, such as the Zealots, who regarded the presence of Romans in their holy city as blasphemy pure and simple and aimed to kick them out. Others were more philosophical, convinced that nothing could be done. And there were even those who thought that since nothing could happen without God's approval, he must have *wanted* Rome to rule over Israel. (Paul similarly suggested that the emperor could have power only if God ordained it, therefore Christians should not oppose him.[25] And ironically the emperor Paul was referring to was Nero.) The Roman presence was a fact of Jewish life in first-century Palestine. Any would-be religious preacher would have been expected to make his views on the issue known, including Jesus.

The succession of conquerors left a variety of marks on Israel—and not just scars. The Greeks after Alexander the Great opened it up to a multitude of cultural influences, a flowering that only increased under the Romans. Many Jews, especially the wealthier classes, adopted Greek lifestyles, and signs of other cultures from across the Empire were everywhere: even Herod the Great's 400-man bodyguard came from Gaul, today's France.[26]

A startling example of this multiculturalism surfaced in 1990, with the discovery in the southern suburbs of Jerusalem of a group of ossuaries belonging to the family of Caiaphas, high priest from 18 to 36 CE, whom the Gospels describe as responsible for the plot that killed Jesus. One of the ossuaries contained his bones, and another those of his son Jehosaf. But the biggest surprise is that one member of this family, a woman named Miriam, had been buried according to *pagan* customs, as a coin (dated 42–43 CE) was found in her mouth. The practice of Hellenized Jews or even non-Jews marrying into Jewish families was by no means unknown in Jerusalem, but a member of the high priest's own family being blatantly buried as a pagan! If such a thing was acceptable so far up the hierarchy, Jerusalem really must have been multicultural.[27]

Even if we regard Jesus as entirely and fundamentally Jewish, he was living and operating in a dual culture. However, some have even proposed that Jesus himself, while obviously operating in a predominantly Jewish environment, was not Jewish at all. As we have seen, Burton Mack argues he was a Cynic philosopher.

Galilee in particular, where Jesus is said to have undertaken most of his mission, was by no means exclusively Jewish. Separated from Judea by Samaria, in the golden age of the reigns of David and Solomon to which the Jewish imagination constantly returned Galilee had once been part of the kingdom of Israel, although it never completely eradicated its previous inhabitants. After Solomon Galilee became part of the northern kingdom, being captured by the Assyrians and then the Persians, although its people were not taken into captivity in Babylon and, like the Samaritans, were looked down upon by those in Jerusalem when they returned from exile.

Under the Greeks Galilee became home to a thriving Hellenistic culture, but, again like the Samaritans, the Galileans generally neither resented nor resisted the coming of the Greeks. It was another story, though, when Galilee was conquered by the Judeans under the Hasmonean dynasty in about 100 BCE. As Burton Mack notes, "it would be wrong to picture Galilee as suddenly converted to a Jewish loyalty and culture."[28] Quite. The Galileans resented Judean domination and the fact that Jerusalem was now in charge of their administration—taking their taxes and being the ultimate arbitrator in legal disputes. In fact the situation actually improved for them under Roman rule, as Galilee became administratively separate from Judea.

The region was known by the Judeans as "Galilee of the Gentiles." Because of its background and resentment of Jerusalem, it is likely that unorthodox and unconventional forms of Judaism had either survived or developed in Galilee, just as they had in Samaria. And as the two countries were geographically so close, it seems probable that Samaritanism was well represented in Galilee. This was also where the mix of cultures would encourage the blending of religious and philosophical ideas.

Jesus the Anti-Christ

The electric tension of Roman domination caused a seething groundswell of apocalyptic expectation. Surely, of all terrible times, this was when the Messiah must return.

Moses had begun the Israelites' tradition of divinely inspired individuals who would step forward at the critical hour to save the race or keep the people on the straight and narrow. Any individual could become a prophet: there was no requirement for them to be priests or of royal lineage. In the Jewish tradition, prophets were God's agents for keeping the religion on track. If something went badly awry among his Chosen People, God would always inspire someone to denounce their failings, and when prophets spoke, even kings had to listen.

The books written by or attributed to the prophets, such as Isaiah and Zechariah, were also used as guides to the future, and in troubled times the Jews would scrutinize them for glimmers of hope and clues about their fate. People had come to believe that when things reached rock bottom, God would send a deliverer, a figure most often associated with the Messiah.

However, although because of the success of Christianity we tend to assume that the Messiah was the only expected deliverer, the situation was more complicated. There were many alternatives: that God himself would descend upon the world or send an angel; such as Michael, or the prophet Elijah—in Malachi God promises, "I will send the prophet Elijah to you before that great and dreadful day of the Lord comes"[29]—or Melchizedek, or a kind of previously unknown superprophet. The Samaritans had their own equivalent of the Messiah, the Taheb, whom they linked with Joshua and Moses—one of whose functions was to bring the Jews under their control.

Besides, ideas about the Messiah were many, varied, and often conflicting. Messiah (*Mashiah*), the Hebrew for "the Anointed," was translated into Greek as *Khristos*, then Latinized as *Christus*, eventually becoming "Christ." In the Old Testament the word is used to describe Saul, the first king of Israel, and priests who are anointed into their office. It was even applied to Cyrus of Persia, who is described as "the Lord's anointed" because he freed the nation from the Babylonian captivity.[30] Sometimes the term was used to personify the whole Jewish nation, but increasingly it was applied to the deliverer God would send in time of need.

Joseph Klausner, in *The Messianic Idea in Israel* (1956), summarizes the stances of the various prophetic books—dating from about 800 BCE to 165 BCE—about the Messiah. Most have no human Messiah at all: deliverance was expected from God himself or the people of Israel collectively. Only five books have an "ideal human Messiah," and Klausner sums up what they expect of him:

> All these prophets describe this human Messiah as replete with lofty spiritual and ethical qualities. He is filled with wisdom and understanding, knowledge and the fear of the Lord. He slays the wicked with the breath of his lips, and executes justice and righteousness in the earth. In general he is righteous and humble; but along with this he is a king of the house of David, a noble ruler, filled with the spirit of heroism, to whom Israel and all the Gentiles submit. He is not a redeemer *per se*, as the Messiah became in later times: the Lord [God] is the redeemer, and the King-Messiah is only the head of the redeemed people, its political and spiritual king; and since he is righteous and free from transgression he is also king of the world, for all the nations submit to Israel because they long to hear the word of the Lord and to learn of his ways.[31]

The problem is that the wholesale destruction of the Jewish lands during the Roman suppression of the two revolts created a void in the historical record. We can see ideas about the Messiah developing over the last centuries BCE as just described, but then everything disappears into a dark tunnel, emerging only when the dust settles after the second revolt, in the mid–second century CE. As we emerge blinking into the light, we can see that many of the ideas about the Messiah had become very different from what they were when we entered the tunnel. Frustratingly, there is no way to be sure exactly how, when, and with whom the messianic concepts relevant to Jesus originated and were developed. That was why the discovery of the Dead Sea Scrolls was so valuable, for they shed a little light on some of the ideas being explored in the tunnel, although many areas remain dark and unknowable.

All that we really know is that different groups were speculating, often wildly, about the Messiah, creating sometimes contradictory permutations of a whole raft of prophecies and dreaming up novel and exotic variations. A famous example is the concept, found in the Dead Sea Scrolls (and elsewhere), that there would be two Messiahs, one a king and one descended from Israel's first priest, Aaron, the nation's spiritual leader. This was not, however, a widespread view.

Before the "tunnel" there was no question that the Messiah had to be a descendant of David; afterwards there are discussions of Messiahs who were not, which could explain some of the contradictions in the Gospels about whether or not Jesus was of David's line (to Mark he wasn't, to the other synoptics he was). There were disagreements about the signs by which the Messiah would be recognized, such as his birthplace—or even whether it would be known at all.

One of the stranger ideas, from the second century, was of a kind of failed Messiah, the "Messiah of Joseph," expected to arise from Galilee yet, bizarrely, destined to die in battle; only when he does so can the Messiah of David appear. There are obvious undertones of Jesus here—a Messiah descended from a Joseph who comes from Galilee and is destined to die—but equally obvious is the difference that he dies in battle without any hint of "atoning power."[32] (An interesting suggestion is that this idea came from a Galilean take on the Samaritan Taheb.)

So Judea was buzzing with the expectation that the Messiah—or another instrument of God's judgment—would be striding forth spitting fire at any moment. And unsurprisingly, there were many who tried to claim one of the titles, or who had the title thrust upon them. Jesus was by no means the only claimant. One, Simon bar Kokhba ("Son of the Star"), who led the second Jewish Revolt of 132–35 CE, was recognized as the Messiah by most of the population and even received the endorsement of the more influential priests but was killed in battle. The fate of the Messiah was to lead the nation's army to victory and certainly not get shamefully executed as a criminal flanked on either side by rebel riffraff.

The Messiah was emphatically never expected to be anything like the Christ of Christianity, as first proposed by Paul. He was supposed to be a king like David, with a divine mandate, but still a king. Some expected him to have the power to work miracles like prophets and other holy men, but then people have always expected such powers of even their secular rulers.

The Messiah was not only expected to drive the foreign oppressors out of the sacred land but also to restore the Kingdom of Israel to its original state. This necessarily involved the rather difficult task of gathering the twelve tribes back together: no one knew their precise location, or even if they still existed as such, and there was the awkward problem of overcoming anti-Samaritan prejudice. (Almost all the prophets envisaged a reunion of the tribes of Judah and Ephraim as part of the messianic program.)

A first-century BCE text, the *Psalms of Solomon*, set out the "six point program" (in the words of James D. Tabor of the University of North Carolina) expected of the Messiah: to establish himself as the ruler of Israel; throw out the foreign rulers; establish the rule of righteousness (i.e., Mosaic Law); separate the sinners from the people of Israel; extend his rule over all the nations of the world; and gather the scattered tribes of Israel. On every single point Jesus failed. He was captured, tried, and executed, in Geoffrey Ashe's words "horribly, disgracefully, and, worst of all, unexpectedly."[33] As the former dean of York Alan Richardson commented:

It is almost impossibly difficult for us to comprehend the offensiveness to Jewish ears of the preaching of a crucified Messiah. Death by hanging brought upon a crucified man the curse of the

Law. A crucified carpenter-rabbi was utterly at variance with the expectation, where it existed, of a glorious and triumphant prince of David's line, who would restore the kingdom to Israel, to say nothing of apocalyptic fantasies of a supernatural Heavenly Man who would slay his enemies with the breath of his mouth.[34]

The disgrace was exacerbated by the fact that the manner of his death was singled out for opprobrium in Deuteronomy: "anyone who is hung on a pole is under God's curse."[35] (This judgment, originally referring to those whose corpses remained unburied after execution, came to apply to crucifixion victims.)

Jesus' followers had a serious struggle on their hands to justify believing in him as something he had manifestly failed to be. Paul dealt with this simply by rewriting the definition of "Messiah," arguing with characteristic chutzpah that God had changed the rules. But it is still a major problem for modern commentators, on different grounds: by rights Jesus should be just as forgotten as all the other "messiahs" who fell by the wayside—so why wasn't he?

In the First Letter to the Corinthians Paul acknowledged that the reason the Jews didn't accept Jesus was that both the fact and the manner of his death meant that he could never be the Messiah. Paul's response is that this was precisely God's point: accepting someone who did the very opposite of what was expected is a measure of faith: "God decided to use the very foolishness of His doctrine to save those who placed their faith in it."[36]

A saner strategy adopted by the early Christians was to comb the Jewish scriptures to find prophecies they could twist to be relevant to their new belief. They found one in Isaiah, in a lengthy but typically enigmatic section about a "servant of the Lord" who would suffer and give his life as a sin offering, but would then be "raised and lifted up and highly exalted":

> Surely he took up our pain
>   and bore our suffering,
>   yet we considered him punished by God,
> stricken by him, and afflicted.
>   But he was pierced for our transgressions,
>   he was crushed for our iniquities;

the punishment that brought us peace was on him,
and by his wounds we are healed.[37]

This text was being applied to Jesus by the time the Acts of the Apostles was written, in the seventies or eighties CE—within fifty years of the crucifixion. However, there is no evidence that this part of Isaiah was taken to predict the coming of a Messiah-type figure who would suffer for the people's sins *before* Jesus had been crucified.

Then there is the greatest irony. Jesus not only signally failed to achieve what was expected of the Messiah but actually created the *opposite* effect. The Jews expected their great longed-for hero who would not only free them and restore their golden age but would make them the greatest nation on earth, reigning supreme over the whole planet. In Jesus, however, they got someone in whose name (through no fault of his own) a religion was created whose devotees ensured that the Jews were reviled as deicides rejected by God—a direct result of which was centuries of repression and the most atrocious, remorseless, and unrelenting pogroms.

In terms of the original meaning of "Messiah," there is no doubt that to millions of Jews over the centuries, purely by an accident of fate, Jesus was actually the anti-Christ.

3

BORN OF A VIRGIN?

The central celebration of every year for most families in the West is Christmas, when even many nonbelievers' greeting cards bear depictions of the baby Jesus swaddled in a manger with his mother, Mary, looking on adoringly, a bearded Joseph lurking in the background. Often also present are the shepherds (bearing a cute and cuddly lamb), the three regal wise men (offering their gifts of gold, frankincense, and myrrh), and assorted dewy-eyed and unfeasibly pristine farm animals. Many who rarely see the inside of a church for the rest of the year find that the sheer emotional pull of the season leads them to enjoy midnight mass or a carol concert alongside more committed believers. Inside the churches there appears to be a peace that does indeed pass all understanding, an all-persuasive token of the ultimate feel-good religious festival. Joy to the world, the Lord is nigh!

Yet sadly for this most evocative of festivals, as with every other aspect of the Jesus story, the nativity is riddled with inconsistencies, contradictions—and just plain fabrications. It is almost completely a fairy story—although the source and inspiration of its various elements can be remarkably telling.

The major sources on Jesus' birth, early life, and family background are the canonical Gospels: few of the other early Christian texts of equal status, such as the Gospel of Thomas, concern themselves with biographical information, and all of them concentrate on his adult life and mission. True, there are some spurious "infancy gospels" of the second century, but they are obviously fables concocted simply to fill the yawning hole in Christ's life story. Although clearly fictitious, a mid-second-century account of Mary's life from her birth to her son's, the so-called *Protevangelium* (also known as *The Book of James* or the *Infancy Gospel of James*), attributed to James the Just, is worthy of a passing mention as it is the source for many Christian ideas about the Virgin Mary not found in the New Testament.

Mark, the first of the synoptic Gospels to be written, says nothing whatsoever about Jesus' birth or early life, beginning with his baptism as an adult—as does John's Gospel. Why do they so conspicuously avoid Jesus' origin? The obvious answer is that the writers knew nothing about it. The more important question therefore is why do Matthew and Luke, the two Gospels based on Mark, contain *added* material on Jesus' birth and childhood? To them, clearly Jesus' birth and lineage is the pivotal point of the whole story: they intended their readers to be in no doubt about the fact that he was special because of his ancestry. His alleged bloodline was all-important. Perhaps we should be cautious about Matthew and Luke's additions from the start.

Caution hardens into suspicion when we see that their respective birth stories are entirely different. With all the authority they can muster, they give completely—and incompatibly—different accounts of the circumstances of Jesus' birth. For example, Matthew tells of Herod's order that all male children under two in Bethlehem are to be slaughtered and the holy family's flight to Egypt, whereas these episodes are literally a closed book to Luke.

It seems that both gospel writers are trying to fill in an embarrassing hole in their stories: early Christians would have wanted to know about the birth and early life of their hero, and no doubt expected his birth to have been attended by as many signs and wonders as possible, but the unpalatable truth was that nobody knew much about Jesus before his baptism. So did Matthew and Luke (or their sources) just make it all up, in the manner of the *Protevangelium*, as a crowd-pleaser? In fact we know they did invent at least parts of it because we can identify some of their sources. But even so, Matthew and Luke's accounts are not simply different, they are actually irreconcilable.

They agree that Mary conceived Jesus through divine intervention and was a virgin at the time of the conception and until the birth. They also agree that, at the time of Jesus' conception, she was betrothed ("pledged to be married") to a man named Joseph, a descendant of King David. But they disagree on whether the couple were married by the time Jesus was born.

Betrothal in their culture was not in fact very different from marriage: legally the couple was regarded as man and wife from the moment of betrothal, the union being complete when they set up house together. This accounts for some apparent anomalies, such as Matthew's calling Joseph Mary's husband while also describing them as betrothed. Whether sex was permitted during the period of betrothal is an open question: it appears that officially it was not, but in practice, human nature being what it always has been, no doubt the rules would have often been bent.

In Matthew, when Mary becomes pregnant, Joseph wants to divorce her—oddly, to avoid *her* being publicly disgraced, which surely would be self-defeating—but is told by an angel in a dream that she has conceived by the Holy Spirit and that the son she is to bear will "save his people from their sins." Accordingly Joseph marries her ("took Mary home as his wife"), though he avoids any "union" with her. In Luke there is no such moral dilemma: we are not told Joseph's reaction to the turn of events, and they are still only betrothed at the time of Jesus' birth.

Luke links the story of Jesus' conception and birth to that of John the Baptist, who is born to Mary's relative Elizabeth, establishing a connection between the two figures from the outset. Matthew, on the other hand, makes no connection with John, and like the other Gospels shows no awareness of kinship between the two.

In Luke, Mary and Joseph are already living in Nazareth in Galilee; in Matthew, they come from Bethlehem in Judea and surface in Nazareth only after their son's birth as the result of fleeing from the evil infanticide Herod. Presumably that explains why Luke felt the need to mention the census—the reason, he claimed, for Jesus' being born in Bethlehem.

Also in Luke, shepherds come to pay tribute to the baby Jesus, whereas in Matthew the worshippers are Magi—magicians or wise men—who have come from "the East," alerted to his presence by a mysterious new star. Both add an element of awe, of adoration of the newborn divine hero. We are expected to share in the magical atmosphere conjured by the story.

Some try to explain the discrepancies on the grounds that one tells the story from Mary's point of view, the other from Joseph's. But this argument collapses with the most glaring difference between the two nativity stories: the massacre of the innocents. It fails to appear in Luke at all: Joseph and Mary simply take Jesus to Jerusalem to be circumcised when he is eight days old, as was the custom, then go home to Nazareth. Only in Matthew do we find the lurid tale of Herod's hunt for the child who poses a threat to his throne, his order that all male children under the age of two in Bethlehem and its environs should be put to the sword, and the holy family's seeking sanctuary in Egypt.

The Year of the Lord

Perhaps bizarrely, given that the Western calendar begins from Jesus' birth and that all previous years are known as "before Christ" and all those subsequent as "anno domini," in the year of the Lord—although we prefer the more neutral BCE (before common era) and CE (common era)—the actual year of his birth is unknown. It is impossible to work it out using the apparently precise references to external events in the two nativity accounts, as they are mutually exclusive. In fact the only certainty is that it did not happen at the turn of 1 BCE/1 CE: there was a crucial error in the sixth century when AD 1 was calculated.

According to Matthew's Gospel, Jesus was born during the reign of Herod the Great, the king of all the Jewish lands. After a thirty-six-year reign, Herod died in 4 BCE, so if Matthew is right, Jesus must have been born before then. But Luke, while still setting the nativity in Herod's reign, more specifically links the birth to a census (a registration of the population for taxation) carried out when one Quirinius was the Roman governor of Syria (the official responsible for the whole region). Sulpicius Quirinius was a real person and governor of Syria, but he held that office several years after Herod's death. And although we know from Josephus that he did organize a census in Judea, that was in 6 CE, a decade after the end of Herod's reign. So, according to one Gospel, Jesus could not have been born after 4 BCE, and according to the other he was specifically born in 6 CE—a minimum ten-year gap between the two.

Indeed there are huge problems with the whole of Luke's account. He states that the census was the result of a decree by the Emperor Augustus that the whole Empire should be taxed. But this decree would not have applied to Herod's kingdom, as Rome recognized his sovereignty. As Joseph lived in an entirely different country, Galilee—which in 6 CE was still ruled by another of Herod's sons, Antipas—the decree simply had no relevance to him at all. As historian Robin Lane Fox states baldly, "Luke's story is historically impossible and internally incoherent. . . . It is, therefore, false."[1]

But does it really matter? Other ancient chronicles have similar inconsistencies, either because of a mistake or erroneous sources. Ultimately this kind of lapse is only a problem for those who totally reject the thought that *anything* in the Gospels could be wrong or subject to human fallibility.

For example, some have attempted to reconcile the anomaly concerning Quirinius' census by suggesting that he actually held office in Syria on two separate occasions, and that an inscription from the rule of Augustus, found at Tivoli, shows that his first tour of duty included the year 8 BCE, therefore during Herod's reign.[2] So, they argue, the census during which Jesus was born could have happened during Quirinius' first term of office and therefore while Herod was still alive. However, it transpires that this theory is based simply on the overwhelming desire to prove the Gospels right on every single point: incredibly, the name of the person involved is actually missing from the inscription. Because of wishful thinking on a massive scale, it is only *assumed* to be Quirinius.[3]

Not knowing the real year of Jesus' birth is frustrating, particularly because it is impossible to work out how old he was at the time of his mission. There are just two references in the Gospels to his age during his ministry, and—predictably—they contradict each other. Luke says that he was "about thirty" at the time of his baptism, whereas John has people commenting that he is "not yet fifty," implying he is in his mid- to late forties, quite old for his day. As we will see, the baptism that marked the beginning of his career could have happened at any time between the years 29 and 33. If he was born in the last years of Herod the Great's reign, he would have been at least in his midthirties, probably somewhat older; if at the time of the census, he would have been in his midtwenties.

Descent from David?

Matthew and Luke both list genealogies that are intended to show that Jesus was descended from David, taken by most Jews to be a requirement of the Messiah. However, the two genealogies give flagrantly different lines of descent, from the beginning to the end of the supposed Davidic line. Matthew traces it from David's son Solomon to Joseph's father, Jacob, whereas Luke begins the line with another son of David named Nathan and gives Joseph's father as Heli. All the names in between are different.

Matthew and Luke's tracing of Jesus' Davidic descent to Joseph leads to a major contradiction with their assertion that Jesus was literally the son of *God*. Both insist on his divine conception but then blithely undermine their own claim by providing evidence of his very mortal descent. The writers were clearly desperate to have it both ways. To be the Messiah, Jesus had to have been descended from David, but to be the Christian Christ he had to be the Son of God. (Paul, in one of his few pieces of information about the earthly Jesus, wrote that he was descended from David "according to the flesh," and said nothing about a miraculous conception or birth.) Mark felt no need to provide "proof" of either claim. Mainstream Christianity, however, has simply ignored the discrepancy—maintaining that both accounts of Jesus' ancestry are true, even though they are blatantly irreconcilable.

Some have attempted to explain the contradiction between the two genealogies by suggesting that one is in fact Mary's, not Joseph's, and shows that she too was descended from David; one of the gospel writers either misunderstood or changed the last generation because he was unhappy about tracing the line through a woman.[4] But there is no evidence for this: it is simply an attempt to reconcile the irreconcilable.

In fact, if Matthew's genealogy is correct, it proves that Jesus could *not* have been the legitimate king of David's line. One of the men listed as an ancestor of Joseph is Jehoiachin, the son and heir of the king of Judah, but not only had he been barred from the king-ship himself but the ban had been extended to his descendants: in the words of the Book of Jeremiah, "none of his offspring will prosper, none will sit on the throne of David or rule any more in Judah."[5] This ban would have disproved Jesus' claim to the throne, and the messiahship, even if the genealogy had been accepted.

There is something else about Matthew's genealogy. Although both he and Luke trace the descent through the male line, Matthew includes four women, whose stories are known from the Old Testament. Why the writer of Matthew (or more likely his source) has highlighted these four alone is unclear, but the tantalizing clue is that all four are outsiders, foreigners, and of dubious reputation. As James D. Tabor points out, "All four women that Matthew mentions in his genealogy had sex out of wedlock and at least two of them became pregnant."[6] Tamar disguised herself as a prostitute in order to become pregnant by her father-in-law, Judah. (This is not quite as outrageous as it sounds, as the widowed Tamar was basically forcing Judah into doing what he was neglecting to do voluntarily according to Jewish custom: marrying her because he was the near-est male relative to her deceased husband.) Rahab was a genuine prostitute. Ruth was a Moabite, and Israelites were forbidden from mixing with Moabites specifically because of "their reputation as sexual temptresses."[7] "Uriah's wife" (Bathsheba, although she re-mains anonymous on Matthew's list) was an adulteress who be-came pregnant by King David while married to one of his generals, Uriah the Hittite. (David subsequently married her, and she became Solomon's mother.) It has been suggested that Bathsheba is included in the genealogy to show that even Solomon was the son of a loose woman, as a rebuff to similar claims about Jesus, but it could just as well be a straight comparison.

Certainly to modern eyes the emphasis on dubious female ances-try has remarkable and unavoidably unsavory implications for Mary's own reputation. But why, when clearly trying to make Jesus out to be the Chosen One, would Matthew make such a lurid point, however obliquely? The fact remains that there is nothing positive about Mary the Mother to be gleaned from the doubtful "female" genealogy.

The conflicts between the two genealogies mean that they are useless as historical information: it is impossible for them both to be correct, and possibly neither of them is. (And even if one is genuine, there is simply no way of telling which it is.) In fact it is not hard to conclude that the suspicious silence of Mark and John on this fundamentally important matter suggests that both genealogies are inventions.

As for Mark, he is at best noncommittal on Jesus' pedigree: only once is Jesus referred to as the "Son of David," although whether Jesus accepted or rejected the name is not mentioned.[8] Later, however, when preaching in the courts of the Temple, Jesus argues against the teaching that the Messiah will necessarily be a "Son of David."[9] John's Gospel casts yet more doubt on the claim of Davidic descent, describing how the people debate whether or not Jesus is the Messiah, the skeptics believing that he is *not* descended from David. Intriguingly, however, the gospel writer says nothing to contradict this, which suggests strongly that he himself was skeptical.

While there are reasons for Matthew and Luke to have invented Jesus' descent from David, it is considerably harder to imagine any reasons Mark and John chose to ignore or suppress it. On that basis one must conclude that the claim of Davidic descent was false—whether or not it was ever actually made during Jesus' lifetime.

Parents of the Son of God

What do we know about Jesus' parents? All the sources agree that his mother was named Mary: the Gospels usually call her Mariam, sometimes Maria—an extremely common name. But beyond that they tell us virtually nothing about her or her background, and what little they do say is suspect. For someone who was to loom so large in Christian, particularly Catholic, belief, she hardly makes an appearance in the Gospels—and her only starring role, in Luke's version of the nativity, can easily be shown to be fictitious.

As we have already mentioned, there is only one nonbiblical text that purports to describe Mary's life, the peculiar second-century *Protevangelium.* This short "gospel" tells the story from her own miraculous conception, through her childhood to the birth of Jesus, ending somewhat abruptly at the massacre of the innocents. Clearly this curious work was cobbled together from a number of separate stories, which came to the author either orally or in writing, but which have been edited together badly; for example, a first-person narrative is suddenly inserted into the third-person text. And anachronisms proliferate, showing that whoever composed the bulk of the story was not familiar with Jewish customs. The author writes of the "tribe of David" and reveals complete ignorance about the geography of Palestine.

Nevertheless, some of the details have taken root in Catholic teachings about Mary, for example, calling her parents Joachim and Anna, now saints. The *Protevangelium* is also the origin (or at least the first recorded telling) of an aspect of Mary's life that not only was to become deeply embedded in Christian belief but was eventually to be elevated into a Catholic article of faith: that of her own miraculous conception from the Holy Spirit, being born to an elderly and barren mother as foretold by an angel, and conceived without the taint of sex and so born free from sin.

Mark says nothing at all about Jesus' paternity. Neither Matthew nor Luke mentions Joseph after the nativity; he is just dropped, his fate remaining unreported. John's Gospel twice refers to Jesus as "the son of Joseph," but there is nothing beyond that. There are telling changes to one passage in Mark when it was retold in Matthew and Luke. While Mark records the people of Galilee, astonished at Jesus' preaching, saying, "Isn't this the carpenter? Isn't this Mary's son . . . ?"[10] Matthew renders this as "Isn't this the carpenter's son? Isn't his mother's name Mary . . . ?"[11] Luke goes even further and has the people ask, "Isn't this Joseph's son?" with nothing about Mary.[12] In the circumstances we must assume Mark to be the most authentic.

So, in the earliest account, the writer obviously did not consider Jesus' father relevant enough to merit a single mention—an amazing omission. Even more astonishingly, Jesus is defined by his *mother*, which was actually an insult in that culture.[13]

Announced and Conceived

Luke begins with the angel Gabriel appearing to John the Baptist's father, the priest Zechariah, and announcing that he and his wife Elizabeth have been chosen to bear a child who will prepare the people for the coming of the Lord. As the couple is childless and elderly, not unnaturally Zechariah expresses his doubts—only to be struck dumb by Gabriel, who tells him he will speak again only when his son is born.

When Elizabeth is six months pregnant, Gabriel appears to her kinswoman Mary to tell her she has been chosen by God to give birth to "the Son of the Most High," even though she is still a virgin—the famous annunciation scene. However, while it is tempting to reject the whole episode as a later fabrication, Geoffrey Ashe has put forward a persuasive argument that not only was this a separate earlier text that Luke incorporated into his account but it might even date from Jesus' lifetime.[14]

Gabriel makes certain predictions about the child that Mary is to bear: "He will be great, and will be called the Son of the Most High. The Lord God will give him the throne of his father David, and he will reign over the house of Jacob for ever; his kingdom will never end."[15] Clearly this fits the conventional Jewish expectations of the Messiah—emphasizing his role as the prophesied warrior-king who will restore Israel's greatness. (The "house of Jacob" refers to the whole of the twelve tribes, relating to the expectation that the Messiah would reunite the lost tribes.)

By the time Luke's Gospel came to be written two things had happened. First, and most glaringly, Jesus had utterly failed to fulfill the conventional messianic role; Gabriel's prophecy had failed. Second, the early Christians, such as Paul, had dealt with this problem by redefining the role of the Messiah. Therefore Luke could never have invented Gabriel's words: why make up a prediction that had already failed? If Luke had felt a need to invent something, surely it would have been that Mary had been chosen to bear a son who would save mankind by dying and rising again. This line of reasoning is confirmed by the fact that this is precisely what Matthew did: he has Gabriel announcing to Joseph that Jesus "will save the people from their sins," fitting the reinterpreted Christian image of the Christ.

Clearly in this case Luke used an older source that—presumably out of respect—he did not dare change, despite the glaring inconsistency with his overall message. And the same argument goes for his source: whoever wrote it would never have invented a failed prophecy either. Ashe concludes that this account of Gabriel's prophecy must *predate* Jesus' crucifixion, when there was still an expectation that he would fulfill the messianic role. This may be going a little too far, as the "prophecy" could have been written very soon after the crucifixion, when Jesus' followers still believed he would be making an almost immediate comeback. Even so, Luke could not have invented what must indeed be one of the oldest passages of the Gospels. This is compelling evidence that at least some of Jesus' immediate followers believed that he had been in some way supernaturally predicted as the Messiah.

Whose Soul Glorifies the Lord?

In Luke's account, after she has been visited by Gabriel, Mary goes to see Elizabeth in her home "in the hill country of Judea." The baby in Elizabeth's womb leaps for joy when she arrives, apparently an early sign both of John's prescience and his subservient role as the one who will recognize the Messiah.

Significantly there is considerable evidence that the opening chapters of Luke, dealing with the nativity, were pieced together from several earlier sources. The style of these chapters is entirely different from the rest of the Gospel, and several passages suggest that they began life as poems or hymns circulated separately and incorporated wholesale into the narrative, such as Gabriel's prophecy.

However, some were written not about Jesus, but about the conception and birth of John the Baptist with the intention of glorifying *him*. In Luke these have been interwoven with Jesus' story in order to stress the point that, while his career and John's were, at least at the beginning, interdependent, John was the lesser of the two. (Matthew has nothing about John in his nativity story.)

Mostly Luke has lifted the John the Baptist material without amendments, since it fits the Christian view that John was chosen by God, although for a task nowhere near as important as Jesus'. But one passage from this material has undergone hugely significant changes.

In response to Elizabeth's words of wonder and praise—"Blessed is she who has believed that the Lord would fulfil his promises to her!"—in today's Bibles Mary sings of her humility and joy at the honor God has shown her, beginning:

> My soul glorifies the Lord
>   and my spirit rejoices in God my Savior,
> for he has been mindful
>   of the humble state of his servant.[16]

Now known as the "Magnificat," this little song or poem is the key liturgy for today's burgeoning Marian movement (which even seeks to elevate the Blessed Virgin to the same level as her son). However, there is a major problem: the overwhelming evidence is that this was originally *Elizabeth's* song and was proclaimed in honor of *her* son, John the Baptist.

In fact the Church Fathers were undecided whether the Magnificat was Mary's or Elizabeth's: some said one, some the other. Many early Church texts—such as the writings of Irenaeus of Lyon, in around 180 CE—categorically state that the song was Elizabeth's.[17] How could there be such a muddle over such a key passage? The answer may be simpler than it first appears. After Elizabeth praises Mary, Luke's Gospel segues into the Magnificat with the words "And Mary said:." It has been suggested that the Gospel originally had the ambiguous "And she said:," leaving it unclear which of the two women was intended. Some commentators therefore took it to be Mary, some Elizabeth, until eventually it was decided to make it clear by changing the "she" to "Mary."[18]

If it was Mary's song, it would make much more sense to find it after Gabriel's visit or the birth, not as part of an interchange with Elizabeth. Moreover, the wording links to—indeed quotes from—the song of Hannah in the Old Testament's First Book of Samuel, and Hannah was, like Elizabeth, barren until being miraculously blessed with a child in her old age.

But beyond being an embarrassment for Marian Christians, does this tell us anything significant? First, we learn that hymns and poems had been composed in honor of John the Baptist, telling of *his* miraculous birth. The "Benedictus," a "prophecy" in poetic form declaimed at his circumcision by an inspired Zechariah (when his muteness is lifted), unequivocally in praise of him, is clearly another such composition that Luke has incorporated.

It is most likely that these hymns and poems were composed not by early devotees of Jesus, but by the Baptist's own followers. Yale professor Carl H. Kraeling has pointed out that this material shows "not the slightest trace of the common Gospel tendency to subordinate John to Jesus and to regard him as Jesus' Forerunner,"[19] adding, "The autonomy and significance of John in the Infancy Narrative demands that the story arose in Baptist circles."[20] Clearly legends about John were being created by his disciples just as they were about Jesus, including a miraculous conception and angelic visitations. (While there is no reason to take these legends any more seriously than Jesus' nativity tales, it is news to most Christians that John was also the subject of such devoted mythmaking.)

So the true origin of the Magnificat hints that there was more to John the Baptist, and his relationship with Jesus, than the Gospels choose to tell us.

Luke's account is the only evidence for the common idea that Jesus and John were related. If Mary and Elizabeth were kin—although we are not told their exact relationship—then so were their children, being cousins of some kind. But none of the other Gospels mentions a family connection, a curious omission if it were true. So there is a strong (though ultimately unverifiable) suspicion that Luke invented the relationship as a convenient device to justify interweaving the "Jesus" and "John" texts, supplying a reason for the two expectant mothers to meet.

An Unprecedented Miracle

As a literal virgin birth would be historically unprecedented, we ourselves are inclined to be skeptical about Mary's miracle, and we are by no means alone in this. Among those who do not simply dismiss the notion out of hand as complete nonsense, the prevailing view—at least among nonbelievers—is that the virgin birth was the product of a mistranslation of a messianic prophecy and that the details of the story were derived from similar tales about pagan gods and heroes.

Although this might be unsettling news to today's conventional Christians—especially Catholics, who tend even now to be literalists on the subject of Mary the Mother—it is uncertain whether the very first generation of Christians believed in the virgin birth. The evidence is fragmentary, although what there is argues against belief. Most significantly, Paul never mentions such an astounding phenomenon; surely if he was aware of the belief, he would have discussed it, either positively or negatively. More conspicuously, neither Mark nor John refers to Jesus as virgin-born either; therefore, as Matthew and Luke clearly did not get the idea from Mark, where *did* they get it from?

According to the mistranslation hypothesis, a word in a prophecy of Isaiah about the birth of the Messiah, *almah*, meaning "young woman," was mistranslated into Greek as *parthenos*, "virgin." [21] Therefore, the critics argue, the virgin birth idea must have been developed after Jesus' death. Unfortunately it is by no means quite as simple as that. Surprisingly, despite the popular misconception, Greek authors—such as Homer, Euripides, and Sophocles—most often used *parthenos* to signify an unmarried girl, but not necessarily one who hadn't had sex, and indeed there are many references to the offspring of a *parthenos*, effectively meaning "love child." In other words, *parthenos* and *almah* do basically have the same meaning—and neither means virgin! [22] The development of the virgin birth idea is more complex than a simple mistranslation.

There are many prophetic verses—for example in Isaiah, Jeremiah, and Zechariah—which depict the people and nation of Israel symbolically as the "Daughter Zion," sometimes suffering the travails of childbirth. Many of the same books also use the image of "Virgin Zion," and occasionally (for example in Lamentations) the two are put together as "Virgin Daughter Zion." Geoffrey Ashe, in *The Virgin* (1976), suggests that this complex of imagery—Israel as virgin and Israel as God's daughter both as virgin and in childbirth—could easily have been transformed into the idea that a literal, rather than a symbolic, virgin mother had to be involved in the coming of the Messiah. [23]

Although that is certainly one possible route by which the idea arose that Jesus, as the Messiah, had to have been born of a virgin, Ashe suggests another possibility. Although many have dismissed the

Christian belief as a copy of pagan myths of heroes fathered by gods and mortal women, the parallel is by no means exact. Although they are tales of "miraculous impregnation," sex is involved: the women or goddesses involved were certainly not virgins afterwards!

Ashe points out that the only specific antecedents of the concept of a "virgin mother" were to be found in the goddess cults of the ancient Middle East, citing specifically those of Egypt: Isis, Anath, and Neith. The last was regarded as both the mother and daughter of the sun god Ra; Anath was known as "the Virgin," "Queen of Heaven"—as was Isis—and "Mother of Nations."[24] The first two were to become attributes of the mother of Jesus, and the last could have been a bridge to the Virgin Daughter Zion who personified Israel. Also, at least in the fifth century BCE, a community of Jewish mercenaries at Elephantiné on the Nile near Aswan had a temple in which Anath was worshipped alongside "Yaho" (Yahweh). Ashe points out that while Neith and Anath were never directly equated (although they were both worshipped at Elephantiné), both were identified with the virgin goddess Athene.[25]

So it is also possible that the accounts of Jesus' conception and virgin birth owe something to the beliefs of heterodox Jews who worshipped a goddess. But were they borrowed by the gospel writers (or their sources), or does the story reflect an idea current in Jesus' lifetime?

On the other hand, inevitably some preferred to explain the doubts over Jesus' paternity in more mundane, not to say scurrilous, ways. By the middle of the second century Jews were spreading the rumor that Jesus' father was unknown simply because the boy was illegitimate and his mother a well-known woman of dubious virtue. Origen, in his refutation of the claims made by a pagan critic of Christianity, Celsus, wrote in about 150 CE that Mary had been thrown out by her carpenter husband for unfaithfulness and later had an illegitimate son by a soldier named Panthera.[26] Surely it is hard to think of a scenario more at odds with the Catholic veneration of Mary the Mother.

British historian Ian Wilson points out that certain references in the Gospels imply that rumors were being spread at least at the time those texts were written. Saying 105 of the Gospel of Thomas has

Jesus declaring, perhaps defensively, "He who knows the father and the mother will be called the son of a harlot," and John's Gospel has a group of Jews saying to Jesus, "We are not illegitimate children," which Wilson interprets as a sly dig.[27]

The earliest explicitly hostile statement from a Jewish source is in the Talmud's Mishnah, in which Jesus is described as "a bastard of an adulteress." Later statements in the Talmud follow Origen/Celsus in describing Jesus as "ben [son of] Pantera," or variations such as "Pandera." Because this name was unknown from Roman times, it was always explained away simply as a corruption of *parthenos,* but in 1859 a Roman tombstone was found at Bingerbrück in Germany that had marked the grave of one Tiberius Julius Abdes Pantera. Not only did it date from the early first century, but this Pantera was an archer from Sidon in Phoenicia and had served in Syria until his transfer to the Rhine in 9 CE. The name Abdes is Semitic (though not necessarily Jewish), and Pantera was a fairly common name among Syrians in the first century.[28] So could he have been Jesus' father? At the very least, this discovery confirms that the name attributed to his father by those hostile sources was real.

But even if evidence shows that slurs of illegitimacy were being spread at any early date, it hardly means they were true, being exactly what Jesus' enemies would have said about a boy with uncertain paternity. It was too obvious a target not to have been used. In the final analysis no one knows for sure. Nevertheless, such stories do highlight the fact that there is a distinct air of vagueness, if not outright evasion, about Jesus' paternity.

O Little Town of Bethlehem

Although Luke and Matthew's accounts of the nativity story agree that Jesus was born in Bethlehem (one of the messianic prophecies that, according to some interpretations, had to be fulfilled), they give different reasons for the couple's being there. In Matthew it is simply their hometown, and the baby is born in a house, presumably theirs. In Luke they have to toil to Bethlehem for a Roman taxation census, and as every Christian child knows, the newborn Messiah is placed in a manger "because there was no guest room available for them." But there is nothing about a stable, and how the manger comes into it remains unexplained.

A prophecy in Micah tells how from Bethlehem will come "one who will rule over Israel"[29]—the Messiah would be born there. Matthew specifically cites this passage in his account of the birth (and uses it to explain how the Magi know where to look—the star only leads them to the specific house). So was Bethlehem chosen as a fictional scene simply to fulfill this prophecy?

Luke's explanation of why Jesus came to be born in Bethlehem can easily be shown to be contrived: he says Joseph had to travel from Nazareth to Bethlehem because it was the town of his ancestors, specifically the great Judaic icon King David. But as Roman taxes were based on land and property owned, not on where an individual's family came from, this makes no sense. Once again, Luke changes the facts to suit his story, melding tales and traditions that associated Jesus' origins with both Nazareth and Bethlehem, and inventing a tale to reconcile the two.[30]

As with the claims of Davidic descent, John's Gospel lets the cat out of the bag, describing how doubts were expressed about Jesus' messiahship on the grounds that the scriptures say that the chosen one will come from Bethlehem, not from Galilee.[31] And even though this is the only mention of Bethlehem in the entire Gospel, John does not use it to make the claim that this is where Jesus came from. Given Mark's lack of mention of Bethlehem, there is a strong suspicion that the whole connection was invented specifically in order to make Christ fulfill the prophecy. The fact that Matthew and Luke came up with entirely different ways of making the link show that it was almost certainly invented.

So baby Jesus is born, swaddled, and laid in the manger. They name him—as instructed by Gabriel (to Joseph in Matthew, to Mary in Luke)—Jesus, or more accurately Yeshu or Yeshua: Jesus is a transliteration of the Aramaic name into Greek characters (Iesos), a shortened form of Yehoshua—Greek Joshua, meaning "God saves."

According to Luke, almost immediately a flock of shepherds arrive to adore him, followed—or so we are told by Matthew—sometime later (it could have been anytime during the infant's first two years) by a clutch of wise men, or "Magi." The two writers seem totally unaware of the details of each other's stories.

Shepherds were not new adorers of infant dying-and-rising gods: they traditionally attended the births of the Egyptian Osiris and the shepherd-musician Orpheus, besides the baby Mithras. In fact it was fully expected of a new god to have horny-handed agricultural workers kneeling before him in simpleminded wonder.

The involvement of the Magi has perplexed people for centuries: it is never spelled out who they are and why the birth of the Messiah is any of their business. The Greek word is *magoi*, the plural of *magos*, a magician and/or learned person, but no explanation is offered about their relevance to the Jesus story. All we are told is that they came "from the East," which is not very helpful. (And Luke never mentions how many wise men there are, just that they bring three gifts. It was only centuries later that they also became "kings" in Christian lore.) They "saw his star" rise when the King of the Jews was born, and so have come to Bethlehem to worship him, as they know that is his destined birthplace. (The star only reappears when they reach Bethlehem, where it performs an extremely unlikely maneuver for a heavenly body in guiding them to the right house.)

The star is always good for a handful of features in the press every Christmastime. Every year someone seems to come up with another idea of what the "Star of Bethlehem" might have been: a comet, a supernova, even a rare astrological conjunction rather than a visible astronomical event. These theories in turn lead to attempts to date Jesus' birth by reference to a particular comet or conjunction. But they all share a basic and very serious flaw—they assume the Gospel story refers to a real event, yet the overwhelming evidence is that it is just another piece of New Testament fiction.

First, the literary convolutions required to get the holy family into Bethlehem suggest strongly they were never there, so if the Magi did turn up, they would have been disappointed. And a miraculous star is exactly what Matthew's readers expected to find in an account of the Messiah's birth: they were a standard aspect of the "signs and wonders" of contemporary Jewish thinking. For example, Josephus, in *The Jewish War*, when discussing portents of the destruction of the Temple, wrote, "First a star stood over the City, very like a broadsword, and a comet that remained for a whole year."[32] As Josephus' book appeared in the seventies of the first century, and the story of these omens was probably well known, it is even possible that this story is what inspired Matthew's account. Indeed a miraculous heavenly body *had* to feature in the life of the Messiah. One of the best-known prophecies, from the Book of Numbers, declared:

> A star will come out of Jacob;
> a sceptre will rise out of Israel.[33]

(The man most widely regarded by Jews as the Messiah, who appeared about a century after Jesus, was Simon bar Kokhba, "Son of the Star.")

It is unclear what Matthew intended his audience to make of the Magi's visit, as uncharacteristically he fails to labor the point about it fulfilling some messianic prophecy (even though the story incorporates two of them, the star and the place of birth). There is not even a word of explanation about the identity of the Magi. It has been suggested that they were intended to represent one of the lost tribes, which the Messiah was supposed to bring back to Israel, but Matthew stops short of making this explicit. "Magi" usually describes the priestly caste of the Parthian Empire (in modern Persia), but why should they be interested in the birth of Israel's Messiah?

However, Keith Prince has pointed out another possible connection to us—an event that took place in Rome in 66 CE, which whipped up great excitement throughout the Empire and was reported by at least three Roman chroniclers, Suetonius, Cassius Dio, and Pliny the Elder. To celebrate the settlement of a centuries-long on/off war with the Parthian Empire, an impressive parade progressed all the way from the Euphrates in the East to Rome led by Tiridates, the Parthian king of Armenia, including the sons of three other Parthian kings, with an entourage of some three thousand. They went to Rome to honor Nero *as their god*. As Tiridates put it (according to Cassius Dio), "I have come to thee, my god, to worship thee as I do Mithras."[34] They were accompanied by their priests—the Magi. In fact Tiridates himself was a magus, besides being a king.

Could this celebrated event have supplied the writer of Matthew's Gospel with an idea for spicing up his story? He needed a device for Herod to learn of Jesus' birth—and the Magi provide it. And in one fell swoop it would also take a sideswipe at Nero, the first persecutor of the Christians, and his claim to be God incarnate. The finale of Tiridates' visit provides the most telling clue: Dio says that Tiridates "did not return by the route he had followed in coming."[35] Matthew's Magi, having been warned in a dream not to return to Herod as they had promised to do, "returned to their country by another route."[36] Given all the problems about Matthew's reliability on this issue, he must have drawn this part of his story from *somewhere*—and Tiridates' visit to Rome seems to have been his inspiration.

The "Dangerous Child"

Perhaps the greatest discrepancy between the two nativity stories concerns the massacre of the innocents. In Luke there simply isn't one. Eight days after the birth and the shepherds' visit, as prescribed by Mosaic Law, Joseph and Mary take their son to the Temple in Jerusalem to be circumcised. Two holy people, a devout man named Simeon and the elderly prophetess Anna, recognise the infant as the prophesied one. Then Joseph and Mary simply take him home to Nazareth.

Matthew is very different. Alerted by the Magi to the birth of the "King of the Jews," Herod determines to preempt this threat to his power, ordering the killing of all male children under the age of two in and around Bethlehem. But in a dream an angel advises Joseph to flee to Egypt with mother and child, and so they escape. After Herod's death another dream angel tells Joseph it is now safe to return to Israel, although rather than returning to their home in Judea, which is ruled by Herod's son Archelaus, Joseph takes Mary and the infant Jesus to Nazareth in Galilee, thereby inadvertently fulfilling a prophecy that the Messiah "will be called a Nazarene." However, this is one prophecy that makes no appearance in any of the Old Testament books. Where the gospel writer got it from is a mystery. (As it happens, Matthew's rationale for the family's going to Galilee because Judea is still ruled by one of Herod the Great's sons shows that the story is contrived: Galilee was ruled by another of his sons, Herod Antipas.)

There are many logical reasons for dismissing the whole story of the massacre of the innocents as another complete invention. First, how could such a key event be known to only one of the gospel writers? It is much more likely that Matthew invented this sensational story rather than that the other three had either not heard of it or deemed it unworthy of mention. Second, surely such an unspeakably brutal act by Herod would have been recorded by some chronicler—Josephus, for example, who gleefully records all of Herod's other excesses.

Finally it rather too neatly echoes the well-worn myth of the "dangerous child" whose existence poses a threat to a cruel and tyrannical leader, but who escapes and returns as an adult to wreak his revenge. At that time readers *expected* any significant figure to have a dramatic nativity. Did Matthew merely concoct his tale as a crowd-pleaser and to justify the fulfillment of yet more messianic prophecies? The first is that the Messiah would "be called out of Egypt": escaping the massacre creates a reason for Jesus to go to Egypt. Matthew also explicitly links the massacre to a passage in Jeremiah that refers to Rachel weeping for her children, which, he says, was a prophecy of the massacre.

Possible supporting evidence for some link with Egypt comes from hostile references to Jesus in the Jewish Talmud, which denounces him as a practitioner of sorcery, learned in Egypt, and who through dark arts attempted to lead the people of Israel astray. But none of the Talmudic references was written before 200 CE at the earliest, and although they clearly drew upon older material, the usual problem remains of determining which, if any, scraps of information come from Jesus' own lifetime, and if so how reliable they are. Obviously, as they come from a hostile source they should be treated with caution, although the emphasis that Jesus had learned magic in Egypt is intriguing. Was this idea simply extrapolated from the single, brief reference to a sojourn in Egypt, or is it based on something more explicit, now lost to history?

There is nothing inherently unlikely about choosing Egypt as a refuge, as it boasted a sizeable Jewish community, particularly in the great seaport of Alexandria, which had in fact the largest Jewish population outside of Palestine. Consequently there were much traffic and good lines of communication between the two countries. Indeed, some commentators, even within academia, have come to see affinities between Jesus' teaching and the Egyptian religion and speculated that an Egyptian sojourn would have allowed him to absorb these influences.

The Lost Years

By now it should be clear to all but the most blinkered Christian that the nativity tales are unreliable, to say the least. But there is another, major reason for concluding that they are more or less fictitious: Jesus' birth stories make little sense *even on the Gospels' own logic.* Bethlehem, if not the whole of Israel, is buzzing with the news that the Messiah has been born. Shepherds arrive to adore him. Wise men travel great distances to bring gifts and pay tribute. He is recognized as the Messiah by two holy people. His birth precipitates a terrible massacre of children that, had it happened, must have haunted the memories of the people of Bethlehem and beyond for generations. Then everyone—including his own parents—forgets about all of this. When he turns up thirty or so years later, nobody knows who he is and he has to prove himself all over again—an extremely unlikely scenario, especially for a proud people with very long memories.

Between his birth and baptism by John, when he was at least thirty, the Gospels tell us nothing about Jesus' life—another astonishing omission—apart from a single mention in Luke of him as a boy in the unlikely tale of his being found in the Temple at the age of twelve after his parents frantically searched for him. When Mary rebukes the boy for giving them such a scare, he replies loftily, even arrogantly: "'Why were you searching for me?' he asked. 'Didn't you know I had to be in my Father's house?' But they did not understand what he was saying to them." [37]

This beggars belief. Luke has just told an elaborate story about an angel appearing to Mary, her giving birth to her son even though *virgo intacta*, shepherds being sent to honor him by another flock of angels, and two holy people proclaiming him during his circumcision at the Temple. If we add in Matthew, we have him being hunted by the king because of who he is, causing his parents to take him into hiding in another country. But now Mary and Joseph *have no idea what he is talking about.*

So what was Jesus doing before he embarked on his public ministry? His first thirty years (at least) are a complete blank. All the Gospels tell us is that he lived in Nazareth, although at some point he moved to the town of Capernaum on the shores of Lake Galilee. We know nothing about the circumstances in which he was brought up; what he did for a living; whether he married and brought up a family. There is just a stark, staring blank.

The only clue is a single reference to him as a carpenter—and even this might not be what it seems. Mark's Gospel describes how the crowd referred to him—just once—as a carpenter, which becomes "carpenter's son" in Matthew and is ignored by Luke entirely. For a start, the Greek word translated as "carpenter" is *tekton*, which actually means "builder"—not necessarily a worker in wood. However, the eminent Jewish New Testament scholar Geza Vermes has suggested that the original meaning was quite different. Although the Greek *tekton* appears in the Gospels, the original word would have been the Aramaic *naggar*, also a colloquialism for a learned man, a scholar. Vermes points out that as this description occurs in a passage where the crowd is expressing amazement at his erudition, it would seem that this meaning of *naggar* would be more logical.[38] If Vermes is right, we can say good-bye to our only clue as to what Jesus was doing for the first thirty-odd years of his life.

Some have suggested that the reason the Gospels are silent on the missing years is that Jesus was brought up within a closed religious community such as that of the Essenes, where he was schooled in the beliefs he would then preach, but there is not a shred of evidence for this. There is a complete mismatch between many of the principles and teachings of the Essenes as documented by first-century writers—particularly Josephus, who dabbled in Essenism as a young man—and the ones attributed to Jesus in the Gospels. The same objection applies to the idea that Jesus spent his missing years in India, where he was trained as a Buddhist. While some of his reported teachings strike a chord with Buddhism, just as many simply do not, most obviously the lack of a personal God.[39]

The (Extended) Holy Family

Do we know anything about Jesus' family background or status? Were they rich or poor? Were they educated? Did they have any strong sectarian orientation? All this is relevant, as some theories about the historical Jesus either have him as a scion of a distinguished dynasty—a descendant of David, Herod, or even the pharaohs of Egypt—or see him as the front man for a family plot with religious or political objectives. However, none of this is supported by the canonical Gospels or indeed any of the nonbiblical sources. Once the claim of descent from King David is discounted, we are left knowing nothing about the background of his family.

By the time the story of the adult Jesus begins, Joseph is absent, but his disappearance goes unmarked from the same Gospels that were so keen to bestow a starring role on him in the nativity stories. It is usually assumed he is dead, but he may not have been. Mary is certainly still alive and seems to outlive her famous son—who, if the Gospels (as opposed to the Catholic and Orthodox Churches) are to be believed, was merely her firstborn.

Although Catholics believe Jesus was Mary's only child, born to her miraculously in her virgin state, the Gospels quite clearly list his four brothers as James, Joses (Joseph), Jude (Judas), and Simon. His sisters are not named but because of the plural obviously there were at least two. James, although never mentioned as a disciple during Jesus' lifetime, was to become the leader of the Jerusalem Church after the crucifixion.

The early Church had no problem with accepting that "brothers" meant blood brothers. Eusebius cites the earlier Hegesippus on the grandsons of Jude, "who was his [Jesus'] brother, humanly speaking."[40] (These grandsons—great-nephews of Jesus—were living in the early first century.) However, two situations led to the airbrushing out of his brothers and sisters from the Christian scenario. The first was the tension between James' Jerusalem Church and the community in Rome that supported Paul's interpretation of Jesus' mission. As the latter won the battle to be mainstream Christianity, anything about the Jerusalem Church had to be played down, especially any hint that appeared to give James an authority equal to that of the apostles to whom the Roman Church appealed. More important from a theological perspective was the doctrine that Mary had not only been a virgin when she conceived and gave birth to Jesus but remained one for the rest of her life. Clearly the fact of Jesus' younger brothers and sisters gave the lie to this notion and was a huge embarrassment.

The traditional Catholic explanation, first recorded in the late fourth century, of this challenge to the doctrine of Mary's eternal virginity is that the "brothers and sisters" were really Jesus' cousins, the children of Joseph's brother and his wife (so without any parental bond with Jesus at all). The Greek Orthodox position (taken from the *Protevangelium*) is that they were half brothers and half sisters, the children of an earlier marriage of Joseph's.

The Catholic Church argues that the Gospels, written in Greek, used the word *adelphos* to describe the relationship, which means "brother" in the literal sense. But Hebrew and Aramaic were more flexible and applied their words for "brother" to a variety of male relations including stepbrothers, half brothers, cousins, and even uncle and nephew. So, the argument goes, when the Gospels were written, the writers were undecided about exactly which of these relationships was intended, and so settled on *adelphos*, thereby fixing a more specific relationship than was truly the case. This has indeed happened on many occasions in the Greek translation of the Old Testament, the Septuagint, where men who are clearly not blood brothers are described as *adelphos*.

True, this argument does stand up when applied to the Gospels—but then it is completely undermined by the writings of Paul and Josephus, both of whom wrote in Greek, and both of whom call James Jesus' *adelphos*. While it is true that *adelphos* can be a figurative term for male relatives in general, had either of these writers known of a more specific relationship, they would have been more explicit. Especially as Paul met James face-to-face, one would think he would know what he was talking about.

The fact is that Jesus *did* have blood siblings and that his mother, Mary, was *not* a perpetual virgin, even if she had been intact at the time of her eldest son's birth—itself an exceptionally unlikely scenario. The Catholic and Orthodox Churches are quite plainly wrong on this subject. One can only conclude that all its arguments on this subject are just fantasy, stemming from its insistence on the embarrassing "perpetual virginity" doctrine, which itself was wishful thinking on the part of the early Church. Surely we have here yet more evidence of an indefensible misogyny and horror of sex and childbirth that is hardly compatible with a respect for all of God's creation.

Did Jesus have a twin brother? Certainly one of the disciples, and subsequent apostle, is called Thomas, Aramaic for "twin." However, in many early sources—such as the Gospel of Thomas—he is referred to as Didymus Jude Thomas. "Didymus" also means "twin" in Greek, essentially just a translation of his Aramaic name. Clearly his real name was Jude, and Thomas a nickname (or cognomen). Twin he may have been, but of course not necessarily *Jesus'* twin.

The tradition that Thomas was Jesus' identical twin developed among Eastern Christians at an early date, although unfortunately there is no way of telling whether it was based on facts or just extrapolated from the name. The theological difficulty here is that if Christ was divinely conceived, then so was his twin. And how could the early Christians who believed that he had a twin brother reconcile this belief with the nativity story that concentrated solely on Jesus?

A Married Man?

Was Jesus married? To the millions of *Da Vinci Code* fans the answer must be unequivocally yes. In Dan Brown's reconstruction it is a fact that Jesus and Mary Magdalene were man and wife, with children, although this information has been ruthlessly suppressed by the Catholic Church for the past two thousand years. However, the idea is not confined to fiction, and the case for a married Jesus is extremely strong. Several commentators have suggested over the years that Jesus may have married and fathered children during the "lost years" between his birth and baptism.

This is hardly a new idea: there were gnostic sects in the second century that believed that Jesus had been married (or at least had intimate female companions). Martin Luther also believed—on the basis that it was impossible for a man to remain celibate—not that Jesus had been married, but that he had been sexually involved with various women in the Gospel stories (Mary Magdalene, the Samaritan woman, and the woman taken in adultery).

The case for a married Jesus was made most cogently by American academic William E. Phipps in the early 1970s, although the strongest argument in his favor seems at first somewhat perverse from a modern perspective: basically neither the Gospels nor any other early Christian source says he wasn't. (In fact, as we will see, at least one early source implies he was.) Following Phipps' dictum that "it is the unconventional practices of a person that are more likely to be remembered and recorded,"[41] remaining single in that culture was so unusual that had Jesus not been married, there is no question that the fact would have been "remembered and recorded" and probably called for some justification or explanation. On the other hand, since being married (or having had a wife—widowers and even divorcés were not uncommon) was the custom, a writer would not have felt he had to spell it out.

Proof comes from the way the Gospels treat the disciples. We are never explicitly told that Peter, for example, was married, and yet Jesus healed his mother-in-law, so he must have been. Had she not been cured, we would never have known he was a married man, at least not from the Gospels or the Acts of the Apostles (although one of Paul's Letters mentions his having a wife).

For a man to be unmarried or celibate was not just unusual in Jewish culture, it was deemed freakishly abnormal. Since the continuation and expansion of God's chosen people was an imperative, it was nothing less than a religious duty to marry and produce children. (Hence the depth of anguish of barren women and childless husbands in the Old Testament.) Mainstream rabbinic thinking viewed celibates "as violators of God's commandment to procreate."[42] And as Phipps points out, "there are no instances of life-long celibacy in the entire Old Testament history."[43]

Those scholars, such as Geza Vermes, who accept that Jesus was celibate and seek to account for it in Jewish terms, look to the mere handful of holy men who did preach celibacy, such as the second-century Pinhas ben Yair.[44] But such examples only serve to *support* Phipps' case, since Pinhas' injunction clearly refers to the preferred state of a man who had already done his duty of marrying and fathering children.

In the Jewish culture of Jesus' time men were usually married at around sixteen—and certainly by twenty—betrothal occurring a couple of years before that, to slightly younger brides. Marriages were arranged, couples often never even meeting before their betrothal, and it was the duty of a father to find brides for his sons, who had no say in the matter. In the absence of a father this task would have fallen to Jesus' mother, Mary. In other words, had Jesus never married, the fact would have reflected a conscious decision by his parents some twenty years before he embarked on his mission. Since (once we reject the nativity stories) nothing suggests that his family considered Jesus to be in any way special, there is absolutely no reason for them to have made such a decision.

Ultimately there is no way that Phipps' case can be conclusively proven, but it does have the weight of evidence and logic on its side. If correct, Jesus would have been married for some twenty years before the beginning of his religious career. By that time he could have been a widower, or even simply have left his wife at home to embark on his mission.

Perhaps the strongest counterargument to Phipps is not the absence of Jesus' wife in the early sources but the absence of children. However, as Phipps points out, "Jesus and his movement belonged to the prophetic stream of Hebraic tradition that did not ascribe significance to an individual merely because of his family status. Even though the prophets married, in most cases no mention is made of their children."[45] And there are alternative explanations: infertility or the high rate of infant mortality at that time. And again there is no mention in any Christian source of the children or descendants of such an important figure as Peter.

Jesus of . . . ?

The connection between Jesus and Bethlehem is almost certainly spurious, but the other place with which he is associated, and which even gives him his name, is equally mysterious. In fact he may not be "Jesus of Nazareth" at all.

In the Gospels, Christ is occasionally described by the Greek epithet *o Nazoraios*, translated as "the Nazorean," or *o Nazarenos*, "the

Nazarene." This apparently small distinction has very far-reaching implications for our understanding of the historical Jesus—not just to fill in the details of his life but also because it might shed light on his own religious orientation. Some academics argue that the term does not mean "of Nazareth."

Nazoraios must have been how Jesus was known during his public ministry, since the Gospels are quite consistent in applying the description to him. They also refer to the town of Nazareth (Nazaret) in Galilee, where he was apparently brought up. (Even though Mark's Gospel has no account of the nativity, it does say that Jesus came from Nazareth to the Jordan to be baptized—its sole reference to the town.) Clearly there is at least an implied connection between the place and the epithet, although it is made explicit only once, in Matthew, where it invokes a prophecy that the Messiah will be called "Nazorean" in order to explain why he had to live in Nazareth—yet as we noted above, this messianic link is not in any of the other Gospels and was not taken from Matthew's primary source, Mark.

Other sources offer little help. In the Jewish Mishnah Jesus is called "Yeshu Hanotzri," but there is the same uncertainty over whether this means "of Nazareth" or "Nazorean." So we have three choices: Jesus came from Nazareth and "Nazorean" simply refers to the town; Jesus came from Nazareth but the epithet means something else—the similarity of the two words being just a coincidence; the whole notion of a connection with Nazareth is a mistake, the result of the gospel writers or their sources misunderstanding "Nazorean," thinking it referred to the town, which confusion then became elaborated as the nativity tales developed.

Some doubt the existence of Nazareth in Jesus' day because it is not mentioned in any sources other than the Gospels until the third century (and even that first allusion is disputed by some historians, who argue that it refers to another place entirely).[46] However, if there was no Nazareth, how could the gospel writers have mentioned it? Rightly or wrongly, they associated Jesus with a town or village called Nazareth, so clearly it must have existed, and have been known by that name, by the time the Gospels were written, therefore before 100.

But this does not necessarily imply that "Nazorean" derives from the place. The major problem is that specialists who think it originates in some source other than the town disagree about the root word. One school of thought links it to *nazir*, "shoot" or "branch"—after all, messianic prophecies referred to a shoot or branch of Jesse.[47] Others relate it to *nazar*, "to observe," in the sense of being religiously observant. A third suggestion links it to a specific sect within Judaism known as the *nozrim* (singular *nazr*), meaning "guardians of the Covenant" or, in the words of the British New Testament scholar Hugh J. Schonfield, "Keepers or Preservers . . . those who maintained the true teaching and tradition, or who cherished certain secrets which they did not divulge to others."[48]

Although all these explanations seem plausible, is it possible to isolate the right one? At the moment perhaps not, but we will return to this word later to try to set it in context with other aspects of Jesus' career.

A Deafening Silence

So to sum up: we know almost nothing about Jesus before he began his public career. Most of the information in the Gospels is demonstrably fictitious, and what is left is questionable and unreliable.

The little that does seem to be accurate makes a very short list. We know his mother's name and those of his male siblings, and probably his father's. We know there was something odd about his paternity, setting the scene for stories of both his miraculous conception and his illegitimacy to circulate. He emerged from Galilee, but whether it was his family home or the place of his birth remains unclear.

There is nothing that can be said for certain about when, where, or in what circumstances Jesus was born, or anything about his family background. Neither is there the slightest clue as to where, or even if, he was educated. Despite the popular belief he was a carpenter, in fact there is no real information about what he did for a living. He may or may not have come from Nazareth.

But even the blanks and the inventions tell us something—that those who made it their job to set down a record of Jesus' life knew nothing about it before he made his debut on the public stage. This must mean that none of his first followers knew about it otherwise some scraps of information would surely have been passed down to the gospel writers. Jesus must have been a mystery even to those closest to him. (This is even odder given that members of his family emerged to take charge of the movement after his departure. Did they fail to tell anyone anything about his background?)

Why the mystery? Was it simply that his origins were too ordinary or too obscure? Or was the secrecy deliberate, either to build an air of mystery about him or because Jesus had a secret that needed to be kept?

4

"Excited to the Utmost"

As we saw in the previous chapter, the well-loved stories about Jesus' birth and early life are, disappointingly, merely literary devices to impress readers of the Gospels with a sense of awe and wonder at the advent of their hero, the man-god Christ. There could have been no virgin birth; there was no new star lighting the path of the mysterious Magi—themselves nonexistent—and even Jesus' being born in "the little town of Bethlehem" is by no means certain. But the beginning of his public ministry is where facts rather than fiction come to the fore and we can begin to take the whole Jesus story much more seriously.

Although at first glance the Gospels seem to vary significantly, in fact they are internally consistent to a remarkable extent. And at last, for the first time, there are independent sources to provide cross-references.

The two main gospel traditions, the synoptics and John's Gospel, agree on the basic shape of Jesus' career, beginning with his baptism by John the Baptist, after which he called together a group of disciples, taking them on the road around Palestine (chiefly Galilee and other places in the north) performing miracles—mostly healings and exorcisms—and preaching to the wonder-hungry crowds. Finally, during a visit to Jerusalem, he was arrested, tried, condemned to death, and crucified.

However, the details—the order of events and even many of the key episodes themselves—are very different in the two sets of gospels. For example, the synoptics have Jesus confining his activity exclusively to Galilee and the northern territories until his final, fateful journey to Jerusalem right at the end, whereas John describes Jesus as beginning his ministry in Judea and visiting Jerusalem several times right from the start. But is it possible to determine which chronology is the more reliable?

As we noted earlier, even the earliest Christian commentators said that the author of the first synoptic Gospel, Mark, set individual stories about Jesus' deeds in very much his own sequence, because he had no idea about their real chronology. This fits precisely with the modern scholars' analysis that Mark is made up of individual story units arranged into a narrative by short linking passages. So not only should we not take Mark literally about the order of events, but neither can we take Matthew and Luke literally, because they followed Mark's plot.

Besides, the synoptics' version makes a more satisfying drama, with its single momentous journey to Jerusalem as the climax, which suggests that John's order of events might well be more reliable. (It makes more sense, for example, that Jesus made many visits to the holy city.) But even here we have to tread carefully: clearly John shaped his story around the cycle of Jewish feasts rather too neatly—so even his chronology is somewhat suspect, although still preferable to the synoptics'.

The difference between the chronology of the two gospel traditions is particularly important when examining the singularly significant relationship between Jesus and John the Baptist and the connection between their two ministries. John's Gospel describes them as overlapping—which must be correct because, as will become clear in this chapter, it could never have been made up.

However, all the canonical Gospels agree that Jesus' public career began when he was baptized by John the Baptist, who is obviously a highly significant figure in this story, and one way or another a major influence on Jesus. But what exactly was his role in the story? And could that throw more light on Christ's own mission and purpose?

A Dramatic Appearance

The one thing that the New Testament Gospels—and all Christian sources—agree on is that John the Baptist's importance is confined merely to his role as the one who sets the scene for Jesus, the divinely inspired—but resolutely not actually divine himself—holy man whose task it is to whip the people up into a state of excited expectation for the arrival of this advanced spiritual being and then, with a huge sense of drama, point him out when he appears among them.

Both Mark and John begin with the appearance of John the Baptist on the banks of the Jordan. If we ignore the fairy-tale nativity, then the Matthew and Luke stories also start with the Baptist.

Many modern scholars prefer "John the Baptiser," a more accurate translation of the original Greek—*Ioannes o Baptistes* or *o Baptison*—Ioannes being Greek for the Aramaic Yehohanan, and Baptizer from the Greek word meaning "to immerse." Even the grammar itself reveals the unique qualities of this man: the construction ("the" followed by an adjectival verb) is highly unusual for the Greek of that time.[1] Whoever he was and whatever he did, John the Baptist/Baptizer was *special*.

Having rejected Luke's nativity story, we are left without any reliable source of information about the Baptist's family background and early life, the date of his birth, or his age when he first strode onto the public stage. As we have seen, Luke's assertion that Jesus and John the Baptist were cousins is by no means certain. The only fact of any significance we have learned from Luke is that his account of the annunciation incorporates passages—most significantly the Magnificat—which were originally composed in honor of John, the first clue that he may have been more important than Christianity has always been so careful to teach. And that, in itself, is hugely thought-provoking.

John's parents' names as given in Luke—Zechariah and Elizabeth—are probably accurate, but it is impossible to be sure. Zechariah was very common, but Elizabeth (*Elisheva*) was not.

Luke states that John came from a long line of priests on both his parents' sides, as Elizabeth was a descendant of Israel's first priest,

Aaron, the brother of Moses—although it must be admitted that Luke is often unreliable on such matters. But even if John was from a priestly family, then surely he must have repudiated his heritage when he began his innovative baptismal mission, which posed at least an implicit challenge to the Temple priesthood. So does his genealogical background really matter?

There are other sources, including a *Life of John*, full of tall stories and miraculous happenings, written by the Egyptian bishop Serapion of Thmouis around 390, but there is no reason to take that source particularly seriously, except perhaps for the fact that it is the first known reference to a tradition that links John the Baptist with Ain Karim (Arabic for "spring of the vineyard"), a large village about five miles west of Jerusalem, which in ancient times was known as Karem and Beth Hacceram. The *Life of John* claims this is where Elizabeth died and was buried, but other writings, from about 530, also claim that Ain Karim was where John was born.

As those texts are very late, perhaps they should be treated with a pinch of salt, but on the other hand they are not based on the Gospels and do not depend on any prophecies or legends (unlike the traditions identifying Jesus' birthplace) so *might* be based on a solid tradition. Also, the link between John the Baptist and Ain Karim has received some support from recent archaeological discoveries, as we will see.

"A Voice Crying in the Wilderness"

In Mark, John appears "in the desert region"—*eremos*, "an uninhabited, uncultivated area, often used for grazing,"[2] not necessarily the grim and desiccated place conjured up by the uncompromising word "desert"—preaching and baptizing. He proclaimed, presumably as loudly as his lungs would allow, that the people should prepare for the coming of the Lord by repenting (literally "changing their minds"[3]). As he made very clear, the outward and visible sign of that internal mind changing, and of the "remission of sins," is baptism—total immersion in the waters of the River Jordan. Clearly his was a message whose time had come, striking a deep and powerful chord in the minds of the masses: "the whole Judean countryside and all the people of Jerusalem"[4] flock to him for baptism, presumably an exaggeration, although perhaps not much of one.

The Jordan marked the border between Judea, which was under direct Roman control, and Perea, ruled, along with Galilee, by Herod Antipas. Both the Gospels and Josephus (as we will see) imply that John was mainly active on the Perean side, to the east of the river.

John's unusual mode of dress and lifestyle are singled out for comment—his distinctive (and presumably malodorous) camel-hair clothing and leather belt being exactly as worn by the prophet Elijah, according the Old Testament.[5] He also ate locusts and wild honey, though this merely suggests that he lived off the land rather than followed an exotic or finicky diet.

So far, so straightforward. But when we turn our attention to his message, other agendas creep into the Gospels' accounts. John preaches that "one more powerful than I" is to come after him, who will baptize not with water but "with the Holy Spirit"—literally "holy breath"—and "the thongs of whose sandals I am not worthy to stoop down and untie."[6] The unfastening of sandals, an image repeated by Matthew and Luke (although Matthew changes it to carrying the sandals), was emphatically a slave's task, and a particularly low-ranking, menial slave at that; in rabbinic literature the taking off and putting on of shoes was exclusively used as an image of a master-slave relationship.[7] So from the start it places John the Baptist in not merely a subordinate but actually an obsequiously submissive relationship to Jesus.

Matthew and Luke develop the story a little, adding details that clearly derive from a common source although they present them in different ways. Both add the passage in which Jesus delivers a stinging attack on his audience as (among other things) a "brood of vipers" and "rotten fruit," for turning away from God's true path. The words attributed to John in Matthew and Luke are near-identical (only four different words out of sixty-four), obviously originating with Q, but the two Gospels have them being directed at different groups: in Luke John's invective is aimed at the people of Israel as a whole; in Matthew it is only Pharisees and Sadducees who come to see him.

The majority of scholars accept that these words were genuinely

John's. There is no reason for later Christians to have made them up and indeed sound reasons for them not to have done so: the rebuke does not relate at all to the basic gospel message (in which Jesus calls for the people to repent before he saves them). But while it is clear that John uttered those or similar words, it is frustratingly unclear whether he was referring to all Jews or just certain groups of Jews.

Luke adds some extra passages in which the Baptist exhorts the people to share what they have, and delivers specific messages to tax collectors and soldiers, some of which are later echoed by Jesus. He tells the taxmen to take no more than is legally due, and the soldiers not to extort money and to be content with their wages. These injunctions indicate that Luke was at least aware that there was a political component to John's message (although he fails to make it explicit): both address the issue of collaboration with the Roman overlords, an emphasis on the political aspect that neatly echoes other sources.

As another indication of the mix of John's following, or the broadness of his appeal, Matthew has Jesus saying (when in debate with the chief priests), "For John came to you to show you the way of righteousness, and you did not believe him, but the tax collectors and prostitutes did."[8]

Luke makes the link with his nativity story by having the infant John the Baptist living in the "desert" until the time of his emergence as a preacher, in the fifteenth year of Tiberius' rule (28 or 29 CE). But can we really take Luke's chronology seriously? The Baptist's living in the desert for his entire childhood seems somewhat unlikely.

There are some telling differences in the way the Baptist is introduced and described in John's Gospel, which tells us more about him, and presents more clues that he was both important in his own right and was a major influence on Jesus, than any other Christian source. But paradoxically it is also the most emphatic that John was merely the forerunner and that Jesus was unequivocally the star of the show.

The Baptist is only ever referred to as "John" in this Gospel—no title or epithet—and unlike in the synoptics' portrayal he has no introduction or explanation. Clearly the writer expected his audience to know who he was, which may explain some of the differences between his account and the other Gospels': if his audience was already familiar with John, he could never have gotten away with embroidering the facts. This is presumably why this Gospel acknowledges the overlap between the careers of John and Jesus, as in the synoptics.

In characteristic style the Fourth Gospel fleshes out the story by identifying the place where John baptized as "Bethany on the other side of the Jordan" (to distinguish it from the Bethany on the outskirts of Jerusalem that features prominently in the story afterwards), also known as Betheraba. This was a small town on the eastern, Perean side of the Jordan, close to the main road that ran east from Jerusalem.

John's Gospel is particularly keen to emphasize that John the Baptist was not *the* One, but only the forerunner who paved the way for the One. The Jews send Pharisees from Jerusalem specifically to ask John if he is the Messiah, to which, unsurprisingly, given the Gospel's agenda, he responds in the negative. (There is a similar denial in Luke.) Then they ask him if he is Elijah, which he also denies, and finally if he is "the Prophet," again denied. (This question refers to an expectation of the coming of a prophet of similar status to Moses who could establish new laws, a figure referred to in some of the Dead Sea Scrolls and called by Raymond E. Brown a "Prophet-like-Moses.")[9]

The Fourth Gospel is the most strident in denying certain things about John the Baptist: he wasn't the Messiah, it was Jesus; he wasn't the light, it was Jesus; Jesus existed before him; John never "did signs" (i.e., worked miracles), and so on. It is clear that these assertions were included because people at the time John's Gospel was written believed these things about the Baptist. As Brown explains (his emphasis), "It is reasonable to suspect that *some* of the negations about John the Baptist in the Fourth Gospel were intended as refutations of claims that the sectarians of John the Baptist made about their master."[10]

This overemphasis on the Baptist's inferiority, coupled with certain paradoxes in the Fourth Gospel, led the eminent German scholar Rudolf Bultmann to an extremely thought-provoking hypothesis. He argues that parts of John's Gospel were adapted—or, more cynically, perhaps just lifted—from texts that were originally composed by the Baptist's followers, including the famous "Word" prologue. In his 1964 commentary on John's Gospel, Bultmann writes of these opening verses (his emphasis), "This suggests that the source-text was *a hymn of the Baptist-Community*." [11]

Bultmann also argued that the "revelation discourses" put into Jesus' mouth in that Gospel also began as texts of the Baptist sect, and concluded that a substantial part was written by John the Baptist's followers and was adapted by Christians. On the strength of this theory he proposed that John's Gospel was written by a former disciple of the Baptist who had converted to the Jesus movement. Be that as it may, the fact that the authors of John and Luke felt it necessary to raise the question of the Baptist's being the Messiah—if only to discredit it—can only mean that at least a significant number of people *at the time those Gospels were written* believed that is precisely what he was.

Not Merely a Warm-up Man

However, where John the Baptist is concerned, at last we have an independent source of information, although tantalizingly still not very detailed. Josephus, in his *Antiquities of the Jews*—in which he calls John *Baptistou*, as opposed to the Gospels' *Baptistes* or *Baptison*, revealing that his version was his own—tells us a little about the Baptist. And unlike his disputed references to Jesus, undoubtedly the passage about John the Baptist is authentic.

After relating how Herod Antipas became embroiled in a war with Aretas IV, King of Nabataea—which ended with the resounding defeat and destruction of Antipas' army—Josephus explains that the people saw the defeat as God's judgment on Antipas for having had John the Baptist put to death. He then explains a little about "John, that was called the Baptist," clearly someone he admires. Josephus, who was born around the time that John was killed, obviously had to depend on hearsay, but it had clearly impressed him, for he wrote (in New Testament scholar Robert L. Webb's translation in his *John the Baptizer and Prophet*, 1991):

> [He] was a good man and one who commanded the Jews to practise virtue and act with justice toward one another and with piety

toward God, and [so] to gather together by baptism. For [John's view was that] in this way baptism certainly would appear acceptable to him [i.e., God] if [they] used [it] not for seeking pardon of certain sins, but for purification of the body, because the soul had already been cleansed before by righteousness. And when others gathered together [around John] (for they were also excited to the utmost by listening to [his] teachings), Herod, because he feared that his great persuasiveness with the people might lead to some kind of strife (for they seemed as if they would do everything which he counselled), thought it preferable, before anything radically innovative happened as a result of him, to execute [John], taking action first, rather than when the upheaval happened to perceive too late [sic], having already fallen into trouble. Because of the suspicion of Herod, he [i.e., John], after being sent bound to Machaerus (the fortress mentioned before), was executed there.[12]

Superficially Josephus' explanation of the purpose of John's baptism clashes with the Gospels', as he seems to be saying it was not about the remission of sins. But the distinction he makes—that baptism symbolized the fact that sins had already been forgiven because of the individual's commitment to righteous behavior—is actually rather subtle, and does in fact sit comfortably with the Gospel definition.

Josephus evokes a picture of John as a religious preacher and leader in his own right: he never suggests that he is only effectively the warm-up man for someone else. To Josephus, and presumably many others, the Baptist was a very special celebrity, not only charismatic but also quintessentially authoritative, *commanding* the people to mend their ways, not exhorting or imploring. When he spoke the masses not only listened but, clearly moved and shaken to the core, instantly obeyed. Given the context, he could only have claimed that his authority came directly from God, and the crowds that thronged to the Jordan obviously believed that to be true.

Josephus stresses the size of his following and, as we have seen, the fact that the people were "excited to the utmost" by his fiery rhetoric, citing his popularity as the reason that Herod Antipas had him arrested. As Webb puts it, Josephus shows that "the people around John were excited to a fever pitch and ready to do anything."[13]

According to Josephus, there were two elements to Antipas' fear:

John the Baptist's hold over the people, and the anxiety that he would use this to cause "strife," which could either mean a rebellion against the authorities or civil unrest between different factions. However, Josephus' description of Antipas' fear yields a clue—the Baptist was seen as a threat because he was a *revolutionary*.

There is nothing in Josephus' outline of John's basic message—that people should behave righteously and repent of their sins—that sounds potentially subversive in an obviously political sense, at least to modern ears. But John's injunction that the people should "gather together"—or unite—through his baptism, when taken with his words to tax collectors and soldiers in the Gospels, suggests that an element of his preaching explicitly or implicitly threatened the political status quo.

The Baptist had also established himself as the man who possessed the power and authority to channel God's forgiveness—quite a claim. And in doing so he had abrogated one of the Temple's main functions, which was at least an implicit criticism of the religious establishment.[14]

"With You I Am Well Pleased"

None of the Gospels mentions how long John had been baptizing before Jesus appeared. Although the compression of the narrative gives the impression that he appears almost immediately, that can hardly be true. John had to have had enough time to build up his following, so Jesus probably went to him for baptism after he had been calling the people to repentance for at least a few years. (If we accept Luke's dating of John's first appearance to 28 or 29 CE, and his arrest—for reasons that we will explain shortly—to 34, then his public career lasted five or six years.)

Mark relates that Jesus comes to the Jordan from Nazareth in Galilee to be baptized by John. At the moment of his baptism a "spirit like a dove" descends on him and a voice from the sky proclaims, "You are my Son, whom I love; with you I am well pleased."[15] However, something is missing from this, the earliest of the synoptic Gospels, which appears in all the others. As Morna D. Hooker points out in her 1981 commentary on Mark's Gospel, "*there is no hint in Mark's narrative that John recognised Jesus as the one whose coming he had proclaimed* [our emphasis]."[16] In the context of the overall message of the canonical Gospels, indeed of the entire Christian religion, this is quite astounding, instantly throwing everything we thought we ever knew about the Baptist's role into confusion.

The synoptics seem to be uncertain how to handle the whole John the Baptist episode. Mark has no problem with Jesus' having to be baptized, unlike all the other gospel writers: clearly he regards Christ as an ordinary man, not God incarnate, and not conceived without sex or sin. On the other hand, Matthew disingenuously adds an exchange between Jesus and John in which the latter at first refuses Jesus' request for baptism on the grounds that *he* should be asking Jesus to baptize *him*. Jesus replies that he should allow it just this once so that they may "fulfill all righteousness" (whatever that means).[17] Clearly Matthew has felt a need to address a question that would have occurred to any intelligent reader of his Gospel: why did Jesus need to be baptized at all, as the purpose of baptism was to remit one's sins?

As Robert L. Webb notes:

> It is quite evident that Jesus' baptism by John was a source of difficulty for some persons within the early church, not only because it suggested that Jesus was a disciple of John's and thus inferior, but also because a baptism of repentance for the forgiveness of sins placed in question the doctrine of Jesus' sinlessness.[18]

However, there is a third reason for early Christians to have felt profoundly uncomfortable about John's true role and authority, which few Bible readers even notice but which, once acknowledged, changes almost everything about our perception of Jesus the Christ.

The fact is that baptism was not a vague ritual unconnected with any sect or cult. On the contrary, baptism in the Jordan was a very specific act, for it *marked an individual's entry or initiation into John's movement.*

When Jesus was baptized by John, dress it up how one may, he was not showing the population merely how to be washed clean of one's sins. *He was becoming a disciple of John the Baptist* and therefore the example he was showing the world was that of a devotee to someone else's sect. So rather than a unique Son of God, chosen for his singular role from the start and deigning to be baptized by the Baptist as an example to lesser beings, in fact what we have is someone who simply began as a member of John's cult. Jesus was subservient to the Baptist—his spiritual superior.

Luke deals with the issue particularly evasively. Although describing Jesus' being baptized in the context of John's activity at the Jordan, seemingly he has a real problem with explicitly stating that it was the Baptist who performed the rite. He separates his introduction of John at the Jordan from Jesus' baptism with an aside about the Baptist's arrest (whereas the other synoptics tell us about this *after* he has baptized Jesus), as if subconsciously trying to write John out of the baptism scene entirely.[19]

If that were not enough, John's Gospel deals with the problem of Jesus' baptism in an even more extreme way: he is not baptized at all. Although he arrives at the Jordan while John is baptizing, and the Baptist, seeing the dove alight on him, recognizes him as the Coming One, nowhere does it actually state that Jesus was baptized, by John or anybody else.[20]

Be that as it may, in this Gospel, when Jesus appears the Baptist is much more fulsome and fawning (some might say sickeningly obsequious) in his praise than in any of the synoptics, stating immediately that this is the One he has prophesied—the Lamb of God. The vision of the descending dove is described by the Baptist himself. And in this version there is no voice from heaven, although there is one in John's head that tells him this is the man he has been prophesying.

However, after the (non)baptism, in John's Gospel events take a radically different course. Where the synoptics have Jesus being led by the "spirit" into the wilderness to be tempted by Satan, in John's Gospel there is no temptation at all. Instead Jesus immediately starts gathering a group of disciples (more accurately, disciples begin to attach themselves to him) *from among John's own following*.

Two of John's disciples, Andrew (the brother of Simon) and the other anonymous, decide to follow Jesus instead. After receiving some teaching from Jesus, Andrew finds his brother and tells him they have found the Messiah. He brings Simon to Jesus, who renames him Cephas (Peter), although no reason for the nickname is given. Jesus then starts gathering his own following and begins his ministry, which initially takes place in Judea, not Galilee.

In order to sort out which version is correct, we need to look at another point on which the synoptic Gospels and John's Gospel disagree: the apparently intimate relationship between John the Baptist's arrest and imprisonment and the beginning of Jesus' ministry.

An Ending and a Beginning

Why exactly did Antipas have John the Baptist arrested? Although John's Gospel ignores the episode completely, Mark—followed by the other synoptic Gospels—takes this line: "He did this because of Herodias, his brother Philip's wife, whom he had married. For John had been saying to Herod [Antipas], 'It is not lawful for you to have your brother's wife.'"[21]

The problems with the marriage, although not explicit in the Gospels, are that Herodias' divorce from her first husband was not legal under Jewish law (she had initiated it using Roman law), and second, she had married his brother, which broke a law of Leviticus. However, Mark makes a major mistake. We know from Josephus (who dwells on the intricate, and sometimes incestuous, relationships of the Herodians in great detail) that Herodias was not in fact the wife of Antipas' brother Philip at all; she was married to Antipas' half brother (he had the same father but a different mother), who was another Herod. Philip, the tetrarch of Trachonitis and Gaulanitis, was actually married to Herodias' daughter (by her first marriage), the notorious Salome. Mark, or his source, seems to have confused mother and daughter.

Even so, Mark's explanation for John the Baptist's execution is that he had angered Herod Antipas by denouncing his marriage to Herodias. She was to have her revenge on John, or so we are told, by engineering his execution against Antipas' own wishes.

But as we saw earlier, Josephus offers what appears to be a conflicting reason for Antipas' plan of action: he was so alarmed at John's great influence over the people that he had him arrested as a

preemptive strike before he had the chance to whip up a fully
fledged rebellion of the masses.

In fact Josephus' account matches Luke's much more neatly than
it first appears. Something else we learn from Josephus is that Antipas' marriage to Herodias was not merely a breach of Jewish law
(because of her divorce from his half brother), but also had important political implications because of whom *Antipas* had to divorce
too—a Nabataean princess named Phasaelis. The marriage had been
part of a deal to end a long-standing territorial dispute between Antipas and her father, the powerful Nabataean king Aretas IV, whose
lands bordered those of Antipas in Perea and those of Philip in
Gaulanitis. Discovering Antipas' plan to divorce her and marry
Herodias, Phasaelis fled home to her father's court at Petra, and the
perceived insult precipitated the war that ended with Aretas' resounding victory, the destruction of Antipas' army, and the capture
of substantial territory (mostly from Philip's former tetrarchy, including Damascus).

We know that Antipas' defeat was widely taken as God's retribu-
tion for ordering the Baptist's execution, and although Josephus
says nothing about John's criticism of the marriage, the fact that
there was a popular association between Antipas' having John killed
and losing a war that happened because of the union certainly implies a connection.

Not only would public condemnation of the marriage (and by
implication the divorce) be tantamount to taking the enemy's side,
but Perea bordered on Nabataea—only a dozen miles east of the
Jordan. By preaching against Antipas and in favor of Aretas, John the
Baptist threatened to swing the people to the Nabataean side—a
real, political act with very far-reaching effects for that place and
time.

In other words, the synoptic Gospels are right to link John's criticism of the marriage with his arrest, but either they deliberately
changed a vitally important part of the story without which it fails
to make complete sense or completely missed the point (possibly
because the Nabataean war was irrelevant by their day).

Here we have a chain of reasoning involving comparisons with
independent sources and external events that, unlike the nativity
stories, leads logically to conclusions that are not only internally

consistent but shed new light on the Gospels' account. Here at least the Gospels are essentially based on real events, even though they have imposed their own meaning and interpretation—not to mention spin—on them.

However, there was much more to John's arrest than even a massive political scandal. Coincidentally or not, it seems to have marked the start of Jesus' own mission. Two of the synoptics certainly imply a connection, as Mark explains: "After John was put in prison, Jesus went into Galilee, proclaiming the good news of God."[22] While Jesus gathers his disciples together and begins his ministry, the Baptist is dropped from the story; it is only later in the narrative that we are told in flashback, almost as an aside, that Antipas has had him killed.

In Matthew the connection is reinforced: "When Jesus heard that John had been put in prison, he withdrew to Galilee" (where he settles in Capernaum, unsurprisingly to fulfill a messianic prophecy).[23] Although he presents it as clear cause and effect, Matthew fails to spell out the exact nature of the connection, but is he implying that Jesus fled to Galilee because he thought Antipas might also come after him? Unlikely: Antipas ruled Galilee too.

Neither is there a link between the two events in John's Gospel— rather the reverse in fact, as it has Jesus going about his ministry while John is still active on his (causing occasional disputes between the two groups of disciples). Their careers overlap for some time, although we are carefully told that Jesus baptized more people than John, making him seem the more popular. And in the same Gospel the early part of his ministry takes place in Judea, involving visits to Jerusalem itself. Although after he has gathered his first disciples, this account has Jesus go to Galilee for the wedding at Cana, afterwards returning to Judea to continue his public work.

This is in sharp contrast to the synoptic Gospels, which expressly have him returning home to Galilee after his baptism, and never venturing near Judea until the very end. In John's Gospel it is only later that Jesus shifts the focus of his activity to Galilee, and then for a very odd reason: because he discovers that the Pharisees have found out that he is baptizing more disciples than John. Why this should precipitate what appears to be a hasty departure from the country is left unexplained, although it may imply that Jesus himself was beginning to be seen as a dangerous, crowd-pleasing political agitator.

Weirdly, nothing is said about either John's arrest or his execution in the Fourth Gospel. There is just one, rather superfluous, aside, in the passage about John baptizing at Aenon, which explains, "This was before John was put in prison."[24] Paradoxically, despite devoting more space to the Baptist than any of the other gospels, the Fourth Gospel completely drops him from the story, saying nothing about his fate. Which is right? Did Jesus begin his ministry in the wake of—or even as a consequence of—John's arrest, or did their missions actually overlap?

As we know, in matters of chronology Mark is less reliable than John's Gospel, which suggests that the latter's version is more likely to be correct. But it makes sense for other reasons too. The Gospels routinely downplay John the Baptist as much as possible, particularly marginalizing any influence he might have had on Jesus, and therefore anything that builds him up is unlikely to have been fabricated. And having John continue to preach and baptize after he has recognized Jesus as the Messiah goes completely against the Fourth Gospel's insistence that his role was solely to pave the way for Christ: once Jesus had appeared and had been baptized, surely his job was done. The synoptics have more of a motive for omitting the overlap between the two ministries than there is for the author of John's Gospel to invent it.

Leaving aside the Gospels' spin, it seems that Jesus' and John's careers overlapped for some time before the Baptist's imprisonment, the former touring Judea while the latter worked Perea on the other side of the Jordan. Frustratingly, however, one searches John's Gospel in vain for clues about the length of time they overlapped.

Does this mean that Mark and Matthew are wrong to link John's arrest directly with the start of Jesus' ministry? Not necessarily. Clearly Mark (or his sources) made some association between the two events, and it is possible to reconcile the two versions if the synoptics refer to the reason that Jesus left *Judea* for Galilee. The Fourth Gospel's bizarre explanation that it was because the Pharisees discovered he was baptizing more people than John smacks of blatant evasion, and the only alternative is the one supplied by the synoptic Gospels.

Even then, the Fourth Gospel's explanation misses out a key link:

if the Baptist had just been arrested as a potential challenge to law and order, not only would anyone connected to him also automatically be deemed a potential subversive, but an emergent leader in his movement who was threatening to become *more* popular would no doubt have chosen that moment to flee for his life. Anyone John himself had singled out for praise would have been on the authorities' "watch list."

So in this scenario, after being baptized, Jesus began his public work in Judea, but when John was arrested, he returned to Galilee. There is, however, one illogical element: Galilee was also governed by Antipas, whereas Judea was not, so it was hardly the best place to hide from him.

The scriptwriter and novelist Donovan Joyce, in his nonfiction *The Jesus Scroll* (1973), outlined what many would consider an outrageous and even blasphemous suggestion to account for the Gospels' connection between John the Baptist's arrest and Christ's return to Galilee: it was Jesus who informed on John to Antipas. Joyce's theory is that Jesus and John were rivals (in his scenario actually both claimants to the throne of Jerusalem), and he suggests that Jesus took the opportunity to remove his rival by denouncing him for spreading sedition. Joyce has him fleeing to Galilee, but not to avoid Antipas: he was escaping from John's vengeful followers.

There is, as we will see, no doubt that John's eventual execution by Antipas, after an unspecified time languishing in prison, gave another boost to Jesus' career. Certainly neither his arrest nor his death presented major problems for the fledgling Messiah: quite the reverse.

The Time and the Place

Because the start of Jesus' ministry relates to John's arrest and imprisonment, the latter event can help us to fix some of the dates. If we can establish a date for the marriage condemned by the Baptist and the start of the war with Nabataea that it provoked, this would give us an anchor point for the rest of the chronology.

The passage in which Josephus describes the origins of the war comes immediately after the death of Philip the tetrarch, which he specifically dates to 33–34 CE. He moves from Philip's death to the Nabataean war by saying that at "about this time" trouble brewed between Antipas and Aretas and explains how it was caused by Antipas' plan to divorce Phasaelis in order to marry Herodias. All this implies that the war began soon after Philip's death, and so the marriage must also have happened at that time.

The war with Aretas, and the destruction of Antipas' army—which the people linked with John the Baptist—definitely happened in 36. Clearly the marriage and divorce that started the trouble took place in 35, give or take a year. So if John was imprisoned for condemning those events, he must have done so at around the same time: certainly not before 34, and not after Aretas' victory in 36, by which time the Baptist was dead.[25]

So at last we have a clear date on which to anchor the chronology of Jesus' mission. As his career overlapped with John's, it is impossible to tell when Jesus' started, but it was certainly well established at the time of the Baptist's arrest in 34 or 35. And, as we will see, it entered a new phase after John's execution. Therefore the crucifixion must have happened around 36, since Pilate's term as governor ended before Passover in 37.

As we saw earlier, Aretas' conquest of part of the Herodian territories also enables us to work out an approximate date for another seminal event in Christian history: Paul's conversion. And now this new date for John the Baptist's arrest allows us to narrow it down yet further.

As we have seen, Paul's escape from Damascus happened during Aretas' occupation of the city—between 36 and 40—and so his conversion, three years earlier, must have happened between 33 and 37. To appear to Paul, Jesus must have been crucified, have been resurrected, and have ascended. But as the crucifixion must have taken place after 35—more likely 36—Paul's own conversion must therefore have happened within about a year or two of the crucifixion.

Therefore three pivotal events—John's arrest, Jesus' crucifixion, and Paul's conversion—must all have happened within a three-year period, 34 to 37 CE, a tiny sliver of time in a backwater of the Roman Empire that nevertheless changed the course of history.

Taking Stock

As the head of a mass movement, with his own inner circle of disciples, John the Baptist would have been a significant religious figure of the time even if Jesus had never appeared on the scene. And Jesus, who was one of John's disciples, emerged from his movement, even recruiting his first disciples from among John's followers. Although the exact connection is unclear at this stage, the idea presented in the Gospels—that the Baptist's role was solely to pave the way for Jesus—fails to work even by its own logic. Jesus' ministry overlapped with John's for a while, and not only did the Baptist's movement continue after Christ's public debut, but the Gospels make it clear that it continued even after its leader's arrest and execution.

By the time the Gospels were written, this rival movement was proclaiming that John was the Messiah (or one of the other traditional end-times figures). The fact that the Gospels felt it essential to include denials of John's messiahship—perhaps even protesting too much—reveals an attempt to preempt the readers who may well have heard rumors that the Baptist himself was the Chosen One. This echoes the references in Acts to "apostles" of John preaching his baptism in competition with Paul and the other missionaries of Jesus. As Hugh J. Schonfield comments, "We are made aware from Christian sources that there was a considerable Jewish sect in rivalry with the followers of Jesus, who held that John the Baptist was the true Messiah."[26] For example, the fourth-century Syrian Christian writer Ephraem refers to the heresy of "disciples of John . . . who claim he is greater than Christ."[27] We should also recall that gospels and hymns were composed by John's followers, fragments of which have survived in the New Testament, mainly in Luke's account of the nativity.

However, what is most significant here is that John's great message could never have been that he was only the Messiah's forerunner. Had he really toured the countryside making such a claim, no one would ever have thought that *he* might be the Messiah. Presumably, then, he never said he was merely the forerunner, unworthy and craven. So why do the Gospels present him as so utterly obsequious to Christ that he almost licks his feet? Clearly to create the belief that while the two preachers might have a great deal in common, it was Jesus, not John, who was the real Messiah, *the* one chosen by God to save the Jews.

If John's whole mission had really just been about warming Israel up for Jesus, then there would never have been a John movement that survived him. Had the Baptist really made his groveling declaration about Jesus, his entire following would have switched their allegiance en masse to Christ, with John's blessing—or even on his orders. As it was, in British-born Israeli archaeologist Shimon Gibson's words, "The career of Jesus only blooms . . . after the death of John the Baptist. But John the Baptist is clearly in command up to that point."[28]

All this leads to only one conclusion: John the Baptist never endorsed Jesus as the Messiah, which immediately prompts two major questions. What, then, *was* the Baptist's connection to Jesus? And what was it about John's message that made those who heard it, as Josephus claimed, "excited to the utmost"?

In the Shadow of the Baptist

The one certainty is that Jesus was baptized by John the Baptist, and only after that did he begin to attract public attention. Clearly this was well known to the gospel writers and, more important, to their audience. In some way Jesus' career was kick-started by his baptism. Because the writers had to account for the relationship, they concocted the "forerunner" idea.

In his 1928 book *Au seuil de l'Évangile Jean-Baptiste* (*On the Threshold of the John the Baptist Gospel*) Maurice Goguel, director of studies at the École des Hautes Études in Paris, first proposed the theory that Jesus began as a disciple of John's and a proclaimer of his message. But then Jesus came to believe he had received a divine messianic calling, causing him to break with the Baptist and his movement. He places this event at the time of Jesus' return to Galilee. Goguel describes Jesus as a "renegade from the Baptist sect."[29]

Since then, many other scholars have accepted at least the first part of Goguel's theory, that Jesus started out as a disciple of the Baptist. Evidence has continued to accumulate, even being found in the Gospels themselves. Several scholars, including C. H. Dodd and Kendrick Grobel, have proposed that John's words about "he who comes after" (*ho opiso mou erchomenos*) mean "follower" or "disciple."[30] (The double meaning of "follow" existed in Greek as it does in English.) Walter Wink of New York's Union Theological Seminary notes (his emphasis):

> The scribe Matthew . . . has a very clear conception of discipleship patterned after the rabbinic example: the disciple follows his master. It is all the more remarkable then that Matthew portrays Jesus as the *disciple of John*. There is no other way to interpret his retention of *opisomou* [translated as "comes after"] in 3:11.[31]

But is this the full extent of their relationship? Did the Gospels invent the idea of the Baptist singling Jesus out for praise as a way of demonstrating to John's followers that they should really be following Jesus?

It seems unlikely. The most logical conclusion is that John did give some kind of endorsement or backing to Jesus. Indeed Jesus must have held a prominent position within the Baptist's circle of disciples—perhaps being selected to spread the movement to Judea and Galilee, effectively as one of John's apostles. He may have been a trusted lieutenant (similar to Peter's later role in Jesus' own movement). It has also been suggested that John appointed him as his second in command, to whom his authority would automatically pass if anything happened to him.

So we have Jesus beginning not merely as a disciple of John's, but holding an important position within his movement (even if we still have to define exactly what that position was). On the other hand, Jesus clearly needed the Baptist too. As Shimon Gibson writes:

> John was regarded as one of the leading prophetic figures of his generation and Jesus needed his stamp of approval so that later on he could press on with his own mission. Apart from the clear respect that Jesus extends to John, there are also other strands of information in the Gospels suggesting tension between the two men,

and there was undoubtedly vocal conflict between the followers of the two individuals as well.[32]

As history proves, Jesus subsequently achieved fame as the head of his own movement, but how did he make the transition from one to the other? Was his ministry essentially a continuation of John's? Or was it a breakaway movement?

John's Message

Although Luke singles out John the Baptist as the heir to the hereditary priesthood, the fact remains that even if this is true, by the very nature of his unique lifestyle and innovative work he must have repudiated such a legacy, so it hardly matters one way or the other.

Some have attempted to identify John the Baptist as a member of the Essene community, although none of the canonical Gospels links him to any sect or school, nor does Josephus, who is usually scrupulous about acknowledging an individual's particular brand of Judaism. Had John belonged to any established school, Josephus would have said so.

Certainly the Gospels explicitly categorize John as a prophet, and so does Josephus implicitly—a religious leader who speaks with the immediate authority of God. There was apparently no prerequisite to be schooled in any specific stream of Judaism—or even to be educated at all. In some ways labeling someone a prophet is like filing them under "miscellaneous": they fit no other category and have no known adherence to a particular sect or school. But at least this tells us that almost by definition the Gospels and Josephus were not aware of a connection between John the Baptist and any specific sect, or if he was he chose to keep his affiliation secret for some reason.

But what was John's message? The Gospels and Josephus agree that a central element was the insistence on repentance, which was intimately bound up with the drama of complete immersion in the Jordan.

Another key feature was John's preparing the way for "one who is to come" who would bring God's judgment on those who fail to repent: a messianic element. In Josephus that element is absent, at least explicitly, so was it purely a Christian invention in order to have John identify Jesus as "the One," an element with absolutely no real connection to the Baptist's essential message? Perhaps strangely, given what we argued earlier about John's never proclaiming Jesus as the Messiah, the answer is probably not.

The words attributed to John about the expected figure apply only very loosely to Jesus and even omit altogether what to Christians is the most important point. If Jesus' followers had simply fabricated the passage, surely they would have ensured the words were tailor-made for him and could never have been applied to anyone else.

However, there is a vital point which is often missed. Although it is fundamental to the Gospels that John the Baptist preached the imminent coming of a special figure who would bring down God's judgment on the people, before Jesus is singled out as the fulfillment of that prophecy, *nowhere does the word "Messiah" actually appear.* Instead the Gospels rather suspiciously—or at least very carefully— employ nonspecific terms such as "the one who is to come." And when John recognizes Jesus, essentially all he says is "That's him, the one I've been talking about." The only time the Baptist is ever said to utter the word "Messiah" is when he denies that he himself fits the role: he *never* claims that Jesus does.

This is very odd. The whole point of the Gospels is to proclaim—and prove—that Jesus was the Messiah, so why should they so pointedly avoid the term when they are quoting the Baptist? This is especially peculiar when they obviously intend their readers to take John's proclamation as the first sign that Jesus *is* the Messiah. The avoidance of the word is so conspicuous that it screams out for further delving. The only possible explanation is that the Baptist's words were too well known to change—and they never included "Messiah."

John *did* prophesy the coming of some iconic figure, but whoever it was, it was *not* the Messiah. As we saw in chapter 2, in the end-times excitement of that era, expectations of some divinely sent figure who would dispense God's judgment were not confined to the Messiah prophesied in the scriptures.

Robert Webb argues persuasively that John was preaching the

imminent arrival of a generic "agent of God" but was deliberately vague about his identity in order to build up a belief in his divine status.[33] He was also careful not to identify him with any particular strand of Jewish expectation, sidestepping the potential problem of alienating other schools. There was one great advantage to this approach: it made his message inclusive, rather than divisive. But did John proclaim Jesus as that mysterious but expected "agent of God"? Without knowing exactly what Jordan's famous wild man was expecting of his "God's Chosen One" (the term used in the Fourth Gospel), this is difficult to answer.

It could be that John was expecting the Chosen One to emerge from within the ranks of his own movement: perhaps he was even grooming someone for the role. If so, he could have marked Jesus out as that person, whom he expected to *become* the One, or thought *might* be the One. Naming him as his chief disciple or second in command would have been a step on the way. Another possibility is that Jesus was given a special role in John's movement as a chief disciple but after the Baptist's arrest or death took it upon himself to be the Chosen One whose coming his spiritual teacher had preached.

However, there is one major point that changes a great deal, certainly in the usual Christian story. Jumping ahead of our story for a moment, the fact remains that *John himself came to have his doubts about singling Jesus out for a special role*, whatever that might have been or have been intended to be. As we will see, when he was in prison John managed to get a message out to Jesus asking, "Are you the one who was to come, or should we expect someone else?" (Part of the Q tradition, this passage is found in Matthew and Luke but not Mark. Again the word "Messiah" is conspicuous by its absence.) It goes without saying that such an unsettling passage is rarely, if ever, read out in church services.[34]

The Man Who Empowered Women

John's call to repentance was closely bound up with baptism, a ritual so fundamental to what he was about that it was literally used to identify him. And it works both ways: not only was he identified as "John *the* Baptist," but his ritual was known as "the baptism of

John," a specific one-to-one, unique relationship between the man and the ritual, which had a specific, profoundly spiritual purpose.

Although the Gospels describe John's rite as "a baptism of repentance for the forgiveness of sins," was this discription nothing more than the truth or perhaps just another example of embroidering the facts for their own agenda? As Webb points out, it is likely to be accurate, because Christians claimed forgiveness of sins as an exclusive prerogative of Jesus and therefore would hardly have invented John's authority to confer it.[35] (For someone other than Jesus to claim the ability to forgive sins should actually have been regarded as heretical.)

We can only guess at the details of John's original baptisms. Certainly the crowds who thronged to the banks of the Jordan would have been whipped into a state of religious frenzy—or perhaps rapture—by the Baptist's fiery rhetoric and towering command. And of course the individual rose newly shriven from the water as an initiate of John's movement.

As we have seen, both the Gospels and Josephus imply that John's baptism had a political, even subversive, connotation—which was clearly regarded as dangerous enough for him to be arrested and executed. As Josephus says, John urged the people to "gather together [or 'unite'] by baptism," although for what purpose remains tantalizingly obscure. But whatever his overall aim, even the composition of his baptizees reveals a remarkable eclecticism—an inclusivity that would automatically put him at the top of several hit lists.

As the Baptist's rite was quintessentially gnostic (in its widest sense)—enabling the individual to forge his or her own relationship with God, without benefit of the priesthood or the heavily formulaic Judaism of the Jerusalem Temple—its secret almost certainly lay in the fact that it bestowed *power* on the ordinary people who flocked to join his movement. That in itself would have worried Herod Antipas and the occupying Romans, not to mention the Sanhedrin, but John's baptism was also available to *women*. Although we have discussed the whole subject of the female role in the early Christian movements elsewhere,[36] we will say here simply that even the implications of *John's* baptizing women are so astounding that even the Church has failed to notice them. To Christians there is only one baptism—entrance into Jesus' Holy Church—but the original rite was clearly quite different, and even in the hands of John the Baptist, or perhaps especially in his hands, it *had no specific reference to Jesus at all.*

This extraordinary man from the desert was standing in the fast-flowing Jordan and empowering both men and women equally with their own intimate connection to God. What he was doing was astonishing, previously unheard and unthought of. He was certainly a revolutionary with a completely innovative approach to saving souls and healing hearts, so where on earth did he learn his rite? Where did baptism come from?

The rite and its meaning were completely unknown in Judaism before John, and have remained so, since Christianity adopted it. Although ritual washings and even full immersions of one sort or another were accepted as an intrinsic part of various streams of the Jewish religion, nothing with anything like this underlying meaning had been known before. All the other washing or immersion rituals were either part of the preparation for praying or eating (for example, those of the Qumran sect as prescribed in the Dead Sea Scrolls, which are often cited as a parallel with John's baptism) or were performed to purify oneself after committing one of the many actions that were deemed contaminatory. They were performed regularly—in the case of the Qumran sect, several times a day—and were not a major life-changing initiation by an exceptional prophet or holy man. And there is no parallel or precedent in Jewish practices for a ritual immersion being *administered.* Apart from very few that involve sprinkling water on the unclean, the rites are all self-administered.

Although baptism has always been regarded as John's own innovation—which is implied by his title of *the* Baptist—even he must have been inspired by something that had gone before. John could have been inspired by one of the washing rituals but then developed it in a completely novel way. But, as we pointed out in *The Templar Revelation*, there are exact—and contemporary—parallels to John's baptism: rituals of the pagan mystery cults. These, too, were immersions that marked initiation or entry, being frequently preceded by a public—and often dramatic—admission of sins. The parallel has been noted but dismissed by a few scholars on the grounds that as they are not Jewish practices, there is no possibility that John could have been inspired by them. The perfect example of such blinkered reasoning comes from Duke University professor W. H. Brownlee:

> One issue strongly debated among scholars is where John got his ideas for baptism. Does it represent a pagan influence, borrowed from some Oriental mystery cult? Was it original with John? Or was it an adaptation of some previous Jewish rite? It will be safer to assume the last position, for originality usually starts with ideas which are not entirely new, and John was not one to borrow directly from the Gentile world.[37]

This is glaringly circular reasoning. It is now acknowledged that the world in which Jesus and John the Baptist lived was much more cosmopolitan than one would imagine from the tight, almost claustrophobic little territory portrayed by the Gospels. In fact, there was a surprising amount of social and religious exchange, with philosophical and spiritual ideas being traded between beliefs. Given the extremely close parallels between John's baptism and the practice of the mysteries, it is not beyond the bounds of possibility that he borrowed certain ideas from them, without necessarily compromising his Jewish roots. Why are scholars so resistant to the obvious?

However, it appears that there were several categories of "Jewish roots"—some considerably more unorthodox than others. As we will see shortly, the latest discoveries suggest that John's own background dramatically diverged from the mainstream religion of his time and place. He was not only an innovator but effectively a missionary for a profoundly heretical sect—and if that was true of him, then at least at the beginning, it was also true of Jesus.

"The Others"

Another aspect of John the Baptist's ministry might yield some clues about Jesus' own mission: his target audience. Who was his message aimed at? The most obvious answer is the Jews of Israel as a whole. Everything that he is reported as preaching in the Gospels and by Josephus can be understood in terms of the Judaism of his day, even though some of it seems to have a deliberately vague gloss. But a few clues hint that John's message was intended to be much more inclusive.

Josephus describes how the Baptist "commanded the Jews" to mend their ways and gather together for baptism, but Antipas became alarmed when "others" joined in, and, as Robert Webb points out:

> there is nothing in the context to suggest that they could not be Gentiles. The location of John's ministry suggests that he could have contact with Gentiles who travelled the trade routes coming from the East, as well as with Gentiles living in the region of the Trans-Jordan.[38]

Could the "others" have been "god-fearers"—Greeks and Romans who were attracted to Judaism but stopped short of actually converting? (Their number even included Nero's wife.) They could have been Gentiles pure and simple, but then why would they of all people become so intoxicated by John's haranguing them about Jews returning to their true religion—or else? That really depends on what the Baptist considered that "true religion" to be. And in any case both Matthew and Luke describe him berating either all the people of Israel or just the Pharisees and Sadducees, for not keeping to their religion, telling them (in a passage taken from Q):

> And do not think to yourselves, "We have Abraham as our father." I tell you that out of these stones God can raise up children from Abraham. The axe is already at the root of the trees, and every tree that does not produce good fruit will be cut down and thrown into the fire.[39]

In other words, he is warning the people of Israel against complacency over the covenant God made with Abraham that made his descendants the chosen people. What Yahweh had done once he could do again: *he can choose another nation.* If he was open to showing favor to non-Jews, then John's rite was open to Gentiles too—which could fit Josephus' "others."

Although the Baptist's core message was of imminent judgment by Yahweh, definitively couched in terms of the Jewish scriptures, many Old Testament references to judgment—in Isaiah and Ezekiel, for example—show that it would apply equally to the Gentiles, so there was room within the Jewish tradition to allow for John to extend his baptism to them, and for them to be interested in what he had to say. And if God's judgment was intended for all people everywhere, perhaps the Gentiles might actually be judged more favorably. As James Tabor comments, "According to the Prophets, God's judgement was to fall not only upon Israel but also upon all humankind. Accordingly Jews as well as non-Jews were called upon to repent of their sins and turn to God in order to be saved from the 'wrath to come.'"[40]

Unfortunately, as the information about John is very limited, the most that can be said is that his system *could* have kept a place warm for non-Jews, at least in theory, but whether or not it actually did in practice is another matter. Even so, the possible Gentile connection may help us to understand Jesus' own career as it gradually unfolds before us.

There is another important clue in the second location, Aenon ("springs"), where the Fourth Gospel tells us that John the Baptist performed his rite, near a town called Salim, where "there was plenty of water."[41] Since the fourth century this town has been identified with a village in the Decapolis, on the western side of the Jordan. However, in 1960 Archibald M. Hunter, master of Christ's College, Aberdeen, pointed out the problems with this identification and proposed a much more plausible location for the New Testament Aenon.

First, the description of Aenon as being "near Salim" would normally mean that Salim was the better-known place, and there is no such place near the Decapolitan Aenon. Secondly, pointing out that "there was plenty of water" there is superfluous when it is beside the biggest river in the country. But there is another Aenon, just seven miles from a Salim, which was renowned for its many springs in an otherwise dry area. This is squarely in the middle of Samaria—close, in fact, to the capital, Sebaste. Hunter argues that *this* Aenon (modern Ainûn) is the one where John baptized, and his case is overwhelming.[42] Indeed, according to tradition, John the Baptist was buried in Sebaste, his tomb there being revered by pilgrims until it was destroyed on the orders of the Emperor Julian the Apostate in the fourth century.

This is all very strange for someone supposed to be purely a Jewish holy man, but perhaps more understandable if he was intent on expanding his mission beyond the Jews. As we will see, Samaria and the Samaritans have a great many surprises in store, and may even provide the key to several of the great New Testament mysteries.

But even though the Baptist comes across as strident, charismatic, and commanding, he still appears to have deliberately couched his message in rather vague terms. Who exactly was he expecting "to come"? And just what was the ultimate aim of his movement?

Although we have teased some fascinating insights out of the—admittedly biased—material in the Gospels and Josephus' frustratingly brief account, we have to acknowledge that there is more about John the Baptist that we *don't* know than we do. The wild man in camel-hair clothes commanding the people to repent and be baptized, the charismatic preacher who may or may not have been related to Jesus, and above all, it seems, Jesus' spiritual teacher and superior, remains an elusive and somewhat obscure figure. However, in recent years intriguing new archaeological evidence has emerged that—against all the odds—has perhaps finally begun to shed light on some of the cloudy areas of John's mission.

The Case for the Cave

In 1999 a team led by Shimon Gibson discovered a man-made cave cut into the side of a valley some five miles from the western suburbs of Jerusalem, and about three-quarters of a mile from what was in ancient times the flourishing town of Suba. They excavated the cave, with growing excitement, over the subsequent three years: pottery and other debris they uncovered showed that it had been used extensively in the first and second centuries.

An opening just large enough to admit one adult led into a chamber, ninety feet long by thirteen wide and sixteen high (24 by 3.5 by 5 meters), with plastered walls and a shaft in the roof. Twelve steps cut into the rock led down to the floor of the cave, at the end of which a deep pool was sunk. There was a sophisticated system of channels and conduits—"an amazing feat of engineering"[43]—to feed the pool with rainwater collected outside to keep it permanently filled. There were also two small pools immediately outside the entrance.

It was immediately obvious that the cave was artificial, and Gibson also quickly realized that it must have been used for some ritual purpose, as its location and design made no sense as a purely functional cave for habitation, storage, or use as a reservoir. And whatever the ritual was, a central element involved a deep pool of water—clearly immersion.

The pool that is the cave's central feature is similar to the ritual bathing pools, *miqweh*, which Jews used to purify themselves after doing or touching something that rendered them unclean. But these came into use in the first century BCE—and, as we are about to see, the one in the Suba cave is *much* older. Besides, the whole point of *miqweh* is that they had to be conveniently to hand: one in a cave in a secluded spot, dug into a hillside far from the nearest dwellings, makes no sense.

A number of Christian symbols had been incised on the plastered walls, most of which relate to John the Baptist: indeed, the largest figure (two feet four inches, or 0.7 meters long) is a stylistic representation of him with his characteristic long staff topped with a cross, and there is also an image of his severed head. A hollow beneath the large figure was probably used to house a small relic associated with him—Gibson suggests a finger bone. And although the carvings definitely date as late as the fourth or fifth century, the Byzantine period, excitingly this is the earliest known cult center dedicated to the Baptist.

The case for the cave becomes increasingly intriguing: with almost uncanny neatness it is located about two miles from Ain Karim, traditionally identified as John the Baptist's birthplace. Besides, it is hard to see why the Byzantine Christians associated the cave with John the Baptist for any other reason: all early Christian writings have him working in the open air in a region some distance from Jerusalem. There are no obvious reasons for anyone to have linked him with this cave, unless it was based on some real memory. (The location could qualify for the vague definition of "wilderness," but it is a long way from the Jordan and the baptismal pool is in an enclosed space.)

The evidence prompted Gibson to conclude that the cave really had been used by John the Baptist. As we have seen, John's baptism had no precedent or parallel in Judaic practices. Neither did whatever immersion ritual took place in the Suba cave. As Gibson writes:

> Clear and unequivocal archaeological evidence was uncovered indicating that complex baptism rituals were being undertaken in the cave of Suba during the first century AD, at the time of John the Baptist and later. These rituals were quite distinct from those practised by the Jews of that time.[44]

A large stone set into the floor of the cave bears a hollowed-out depression in the shape of a right foot—presumably in which would-be initiates placed their right feet—beside a cup-shaped depression, where presumably some kind of jar of anointing oil was kept handy.

Gibson points to what appears to be an obsession with feet and footwear in the Gospels—for example, the Baptist's words about undoing sandals, Jesus washing his disciples' feet, and his own feet being anointed and wiped by a woman—and speculates that these may be garbled references to some foot-anointing ritual similar to the one apparently performed in the Suba cave.[45]

All this seems very clear and consistent, but there was a sting in the tail of Gibson's work on the Suba cave which threw the whole affair into confusion.

Early in their project the team established that the composition of the plaster covering the walls was characteristic of a period from the eighth to the sixth century BCE. To begin with, this did not seem too much of a problem, as all the earliest—and the vast majority—of the astonishing cache of over 100,000 pottery fragments came from around the first century CE, and it seemed reasonable to see this date linking with their working theory that the cave had not only been used, but basically founded, by John the Baptist. (On the logic that if he had invented baptism, and instituted the ritual at Suba, the cave must have been specially constructed for him.)

However, toward the end of their excavation pottery from the same eighth- to sixth-century BCE period *was* found, as well as some examples from between the late second and late first centuries BCE. And two dating techniques confirmed the antiquity of the plaster. In other words, as Gibson acknowledges, "The new evidence showed that the cave at Suba was already more than seven hundred years old at the time of the birth of John the Baptist." [46] And it had been used more or less constantly during all that time—although as the vast majority of material in it comes from between the first century BCE and the beginning of the second century CE, apparently that was when it was most used.

From its design and construction clearly, as Gibson notes:

There can be no doubt that this artificial cave was pre-planned and not created in stages: in other words, the shape of the cave today is the same as those hewing it originally conceived it. . . . There is absolutely no evidence that the cave was ever enlarged or expanded. [47]

In other words, it could not have been created in one era for a particular purpose and then converted to a quite different use at a later time.

Clearly at a loss, Gibson is compelled to argue that "it was a place, I believe, that must have possessed a hoary Israelite tradition of ritualistic bathing going back to the mists of time" and that "John the Baptist and his followers would have chosen the cave precisely because of the ancient traditions of ritual bathing associated with it." [48]

But we believe that the implications go way beyond that. First, as we know, no such "Israelite tradition of ritualistic bathing" is known from the historical record. So if it was a "tradition," it was one that existed outside the mainstream religion and must have been practiced by a specific sect. The secluded location of the cave—in the side of a valley some distance away from the nearest habitation—even suggests a degree of secrecy, or at least privacy. Since the cave exists and was clearly created for ritual bathing, the sect that created it must have been around for many centuries before John the Baptist.

More significantly, if John used the cave, he must have been a member of the same sect—so despite the implications of the New

Testament, he was *not* an innovator but an adherent of a long-established group, which nevertheless remained outside mainstream Judaism, and which had—at the very least—chosen to keep a low profile.

But according to the Gospels and Josephus, John himself can hardly be said to have kept a low profile, and he was certainly regarded by most people as an innovator. The obvious deduction is that whatever John the Baptist was part of, it had been decided that the time was right for it to go public. Whether this was a policy decision made by the sect, or John's decision alone, is impossible to tell. But it does explain why neither the Gospels nor Josephus was able to place the Baptist in any specific Jewish tradition.

The Suba cave provides evidence of a hitherto unknown, and by definition secretive, group that had existed in Judea for several centuries before John and Jesus' day and whose rituals centered on baptism (or at least some kind of immersion). It would be an enormous coincidence if such a baptismal sect had no connection with the mysterious baptizer named John. And the presence of a shadowy sect behind him would indeed explain a great many of the mysteries that surround him. But who were these people? What did they believe and when was their sect founded? What happened to them?

Although the answers to those questions remain tantalizing, we can bear them in mind as we continue our investigation. First, however, we turn our attention to the more pressing question— what was Jesus like?

5

THE MAN BEHIND
THE MISSION

The powerful imagery of the parables and the strange immediacy of the miracles have a profound hold over the imagination, lingering long even in the minds of those who have abandoned their faith. But what do we know about Jesus' early days after he emerges from John the Baptist's disciples and sets up on his own?

Matthew, Mark, Luke, and John are still our main sources, as only they are concerned with the details of Jesus' early mission, and all tell basically the same story: in Galilee Jesus gathers a band of disciples, who then tour the country together (with excursions into neighboring lands) spreading his message. He performs healings and exorcisms, and when the wonder-hungry crowds flock to see him, he seizes the opportunity to preach to them. Finally he takes his mission into Judea, to the holy city of Jerusalem, with fatal consequences.

Although to the average believer the Galilee and Jerusalem phases may seem a homogeneous blur of miracles and heady spirituality, in fact they are entirely different in character, and so are even Jesus' actions and apparent objectives in the two locations. In Galilee he is basically an itinerant healer who also preaches the coming end-times; when the scene shifts to Jerusalem, he comes across as a more proactive figure with a specific political and even seditious intent. The issues that concern him most are different in the two phases, and apparently even the reasons the people listen to him differ.

The entire ministry, from baptism to crucifixion, seems to have been compressed into a remarkably short period. In the synoptic Gospels, the general impression is that it took place within about a year—which seems unlikely, as surely that was nowhere near enough time for Jesus to build up his reputation (either among his fans or his detractors). John's Gospel specifies that it lasted three years, as it mentions three Passover festivals, which seems more reasonable, although of course his chronology might have been contrived to fit the cycle of religious festivals in the first place.

We have argued in our reconstruction that Jesus was active in John the Baptist's movement before emerging as a leader in his own right, so some of the Gospel stories might refer to his activities during that time. But how long was Jesus preaching his *own* message— as opposed to John's?

Dating the beginning and end of his ministry with any precision is notoriously difficult, but it must have started after John the Baptist first became a star preacher in the late twenties CE, and, if the crucifixion took place at the time of Passover during Pilate's procuratorship, then the latest it could have happened was 36. So the maximum duration of Jesus' ministry is from about 30 to 36, although we favor a start date of ca. 33 or 34, following the Baptist's arrest.

The Man Behind the Halo

To the average Westerner of the twenty-first century, a celebrity's looks, personality, and lifestyle are supremely important. The more famous the person, the more his taste in clothes, changing hairstyles, and circle of friends are hot topics for discussion. Therefore it is astonishing—as well as hugely frustrating—that the gospel writers display not the remotest interest in Jesus the man.

The Gospels are totally silent about Jesus' physical appearance, but obviously they chose to rise above such worldly considerations, since there are no descriptions of anyone else, either. We can make a few deductions, however, based on the reasonable assumption that had there been anything about him that was so unusual as to make him distinctive, it would have been remembered and recorded.

One thing is certain: Jesus would have had the typically Semitic dark olive skin. It is highly improbable that he was the strapping blond-haired and blue-eyed all-American boy so beloved of today's fundamentalists and members of the Mormon Church, in whose vestibules a favorite painting showing a positively peroxided Christ is proudly displayed.

At the other extreme, early Christian traditions from Syria describe Jesus as a small man, even for his time and place. In the Acts of Thomas (about the alleged deeds of Jesus' alleged twin brother), Thomas describes himself rather pathetically as "me, who am small." For a writer who believed that Thomas and Christ were identical twins to put these words into the former's mouth, he must have thought that Jesus was small, too. None of the Syrian sources is earlier than the fourth century, but they could represent a real memory of his stature.[1]

Even Jesus' age is uncertain. By contrast with the Fourth Gospel's anomalous "not yet fifty," the synoptics suggest he was in his early to mid-thirties when John baptized him. He was unlikely to have been much younger, as in that culture respect very much depended on age: he simply would never have been taken seriously had he been any younger. (Or if he was such a prodigy that he *was* taken seriously at an early age, the Gospels would have said so.) The thirties were also an age by which a man would be expected to be free of his immediate family responsibilities—his children, particularly sons, having reached adulthood (marriage usually took place in mid- to late teens). Thirty in those harsh days would have been mature middle age—probably the equivalent of being in one's fifties or even sixties in today's West.

As with his physical appearance, the early sources are disappointingly unenlightening about Jesus' personality. The presentation of Jesus' character differs wildly between the synoptic Gospels and John's Gospel. He is more recognizably human in the former, while the latter portrays him, in Schonfield's words, as a "pathological egoist"[2] and a coldly aloof superman, always in control.

It is often noted that while Mark's Gospel frequently attributes human emotions to Jesus, these passages were downplayed—if not completely erased—when used by Matthew and Luke. Although the first generation of Christians—those who produced Mark—considered Jesus to be basically human, evidently the next wave found this idea too uncomfortable, rewriting his character to marginalize or even deny his human-ness. The Christian image of Christ was being carefully stage-managed from the very earliest days. As Bruce Metzger of the Princeton Theological Seminary sums up Mark's depiction of his character:

> No gospel brings into clearer light the full humanity of Jesus. . . .
> Jesus asks questions, apparently for the purpose of gaining information, and displays such human emotions as grief, anger, and amazement. He sleeps from fatigue and declares that he, though the Son, is ignorant of the Father's appointed time.[3]

This Jesus is not perfect or all-knowing and even has the power to shock today's politically correct. In fact at one point, as we will see shortly, in a brutally bigoted manner he insults a woman who pleads for him to ease her little girl's suffering—simply because of her ethnic background.

A good example of the way Mark depicts Jesus—and how the later Gospels changed it—is the description of his first public healing, that of a leper. Three words are used in this short episode that "suggest agitation or strong emotion on Jesus' part."[4] When the "leper"—the Greek word covered a variety of skin diseases, not just leprosy—approaches Jesus, Christ is "moved with anger" (the TNIV has "indignant"). Exactly why is far from clear. Was it because the leper had broken Mosaic Law, which forbade the unclean from approaching the whole and healthy? But Jesus is frequently portrayed as mixing with social outcasts, and in any case he then touches the sufferer. Was he angry because the man seemed to doubt he could heal him? Or was his ire directed at the evil spirits that caused the man's anguish? We are left guessing, but for our present purposes it hardly matters: Jesus must have genuinely been angry and indignant, precisely because the reason for it is so vague. (As Mark seems to have been unsure about the cause himself, he was obviously just passing on the story he took from his source.)

As part of their image damage limitation, some early manuscripts of Mark have totally transformed "moved with anger" into the much more acceptable "filled with compassion." But while it is easy to see why early Christians changed anger to compassion, it would be very odd to do it the other way round. Nevertheless, many modern translations use the "compassion" version, which is no doubt more comforting for their readers.

Although Matthew and Luke took the story of the healing of the leper from Mark, they both omitted the sentence about Jesus becoming angry, and "thus avoid all reference to emotion on Jesus' part."[5] On the other hand, John's Gospel also attributes normal human emotions to Jesus, although not as much as Mark. For example, during the raising of Lazarus he becomes angry—again for obscure reasons. Once more, some English versions translate this as "deeply moved in spirit and troubled" (TNIV) or "greatly disturbed" (New Revised Standard Version), although the word *embrimaomai* is used everywhere else to mean angry or indignant.[6]

None of this helps much in establishing what Jesus the man was really like, but it does tell us he had recognizably human characteristics. Apart from getting angry, he must also have possessed a special charisma, otherwise no one would have followed him and no one would have remembered him for two thousand years.

Some aspects of his character do still shine through even in the Gospels' heavily edited stories. For example, beginning a sentence with the word "truly"—"amen," the Hebrew for "true"—rather than at the end is very unusual, and the fact that this characteristic of speech is ascribed to Jesus (and nobody else) in all the Gospels makes it virtually certain that it really was a memorable idiosyncrasy.

It also appears that Jesus had a reputation, as one eminent scholar discreetly put it, as "a person likely to contribute to the success of a convivial occasion."[7] Several of the Gospel stories are set while he is at dinner with numerous other guests, and Jesus himself is said to have acknowledged—while denying it—that he was often accused of being "a glutton and a drunkard."[8] It seems highly unlikely that the gospel writers would invent such a slur, and that suggests it was common knowledge at the time they were writing that Jesus had a reputation for unrepentant partying.

Galilean Troublemakers

The fact that Christ's mission began in Galilee is so entrenched in Christian thinking that few think to ask why. Yet clearly the location was a deliberate choice, presumably for good reasons.

The canonical Gospels associate the beginning of Jesus' mission with Capernaum, a fishing town on the southern shore of the Sea of Galilee, where he began preaching and gathered his first disciples, although it is unclear whether this was where he lived or simply where he made his first impact. But there is no reason to doubt the connection with Capernaum: it was hardly a significant place and was not associated with any messianic prophecies.

Most of the Gospel stories take place in Galilee, too, although Jesus made occasional forays into the neighboring countryside. Frustratingly, but as usual in this story, Jesus' choosing to begin his mission in Galilee could be explained by one of two diametrically opposed motives. As we have seen, that country was not an entirely Jewish land and enjoyed a mix of cultures and religions. Judea would have made more sense as a place in which to begin a mission to the Jews, but "instead, he travels around semi-pagan Galilee, and preaches there."[9]

But Galilee was also known as a center of Jewish nationalist resistance to Roman rule.[10] This is not quite the paradox it might seem. Galilee was distant enough from Jerusalem to allow nationalists to hide away, and there were plenty of remote locations to choose from, while being close enough to maintain contact with Judea. It was also beyond the Romans' direct control. Of course the nationalists, such as the Zealots, were also opposed to the Herodians who ruled Galilee on behalf of the occupying forces, but it was easier to seek refuge in such a rural and hilly land.

Even Galileans born and bred were hardly famed for their softheartedness. Josephus (who held an administrative post in Galilee before switching to the Roman side during the Jewish Revolt) returns time and again to the aggressive nature of the Jews of Galilee, writing that "the Galileans are fighters from the cradle and at all time numerous, and never has cowardice afflicted the men or a declining population the country."[11]

It could be that Jesus began his work there because it was not predominantly Jewish: what he was preaching could be extended to its other cultures—the view taken by, for example, Burton Mack. To Mack, the majority of Galileans were apathetic about matters of Jewish nationalism or criticisms of the Temple authorities, so if a significant number were caught up by Jesus' teaching, it had to be for other reasons.[12] Conversely Galilee might have been chosen because it was a hotbed of opposition, albeit underground, to either the Romans and the Jewish Temple authorities or both. This is the view of, for example, Robert Eisenman, professor of Middle Eastern religions and director of the Institute for the Study of Judeo-Christian Origins at California State University.[13] Which is correct? In order to reach a conclusion we will need to know exactly what Jesus taught and at whom his message was aimed, which we will come to later.

However, there is no denying that the canonical Gospels set the Galilee mission in a firmly Jewish context. Mark, followed by the other synoptics, has Jesus first beginning to preach in the synagogues of Galilee, which makes sense: someone with a message to spread among the Jewish community would start there. In the days of the Temple, synagogues were effectively community centers run by the town or village elders, not priests, where any man could, with permission, speak and sermonize.

One puzzling aspect of the Gospels' story is the lack of references to the major cities of Galilee—another reason for the Christian image of Galilee as an almost exclusively rural environment. Excavations have showed that Sepphoris, for example—just a few miles from Nazareth and known as "the ornament of all Galilee"—was a predominantly Jewish town (unusual for that region), although its inhabitants had adopted largely Greek lifestyles. This makes its complete absence from the Gospel accounts, indeed from all early Christian texts relating to Jesus, even more intriguing. Most commentators account for this absence by assuming that he kept away from the cities because they were inhabited by Gentiles, preferring the country villages populated by Jews, but with Sepphoris he avoided a major center of Jewish population.

It could be that Jesus deliberately avoided the cities because of his association with the "seditious" John the Baptist, which would earn him a place on the authorities' watch list.

Other Destinations

But where did Jesus go outside Galilee? As we have already noted, the synoptic Gospels have him returning to Judea only once, at the end of his mission. John's Gospel states explicitly that from the beginning the Jewish leaders in Judea wanted Jesus dead, but it does have him making a couple of secret visits to Jerusalem. Once there, he preached to crowds gathered in the Temple before returning to Galilee.

Individual stories place Jesus in the lands neighboring Galilee, such as the Decapolis and the vicinity of the coastal towns of Tyre and Sidon. Again, they were not predominantly Jewish, so the same questions about Jesus' motivation arise: did Jesus work in these locations because they were not predominantly Jewish, or was he forced by expediency—the danger of preaching openly in Judea—to confine his mission to their Jewish communities?

Mark declares that as his fame spread "many people came to him from Judea, Jerusalem, Idumea and the regions across the Jordan [i.e., Perea] and around Tyre and Sidon." [14] This list is significant because it includes all the lands that had formed part of Israel *except* Samaria and the Decapolis—i.e., all those that were at that time considered Jewish (even if they were not exclusively inhabited by Jews). This emphasis on the Jews is shown by the statement that people came from the region "around Tyre and Sidon"—not *from* those cities (which were almost completely inhabited by pagan Gentiles) but from the country *around* them (which had a large Jewish population). Samaria and the Decapolis were the two regions that were not considered Jewish, the former because it was the land of the hated Samaritans and the latter because it was almost exclusively Greek. (The "Ten Cities" was an area of city-states founded during the Greek period that were autonomous but whose independence was underwritten by Rome—meaning that they were protected by the Roman army.)

In this way, Mark stresses, if only subliminally, that Jesus' message was aimed primarily at the Jews. But is this just because that was what Mark (or his sources) *wanted* his audience to think? What about Samaria, for example? Its absence from his list highlights a definite conflict in the early sources over whether Jesus had visited the region.

As we have seen, there is persuasive evidence that John's Gospel was aimed specifically at an early Samaritan Christian community and John the Baptist had included Samaria in his mission. Where Jesus and Samaria is concerned, however, the Gospels conflict. Mark

pointedly excludes Samaritans from his list of the peoples to whom
Jesus' message appealed. And Luke (alone of the Gospels) describes
an episode when Jesus starts his final journey from Galilee to
Jerusalem:

> And he sent messengers on ahead, who went into a Samaritan vil-
> lage to get things ready for him; but the people there did not wel-
> come him, because he was heading for Jerusalem. When the
> disciples James and John saw this, they asked, "Lord, do you want
> us to call down fire from heaven to destroy them?" But Jesus
> turned and rebuked them [i.e., James and John]. Then he and the
> disciples went to another village.[15]

The passage is obviously included to show that Samaritans were
hostile to Jesus and his mission, but it is clearly selective (unless Luke
thought that Samaria consisted of a single village). If the event really
happened, it only shows that *one* Samaritan village rejected Jesus—
the "other village" he and his entourage moved on to must also
have been Samaritan, since it would have taken more than a day to
pass through the country. Luke has singled out a group of Samaritans who refused to help Jesus but left out the fact that other Samaritans did help him: obviously he is not overkeen for his readers to
think well of them. But paradoxically Luke is also the sole source for
two other stories involving Samaritans, both of which show *individual* Samaritans in a good light.

The first is Jesus' famous parable of the Good Samaritan, given in
a discussion of the Levitical injunction "Love your neighbor as
yourself" and the consequent question (posed by a Jewish canon
lawyer) "Who *is* my neighbor?" A victim of robbers (by implication
a Jew) left injured by the side of the road is ignored by two
fellow Jews, a priest and a Levite, but taken care of by a kindly
Samaritan, revealing himself to be the man's true neighbor.[16]

Jesus' point is that it is altruistic actions that define fellow feeling,
not kinship or ethnic identity. The parable openly plays on the
Jews' anti-Samaritan prejudice, as it is the man a Jew would least expect to be helped by who actually does so. But as far as Luke is concerned, this account is far from a wholesale repatriation of all
Samaritans; *this* one is very much an exception.

Later in the story—although apparently not later in the journey to Jerusalem, as he is somehow back on the border of Galilee and Samaria—Jesus heals a group of ten lepers but is dismayed when, after going to the priests to be pronounced ritually clean, only one can be bothered to come back and thank him—and that one is a Samaritan (by implication the only one in the group).[17] Again, though, the whole point of the story is that the Samaritan would be least expected to show gratitude.

Luke's inclusion of these two passages does go a little way to countering the prejudice that is so evident in the Samaritan village episode. Even so, clearly both the parable and the healing story work on the understanding that Samaritans are usually not very nice people. As an ethnic group they are not exactly the heroes of the synoptic Gospels.

Matthew includes in Jesus' instructions to the twelve disciples, "Do not . . . enter any town of the Samaritans" (the only gospel writer to have such an injunction).[18] Since Jesus and John the Baptist both went there, as did (according to Acts) his postcrucifixion apostles, including Peter and John, this passage is clearly a product of Matthew's own anti-Samaritan prejudice.

By contrast, the Fourth Gospel was written for an early Samaritan Christian community, showing Samaritans in a much more favorable light and even linking Jesus himself with their land. There is even a scene where a Jewish crowd yells at Jesus, "you are a Samaritan and have a demon."[19] While indignantly denying he has a demon, he pointedly avoids denying the Samaritan accusation. In fact in the Fourth Gospel it is the Samaritans—or at least "many Samaritans"—who are the first people besides the disciples to recognize Jesus as the Messiah, even before he arrives in Galilee to begin his mission.

It is a Samaritan, too, who features in one of the strangest episodes of the New Testament. It happens when Jesus leaves Judea for Galilee (because of the hostility of the Pharisees), passes through the buffer state of Samaria, and encounters a woman at a well—to be precise, Jacob's Well near the town of Sychar.[20]

Although the passage points up specific parallels to the wellside meeting of Jacob and Rachel in Genesis that ends in their betrothal—driven home by the setting of the story at the very same well—and also has elements of the Old Testament episode in which a servant sent by Abraham to find a wife for his son Isaac meets Rebekah by a spring, which also ends in their betrothal,[21] it also contains a very unexpected subtext. It may be the last thing one would expect in the story of Jesus Christ, but as Andrew Lincoln points out, the story is heavy on sexual double entendre: "Readers are being led . . . to interpret the narrative on the usual level of an encounter between a man and a woman with a physical betrothal in view."[22]

To a Jewish or Samaritan reader at the time the words were written, the "physical betrothal" would have been startlingly blatant, being compounded by sexual metaphors and euphemisms in the exchange of words between Jesus and the woman. Lincoln explains:

> At this level the giving and receiving of water also carried sexual overtones and represented the exchange of fluids necessary for the procreation of life. The betrothal with its conversation between a man and a woman at a well about water means that this possibility should not be ignored. Again, the Jewish Scriptures indicate clearly how such terminology was a well-known euphemism for sexual relations. . . .
>
> Drinking water from a cistern or well refers to sexual intercourse, with springs specifically having in view semen, and wells and fountains the vagina and its emissions.[23]

Coupled with the betrothal associations, the suggestive subtext would have screamed out to the Gospel's original, Samaritan audience. But it should be stressed that this imagery was chosen by the writer of John's Gospel; it is unlikely that either Jesus or the Samaritan woman consciously employed such startlingly suggestive metaphors. (In any case, as they were alone during the encounter, how does anyone know about their smutty conversation?)

A contemporary Jew or Samaritan reading this story for the first time would have expected it to end with Jesus and the woman going off hand in hand either to get betrothed or to satisfy themselves in some more immediate way. But instead the author turns the story by having Jesus comment on the sexual morality of the woman. He asks her to fetch her husband, and when she replies that she has none, he tells her that although she has had five husbands, she is not married to her present partner.

The woman is impressed with Jesus' psychic abilities and starts a discussion between them about the root of the Jewish–Samaritan split, which is a disagreement on the appointed place to worship God. The woman says it is the very mountain on which they are talking—Gerizim—while the Jews insist it is Jerusalem. Jesus' response is that, while salvation is from the Jews, soon such considerations will no longer matter, since "true worshippers" need only worship God in the spirit.

The woman, obviously perplexed, replies, "I know that the Messiah is coming. When he comes, he will explain everything to us." Choosing her as the first person to whom he makes his great revelation, Jesus declares unambiguously, "I, the one speaking to you— I am he." The woman then goes and tells others, who come to him for teaching. He remains with them for two days, after which at least these Samaritans believe in him as the "Savior of the world."

The sexual imagery is quickly forgotten, but why use it in the first place? While it is impossible to be certain, as we will see, there are some intriguing potential explanations.

If John's Gospel was written for a Samaritan audience, the point of the story is transparent: not only did Jesus carry his message into Samaria, but he dissolved the traditional differences between Samaritans and Jews. Since his crucifixion and resurrection the rules had changed and there was no longer one particular hallowed place where God had to be worshipped. So did John just invent the story to make this point?

It is impossible to be sure. Lincoln, for example, thinks that it could well be based on an real encounter between Jesus and a Samaritan woman, but the gospel writer has "massively elaborated" it so that it is impossible to tell now what really happened and what comes from the writer's imagination.[24] The leading American theologian Ben Witherington III agrees with Lincoln and further argues that the story was based on a real occurrence.[25]

It is in fact impossible that Jesus' declaration of himself as the Messiah is accurate. For a start, it is very clear, as we will see, that he avoided making such an open declaration. Secondly, although the Samaritans were expecting a savior figure, the Taheb, he was irreconcilable with, even the opposite of, the Davidic Messiah. One of the functions of the Taheb was to restore the supremacy of the Samaritans—or rather the tribe of Ephraim, the Samaritans' ancestors—which actually involved conquering the Judeans and removing them from their position of power. The Samaritan woman would never, therefore, have used the words attributed to her, showing that at the very least she is made to speak from a different script.

However, the most significant point for our present purposes is the contrast with the synoptics' attitude to Samaritans. Even though this account still emphatically depicts Jesus as a Jew among them, it does show them in a more favorable light and does suggest that he (like John the Baptist) had spent some time preaching in Samaria. After all, he must have passed through on many occasions, if the Fourth Gospel's statement is correct about his making several visits to Jerusalem.

It would hardly be surprising if the synoptics omitted any mention of Jesus' activity in Samaria, not only because of their prejudice but also because from a Jewish perspective it would simply have been irrelevant. There is another reason, however, for their neglect of Samaria. As we will see, in the earliest days of Christianity a rival form of the new religion, with which Jesus' following was in conflict, had sprung up there. It was therefore safest to avoid all mention of Samaria—far too controversial otherwise. People might ask awkward questions.

Disciples and Other Followers

Whereas the Fourth Gospel has Jesus recruiting his first disciples from among the Baptist's followers by the Jordan, in the synoptics he calls them in Galilee after John's arrest. Andrew Lincoln makes the important point that in the Fourth Gospel joining Jesus means not only leaving behind one's former life but also "a previous religious commitment—to John the Baptist and his mission."[26] From now on they are Jesus' men, not John's.

The version of events in John's Gospel makes more sense, as the synoptics' description is deeply unconvincing: when Jesus calls the disciples and they drop everything to follow him, he has done nothing to merit such a life-changing snap decision. All the Gospels agree that where the Galilee ministry is concerned, Jesus gathers his first disciples and *then* embarks on his career of miracle working, which begs the question of why the disciples should have been impressed enough to sign up in the first place. Only the Fourth Gospel supplies an answer—that the first to join him had already seen him in action, in Judea.

It is entirely possible that both versions are correct in their own way. When he began his own ministry, Jesus may well have called upon people he had known when he was with John the Baptist but who had returned to Galilee to escape the fallout after his arrest. Dropping everything to join Jesus when he called could even have been prearranged: after lying low for a time and returning to their previous lives, they would be ready for action when they received the word. But whatever the case, from that nucleus Jesus built up a band of disciples who traveled with him.

But what kind of people were the disciples? What did Jesus expect of them—and what did they expect of him? Given their importance in the story and the origins of Christianity, it is astonishing how little understanding the disciples have of Jesus' objectives and even how downright stupid they often appear to be.

The Galilee recruitment begins with four fishermen, two pairs of brothers: Simon (nicknamed Peter) and Andrew, and James and John, the sons of Zebedee. (John's Gospel agrees that Peter and Andrew were two of the first three people to join Jesus. The third is unnamed, and opinions are divided on whether this is because the person is this Gospel's beloved disciple, but had it been, surely the fact would have been spelled out more clearly.) As members of a family fishing business these four men would have been quite prosperous; Zebedee, father of James and John, also employed men other than his sons.

Simon's nickname of Peter is left unexplained in the two root Gospels, Mark and John. Only in Matthew do we find the pun "on this rock I will build my church," which basically doesn't work. Jesus' speaking of "my church" is an anachronism, since there could have been no concept then of a church either as an organized entity or as a building. The word used, *ecclesia*, referred to a local *community* of Christians, not the building where they met. So the pun is clearly back-projection by later Christians to explain Simon's nick-name.

So why *was* he called "Rock"? A reasonable guess is that it was a reference to his physique. As Michael Baigent, Richard Leigh, and Henry Lincoln point out in *The Messianic Legacy*, the name is the equivalent of the modern "Rocky." [27]

Other disciples had nicknames bestowed on them by Jesus: James and John became the "Sons of Thunder," but we never learn why; presumably, like Peter, they had a short fuse. (As we have seen, Jesus had to restrain them from "calling down fire" on the Samaritan village.) In any case disciples with nicknames like "Rocky" and "Sons of Thunder" hardly make the band sound meek and mild. It seems they were a rough lot.

In some cases, apparently they were considerably more than merely unsophisticated and irascible. Controversially, some of their epithets appear to point to radical, even militant, associations. This is another one of those issues that could seriously alter our view of Jesus, depending which side of the argument we take.

The militants are apparently Simon the Zealot, a member of the fanatical nationalist group sworn to overthrow the Romans, and Judas Iscariot. In Mark's Gospel Simon's identification is fudged, the writer implying it means "Canaanite": the Aramaic word translated as "zealot" was *qan'ana,* transliterated into Greek as *Kananaios,* which could easily be understood as "Canaanite" (*Kananaia*).[28] If, as seems to be the case, Mark was written in the early Christian community in Rome at a time of particular tension between Romans and Jews (either just before or after the first Jewish revolt), then there were good reasons to downplay Simon's affiliation.

But did Simon join the Jesus group *because* he was a Zealot, or was his nationalist background just incidental? If the former, there are certain unavoidable implications for our understanding of Jesus: as the Zealots were known for their violence, did he approve? Did he go so far as to actively support their cause? Of course, if Simon was an ex-Zealot, those questions no longer apply.

The questions surrounding the other "political" disciple, Judas Is-cariot, are less clear-cut, because whatever his epithet means, it has definitely been garbled; "Iscariot" itself is meaningless. The argument was advanced back in the early twentieth century, and championed more recently by S. G. F. Brandon, that "Iscariot" is a garbled rendering of "Sicarii" or its Latinized version *sicarius*, referring to an even more fanatical and violent group of freedom fighters—or terrorists, depending on whose side you were on—within the Zealots who carried out assassinations of Romans and "collaborators" using short, curved knives called *sica*.[29]

The traditional explanation, however, is that Iscariot comes from *ish qeriyoth*, "man of Kerioth"; two villages of that name are known, one in Judea and the other in Moab. However, this too is a guess. No other character in the Gospels is called "man of . . ."

What makes the "Sicarius" interpretation more likely is that, unusually, the writer of Mark's Gospel failed to translate the word for his Greek-speaking audience. This means either that he himself had no idea what it meant or that he *did* know but had no intention of telling his audience. The fact that he deliberately fudged the description of the other extremist in Jesus' inner circle, the Zealot, strongly suggests the latter.

Even so, the presence of a Zealot and a Sicarius in Jesus' inner circle is only suggestive. We would need considerably more evidence that Jesus' own motivation and ambitions were essentially political before we can conclude that was definitely the case.

That is all the information we have about Jesus' disciples—the male ones anyway. We know the former occupations and a few details about five of them, and the *possible* political affiliations of two, but beyond that nothing apart from their names. Two, Andrew and Philip, had Greek names, but then many Jews, especially in Galilee, had become Hellenized.

Famously, Jesus established an inner circle of twelve disciples to whom he later delegated his authority and power, passing on his ability to drive out evil spirits (presumably a secret technique), and sent them out in pairs to work in his name, after giving them detailed instructions.

While Jesus probably did create an inner circle or top rank within his disciples, did it really consist of the magic Twelve or was the number chosen by later mythmakers? Or was the whole thing invented retrospectively to bestow his authority on the missions of contemporary apostles?

The evidence points to the former. One of Jesus' instructions to the Twelve supports the idea that he was consciously evoking the twelve tribes of Israel. He tells them that if any town or village should refuse to accept them in his name, then as they leave they should shake the dust from their feet. This was not just a somewhat melodramatic turn of phrase: it was a symbolic act that Jews carried out when re-entering Israel, preventing its sacred soil from being contaminated by foreign dust. Basically Jesus meant that any town or village that refused to accept his disciples—and therefore him—was no longer considered part of the Jewish nation, regardless of its geographical location.[30] As this would not have been important to the movement when the Gospels were written, it shows that the idea of twelve disciples representing the twelve tribes was Jesus' own idea and intention, which in turn indicates that he saw his mission as in some way connected with gathering together the scattered twelve tribes.

Even within the Twelve, certain disciples stand out. In Mark's Gospel, Peter, James and John, and sometimes Andrew form a kind of inner-inner circle: they accompany Jesus on occasions when he goes off by himself and sometimes receive special teaching.

Not everything was always sweetness and light. John's Gospel tells of a large-scale desertion of disciples (because of issues raised by Jesus' "bread of life" discourse). This is one of the parts that is likely to be true, because it hardly reflects well on Jesus or his powers of persuasion. To the average Christian, however, the fact that Christ lost a significant number of disciples because he annoyed or upset them—and certainly failed to hold their attention—will come as something of a shock.

Jesus' Women

Largely thanks to *The Da Vinci Code*, there has been a great deal of debate in recent years about the role of women in Jesus' movement—especially the enigmatic but strangely compelling Mary Magdalene. Conventionally the discipleship has been regarded as an all-male affair, and to traditionalists—against the most persuasive evidence, it must be said—it still is. Although to a large extent this belief is a consequence of how the canonical Gospels tell the story, even in their pages there are clues that female followers played an important role.

While Mark's Gospel makes no mention of female followers in its main narrative, there is an aside when it comes to describe the women who are watching Jesus' crucifixion:

Among them were Mary Magdalene, Mary the mother of James the younger and of Joseph, and Salome. In Galilee these women had followed him and cared for his needs. Many other women who had come up with him from Jerusalem were also there.[31]

Perhaps the most intriguing element is the statement that those particular women had been with him in Galilee, since Mark said nothing about them when telling that part of the story.

Matthew's Gospel simply repeats this passage almost word for word. Luke's account of the crucifixion shrinks this to "women who had followed him from Galilee," but alone of the synoptics, it presents more information about the women earlier in the story. (John's Gospel has the women at the cross but fails to explain who they are or how they came to be there.)

Luke tells us that as Jesus traveled around the villages of Galilee proclaiming the coming of the Kingdom of God,

The Twelve were with him, and also some women who had been cured of evil spirits and diseases: Mary (called Magdalene) from whom seven demons had come out; Joanna the wife of Chuza, the manager of Herod's household; Susanna; and many others. These women were helping to support them out of their own means.[32]

As this account is conspicuous by its absence from the other Gospels, Luke's source could not have been Mark or Q, and there are no other clues about where he got it.

As with the male disciples, we are given virtually no background information about these women. The most interesting statement concerns Joanna, who it transpires is the wife of one of Herod Antipas' most important officials: the story of how she came to be traveling with Jesus would no doubt be fascinating, but frustratingly it is left to our imaginations. (Did her husband approve? Did she have a special role in the following? Sadly, we will never know.)

The female devotees, at least in Galilee, traveled with Jesus and his male disciples, and some followed him into Judea. There is no doubt that they had a major role to play, as it is stated unambiguously that they supported Jesus and the male disciples financially and materially. Marks says that they "cared for his needs" and Luke that they supported the men "out of their own means." (Again one wonders about Joanna: did she donate her husband's money to the cause?)

The very fact the canonical Gospels are so vague about the female followers—acknowledging they were important but saying virtually nothing about them—suggests these passages were accurate. After all, the early Christians would hardly have gone to the bother of inventing characters and relationships just to downplay them. Either the writers had no particular interest in the women of Jesus' movement or were uncomfortable about them for some reason. There is a distinct impression that it is only because the women, particularly Mary Magdalene, take center stage in the events immediately after the crucifixion that the gospel writers have reluctantly acknowledged their presence at all.

It should be stressed that for a Jewish teacher to include women among his disciples was not just unusual but literally unprecedented. On the basis that the unusual is most often recorded, it is surprising that the Gospels make such little comment about this. In fact one would expect it to be one of the reasons Jesus' group was singled out for criticism by the Jewish leaders, but it isn't. As Witherington writes, "For a Jewish woman to leave home and travel with a rabbi was not only unheard of, it was scandalous. Even more scandalous was the fact that women, both respectable and not, were among Jesus' traveling companions." [33]

Without doubt the most important of this female group was Mary Magdalene. She is always listed first (except on one occasion in John's Gospel where she takes second place to Jesus' mother), and the fact that the gospel writers feel no need to explain who she is implies that their readers already knew both her identity and clearly extraordinary status. This makes it all the more remarkable that she should play so little part in the story before the crucifixion.

Many commentators, including Catholics, have come to the perfectly logical conclusion that Mary Magdalene was the leader of the female disciples, i.e., the equivalent of Peter. But despite her obvious high standing in the group—perhaps even her celebrity in the wider world—we learn very little about her.

In Mark, Matthew, and John she is "Mary the Magdalene" (*Maria e Magdalene*), an unusual construction if "Magdalene" simply refers to her home town. Luke has the even more peculiar "Mary who is called Magdalene" (*Maria e kaloumene Magdalene*), apparently implying something even more significant, but which is lost on us today, although it is póssibly some kind of a nickname—or even a title. It is reminiscent of the ambiguity about Jesus' being described as "the Nazarene."

Her name is traditionally thought to derive from the town of Magdala in Galilee, although in his commentary on Luke's Gospel, A. R. C. Leaney says this is only "probably" true and points out that the town is not otherwise mentioned in the New Testament.[34] Neither does it make an appearance as such in Josephus, except under the name of Tarichea.

Significantly for such an obviously important woman, she is never identified, as was customary, by her relationship to a man (as wife, daughter, sister, or mother). Even if we assume that Mary Magdalene was already very familiar to the Gospels' first readers, this is still unusual. Obviously she was a woman whose status was somehow beyond question or even outside normal social rules.

Just as intriguingly, no clues are offered about the significance of Luke's statement that "seven demons" had been cast out of her, although the obvious implication is that she had been exorcised by Jesus, which perhaps was why she joined his following. If so, it is odd that no surviving sources actually describe what must have been one of Jesus' most dramatic exorcisms, but the way the allusion is phrased suggests it was probably already well known to Luke's readers.[35]

Is this marginalization of the women in general and Mary Magdalene in particular due merely to a basic misogyny on the part of a man writing for a predominantly male audience, or is there something else going on, some kind of cover-up?

Paul's Letters make it clear that women held prominent and respected positions in Christian communities in his day—when the Gospels were taking shape—so there was no obvious reason to suppress the fact that they also enjoyed high status in Jesus' original following. This suggests there was something about these women that the gospel writers were trying to evade, something that their audience would have been uncomfortable with, yet unfortunately there is no clear-cut evidence to suggest what that might be.

Famously, however, the situation is very different when we turn to the gnostic sources, in which Jesus' female disciples figure prominently, particularly Mary Magdalene. Even more famously—or notoriously, depending on one's point of view—those sources attribute an intimate personal relationship to her and Jesus.

Because the majority of the gnostic gospels are known only from fourth-century Coptic copies, many commentators reject the image they paint of Mary Magdalene and the other female disciples as a much later invention by Christian sects who had their own axe to grind and no access to authentic sources. But that is manifestly not the case.

Mary Magdalene, along with Salome, appears as a key figure in the Gospel of Thomas, which is at least contemporary with, if not earlier than, the canonical Gospels. So she was already, at that early date, considered a prominent member of Jesus' following; whatever the historical reality, her importance was *not* a fourth-century invention.

Another source, *The Sophia of Jesus Christ*, from the Nag Hammadi collection but previously known from other copies, and which has been dated on linguistic and paleographic grounds to before 100 CE—so again approximately contemporary with the New Testament Gospels—refers, without any further explanation, to Jesus' "twelve disciples and seven women."[36] Why did one very early group of Christians associate Jesus with such a specific number of female followers? And again, Mary Magdalene is presented as a leading disciple, one of the select few (along with Matthew, Philip, and Thomas) who ask questions of Jesus about his teaching, a format that was to become popular with gnostic Christian writers. Similarly, in *The Dialogue of the Savior*, another Nag Hammadi book, believed by scholars to be based on a text that dates from before 100 CE, Mary Magdalene appears as one of the leading disciples.[37]

There is no doubt that the idea of Mary Magdalene as a leading and active disciple was around as early as Matthew, Mark, Luke, and John. So why does she figure so little in the New Testament books?

It is tempting to think that the gnostic writers simply invented her status, perhaps because for reasons of their own they wanted to have a female leader and just happened to pick the Magdalene, were it not for the fact that her role is acknowledged, albeit grudgingly and obliquely, in the New Testament Gospels. And this emphasis on Mary Magdalene's importance remains whether or not the specific exchanges between her and Jesus in the gnostic dialogues ever really happened.

It seems likely that the canonical Gospels' reticence about the elevation of Mary Magdalene and the status of the women in the gnostics' books are two sides of the same coin: the biblical texts downplayed the women *because* they were held in high esteem by groups within early Christianity that held a radically different view of Jesus, and which developed into a heretical alternative. In other words, the two sources represent a basic split in the first days of the new religion. But which view represents the reality of Jesus' mission?

The Woman Christ Often Kissed

Concerning Mary Magdalene, however, there is another level of controversy: did her relationship with Jesus go well beyond a special spiritual bond? Were they at least lovers, perhaps even man and wife? Some believe their love—sexual and intense, not merely that of soul mates—was the reason she played such a prominent part in the events following Jesus' crucifixion. Their relationship is of course the major revelation of *The Da Vinci Code*, which galvanized millions worldwide, sparking an incandescent debate that looks set to rumble on wherever Christianity has planted its flag.

Some explain the process the other way round: it was the Magdalene's part in the resurrection story that led to the development of the idea that she was Jesus' lover. The gnostics had wondered why this enigmatic woman was portrayed as so close to Jesus and had been chosen to be the first witness to his resurrection, and their imaginations had done the rest. Which is correct?

Obviously much depends on the relative dating of the sources. If the New Testament Gospels were written in the first century and the gnostic texts not until the fourth, then it would seem that the parts about Mary Magdalene were the product of later imaginations. However, as we have seen, this simplistic reasoning about the dates fails to stand up. Mary Magdalene was written of as one of the leading disciples—and not just of the women—in works contemporary with the canonical Gospels. But what about her *personal* relationship with Jesus: when did it first surface?

One of the primary sources is the Gospel of Philip, another Nag Hammadi text, which, although translated into Coptic, came from a Greek text that dated from ca. 150.[38] It is basically a compilation of sayings of Jesus taken from a number of earlier sources, including the New Testament Gospels, but what is still unknown, frustratingly, is how much earlier are the sources of the non–New Testament passages, which include two now-famous statements about Mary Magdalene. The first is: "There were three who always walked with the lord: Mary his mother and his sister Magdalene, the one who was called his companion. His sister, his mother, and his companiom were each a Mary."[39]

As many millions now know thanks to Dan Brown (and Ian McKellen), the first word translated as "companion" (*koinonos*) implies a more intimate, even sexual relationship between Jesus and the Magdalene.[40]

While it is true that *koinonos* can have a more innocent meaning, in the sense of "colleague," as with many other words context is everything. In fact the best translation into modern English is "partner," since it has all the same range of meanings, from a business partnership to a sexual liaison, even including a spouse. After all, if a man introduced a woman as his partner at a business conference, we would have a different understanding of their relationship than if he did so at a cocktail party.

Even more difficult for traditionalists is the Coptic *hotre*, the second word translated as "companion" in the above quote, which certainly means an intimate partnership but can refer to a spouse.[41]

The writer of the Gospel of Philip clearly understood the relationship between Mary Magdalene and Jesus to be essentially sexual. But what we most want to know—what "Philip" used as sources and whether or not they were at all reliable—is the one thing that is omitted.

Then there is the other (in)famous verse from the Gospel of Philip: "And the companion [*koinonos* again] of the [. . .] Mary Magdalene. He [. . . loved] her more than [all] the disciples, [and used to] kiss her [often] on her [. . .]. The rest of [the disciples]. They said to him 'Why do you love her more than all of us?' "[42]

Although most modern translations give it as "he . . . used to kiss her often on the mouth," the last word has to be a guess as, tantalizingly, that particular fragment is missing from the original. Traditional Christians usually explain any assumptions of intimacy between Christ and the Magdalene by declaring that obviously he kissed her on the cheek, as this was how the early Christians customarily greeted each other. But as this passage makes clear, wherever he kissed her, it offended the male disciples profoundly, so it was hardly the greeting of a brother and sister in God.

As we have seen, many commentators dismiss much of the teachings attributed to Jesus in the gnostic Nag Hammadi texts simply because these teachings present an image of Christ very different from the one we know from the Gospels. (In fact this is precisely the kind of objection that could be made about the Gospel of John.) But this passage continues in a way that is extremely reminiscent of the New Testament Jesus:

> The savior answered and said to them, "Why do I not love you like her? When a blind man and one who sees are both together in the darkness, they are not different from one another. When the light comes, then he who sees will see the light, and he who is blind will remain in darkness."[43]

So, by the critics' logic, this verse should be taken as authentic because it sounds like the sort of thing Jesus would have said. Trying to have it both ways is not an unusual situation in the theological world, however.

As we have seen, the gnostic texts even include a Gospel of Mary (Magdalene), although, unlike the canonical Gospels, the title refers to the fact that it is *about* her, not supposedly by her. Scholars place the original composition as 150 or even earlier—making it possibly contemporary with the canonical Gospels.[44]

Another crucial gnostic work featuring Mary Magdalene is the *Pistis Sophia*, which was acquired by the British Museum in 1785.

Although this typically complicated gnostic book—littered with the most convoluted, in some cases unintentionally comical, cosmologies and featuring Mary Magdalene as Jesus' most tenacious questioner—certainly dates from a later period, probably the fourth century, most academics believe it is a reworking of *The Questions of Mary*. Now lost, we know about the latter because it was quoted by Epiphanius in the fourth century. Described by one authority as "a sort of erotic–mystical novel,"[45] it too placed Mary Magdalene in a specifically sexual relationship with Jesus. Ironically, the purpose of rewriting it as the *Pistis Sophia* was to *downplay* this aspect. How much earlier *The Questions of Mary* was written is uncertain, but significantly the French editor of the Gospel of Mary argued that the Gospel was also written "to counter the excesses of *The Questions of Mary*."[46] Since the Gospel of Mary dates from 150 CE—possibly earlier—*The Questions of Mary* must be even older.

Even if this is not the case, other texts, such as *The Sophia of Jesus Christ* and *The Dialogue of the Savior*, which *can* be traced back to that early time, show that the image of the Magdalene as a feisty, important woman with a special place in the Jesus movement that developed into the Gospel of Mary does indeed date back to the earliest days of the religion.

Another highly intriguing aspect of these texts about Mary Magdalene is the portrayal of her relationship with Peter, one of jealousy and even intense rivalry. The gnostic gospels do seem to have inside information not only about the relationship between Jesus and the Magdalene, but also that of the Magdalene and Peter, which was clearly stormy. As Jesus' truly beloved disciple, she is described in, for example, the later *Pistis Sophia* (although it drew on much earlier works) as always being at the forefront in the group's question-and-answer sessions, which seriously annoyed the men, especially Peter. At one point Mary tells Jesus, "I am afraid of Peter, because he threatened me and hateth our sex."[47] Peter's obvious jealousy and visceral misogyny has finally spilled over into personal threats. His detestation of the Magdalene is a constant undercurrent of many gnostic texts and suggests that on this issue at least they were highly accurate. After all, if the authors were inventing interchanges between the disciples, the picture would have been all sweetness and light. The fact that it is anything but suggests we should take them seriously, at least on this issue.

Were the gnostics trying to elevate Mary retrospectively simply to dissociate themselves from the mainstream church that claimed its authority from Peter—perhaps even to explain the origins of the split? Or was their account based on a real, if embroidered and subjective, memory of personality clashes between the feisty, no-nonsense Mary and Peter, otherwise known as the Rock, with his notoriously short fuse?

There is also a curious echo in the Fourth Gospel of the disciples' complaints about Mary in the Gospel of Philip. When the resurrected Jesus appears to Peter and the other fishermen disciples, he asks Peter, "Simon son of John, do you love me more than these?"[48] The writer seems to have been aware of the dispute between Peter and the Magdalene, the wording perhaps even suggesting he was implicitly responding to the Gospel of Philip.

The Messianic Secret

None of the above answers the most fundamental of all questions: why exactly did the disciples follow Jesus? There may be a clue in the Greek word, which is more accurately translated as "pupil" or "student': those who dedicated themselves to a teacher in order to learn from him. (Rabbis at the time customarily gathered a circle of pupils, although so did non-Jewish philosophers and religious leaders.) It suggests that Jesus was considered by his immediate followers primarily as a teacher—perhaps what we could call a guru—whose message fundamentally captured their hearts and minds. Paradoxically, though, they are consistently portrayed as not understanding his mission, which is why they appear so resolutely dim.

One consideration, however, should be uppermost but is rarely even touched upon. Whatever the reason people followed Jesus, or for that matter opposed him, it could *not* have had any connection with why people have become Christians since Paul's day and still do today.

What was obvious to a *postresurrection* Christian—Jesus' destiny to make an atoning self-sacrifice—would have meant nothing to his contemporary followers, since it went against their entire expectations about the Messiah, or for that matter any other end-times figure. The whole point of Christianity as a religion is Jesus' death and resurrection. Leaving aside theological arguments about the accuracy of Paul's interpretation, he could only have worked it out *after* Christ had been crucified and had returned from the dead. If Jesus had proclaimed in advance, "You should follow me because I'm going to be arrested, tortured, and killed, but don't worry, I'll rise from the grave and it will all be fine—trust me," with immediate effect he would have had no disciples left.

Indeed the Gospels have Jesus making just such statements to the disciples—explaining that when they get to Jerusalem he will be taken, made to suffer, and killed—but obviously they have no clue what he is talking about. Those passages are unlikely to be historically accurate, being a classic example of back-projection by post-resurrection Christians. As has been pointed out, if Jesus really had predicted his fate in such detail, then his disciples, even if they were baffled at the time, would hardly have been so bewildered when it actually happened.[49]

The disciples' expectations of what Jesus would do for them, and what his mission was intended to achieve, must have been quite different from the reason people become Christians today. They emphatically were *not* following him because he was "the Christ" in modern terms. In fact from a traditional Christian perspective the disciples were following Jesus for the *wrong* reasons. So why *were* they following him?

Our reconstruction of events leads logically to what is at this stage something of a sketchy answer, but an answer nonetheless. The first disciples had previously been disciples of John the Baptist, and then worked with Jesus in Judea before returning to Galilee. So, at the very least, Peter and his early colleagues followed Jesus because they thought he was continuing or reviving John's cause—whatever that might have been.

To go beyond this point raises the vexed question of what Jesus himself said he was—and particularly whether he ever actually claimed to be the Messiah.

In 1901 Wilhelm Wrede of Breslau University caused a sensation with *The Secret of the Messiahship*, in which he argued, on the basis of Mark's Gospel, that Jesus had never claimed to be the Messiah and that his disciples had never regarded him as such.

Wrede's view was based on the simple observation that while the synoptic Gospels were written from the viewpoint that Jesus *was* the Messiah/Christ, they never have him declaring this publicly, even portraying him as reticent and ambiguous about it in private. (Also Jesus never actually did what was expected of the Messiah, which is why the first Christians had to redefine the title.) The only explanation for the absence of an explicit public statement in Mark is that it was well known that Jesus had never made such a claim—too well known for the gospel writer to pretend otherwise. Equally significant is that it was never given as one of the reasons that those in power opposed him in Galilee; it only becomes an issue in Jerusalem at the end of the story.

Mark's resolution of this problem was the concept of the "messianic secret": that Jesus was the Messiah but had to keep quiet about it until the appointed time. Only his closest disciples knew, and even they were not aware of it at the start. Wrede, however, argued that this notion was pure invention by Mark (or one of his major sources), and that Jesus had never staked a claim to the title of Messiah at all, either in public or private.

Mark's messianic-secret explanation was basically followed by Matthew and Luke, although not John, which as usual takes a completely contradictory position. It has the first disciples immediately recognizing Jesus as the Messiah (which is why they leave John the Baptist for him) and Jesus making an open declaration of his messiahship to the Samaritan woman before even arriving in Galilee to start his ministry. But even John's Gospel stops short of having him make a messianic declaration as part of his *public* preaching.

Although there is no doubt that Jesus never made a great announcement that he was the long-awaited Messiah, did he ever do so privately, to his closest followers? Since it is impossible that the synoptics and Fourth Gospel could both be correct about when the disciples recognized him in that role, one or other of the gospel traditions must have essentially back-engineered the story. But which? The evidence strongly favors the synoptics: it is much easier to imagine that the writer of the Fourth Gospel invented the disciples' early recognition (to drive the point home from the start that Jesus was the Messiah and avoid any awkward questions) than that Mark pretended they had no idea why they were following him.

The key moment in the synoptic version is the scene in which Peter recognizes Jesus as the Messiah, as told somewhat tersely in Mark:

Jesus and his disciples went on to the villages around Caesarea
Philippi. On the way he asked them, "Who do people say I am?"

They replied, "Some say John the Baptist; others say Elijah;
and still others, one of the prophets."

"But what about you?" he asked. "Who do you say I am?"

Peter answered, "You are the Christ."

Jesus warned them not to tell anyone about him.[50]

This episode crucially shows that (at least as far as the gospel
writer was concerned) up to that moment the disciples have *not*
been following Jesus because they think he is the Messiah. And even
when it does dawn on them, Jesus makes it abundantly clear that
they must not make it general knowledge. In fact in Luke the same
word, *epitimesas*, is used for his "strict instructions," as when he
commands unclean spirits to be silent about his identity.[51] He *orders*
them to keep quiet about it.

But there is one other vital point: *if* Peter did recognize Jesus as
the Messiah, then at that stage of the story it could only have been
the iconic figure expected by the Jews, the divinely mandated—but
not divine or supernatural—man who would lead the children of Israel against their foreign oppressors and establish a terrestrial kingdom, gathering together the remnants of the scattered tribes and
eventually becoming the dominant power in the world. So, in understanding Jesus' motives, it is vital to know whether this scene really took place—and especially whether, as Mark has it, Jesus
accepted Peter's acclamation—or if was a complete invention to
justify the messianic-secret concept.

Was Wrede right? Or was Mark's solution of the messianic secret
essentially correct? As so often happens with the Gospels, a plausible case can be argued for both alternatives, depending on which
parts of the Gospels are judged to be historically reliable. But there
is one revealing episode that swings the argument in favor of Mark.
This is the episode in his Gospel (once again softened by Matthew
and omitted entirely from Luke and John) in which, when Jesus begins his fateful journey toward Jerusalem, the sons of Zebedee ask
for favored positions in his movement, for "one of us to sit at your
right hand and the other at your left in your glory."[52] However, the
two-thousand-year-old Christian gloss obscures the true meaning of
the men's request for favoritism in the glory days to come. It does

not, as might be thought, refer to favored status in some nebulous heaven. As Morna Hooker points out, the passage that James and John have purely *terrestrial* ends in sight: "what they have in mind is nothing less than the best positions in the messianic kingdom which they believe Jesus is about to set up. They perhaps imagine that Jesus is entering Jerusalem in order to claim the Davidic throne and rule the nation."[53] The brothers are not, as we might imagine when reading this Gospel today, asking for favored positions in the movement that Jesus is going to leave behind, because (even in Mark's telling) they have no glimmering that he is going to leave them.

This episode must be authentic, because the sons of Zebedee are appealing to the *Jewish* messianic concept, which had been replaced by the Christian interpretation that was the entire basis for Mark's Gospel. The request causes bad feeling among the other ten disciples that Jesus has to quell with some stern words, another authentic-seeming element that the other Gospels downplay or omit. The suggestion of disharmony and power struggles within the ranks of the Twelve also adds a touch of verisimilitude. The fact that Matthew and Luke were uncomfortable with it—Matthew made it into a request from James and John's *mother* for favors for her boys and Luke left it out completely—only serves to reinforce the point.

If this passage is authentic, it shows that, at least by the close of the Galilee mission and the beginning of the Jerusalem phase, the disciples were following Jesus because they believed he was the Messiah *according to the classic Jewish model*, the kingly hero who would take power in Jerusalem. Whether they had always believed it, or whether Mark's tale of Peter's moment of revelation is accurate, remains obscure, but the passage certainly goes a long way toward explaining why the disciples followed him.

For us, the "sons of Zebedee" episode establishes that the Twelve (at least) thought their master was the Messiah. However, we learn nothing about whether they believed it because Jesus told them, or just because they worked it out for themselves. But another factor needs to be taken account, which strongly suggests that Jesus *did* make such a claim, or at the very least allowed his disciples and others to continue thinking he was the Messiah.

Given the apocalyptic fervor of the times, simply standing up and preaching would make people wonder if you were the Messiah or one of the other expected end-times figures. Had Jesus not wanted people to think he was the Jewish deliverer, he would have explicitly denied it, and had this been a prominent part of his message, unquestionably it would have found its way into the Gospels. (Since the religion was founded on the belief that Jesus had died and risen again, they would probably still have been written, but they would have had to have found some other title for him.) In a bizarre twist, not denying being the Messiah was tantamount to admitting you were. In that sense Jesus was employing "dog-whistle" tactics, allowing people to think of him in the great role while not actually saying he was.

The keeping of the messianic secret makes sense for other reasons. Staking a claim to messiahship would have been guaranteed to invite the authorities' attention, for whom such declarations were a sure sign of subversion and troublemaking, and to invite a robust response to preempt the building up of a mass following (as with John the Baptist). Not making the claim explicit provided "plausible deniability": if he found himself before Herod Antipas, Jesus could say he was merely an itinerant healer. Declaring himself Messiah to all his followers in Galilee would quite simply have meant he would never have made it to Jerusalem.

As mentioned previously, there were other "agents of God" whom different groups of people expected to arise or return, such as Moses and Elijah. So while the evidence shows that the disciples thought of their Lord as the Messiah, his public silence implies that the people might have imagined him to be any one of the other figures. As with the Baptist's proclamation of the Coming One, Jesus' not being specific about *which* "agent of God" he was referring to ensured that those expecting *any* of them would be equally open to his message.

The Prodigal Son

Despite the largely Catholic belief that Christ was the archetypally perfect son, there is no doubt that during his Galilee ministry Jesus was on very poor terms with his family.

Mark, in typical fashion, weaves together two stories with a similar point.[54] Early in the Galilee days, when they hear that he is going about preaching to crowds, his family set off "to take charge of him, for they said, 'He is out of his mind.'" We are left guessing about whether it was the fact that Jesus was preaching at all or *what it was* he was preaching that made them think he had gone mad.

In the meantime Jewish "teachers of the law"—the important religious authorities who came all the way from Jerusalem to watch him—accuse Jesus of being a servant of the demon Beelzebul (or Beelzebub), who is the source of his power. He counters with the clever question "How can Satan drive out Satan?"

Then his "mother and brothers" arrive (although "brothers," *adelphoi*, should really be translated as "relatives," since the term could also cover other, male or female relations), but perhaps understandably in the circumstances he refuses to go out to meet them. Instead he asks, "Who are my mother and my brothers?" adding, "Whoever does God's will is my brother and sister and mother." The implication is often missed: clearly he thinks that his mother, brother, and sisters do *not* do God's will.

The family's belief that Jesus is insane links with the "Beelzebul" accusation, since madness was considered to be caused by demonic possession, which is why Mark has interwoven the two stories thematically.

Right from the start, the idea that Jesus' family considered him insane has made Christians so uncomfortable that they have tried to downplay it in various ways. Matthew and Luke simply suppress the whole episode where his family accuse him of insanity, retaining only the second part of Mark's story, where Jesus snubs his mother and brothers and makes the point that the community of Christians is his real family. In doing so they remove the one thing that makes sense of Jesus' refusal to meet his family: that they have come to have him put away. Matthew and Luke make it sound as if he simply can't be bothered to go and talk to them.

But the full version clearly lies behind another episode in Luke, set much later, which tellingly is also linked to the accusation that Jesus was an agent of Beelzebul. He responds to the accusation as he does in Mark—if he is working for the "prince of demons," why would he be driving other demons out? However, then we are told, in an apparent non sequitur:

As Jesus was saying these things, a woman in the crowd called out, "Blessed is the mother who gave you birth and nursed you."

He replied, "Blessed rather are those who hear the word of God and obey it."[55]

Luke is clearly following the same train of thought as in Mark, linking an accusation of demonism to Jesus' delivering a put-down about his mother. So much for early worship of the "Mother of God."

Attempts to overcome this embarrassing situation continue to this day. Even some modern translations of Mark change "family" to "friends." The Greek phrase *par autou*, literally "those beside him" (the equivalent of "nearest and dearest"), can mean friends or family, depending on the context. But really there is no getting away from it: in *this* scenario the term clearly means family, since when they arrive to take him away, they are described as his mother and relatives, so the "friends" translation is a deliberate attempt to obscure the truth.

John's Gospel omits this episode but still states that "even his own brothers did not believe in him."[56] It may also be significant that Jesus' mother is never referred to by her name throughout the entire Gospel.

Some try to explain this rupture as an invention of the early Christian groups who were Mark and John's source. They argue that because of the split in early Christianity between Paul and the Jerusalem Church led by Jesus' brother James and other close kin, there was a conscious effort by those who accepted Paul's version to denigrate the family, even inventing passages in which Christ effectively insults them. In other words, these sections were written to turn Christians away from the version of the religion propagated by James and the family.[57]

This is not very convincing. There was no need for Paul's supporters to have gone to such lengths if they only wanted to show that Jesus' family had no idea what he was about. In particular the part about their believing Jesus was mad has the ring of truth, being such an unlikely invention by an early Christian. And the fact that Matthew and Luke simply dropped the whole episode shows they considered it unnecessary to make that point.

In fact the evidence is that, after Mark, the gospel writers actually *downplayed* the depth of animosity between Jesus and his family, making it into a simple lack of understanding that could be transmogrified into the glorious concept that those who follow Jesus are one big happy family.

In the synoptic gospels Mary disappears completely from the story after the snub from Jesus. Only in John's Gospel does she reappear (unnamed) as a witness to her son's crucifixion. Such an omission in the synoptics is remarkable if she had really been among the women watching Jesus' death. But which is correct: was she there or not? We have no way of knowing.

There is another omission that worried Christians from the very beginning: the risen Jesus never appears to his mother. Even if the postresurrection stories are complete fiction, we would expect such a scene to be included; after all, he allegedly appeared to the "other Mary" who was with Mary Magdalene at the tomb. The only explanation is that the coolness between Jesus and his mother was genuine: either he chose not to appear to her, or the authors saw no need to pretend he did. This should have been the final nail in the coffin for Catholic Mariolatry.

Great Expectations

Many, both in academic and alternative circles, consider Jesus' family to have been intimately involved in his mission, perhaps even grooming him from birth for his momentous adult role. Obviously the apparent friction between him and his family presents a big problem for such theories.

Some suggest that Jesus was brought up in the expectation that he would fulfill an important role but his own understanding of it differed from his family's and led to a rift.[58] While such a scenario would reconcile the contradiction between his family's expectations and the frostiness between them once Jesus became an established preacher, it is only needed on the assumption that the family *had* such expectations. For these theories to work there has to be something to the nativity stories, even if hidden behind the myth that has come down to us—i.e., that Jesus had in some way been singled out as special from birth. But we know there is no reason to take anything in the nativity and childhood stories seriously (and many reasons not to).

The most recent advocate of the theory that Jesus' mission was a predominantly family, *dynastic* endeavor (in *The Jesus Dynasty*, 2006) is James D. Tabor of the University of North Carolina (who was co-director of the excavation of the Cave of John the Baptist along with Shimon Gibson). Comparing our thoughts on this issue with his is also a good illustration of how taking one position on one issue can affect our overall view of Jesus. Tabor accepts the basic veracity of the nativity stories and the Gospels' genealogies, and because he does, he ends up with a completely different idea of Jesus from those, like ourselves, who don't.

Tabor accepts that Jesus was a genuine descendant of King David, and that his mission aimed at establishing him as the king of the Jews. The twelve disciples were intended to be his regional officials, and after Jesus was killed, his brother James, as next in line to the throne, succeeded him as leader. Tabor summarizes his conclusions (his emphasis): "*Rather than being the founder of a church, Jesus was a claimant to a throne.*"[59]

The common ground between our position and Tabor's, however, is that John the Baptist was a much more influential figure on both Jesus and the movement the latter came to control (which was basically the one that John had set up), and that his true role has been deliberately obscured by the Church from the earliest days.

However, there is an apparent paradox. If there was friction between Jesus and his family, why after his death/ascension did the family take over the leadership of his movement, at least in Jerusalem? In particular, how did Jesus' brother James the Just—never mentioned once as a disciple throughout the Gospels—become the head of the Jerusalem Church? (Even if the Catholic explanation that he was Jesus' cousin is correct, the same question applies.)

There are two Jameses in the Gospels' list of disciples, but neither can be Jesus' brother. The first, along with John, is one of the two sons of Zebedee who were among the first to join the group, and the other is known as James the Younger (or the Less), presumably to distinguish him from the first, and is also identified as the son of Alphaeus. Some, such as James Tabor and Robert Eisenman, have argued that James the Just *was* one of the Twelve—disguised as either James, son of Zebedee, or James the Younger— but the gospel writers obscured his relationship with Jesus because they supported Paul's authority against the family's.

However, such a deliberate obfuscation would require too much coordination among the writers (or later editors) of not only the canonical texts, but also the other sources rejected from the New Testament. None of the apocryphal, gnostic, or other texts has Jesus' brother James as a disciple. The Gospel of Thomas, for example, has Christ telling the disciples to follow James after he has gone, but there is no suggestion that he was already a member of the inner circle—in fact Jesus tells the disciples to go to James, implying he is somewhere else, outside of their group. And, as we have seen, a tradition grew up in some early Christian circles that the disciple Thomas was a brother of Jesus—his twin, in fact—so they were hardly shy of including his brothers in their writings. If James really had been one of the Twelve, surely someone somewhere would have said so.

However, the very fact that researchers seek such disguised characters is based on a need to justify two assumptions: that Jesus *must* have been on good terms with his family (but why?), and that his family in general, and James in particular, must have been part of whatever it was Jesus was about (again, why?). Eisenman, for example, sees James the Just as being Jesus' "true heir and successor." [60]

We can dispense with the idea that James the Just was a member of the original group of disciples. But how then did he come to be effectively Jesus' successor as head of the movement in Jerusalem? We will return to the question in the aftermath of the crucifixion.

Jesus' attraction for his immediate circle of disciples is understandable, but what was it about either him or his message that made so many others flock to him? Conversely, what was it about him that made some oppose him and eventually seek to kill him? In order to answer these questions, we must now turn our attention to his public ministry during the early days in Galilee.

6

SIGNS AND WONDERS

In Galilee, Jesus' public mission took the form of miraculous healings and preaching. The way this is reported in the Gospels, the first was a "hook" for the second, drawing people in and establishing his credentials as a holy man. The crowds flocked to him because they had heard he could cure them or their relatives; only after he had proved his magical powers did he begin sermonizing. Although he is said to have performed other miracles that fly in the face of the laws of nature, such as walking on water and quelling a storm with a word, these were witnessed solely by his disciples. Even in the Gospels these marvels were not why the people clamored for Jesus.

Gerd Theissen has discerned a significant pattern in the narrative of the synoptic Gospels, primarily (as one would expect) Mark. The individual stories can be categorized into different types, two of the most important being, first, those about the cures, and second, "apothegms"—events that illustrate an aspect of Jesus' teaching or mission, such as a dispute with a Pharisee, the Mary and Martha episode, or the anointing by the unnamed sinner/Mary of Bethany. Something happens and is turned into a lesson or used to point up a moral. And as Theissen observes, the cure stories and apothegms are told in very different ways; indeed, the contrasts are striking.[1]

For a start, the stories of healing and exorcism in the synoptics could have come from any culture of that time; they are not particularly Christian or Jewish, being largely universal in their relevance and appeal, and generally there is no attempt to link them with Jesus' overall message. On the other hand, the apothegms are by definition Christian: their whole purpose is to illustrate his teaching. The stories of healing and exorcism are nearly always set in a specifically named town or village, whereas with the apothegms the location is much vaguer, as "in Simon the Leper's house" or "in a certain village." Although the disciples are sometimes present at healings and exorcisms, they are largely anonymous; in the apothegms, particular disciples play specific roles, besides others who follow or are close to Jesus, such as Mary and Martha of Bethany: "All those named [in apothegms] are among Jesus' closest associates."[2]

Theissen's conclusion—and an alternative explanation is hard to find—is that the differences in the way the two sets of stories are told reflect the different ways in which they were passed down until they were put together in the Gospels, beginning with Mark. The stories of healing and exorcism were passed on *outside* the Jesus movement, whereas the apothegms were handed down *within* what became the very early Church. The teachings were probably passed on by the earliest proclaimers of his message: John, Peter, the sons of Zebedee, Mary and Martha of Bethany, and so on. So it seems that at a popular level Jesus was regarded as first and foremost a healer and exorcist, whereas within his movement his pronouncements and promises were more important.

The Enigmatic Teachings

Although many people today believe Jesus' teaching was the most important aspect of his life on earth, reconstructing exactly what he taught is probably the most problematic aspect of the Galilee mission, since it is obscured by so many layers of confusion.

The debate over the authenticity of individual sayings attributed to Jesus in the early sources—there are about five hundred in the first four centuries of Christian literature—has been endless, as have the attempts to use them to reconstruct and define his basic philosophy, theology, and ethical system. The results have often been startlingly contradictory, the only agreement being that a large percentage of the alleged sayings are not authentic and should be rejected. The big disagreement is about which ones.

Since the nineteenth century a basic division has been recognized between general wisdom or ethical teaching on the one hand, and apocalyptic warnings and declarations about the immediate future on the other. The two categories are not just different in style but actually contradictory, being based on entirely different premises. Wisdom sayings assume that this and subsequent generations will need this kind of moral instruction to improve themselves and their world, whereas apocalyptic teachings start from the premise that everything is about to change—initially for the worse but ultimately for the better—in ways completely outside human control.

Some scholars (such as Burton L. Mack) argue that only the wisdom teaching is authentic and reject all the apocalyptic material as later additions. Others, such as Rudolf Bultmann, keep the end-times passages and reject the sayings. The very same source material has prompted theories as diverse as that Jesus was a Cynic philosopher, a Buddhist, a Pharisee, an Essene, a pacifist, and a rebel. The same words of Jesus have been used to portray him as a king and as a champion of the workingman. The identical teaching has inspired socialists and extreme right-wingers, and is used to justify both wars and conscientious objections to the same conflicts.

In fact it is temptingly easy to make Jesus into more or less anything by a simple process: if you want him to be a Buddhist—the theory of German researcher Holger Kersten—pull out the parts with an affinity to Buddhist teaching, exclude the rest, and there you have it: he's a Buddhist. Researchers and scholars are rarely conscious of such bias and usually take care to justify their choices. However, because there is so little available information, inevitably they end up with circular reasoning: material is excluded simply because it fails to fit their theory.

Paradoxically, therefore, a quest for the real Jesus may actually be hampered by focusing too much on his teachings. After all, if the greatest minds in New Testament studies are at loggerheads about what to include and reject, what chance do the rest of us have? Perhaps it makes more sense to work the other way round, to look at what he did and see which of the teachings attributed to him best fit his actions.

Indeed, surprising as it might seem today, Jesus' appeal sprang not from his teaching but from his deeds. To the Galileans his healing was significant; the image of Jesus surrounded by an awestruck and silent crowd, as at the Sermon on the Mount, may well be a complete misapprehension.

Many of the ethical injunctions attributed to Jesus in the Gospels did not originate with him anyway, even the much-loved line in Matthew: "In everything, do to others what you would have them do to you, for this sums up the Law and the Prophets."[3] The second-century BCE Book of Tobit has "Do to no one what you would not want done to you," and the Jewish teacher Hillel the Elder, approximately a generation before Jesus, rendered the thought as, "Whatever is hateful to you, do not do to your fellow man. That is the whole Law."[4] Similarly, Jesus' "Love your neighbor as yourself" comes from Leviticus, having underpinned Jewish ethics for centuries.[5]

Another basic problem is that some traditional Christian ideas about Jesus' teaching are based on simple misreadings of the Gospels. Take, for example, his famous declaration or warning "If anyone causes one of these little ones—those who believe in me— to stumble, it would be better for them if a large millstone were hung around their neck and they were thrown into the sea."[6] How many people realize—as New Testament scholars and theologians have known for decades—that the "little ones" are not children but his *disciples*? In all four Gospels Jesus frequently calls them his "little ones" or "children,"[7] and in Mark the line comes in a section about the disciples remaining steadfast and not "stumbling" (losing faith) either through lack of resolve or because of others' influence. Jesus is saying that anyone who causes them to lose faith in him would suffer a fate worse than drowning, as opposed to those who accept them (who will be rewarded), as is apparent when read in the full context.

Matthew moved this sentence to a later section where Jesus stands a child before his disciples to demonstrate that unless they become like children, they will never get into the kingdom of heaven, which slightly confuses the issue, although the words about the millstone are still obviously about the disciples.[8] But Matthew clearly understood Mark's original meaning, since he included the words "one of these little ones who is known to be my disciple."[9] In Luke it even becomes an injunction to the disciples not to cause "little ones" to stumble, otherwise *they* will be worse than drowned (there are no children at all in this scene, so it makes very little sense).[10]

The whole notion that Jesus had a special love for and offered special protection to children has been extrapolated from an entirely false premise, although it still features in sermons the world over as evidence of his child-friendly message.

Similarly, the modern Christian idea that Jesus taught us to respect and encourage happy families gets precious little support from the Gospels. As we have seen, Jesus' relationship with his own close relatives seems to have been at best fraught. And he clearly expected his disciples to leave their homes and families to follow him, as Matthew has Jesus state, "Anyone who loves their father or mother more than me is not worthy of me; anyone who loves a son or daughter more than me is not worthy of me."[11] Luke goes further: "If anyone comes to me and does not hate father and mother, wife and children, brothers and sisters—yes, even life itself—such a person cannot be my disciple"[12]—which is chillingly reminiscent of the demands of modern cult leaders. Despite the evidence to the contrary, Christians today insist that a major focus of their religion is the encouragement of family values. But although home and hearth may indeed be sacrosanct to modern Christians, any connection with Jesus' own teaching is entirely imaginary—and really rather ironic.

Sifting through all the contradictions can be a thankless task. How does Jesus' being the "prince of peace" square with his reported declaration (from Q):

Do you think I came to bring peace on earth? No, I tell you, but division. From now on there will be five in one family divided against each other, three against two and two against three. They will be divided, father against son and son against father, mother against daughter and daughter against mother, mother-in-law against daughter-in-law and daughter-in-law against mother-in-law.[13]

(The last sentence is a paraphrase of a prophecy in Micah, which Matthew has Jesus quote directly.) Matthew has Jesus say he comes to bring "a sword" instead of "division," but Luke is probably more faithful to Q as Luke's wording also appears in the Gospel of Thomas. In any case the gist is the same.[14]

As the "not peace but division/sword" statement embarrassingly clashes with the popular image of Jesus the pacifist, it is usually assumed to be symbolic, often even by Christians who accept the whole Gospel package as genuine. However, this highlights another huge potential problem: taking a pronouncement Jesus made about a specific situation and turning it into a universal truth. For example, Hugh J. Schonfield suggested that Jesus' pacifist statements in Galilee—love your enemies, pray for your persecutors, and so on—were intended to reassure Herod Antipas' men that he posed no threat and to warn the populace to do nothing that would precipitate action against them.[15] In other words, they were only *temporary* instructions for that phase of the mission, to prevent its being nipped in the bud, like John the Baptist's.

It is not possible to say conclusively that Schonfield is correct, but his theory is plausible. It might well be a grave error to take the "pacifist" statements at face value. And, as we will see, in the final days in Jerusalem, Jesus undoubtedly acted in ways that would inevitably have precipitated violent outbursts among the people—not necessarily with his approval, although he must have been aware of the likelihood of trouble.

One of the fundamental questions for anyone searching for the real Jesus is whether his teachings agreed with or contradicted Jewish Law and customs, another area of massive contradiction in the Gospels. Jesus is said to claim to work strictly within the Law, commanding his followers to obey it:

Do not think that I have come to abolish the Law or the Prophets; I have not come to abolish them but to fulfill them. Truly I tell you, until heaven and earth disappear, not the smallest letter, not the least stroke of the pen, will by any means disappear from the Law until everything is accomplished.[16]

But elsewhere he defies at least certain aspects, even instructing his disciples to contravene the Law; for example, the "cult leader" injunction to abandon one's family flies directly in the face of the fifth commandment. So does his teaching on divorce, in which he insists on stricter rules than those decreed by Moses.[17] Whether these represent a genuine inconsistency in Jesus' teaching, or were introduced by the first generations of Christians (who were embroiled in the controversy over how Jewish the new religion should be), is impossible to tell.

For all these reasons, sifting through Jesus' teachings saying by saying to decide which to keep and which to reject would be both lengthy and fruitless. However, some aspects of his teaching are worthy of special attention.

Pungent and Absurd

Earlier we looked at the similarity between Jesus' teachings in Q and the punchy style of the Cynic *parresia*. Q was made up of a series of aphorisms and analogies, each built around a single short, terse statement, such as "Treat others as you would be treated." As Burton L. Mack summarizes:

> These sayings are not uniquely brilliant, but they are pungent. Some observations are keen, others are mildly humorous, and some are laughable in the sense that the inversion of standard practices or attitudes has been pressed to the point of absurdity. Life in general is under review and conventional values are under critique.[18]

As it is hard to imagine a later follower using such a technique to codify Jesus' teaching, it probably does reflect his own style, which perhaps he copied from the Cynics. But what does it tell us about Jesus' religious and social philosophy? Mack summarizes all that can be said:

> One has only the sense that simplicity is better than pretension, that realistic assessment is a better guide than status, and that life would be more rewarding if lived another way. In general it is clear that sympathies lie with the poor, the least, the humble, the

servant, and those consigned to positions without privilege, more than with their social opposites. But more than this cannot be said without additional information.[19]

In the synoptic Gospels Jesus characteristically delivers his ideas in the form of the parables—Greek *parabole*, literally "setting beside" or an analogy—stories illustrating a moral or ethical point. The style is so unusual that it probably reflects Jesus' customary practice.

In Mark the parables "both reveal and conceal."[20] Jesus may deliver a parable in public, but he has to explain it to his disciples in private: "With many similar parables Jesus spoke the word to them [the crowd], as much as they could understand. He did not say anything to them without using a parable. But when he was alone with his own disciples, he explained everything."[21] This serves two purposes in Mark: the parables set out Jesus' teaching, but also explain why the Jews failed to understand and ultimately rejected him. But why deliberately make the message incomprehensible and then condemn people for not getting it? In Mark's hands the parables seem a kind of test set by Jesus to see who should be saved and who should not, contradicting Mark's basic position that Jesus came to offer salvation to all mankind and that an individual's faith and deeds determined his or her fate; understanding the minutiae of the Kingdom of God was never part of the deal.

Could Mark have gotten it wrong? Did the full explanation come first, before the parable was given as an aide-mémoire? That would make much more sense. In which case, were the parables ever delivered to outsiders at all? In the Gospels Jesus rarely makes public statements; when he does it is usually in the context of a dispute with his Jewish opponents. What appears to be the major exception, the Sermon on the Mount, is really a convenient device used by Matthew to incorporate Q into his story. And despite the popular impression, even the way Matthew tells it is very different: "Now when Jesus saw the crowds, he went up on a mountainside and sat down. His disciples came to him, and he began to teach them."[22] Instead of preaching to the crowd, Jesus is actively avoiding them. Matthew is implying that he revealed his innermost teaching only to his disciples, while the more general message was confined to the simple and sensational: the Kingdom of God is almost here and will be manifested through him.

Gnostic Secrets

Although Mark's explanation of the secret aspect of the parables makes little sense, the notion that Jesus taught certain things privately to his disciples runs through all the early Christian works. All the sources make it clear that there were at least two levels to Jesus' teachings: the public message, which probably consisted of only the most general awareness of the imminence of the Kingdom of God—and private lessons for the disciples. And of course there is the "Secret Gospel" of Mark, which according to Clement of Alexandria had passages removed because Mark considered them for the eyes of initiates only.

Clement said there were (at least to the Alexandrian church) *three* levels to Jesus' teaching: one for public consumption, as in the canonical Mark; more spiritual wisdom for initiates only, as in the Secret Gospel; and a third category that could never be committed to writing, being presumably reserved for the most elevated followers and passed on orally.

The issue of secrecy is relevant to whether we should include the gnostic books in Jesus' teaching. Most commentators have dismissed them as of no value whatsoever, being at best much later extrapolations going off in directions that Jesus never intended and at worst complete flights of fancy with absolutely no connection to him. However, the situation isn't quite that simple.

Clearly the ludicrously complicated and abstruse gnostic concepts had been grafted onto Jesus' teaching in some of the Nag Hammadi texts, but as even the antignostic Ian Wilson acknowledges,

It is most unlikely that Christian Gnosticism sprang out of nothing. Just as . . . the Gnostics' favourite themes are not totally alien to the gospels, so there is likely to have been at least something in Jesus' original teaching that provided the root-stock to which Gnosticism's weeds latched themselves.[23]

They may have developed these ideas in their own idiosyncratic way, but the core is based on a genuine connection to Jesus—and the bridge between the two may lie in the secret teachings. In his *Are These the Words of Jesus?* (1990) Wilson suggests that Jesus' inner teachings were essentially gnostic, and that "leaks" gave rise to the complex ideas incorporated into the gnostic gospels.

The problem lies in teasing out the original kernel from the mass of wild surmise and bizarre cosmologies superimposed by the gnostics. Wilson identifies one of their recurring themes that seems to have originated in Jesus' secret teaching: the focus on a sacred androgyny in which the differences between male and female disappear. For example, he cites certain passages in the now-lost gnostic Gospel of the Egyptians, of which—although it was suppressed as heretical—parts survived by being quoted by Clement of Alexandria. Although there is very little to go on, scholars assign this text to the late first or early second century. The earlier date would mean it is roughly the same age as the New Testament Gospels.[24]

In the Gospel of the Egyptians Jesus talks to a disciple named Salome about the need for men and women to become neither male nor female, which is also in the Gospel of Thomas. And again, in a late second-century Church letter (incorrectly attributed to Clement of Rome) Jesus is quoted in almost exactly the same words.[25] But which came first, or did they both draw on a single source—now lost?

Intriguingly, Origen stated that the Carpocratians—the sect that stole the Secret Gospel of Mark—"follow Salome." Although a disciple of that name appears in the canonical Mark, but in that Gospel alone, judging from the extract quoted by Clement of Alexandria she seems to have had a more substantial role in the secret version. The appearance of the disciple Salome in the Gospel of the Egyptians may imply that certain gnostic sects shared a common heritage that they believed originated with her.[26] Given the other major strand that runs through most of the known gnostic gospels, in which Mary Magdalene reigns supreme over the disciples, could Jesus have reserved special teaching for women?

The Core Message

Having examined the style of Jesus' teaching, is there any way of working out exactly what his message was? Sadly, without wasting an enormous amount of time and energy, it seems not—at least not definitively—but a couple of core concepts are essential to our understanding of the man believed to be the Christ.

According to Mark, Jesus' fundamental message was expressed in his declaration "The time has come. The Kingdom of God has come near. Repent and believe the good news!"[27] What exactly was the "Kingdom of God"? A new kingdom of Israel under his rule? Or, in Jesus' words in John's Gospel, was it a "kingdom not of this world"?

First used in the Book of Daniel, the original Aramaic of the term "Kingdom of God" should really be rendered "kingship of God," which subtly changes the meaning: "the emphasis is on the rule of God, rather than on the territory where this rule is exercised."[28] This emphasis matches Jewish end-times expectation: God would not merely restore Israel but establish his rule over all nations. It was both a literal kingdom and the decisive change in the earthly order, the culmination of God's promise.

There can be little doubt that Jesus was declaring that the manifestation of the Kingdom of God was imminent, and that he himself would make it happen, a message made explicit when he says some of those he was addressing would not "taste of death" before the Kingdom arrived.[29] As Morna D. Hooker writes:

> Part of the difficulty is the fact that it contains an apparently unfulfilled prophecy, since, almost twenty centuries after the words were spoken, there is little sign of the Kingdom of God being established in the world, let alone of its coming "with power," a phrase which indicates the finality and universality of its coming. Was Jesus then wrong? Many of the contorted explanations which exegetes have managed to twist out of these words have been based on the conviction that Jesus could not have been mistaken, and that some fulfilment of his words must therefore be found in history.[30]

So the essence of Jesus' teaching is clear: his mission was to prepare people for, and then bring about, the Kingdom of God as
prophesied in Jewish scriptures. What is not clear is how he intended to do it. Would he oust the current regime in the usual
way—by force? Did he expect that through some momentous act of
his that God would manifest himself in the world? Or would it be
something less dramatic: if he managed to persuade the people of
Israel to live righteously, would this create the right conditions for
God's intervention?

What can be said with certainty is that, however the Kingdom
might be established, just preaching it had real political implications.
As the American professor of Jewish History Ellis Rivkin put it,
"God's kingdom in was Rome's kingdom out!"[31] There was no way
Jesus' preaching could be disentangled from politics, even if he had
no *overt* political intent or agenda.

Of the various titles the Gospels gave Jesus, the two most
interesting—after "Messiah," which we have already discussed—
are "Son of God" and "Son of Man." Were these used during his
lifetime, and, more important, were they how he described himself?

It does seem that Jesus did describe himself as the "Son of God"
(*Huios Theou*), meaning he had a special relationship with Yahweh.
But does this necessarily mean he used the term as in the Christian
tradition? Jews of his time probably would have taken it to mean
royalty, as the Old Testament described the kings of Israel and
David's descendants as "sons of God."[32] Non-Jews would have immediately associated it with the Roman emperor, who was also
considered a son of the gods.[33] (There is, however, a third interpretation, based on comparisons with Greek magical texts, as we will
see shortly.) But in the end we can argue about which interpretation
fits Jesus until water turns into wine, but we can never be sure
which one is right.

A more interesting phrase is "Son of Man" (*bar nasha*), which all
four Gospels suggest was Jesus' preferred term for himself. Although
simply meaning "man," the Book of Daniel uses it to describe a divinely sent being who was "like a son of man"[34] (i.e., he had a
human form while being something more), to whom God would
give dominion over the entire world, establishing a kingdom that

would endure for all time. This seems to be where Jesus first found the phrase, using it as a kind of title for himself, as *the* Son of Man. Maybe it was an adroit way of avoiding problems with the authorities for claiming any of the popular messianic titles.[35]

That is as much as can be said with any certainty about Jesus' teachings, but what about his deeds, particularly the miracles?

Casting Out Demons

The overwhelming majority of miracles ascribed to Jesus in the Gospels and other early writings are healings and exorcisms (although the dividing line is thin).

There was nothing unique in the fact or manner of Jesus' exorcisms: Josephus, for example, mentions witnessing such dramatic healings, and one, which can be dated to 67 or 68 CE, took place in the presence of the future emperor Vespasian. A Jew named Eleazar used commands, incantations, and herbs, all of which were supposedly derived from Solomon, to drive out demons from possessed men.[36]

What is unusual is that in Mark a recurring feature is that the demons recognize Jesus as being from God, but he commands them to be silent. Although we might be tempted to think that Mark contrived Jesus' injunctions to silence to fit his cherished messianic secret (especially as it makes no sense internally: if Jesus succeeded in his demands for silence, how did Mark know about them?). But it seems that Mark's explanation conceals something far more significant. He used the idea of a messianic secret to account for something mysterious or even unacceptable about the way Jesus worked. The command he says Jesus gave to the spirits, "Be silent!" (*Phimotheti!*), was common in magical acts (not just exorcisms), being "used in the ancient world for binding people and demons."[37]

Jesus' command was intended to freeze the power of the spirits— *not* to prevent them from blurting out his identity. And although Mark tried to give it a less occult gloss, the specific word suggests that his source preserved a genuine memory of how Jesus operated— essentially casting out demons using a contemporary magical formula.

Neither was there anything unique about Jesus' cures of physical ailments. Many others were alleged to do more or less the same—even using the same techniques—both within and outside the Jewish world.

In his healing of the deaf man in the Decapolis, in Mark,[38] the method may sound novel, but again, as Andrew Lincoln notes, "Jesus' use of spittle . . . is in line with the practice of healers of the time, in which spittle was widely held to have curative powers."[39] Tacitus records a similar cure performed by Vespasian in Alexandria in which he healed a blind man by rubbing his saliva into his eyes.[40] On other occasions Jesus touches those he is healing, or mutters invocations over them—well-known practices of his day. Such cures—even including raisings from the dead—were ascribed to rabbis, such as Hanina ben Dosa, a fellow Galilean and near contemporary.[41]

There are a couple of occasions—the Syro-Phoenician woman's daughter and the centurion's servant—when Jesus performs "absent healing," curing someone who was not physically present. But this ability, too, was ascribed to others, for example Hanina ben Dosa, and it is still a standard practice among today's New Age and spiritual healers.

There is sometimes, although not always, the implicit (and sometimes explicit) understanding that disease and physical infirmity are the result of sin; Jesus heals by forgiving the sinner. However, this was by no means a new or uncommon idea: both Jews and Gentiles believed it at that time.[42]

Jesus says that he even finds it impossible to heal where there is no faith, and there are episodes in which he fails to perform. The fact that the Gospels acknowledge this at all—no matter how briefly—means it must be true; they would have been unlikely to invent something that conflicts with the idea of a world-beating messianic figure.

The most extreme cures are the three cases of resurrection from physical death, only one of which appears in all the synoptic Gospels—the raising of the daughter of Jairus, a synagogue official in Galilee. The other two are unique to specific Gospels: the raising of the son of the widow of Nain in Luke, and that of Lazarus in John.

The Lazarus episode is conspicuous, as the Secret Gospel of Mark suggests his "raising from the dead" was actually some kind of symbolic death and rebirth ritual. The Fourth Gospel either got it wrong, ingenuously presenting it as a literal resurrection, or deliberately hid the real meaning. Owing to the ritualistic element, we will deal with this event in detail separately.

Luke's story of the raising of the widow's son seems to be basically folklore about Jesus, based on an Old Testament antecedent. Nain is between Endor and Shunem, where Elisha is also said to have raised a woman's son from the dead.[43] Mark and Matthew make no mention of Jesus' act, probably because it never happened and was modeled on the older tale. Clearly, though, raising the dead associated Jesus with the venerable religious figures of the old days, which is precisely Luke's point: by raising the young man, Jesus is recognized as a prophet.[44]

The raising of Jairus' daughter, told in Mark and followed by Matthew and Luke,[45] includes apparently authentic circumstantial details, particularly Jesus' Aramaic command to the girl, "*Talitha koum!*"—literally "Lamb, get up!"—which suggests that it was remembered by an eyewitness. But did Jesus really bring a young girl back from the dead, or was she merely very sick and assumed to be dead?

The stories of Jesus raising the dead are less impressive when analyzed closely. However, the amount of space the Gospels allot to the healings and exorcisms during the Galilee phase shows that Jesus' reputation among the people was based on these supernatural abilities. As we have seen from Gerd Theissen's analysis, the healing stories were passed on at a popular level *outside* his movement. But does this mean that these miracles really happened?

The problem in answering this question is that the accounts we have today were written long after the event by people who were not present, and while undoubtedly they were reported in good faith, without credible firsthand testimony it is impossible to ascertain exactly what happened.

Any analysis of the miracles will always depend on personal bias—for or against the possibility of the paranormal. Some accept that miracles can and do happen, that faith and spiritual healing work. Others would explain such phenomena as being essentially psychosomatic or psychological, or an effect of the still poorly understood connection between mind and body. Ian Wilson, for example, noting that hypnosis can be used to treat *physical* ailments—especially skin conditions, which seem to have been something of a speciality with Jesus—argues that he performed his cures through hypnosis.[46] Those who deem any form of unconventional cure impossible argue that the Gospels' accounts are pure fiction, based on folktales about Jesus that sprung up after his death. Some might even suggest the healings were shameless fakes to pull in the punters.

However, there is no need to become bogged down in that controversy, because whatever the explanation of the healings, the important point for present purposes is that nothing about them was unique to Jesus. Others at the time, both Jewish and pagan, were reported to perform cures and drive out demons using exactly the same techniques. So whatever explanation we prefer for Jesus—real, psychological, hypnotic, folklore, or fake—we must also apply to them, and vice versa.

Angels and Demons

Isolated examples of language such as Jesus' command "*Phimotheti!*" being used when casting out demons have long been recognized; indeed, as far back as 1922 the German specialist in ancient Greek documents, Friedrich Preisigke, explored some of the parallels between his cures and contemporary magical and pagan ideas. But it was in the mid-1970s that two academics published major studies on the correspondences between Jesus' miracles and the formulae found in magical texts from the contemporary Hellenistic world—especially Egypt of the Greek and Roman period.

The two groundbreaking academics were John M. Hull in *Hellenistic Magic and the Synoptic Tradition* (1974) and Morton Smith in *Jesus the Magician* (1978), whose discovery of the Secret Gospel of Mark, and the implications of the ritual it apparently described, naturally led him in this direction. As the two researchers proved, the correspondences between Jesus' miracles and the magical texts are undeniable: in fact, they often used exactly the same words. It is hardly surprising that healing diseases and exorcising evil spirits should be common ground between Jesus and pagan magicians, given that overcoming sickness and infirmity has always been a basic human aspiration, and that the belief, in that time and culture, in the reality of malign spirits was widespread. But it *is* unexpected to find such specific details of the techniques and words Jesus used in texts that predated him and came from another culture.

As Josephus' story of the exorcist Eleazar shows, Judaism had its own strong magical traditions, mostly supposedly derived from the esoteric wisdom of Solomon. But the magic in the Gospels is recognizably not from Jewish but Greek-based traditions. Apparently Jesus was happy to employ *pagan* techniques. However, because magical practitioners deal in secret knowledge and are always seeking to acquire more, occult ideas are readily, if covertly, exchanged between cultures, and given the blending of Hellenistic and Jewish cultures, it would hardly be surprising if Greek and Egyptian magical practices were seized on by Jewish sorcerers and exorcists. Certain magical Jewish texts include "workings" to create a mystical union between the magician and a familiar spirit that involve very un-Judaic concepts.[47] Even so, the indication that *Jesus* should be part of such a dubious scene does come as something of a shock, implying that he had been trained in what we today would consider some very dark arts. And in that case, when and by whom?

Both Hull and Smith also point out that the earliest Jewish traditions about Jesus claimed he was a magician, and even that he was executed for being a sorcerer. Sorcery was clearly one of the authorities' complaints about him during his lifetime, as can be seen from the accusation that he used demons to cast out demons. Less obvious to a modern reader is the Jewish leaders' objections to Jesus' healing on the Sabbath: as Hull shows, the objection was not to the healing as such but to Jesus' use of magical operations on the Sabbath.[48]

In any case the fact that Jesus used the same techniques as the other holy men and magicians presents a problem for conventional Christians who believe Jesus healed simply through grace. But if he did so, why copy other healers, as in his use of saliva? Even if it were merely a canny use of a psychological prop to encourage the faith that moves mountains, why would Christ need to use it?

Overturning Nature

Added to the cures and exorcisms are the miracles where Jesus appears to control and subvert the forces of nature—walking on water, quelling storms with a command, changing the substance of liquids, and multiplying food. There is a significant difference between these miracles and the cures: they are reported only when the disciples alone were there to witness them. Jesus never performs them in front of crowds (or if, as with the turning of the water into wine, other people are present, only the disciples are allowed to know the miraculous nature of the occurrence). This seems rather suspicious. Were these stories just invented?

Although the wedding at Cana is a major event in John's Gospel—the very first miracle that Jesus performs—it is conspicuous by its absence from the synoptic Gospels. The story goes as follows: Soon after recruiting his first disciples, Jesus goes with them to Cana, a small town in the hills of Galilee—generally accepted as the modern Khirbet Qana, about ten miles north of Nazareth—to attend a wedding at which his mother is also present. We are never told the identity of the bride and groom. There he turns water into wine, to the predictable delight of the partygoers (and, given his reputation, probably also his own), then returns to Judea.[49]

The Fourth Gospel calls this "first of the signs" (oemeion), meaning portent or omen. It is noticeably different from Jesus' other miracles: he does it at the bidding of his mother, and there is a strong suggestion, especially in John, that he is reluctant to do it, retorting to Mary's request, "Woman, why do you involve me? My hour has not yet come."

Various attempts have been made to extrapolate information about Jesus from this story. For example, as wedding parties at that time were held only by the rich, Jesus' presence on their guest list suggests he was well heeled. Then there is the suggestion that the wedding was Jesus' own, famously proposed in The Holy Blood and the Holy Grail by Baigent, Leigh, and Lincoln as evidence for their claim that Jesus was married to Mary Magdalene.[50] As it was normally the job of the host—in practice the groom's family—to provide the food and wine, the argument is that as Jesus provided the wine, and at his mother's bidding, he must have been the groom. Baigent, Leigh, and Lincoln also point to the fact that the master of the banquet, on tasting the wine, commended the groom on keeping the best until last, showing that Jesus, who had provided the wine, was the groom.

However, Jesus' response to his mother—basically "What's that got to do with me?"—acknowledges that he, as a guest, was not expected to provide the wine. And there is no reason to suppose that the MC's words were addressed to Jesus, as it is clear that nobody knew he had provided the wine miraculously. Everyone would have assumed the groom did so by normal means.

The "Christ's Wedding" theory may in fact fall at the first hurdle, as it assumes the story was based on a real event. Sadly, perhaps the situation is quite different. First, why is the story only in John's Gospel? Surely it is too important for the others to ignore. So if it happened, why do they leave it out—and what was John's source? As nobody apart from Jesus and his mother, not even the disciples, was aware of what had happened at the time, one or both of them must have mentioned it, but in that case why wasn't the story more widely known, ending up in the other Gospels? And as Jesus' first-ever miracle, it is inconceivable that the other evangelists could have known about it and not thought it worth including.

In fact the real inspiration seems clear. Turning water into wine was firmly the province of the Greek god of wine Dionysus (and his Roman counterpart Bacchus). In abundant and widespread pagan myths, sometimes water turns to wine, sometimes empty but sealed jars are found to be filled with wine. The story was known in the Greek parts of Palestine; in fact one of the legends of Dionysus turning water into wine was related during the annual festival held in his honor in the coastal city of Sidon.[51]

The parallel is acknowledged by most, if not all, specialists on John's Gospel.[52] For example, Andrew Lincoln notes, "The closest parallels to the actual miracle and its significance are in fact found in the Dionysus legends,"[53] and Marvin W. Meyer (director of the Coptic Magical Texts Project of the Institute for Antiquity and Christianity in Claremont, California) points out, "Jesus performs a Dionysian 'sign' by changing water into wine."[54] This was no coincidence. Ben Witherington III suggests, "It is possible that the

Evangelist or his source had adopted or adapted a Hellenistic and pagan miracle story and applied it to Jesus."[55] Even the early Church seems to have been well aware of the parallel, for the Cana episode was read out as part of the Epiphany liturgy on January 6, the old pagan feast of Dionysus.[56]

How did a legend associated with a pagan god end up in the New Testament? As we have seen, the Fourth Gospel draws a few parallels between Jesus and pagan deities, which would have been much more obvious to his audience than they are today.

C. H. Dodd made the interesting suggestion that the Cana tale began as a parable told by Jesus but somewhere during the process of transmission was mistaken for a real event.[57] Dodd pointed out that it incorporates two of the recurring themes used by Jesus in his parables: weddings, brides, and bridegrooms; and wine and vineyards. He may have based such a parable on the Dionysus legend, or the gospel writer could have added the pagan motif as he did with other episodes. Sadly, we can discount the story of the wedding at Cana. It seems it simply never happened.

Much more dramatic is the occasion (in the synoptic Gospels) when, during one of the many crossings of the Sea of Galilee and while Jesus is asleep, a violent storm erupts, terrifying the disciples. He wakes up, commands the storm to stop, and the elemental tumult abruptly subsides. The disciples are amazed.[58] As the Sea of Galilee is prone to sudden storms that abate almost instantly, local weather might explain the "miracle," but surely local fishermen would be only too familiar with all its moods, and presumably not too impressed by the storm's dying down coincidentally the moment Jesus spoke.

On two occasions Jesus is said to have fed enormous crowds with tiny amounts of food, miraculously multiplying loaves and fishes. In the synoptic Gospels it happens once to a gathering of five thousand, then again to four thousand, whereas John only has the first. It is a very different type of miracle and, as one of the few events before the entry into Jerusalem that features in both the synoptic and Johannine tradition, it is also marked out as important. Significantly, it is also the only miracle for which Morton Smith was unable to find a parallel in the Greek and Egyptian magical texts.

However, as we will see, although this was an enormously

significant event, it was no miracle.[59] What was important was the gathering of the multitude under Jesus' leadership, but the point had been lost (or deliberately mislaid) by the time the Gospels were written, so the writers attempt to explain it as a paranormal event.

The only miracle Jesus is said to have performed that has absolutely no point to it other than to demonstrate his power is the walking on water. Not only does it appear in all four Gospels, but in both traditions it is intimately linked with the feeding of the five thousand, which immediately precedes it. It, too, seems to have a hidden significance, suggesting a symbolic rather than literal event. We will discuss it when we analyze the feeding of the five thousand.

These miracles are less impressive than the healings and exorcisms. The only witnesses are the disciples, and it seems that each example is either fictional or has a symbolic rather than literal significance.

Jesus' Legacy

Besides memories of the miracles and his teaching, Jesus is said to have left another sort of legacy: he taught one prayer and performed two acts on which Christian sacraments were modeled, baptism and the Eucharist, the mystical communion with him through the symbolic—or, in the case of Catholic transubstantiation, believed to be the actual—eating of his body and drinking of his blood that is still at the heart of Christian worship. Based on his discovery of the Secret Gospel of Mark, Morton Smith has proposed a third ritual, a secret nocturnal ceremony in which his closest disciples were "taught the mystery of the Kingdom of God."

The Lord's Prayer is supposed to encapsulate the essentials of Jesus' teaching and is special to Christians because it is the only one that he personally taught his disciples. However, it may not have originated with Jesus at all.

The prayer itself comes from Q, since it is found in Matthew and Luke—although in entirely different contexts—but no other gospels. (So Mark and John knew nothing about it—very odd for such an apparently crucial part of Jesus' teaching.) Almost the full text of the familiar prayer is in Matthew, as part of the Sermon on the Mount, allegedly Jesus' lengthy discourse but which was, in reality, a convenient device for inserting a compilation of his sayings into the Gospel.[60]

Luke has a shorter version, with only seven of the ten lines, missing the parts about the Father's will being done on earth as it is in heaven and the plea to be delivered from evil.[61] But it is in a different context, happening "one day . . . in a certain place" when one of the disciples asks Jesus, "Lord, teach us to pray, the same as John taught his disciples." This is the literal translation that preserves the same ambiguity as in the original Greek.[62] It could be read either as a request for Jesus to teach them a prayer because the Baptist did it for his disciples, or for Jesus to teach them *the same prayer* that John taught.

Both Matthew and Luke took this passage from Q, but without an original copy of that book it is impossible to determine which has retained the original context and which has changed it. But some scholars—for example, James D. Tabor[63]—accept Luke's reading and conclude that the Lord's Prayer came from the Baptist. Given John's influence over Jesus, this would hardly be surprising.

Born Again

Obviously the Christian rite of baptism unequivocally owes its origins to John the Baptist, but the question of whether it came into Christianity via Jesus is not as straightforward as it might first appear.

There are two certainties. First, John the Baptist performed a ritual of immersion that was unique to him and so central to his movement that he was named after it. Until recently it had always been assumed that this rite was his innovation, but the discovery of the Suba cave suggests that baptism was a practice of the little-known sect to which he belonged and which had been around for a long time before him. Secondly, from the start baptism was the key rite of passage into the Christian religion: it was already established in Paul's Letters, within twenty or so years of the crucifixion. For the early apostles, persuading people to accept baptism was the sign that they had converted them to the Way. But it is Jesus' own relationship with baptism that is unclear. If the ritual started by John the

Baptist was being used by the first known worshippers of Jesus, then it must have played a part in his own movement: the first Christians baptized because Jesus did, not because John did.

However, in the synoptic Gospels, baptism is only ever associated with John, and the last we hear of it is when he baptizes Jesus. We never learn that Jesus baptized any of his disciples, or that they baptized the crowds that came to hear him. When he sends the Twelve out on the first missionary forays, baptism is not listed as one of their tasks. But then how did it reach the earliest Christians? The Fourth Gospel manages to get itself in a complete mess over this issue, referring at some points to Jesus baptizing but stating baldly at another, "it was not Jesus who baptized, but his disciples." [64]

So the ritual of baptism was at least transferred from John the Baptist to Paul via Jesus' disciples such as Peter, if not Jesus himself. But it would have been *John's* baptism, not his own. In fact after John the Baptist's arrest there was a very good reason for Jesus to discontinue public baptisms. Herod Antipas' men would have descended on him and his disciples like the wrath of hell for their blatant association with the "seditious" Baptist. Big public gatherings like those John had presided over at the Jordan were out of the question.

By the time the Gospels were written, there was another very sound reason to distance Jesus from baptism: the existence of a rival movement that upheld John the Baptist as the Messiah. Admitting that Jesus baptized would have been too potent a reminder that he had once been a disciple—and subordinate—of John, handing too much potential ammunition to the competition. But this assumes that the form of the ritual that the Jesus movement used, and which became Christian baptism, was the same as the one instituted by John the Baptist. Some argue that either Jesus or the early Christians changed it significantly.

Paul describes a mystical significance not explicitly recorded about the Baptist's rite, depicting it as an act, rather like Communion, in which the participant enters into a spiritual union with the resurrected and ascended Jesus—which for obvious reasons of chronology could never have been part of John's rite. However, the controversial issue is whether the whole idea of a mystical, experiential baptism was added after John the Baptist's time—his rite merely symbolizing spiritual cleanliness—and if so whether Jesus added it or it was an innovation of the early Church, perhaps of Paul himself.

Frustratingly for such a crucial rite, on the evidence available it is impossible to reach any firm conclusions about how Jesus himself may have used it.

The Mystery of the Kingdom of God

As we have already discussed, Morton Smith discovered a letter written by Clement of Alexandria toward the end of the second century that included extracts from what he described as a "more spiritual Gospel" by Mark, used by the inner ranks of the Christian community in Alexandria. As discussed in chapter 1, we believe that the weight of evidence shows that there were two versions of Mark's Gospel, one that was accessible to the wider Christian community and one reserved for those deemed to have reached a higher spiritual level. Indeed, the evidence is that the Secret Gospel was Mark's *original*, and that the one now in the New Testament was a version with all the "initiates only" material edited out. The allegation that Clement's letter was a hoax by (or perhaps on) Smith, whispered during his lifetime but voiced publicly since his death, simply does not stand up.

Only two extracts are quoted by Clement, the more significant of which describes Jesus bringing a youth back from the dead, in what is clearly the same story as the Fourth Gospel's raising of Lazarus (although in Secret Mark the youth is unnamed). What is different from John's Gospel is that the youth's resurrection is followed by an odd little drama between him and Jesus: "And after six days Jesus told him what to do, and in the evening the youth comes to him, wearing a linen cloth over his naked body. And he remained with him that night, for Jesus taught him the mystery of the Kingdom of God."[65]

This is totally unlike anything else in the Gospels or indeed in any early Christian source. But it does have an echo in a strange, unexplained aside in Mark's Gospel—the other synoptics ignore it, probably because they were just as baffled as everybody else—that, when

Jesus was arrested in the Garden of Gethsemane, "A young man, wearing nothing but a linen garment, was following Jesus. When they seized him, he fled naked, leaving his garment behind."[66] Where did this young man come from? Whatever it means, this weird little aside does provide support for Secret Mark, showing that youths wearing only linen cloths were not unknown in association with Jesus.

The passage in Secret Mark clearly refers to a ritual of some kind: held at night, requiring a period of preparation and a special garment. Its purpose is for the youth to be "taught the mystery of the Kingdom of God"—whatever that might mean.

"The Kingdom of God" is a phrase that, as we have seen, represented Jesus' essential message: "The time has come. The Kingdom of God has come near." Several explanations have been proposed, from establishing a secular rule under him as the King-Messiah, to the end of the world and its replacement by a new, perfect world into which only the elect will be admitted. All these suggestions, however, rely on the understanding that the coming of the Kingdom of God will affect everybody, which is at odds with the concept of something that has to be taught on a one-to-one basis over the course of a night. (It would take eons to get round to everybody if it did.)

But as Morton Smith observes, Secret Mark's phrase is "the *mystery* of the Kingdom of God," which is slightly different. The implication is that the nocturnal rite of the mystery of the Kingdom of God was one in which understanding of, or entry to, the Kingdom was imparted in a mystical way, analogous to the union with Jesus in the Christian Eucharist.

Morton Smith suggests this "mystery of the Kingdom of God" ritual was Jesus' baptism, the initiation into his following, the "baptism with the Holy Spirit" that was supposed to supersede John's watery baptism. However, although it was clearly an initiatory rite, it seems more likely to have been reserved just for the disciples, or even an inner circle. If it required Jesus' personal attention for an entire night, it seems he envisaged his movement remaining relatively small and select.

The clear implication is that the preceding "raising from the dead" was part of the ritual—a symbolic, rather than literal, death and rebirth that was a very common element of the mystery cults from all periods of history. Although Secret Mark, as quoted by Clement of Alexandria, portrays the two as separate events that just happened to involve the same youth, and the Fourth Gospel has no equivalent of the nocturnal ritual, the whole of this section was removed from the "public" version of Mark because it represented inner doctrine, suggesting that the youth had to "die" and return to qualify for participation in the rite of the mystery of the Kingdom of God.

The Ritual Paradox

There is one of Jesus' supposed deeds that not only stands at the core of Christian worship but is also fundamental to our understanding of him. Depending on the conclusion we reach about it, we are faced with one of two not merely different but *mutually exclusive* views of Jesus.

The Gospels tell us that Jesus instituted a sacrament in which, during a ceremonial communal meal, his followers symbolically ate his body and drank his blood in order to unite with him. But the drinking of any blood has always been a fundamental taboo for Jews, which is the whole basis of kosher foods. And drinking *human* blood is the direst abomination. Even as a metaphor, Jews would never contemplate such an abhorrence. Moreover, the symbolic eating of a god's body and drinking of his blood in order to enter into a mystical communion with him was a common element of the pagan mystery cults of the Greek and Roman world, which were practiced by the Greek communities in Palestine itself. It would have been anathema for a Jew to import those idolatrous practices into his religion.

Either Jesus was, at best, such a peculiar and unconventional—indeed heretical—Jew as to call into question whether he actually qualified as one at all, or the ritual had nothing to do with him. As the overwhelming view is that Jesus was a devout Jew, the vast majority of historians have gone for the second option.

In fact, the evidence is not only overwhelmingly in favor of Jesus' really presiding over such a meal and saying what the Gospels say he said, but actually demonstrates that it is the *most authentic* part of the Gospels, the very core of the Jesus movement and early Christianity. It was so fundamental that it is the *only* concept to appear virtually unchanged in not only all four Gospels but also in Paul's writings.

The synoptic tradition associates Jesus' institution of the Eucharist with the Last Supper, the final meal he took with his disciples in Jerusalem before his arrest and crucifixion. Although we will deal with the iconic Christian meal at the proper place in the story, at this point we are concerned with its meaning, and whether Jesus really instigated it—and if so with what significance he invested it.

The academic consensus is that since the Eucharist is both un-Jewish and so similar to mystery cult practices, it must owe nothing to Jesus but must have been developed by early Christians in the Gentile world, who were unconstrained by Jewish taboos and borrowed from the pagan rituals all around them. The academic finger points at Paul as the inventor of the Eucharist, as part of his campaign to adapt the fledgling religion for a Gentile audience. One of the major cults to use the blood/wine identification was that of Mithras, whose worship included the symbolic drinking of wine as bull's blood; one of its main centers was Tarsus—Paul's birthplace.[67]

Perhaps the foremost exponent of this view is Hyam Maccoby, who argued in *Paul and Hellenism* (1991) that "Paul, not Jesus, was the originator of the eucharist, and that the eucharist itself is not a Jewish, but an essentially Hellenistic rite, showing principal affinities . . . with the ritual meal of the mystery religions."[68] That might be the conventional position, but what is the actual evidence?

The earliest references to the Eucharist are in Paul's First Letter to the Corinthians, written in the midfifties CE, which predates the Gospels (with the possible exception of Mark): "Is not the cup of thanksgiving for which we give thanks a participation in [or "share of"] the blood of Christ? And is not the bread that we break a participation in the body of Christ?"[69] Later in the same letter he elaborates:

> The Lord Jesus, on the night he was betrayed, took bread, and when he had given thanks, he broke it and said, "This is my body, which is for you; do this in remembrance of me." In the same way, after supper he took the cup, saying, "This cup is the new covenant

in my blood; do this, whenever you drink it, in remembrance of me."[70]

Obviously this passage refers to the sacrament of Communion, clearly already well established as part of Christian worship, and to the Last Supper. (And tellingly, it is the only reference Paul ever makes to a specific event in Jesus' earthly life.)

However, as Albert Schweitzer pointed out as long ago as the late nineteenth century, there is evidence in Paul's own works against the argument that he made it up. For the indefatigable saint, the flesh-and-blood Jesus who had once walked Palestine was not only irrelevant but no longer existed physically anyway, having assumed a purely spiritual body that no one could eat. As Schweitzer put it, "To speak of the body and blood of Christ is, from the standpoint of the Apostle's doctrines, an absurdity."[71] And yet Paul *does* include it in his doctrine, although clearly he had to juggle his own logic to do so.

For Paul a mystical communion between the believer and the risen Christ was fundamental—the very definition of the faith—but that was achieved through *baptism*, needing no props such as bread and wine, nor their repeated ingestion to maintain the bond (any more than a Christian had to be baptized anew every day). In Schweitzer's words, "He cannot in his doctrine of the Supper bring the historic words into harmony with his Christology and yet is obliged to do so. The compromise remains for us obscure."[72] In other words, much as he wanted to, it was impossible for Paul to leave the Eucharist out of his grand scheme, because the fact that Jesus instituted such a rite—Schweitzer's "historic words"—was simply too well known.

For Paul, the significance of the "Lord's Supper" was Jesus' injunction that it should be held in memory of him, not that it induced a mystical union with him. This is the crucial *difference* between Paul's interpretation of the Eucharist and the similar rites of the mystery schools.

The next explanation of the Eucharist is in Mark's account of the Last Supper, which most theologians have to assume was influenced by Paul's innovation:

While they were eating, Jesus took bread, and when he had given thanks, he broke it and gave it to this disciples, saying, "Take it; this is my body."

Then he took the cup, and when he had given thanks, he gave it to them, and they all drank from it.

'This is my blood of the covenant which is poured out for many," he said to them, "Truly I tell you, I will not drink again of the fruit of the vine until that day when I drink it anew in the Kingdom of God."[73]

Admittedly this is strikingly similar to Paul's description—and it is very unusual to find any direct correspondences between the Gospels and his writings. But there are differences, too, most significantly that Paul has Jesus' injunction to do these things in remembrance of him, which is conspicuous by its absence from Mark. But, if that had been what Jesus actually said, it is hard to imagine Mark leaving it out, so its absence suggests that he is relating an *earlier* form of the story than the one in Paul's Letter, before the "in memory" aspect was added.

The Fourth Gospel says nothing about the body/blood rite in its account of the Last Supper, which is by no means the same as evidence that Mark or Paul invented it—quite the reverse. Most scholars place John chronologically as the last of the Gospels, so by their logic it *should* have this element. Moreover, this Gospel suggests that the practice was instituted by Jesus *earlier* in his mission, in Galilee.

In John the symbolism comes in the "bread of life" discourse that Jesus delivers after the feeding of the five thousand (which, as we will see, marks his fundamental change in direction). According to John, it was delivered to the congregation of the synagogue in Capernaum, when Jesus declares:

"I am the bread of life. Your ancestors ate the manna in the wilderness, yet they died. But here is the bread that comes down from heaven, which people may eat and not die. I am the living bread that came down from heaven. Whoever eats of this bread will live for ever. This bread is my flesh, which I will give for the life of the world."

Then the Jews began to argue sharply among themselves, "How can this man give us his flesh to eat?"

Jesus said to them, "Very truly I tell you, unless you eat the flesh of the Son of Man and drink his blood, you have no life in you. Whoever eats my flesh and drinks my blood has eternal life, and I will raise them up at the last day. For my flesh is real food and my blood is real drink. Whoever eats my flesh and drinks my blood remains in me, and I in them."[74]

Although this account only makes the "bread = body" equation, it still has Jesus talking about his followers drinking his blood (although not specifically as wine) and obviously is basically the same as the synoptic imagery.

Joachim Jeremias, author of the classic and exhaustive study *The Eucharistic Words of Jesus* (translated into English in 1966 from the German original of 1960), points out that although the words in John's Gospel are very different from Paul's description of the Lord's Supper, the underlying *structure* of the two is the same, showing that they came from a common source which the author of the Fourth Gospel has, as usual, worked over more thoroughly.[75]

There is also evidence that John's Gospel shared a common source with *Mark*, too, where the Eucharist was concerned. Mark has the bread being Jesus' "body" (Greek *soma*) and John his "flesh" (*sarx*). But while the two Greek words (as in English) have rather different meanings, in Aramaic a single word covered both. Clearly Mark has chosen one translation and John the other (or their sources did), but since both wrote in Greek, the original form of *both* traditions must have been Aramaic.[76]

So it seems that all three early traditions about the Eucharist—the synoptic, the Johannine, and the Pauline—all derived from the same common source. And given their usual disagreement, anything they have in common must have been established at a *very* early date. Right at the beginning, in fact. But the big difference between John and Mark is that the former implies that the body/blood imagery was part of Jesus' teaching some time before the Last Supper. Which is correct?

In John, Jesus' words are not only questioned by the Jews he is addressing but also create division among his disciples, many of whom "turned back and no longer followed him" because of it. It implies that *most* of them abandoned him at this point, only Peter and the rest of the Twelve remaining loyal. They find this "a hard teaching" too far, which, given his much more intimidating instructions—such as being persecuted in his name—fails to add up in a purely Christian context, but does make perfect sense for conventional Jews. As Hyam Maccoby explains:

> This declaration might be expected to offend the Jews, not only because of the cannibalistic imagery and the strict prohibition in Jewish law against consuming any blood, but also because such religious language was typical of the communion meals of paganism. But what is stressed, rather, is that it offends many of Jesus' own disciples.[77]

As we noted earlier, the very fact that John's Gospel even includes a mass desertion of disciples points to its being a genuine event, as it rather undermines the image of the infallible Jesus the writer is trying to promote. And if the teaching caused a mutiny in Galilee, then obviously the concept of the mystical union through eating bread and drinking wine that symbolized body and blood must have been around at that time. All of which is almost impossible to account for if the rite is complete fiction.

In John this is the first occasion that Judas Iscariot's future betrayal is mentioned. After the desertion of the majority of disciples and Peter's statement of loyalty on behalf of the Twelve, Jesus responds, "'Have I not chosen you, the Twelve? Yet one of you is a devil!' (He meant Judas, the son of Simon Iscariot, who, though one of the Twelve, was later to betray him.)"[78]

In the synoptics the two significant aspects of the Last Supper—the institution of the Eucharist and the betrayal—are portrayed as if they just happened to be connected with the same meal. But the placing of the same association in a different context in John's Gospel suggests that Judas may have betrayed Jesus *because* of the Eucharist.

If the group was already participating in such meals before the Last Supper, that fact would explain why the writer of this Gospel felt no need to make a special mention of it in his telling of the iconic meal. Alternatively, Jeremias suggests that "the fourth evangelist consciously omitted the account of the Lord's Supper *because he did not want to reveal the sacred formula to the general public* [his emphasis]."[79]

A concern for secrecy about the Eucharist has also been discerned in Luke's Last Supper, where Jesus passes the wine around twice, once at the beginning of the meal with the bread, and again at the end. The first time, however, he merely blesses the cup and tells the disciples to drink from it, only declaring the bread to be his body. The second time he passes the wine around, he says it is his blood.

A specialist on Luke's Gospel, A. R. C. Leaney, demonstrates that the second passing of the wine was actually inserted by an editor to make it accord with the other Gospels. (Early Christians seemed reluctant to *delete* anything, while quite happy to add bits, even if they created glaring anomalies in the text.) Although, in Luke's original, Jesus made no association between the wine and his blood, Leaney argues that Luke deliberately left it out "in order to preserve the secret core of the rite from the uninitiated."[80] The Eucharist was originally a *secret* ritual, reserved—like Morton Smith's Kingdom of God ritual—for the inner circle.

Jeremias, after an exhaustive analysis of the four accounts of Jesus' alleged words when instituting the Eucharist—the three synoptic Gospels and Paul's in First Corinthians—concluded that Mark was the closest to the original form, mainly because "The words 'this is my blood' were susceptible to the misunderstanding that they spoke of the drinking of blood, which, particularly for born Jews, was a dark animistic abomination."[81] Matthew followed Mark's wording, but both Paul and Luke rewrote to try to avoid—or hide—the blood-drinking connotation, although in doing so both had to come up with, in Jeremias' words, a "strange complicated formulation."

So Paul was keen to *remove* the very aspect he is supposed to have taken from the mystery cults, in which the drinking of blood, even though symbolic, was not charged with the taboo it had in Judaism. And paradoxically, the two most Jewish gospel writers, Mark and Matthew, retained it.

But there is a "strange complicated formulation" in Jeremias' explanation, too, no doubt owing to his unwillingness to challenge the consensus on Jesus' Jewishness. Part of his argument is that Mark's words are likely to be closest to what Jesus actually said, as a Jew would never have invented the blood-drinking connotation: Mark is reporting the words faithfully, even though they might be distasteful to him. But Jeremias then describes the apparent connotation of drinking blood as a "misunderstanding"—it might sound like Jesus said it, but that's not what he meant. In the context, however, surely he meant what he said: the wine represented his blood and had to be drunk with this fully in mind.

After an exhaustive analysis of the language of the various accounts, Jeremias sums up (his emphasis):

> The Markan tradition and the Pauline/Lukan tradition are independent of each other and do not go back to the same Greek source: the variations are too great for such a conclusion. On the other hand . . . in their main features both forms are essentially the same. They go back therefore to a *common eucharistic tradition lying behind both forms of the text.* . . . This *primitive tradition*, as the linguistic study of Mark shows, was formulated in *Aramaic or Hebrew.*[82]

So Jeremias established that the form of words in Mark, Matthew, Luke, and Paul all came from an Aramaic or Hebrew version, and as Andrew Lincoln has shown that Mark's and John's account also share an Aramaic origin, *all* five accounts derive from an Aramaic or Hebrew original, which argues against Paul's inventing the Eucharist, since his first language was Greek. Jeremias points out that "we have every reason to conclude that this common core of the tradition of the account of the Lord's Supper—what Jesus said at the Last Supper—is preserved to us in an essentially reliable form."[83]

More internal evidence against the conventional view comes from the use of Judas Iscariot in the synoptics' Last Supper. As we will see, there is a strong case for the details of the betrayal being basically fictitious, because the presence of a traitor at the institution of the Eucharist was necessary to link it with Jesus' sacrifice. In the mystery cults the blood/wine rite was intended to create a mystical communion between a master—representing the god—and his disciples, and John's Gospel suggests that this was the way in which Jesus, too, used the rite. However, in Christianity this awkward fact was dealt with by turning the Eucharist into a devotional commemoration of Jesus' great sacrifice. In order to justify the transformation, an act of betrayal had to be added to the scenario: in Maccoby's words, Judas Iscariot is "the arch-betrayer needed for the story which gave the Eucharist its sacrificial significance."[84] Without the betrayal, the Eucharist remains an embarrassingly blatant pagan ceremony.

The point that Maccoby misses, however, is that the literary device of Judas' betrayal is only needed *if* the rite actually performed at the Last Supper was a purely mystery-cult one. (This also explains why the synoptics have the Eucharist being instigated only at the Last Supper: any earlier and its association with his sacrifice would be meaningless.)

Either Judas really was prompted to betray Jesus because of his "pagan" teachings, enshrined in the Eucharist, or his betrayal was invented to transform a pagan rite into one of sacrifice. In either case the basis is the same: Jesus used it in the same way as the pagan mystery cults.

Laying Down the Law

The evidence of the New Testament shows that the Eucharist was initiated by Jesus himself and was not an invention of Paul. But there is one nonscriptural text that all proponents of the conventional position appeal to as the final proof: the *Didache* ("Teaching" or "Doctrine"), the shortened *The Teachings of the Twelve Apostles*. Written in Greek, it was a kind of early handbook on how Christians should conduct themselves and on the rules and rituals of the community, used by groups in Syria and perhaps Egypt in the early common era. Apart from a few scattered references in early Church works it remained largely unknown in the West until 1883. It clearly comes from a "Jewish Christian" or Jerusalem Church background, as many of the words derive from Aramaic and also have clear parallels with Jewish prayers.[85]

Naturally, the *Didache* includes instructions on the Eucharist, but the blessings to be spoken over the bread and wine are very different:

> Concerning the eucharist you shall give thanks as follows: first concerning the cup: We give you praise and thanks, our Father, for the holy vine of your servant David, which you have revealed to us through Jesus, your servant. To you be the glory for ever! But over the broken bread thus: We give you praise and thanks, our Father, for the life and the knowledge, which you have revealed to us through Jesus, your servant. To you be the glory for ever! As this bread was scattered over the mountain and became one, so let your church be gathered together from the ends of the earth into your kingdom. For yours is the glory and the power for ever! But none shall eat or drink from your eucharist except those who are baptised in the Name of the Lord. For the Lord has also spoken concerning this, "You shall not give what is holy to the dogs!"[86]

There is no reference to the bread and wine being Jesus' body and blood, which is claimed as proof that the concept was only developed later in a Gentile environment. This argument depends on the *Didache*'s age, which makes for a complicated scenario. Although the full text discovered in the nineteenth century bears the date 1056, fragments from the fourth century subsequently came to light. But—the usual question—when was the work originally composed? Estimates have varied from 70 CE to 200 CE, although most scholars plump for between 100 to 125 CE, so slightly later than the Gospels.

However, one of the major reasons for dating it early is precisely its "nonpagan" form of the Eucharist, which fits the belief that the New Testament form was a later development. The *Didache* is seen as preserving the original—which is rather circular reasoning. A theory about the origins of the Eucharist was used to date the *Didache*, and the date of the *Didache* was used to support the theory. But why couldn't the *Didache* have been written by a Jewish-Christian community whose horror at the body/blood symbolism was so raw that they rewrote it? After all, we are supposed to believe that Western Christians rewrote one of their most sacred rites to *include* the same elements.

There is an ironic contrast to the gnostic gospels. The evidence for the age of both those texts and the *Didache* is strikingly similar, even down to the fact that the earliest available copies of the *Didache* are fourth-century Coptic translations. Yet many of the same people who routinely dismiss the gnostic works as being too late to tell us anything about the historical Jesus happily invoke the *Didache* in support of their position.

There is internal evidence in that the *Didache* itself conflicts with the conventional position on the Eucharist. The Gospels make no mention that Jesus told the disciples to repeat the meal in his memory, but Paul does, suggesting that he or whoever he learned the rite from added this aspect. Yet as this is precisely the purpose of the *Didache's* Eucharist—being all about remembering and honoring Jesus—it appears to be following *Paul's* idea. This is the *complete opposite* of the conventional argument.

There is something even more significant. The *Didache* includes two references to the Eucharist: the main one giving the rite itself and a later brief allusion that explicitly calls it a "pure sacrifice."[87] Yet in the main description there is no suggestion that there is anything sacrificial about the bread and wine, and this discrepancy led one authority on the *Didache*, Jean-Paul Audet, to argue that the main rite in the text is *not* the Eucharist as we know it but what he terms a "minor eucharist" performed during the meal, and that the "major eucharist" (the familiar Christian version) followed the meal as a separate rite, held in another room because of its intensely sacred—and therefore secret—nature.[88]

Contrary to the consensus view, the evidence is overwhelming that the words attributed to Jesus at the institution of the Eucharist formed part of the earliest and most fundamental Christian traditions. It is so early and so basic to the Jesus movement that it is the *only* text to have influenced not only all four Gospels but also Paul's writings. Even so, some scholars still reject the idea purely on the grounds that it "seems impossible"[89] that Jesus, as a Jew, could have uttered such words—surely not the best example of historical reasoning.

Yet even if the sacrament originated with Jesus, not Paul, then the parallels with the Hellenistic mystery cults remain, which have often been explored, but only on the understanding that Paul invented the words of the Eucharist. For example, James Tabor writes:

> The closest parallels are certain Greco-Roman magical rites. We have a Greek papyrus that records a love spell in which a male pronounces certain incantations over a cup of wine that represents the blood that the Egyptian god Osiris had given to his consort Isis to make her feel love for him. When his lover drinks the wine, she symbolically unites with her beloved by consuming his blood. In another text the wine is made into the flesh of Osiris. The symbolic eating of "flesh" and drinking of "blood" was a magical rite of union in Greco-Roman culture.[90]

One of the few academics to explore the association from the point of view of what it tells us about Jesus was Morton Smith. In *Jesus the Magician* he reproduces the texts of two magical papyri and comments (his emphasis): "*These texts are the closest known parallels to the text of the eucharist. In them as in it a magician-god gives his own body or blood to a recipient who, by eating it, will be united with him in love.*"[91]

However, if these texts are the closest parallels to the words of the Eucharist, and, as we have just seen, the evidence is that the words of the Eucharist are authentic to Jesus, logically there must be a connection—at least a borrowing of ideas—between him and the cults that produced those texts. This fits with the evidence that Jesus' healings and exorcisms reveal more than a passing acquaintance with pagan magic. But *Jesus* and *paganism*? The idea seems totally at odds with the strictly Jewish—not to say apocalyptic—context in which Jesus operated.

In fact it is simply not true that all streams of Judaism remained completely quarantined from "contamination" by the pagan mystery schools. Some of the Dead Sea Scrolls, for example, use "terminology similar to that of the mysteries."[92] Also ideas and practices from the mysteries specifically concerning wine drinking had been absorbed by the Therapeutae, a protomonastic Jewish community in Egypt who are known only through the writings of Philo of Alexandria (himself an Egyptian Jew), who associates them with the more famous Essenes. Philo notes the similarity of their rites—particularly involving wine—to those of Bacchus (the Roman

Dionysus). These rites were part of the Therapeutae's commemoration of the Exodus and therefore the Passover—perhaps significantly the time of year when the Last Supper was also held.[93]

The influence of the Therapeutae, and particularly their mystery rites, apparently runs through an obscure text that some see as a possible inspiration for Jesus' Eucharist.[94] It is *The Book of Joseph and Asenath*, produced by an—apparently—Jewish writer living in Egypt. It is impossible to date precisely but seems to go back to the last couple of centuries BCE or first century CE.

This folktale tells of the romance and marriage of Joseph—of "dreamcoat" fame—and the Egyptian beauty Asenath, daughter of the priest of On (Heliopolis). Although she appears only briefly in Genesis,[95] *Joseph and Asenath* is a fully fledged tale of star-crossed lovers, in which eventually, with God's help, love finds a way. What drew scholars' attention was that its central feature is a ritual performed on Asenath by the archangel Michael—to change her from an "idolator" into an acceptable bride for Joseph—which involves her eating "the bread of life," drinking wine from "the cup of immortality," and being anointed with the "unction of incorruption."[96]

Strangely, in this account eating the bread of life and drinking from the cup of immortality are claimed to distinguish a Jew in a religious sense: this point is made five times in the text. This is not the case, of course, so where did this peculiar concept come from?

This little tale has more that is worth musing on. Although it is always referred to as a product of the *Jewish* community in Egypt, Joseph and Asenath were the parents of Manesseh and Ephraim, the legendary progenitors of two of the twelve tribes of Israel. And it was from the tribes of Manesseh and Ephraim that the Samaritans descended. Therefore the tale that focuses on a rite of bread, wine, and anointing seems rather to be *Samaritan*. There was a sizeable Samaritan expatriate community in Egypt.[97] And a surprisingly persistent Samaritan theme surfaces repeatedly in our story.

Jesus Magus

Morton Smith and John M. Hull have shown that there are many affinities between the way Jesus is depicted in the Gospels and the practices of magicians of the Greco-Roman world, not just in the healing and exorcisms, or in rituals such as the Eucharist and "mystery of the Kingdom of God," but in many other aspects of his mission. The repeated claim—at least the one put into his mouth in the Gospels—that he had such a special relationship with God that he *was* God, or the Son of God, had no precedent in Judaism. (The Old Testament describes some "sons of God" but simply referred to those specially favored by Yahweh, mainly kings.) But the term "Son of God" was used for a magician who had successfully achieved oneness with the deity, albeit transitory, when he could channel the god's essential spirit.

Whichever one of three groups one picks, the same image of Jesus emerges. The first is the Jewish opponents of Jesus during his lifetime, on the evidence of the Gospels themselves. We are told that one of the major accusations leveled against him was that he had control of a spirit or spirits. As Hull writes, "The belief that Jesus was a magician is an ancient one. It goes back at least as far as the middle of the first century, as is shown by the Beelzebub story in Mark."[98]

The same image dominates early non-Christian views of Jesus by Jewish and pagan critics of the new religion. The Talmud denounces him baldly: "Jesus wrought his miracles by means of sorcery, which he brought from Egypt," and says elsewhere that he "corrupted and seduced Israel" through occult means.[99] Note that the objection was not so much that he was a magician but that he used a *foreign* form of sorcery, which necessarily involved a reverence for other gods. Origen reports the same accusation being made by the pagan opponent of Christianity Celsus.[100] The most logical explanation of these later views, particularly the Jewish ones, is that they developed out of Jesus' detractors' during his lifetime, as recorded in the Gospels.

Of course, these are the views of Christians' enemies and might have been taken with a pinch of salt, but Smith and Hull also demonstrate that this was how Jesus' *followers* saw him, too. They attribute the same powers to him as belonged to a magus and the same claims regarding the source of his power. As Smith summarizes:

> What really proves Jesus practised magic is the essential content of most of the major stories in the Gospels. In Mark Jesus appears as one possessed by a spirit and thereby made the son of a god; so do

magicians in the magical papyri. Other stories say he was fathered by a god; the same was said of other magicians. Like them, he was driven by the spirit into the wilderness and there met and repulsed evil spirits; this is a typical pattern of shamanic initiation. And like the shamans he is sometimes represented as possessing a spirit, sometimes as himself possessed. Like other ancient magicians he lived as a wandering preacher with a circle of disciples, but was distinguished from ordinary preachers by his miraculous powers. Most of the various stories told of him are told of other magicians, and directions for their performance are given in the magical papyri.[101]

So, says Smith, on the evidence of any of those groups *alone*, the same conclusion is unavoidable.

What makes the "Jesus magus" theory so compelling is that only in the twentieth century has detailed study of Greek and Egyptian magical texts enabled scholars to reconstruct the practices of magicians contemporary with Jesus. The findings match exactly what the Talmud and Celsus claimed about Jesus in the second century. It has taken two thousand years for them to be independently corroborated.

Smith lists a great number of formulae in magical papyri, to be spoken by the magician when casting a spell, which are the *exact* words attributed to Jesus in the Gospels: "I am the Son of the living God"; "I am the one come forth from heaven"; "I am the truth"; "I am . . . light for men"; and so on.[102]

Certainly on the basis simply of Jesus' words and deeds during his Galilee phase, Smith's theory that Jesus was a magician of the type described in the Greco-Egyptian magical papyri would be by far the best description. But there is one glaring problem: this description utterly fails to fit the Jewish nationalist scenario and messianic claims that characterize the Jerusalem phase.

Once again we are faced with what appears to be an insurmountable paradox. Jesus is both a typical—and possibly Egyptian-trained—magician who practices the mysteries *and* a typical Jewish nationalist, even a would-be Messiah. Is there any way to reconcile this paradox?

One way of approaching this problem is by examining Jesus' target audience: who was he preaching to? And who was most fired up by his message?

Jesus and the People

As previously discussed, Jesus could have chosen to begin his mission in Galilee—with its mixed population—either because it was less than totally Jewish or, paradoxically, because it was a hotbed of Jewish nationalism. However, the Gospels were clearly written from a Jewish perspective—he is portrayed preaching to the people using familiar references to their Law and scriptures—and so the academic consensus, as summed up by Morna Hooker, is that "the evidence is firmly in favor of the theory that he confined his attention to the Jews."[103]

However, we suggest a subtle but important modification to Hooker's statement: Jesus confined his attention to the *people of Israel*, i.e., those perceived as belonging to the scattered twelve tribes. Although the term "Jews," technically referring only to the predominant tribe of Judah, had become synonymous with the whole people of Israel, it is helpful to bear the distinction in mind. Some at the time, for example, would have included the Samaritans within "Israel," although this would have appalled most Jews and vice versa. Others might have excluded Gentile converts, on the grounds that Jewishness was defined by ethnicity, membership in one of the tribes being quintessential.

The major question for Christians right from the very beginning was whether Jesus' message was reserved exclusively for Jews or whether he envisaged extending it to Gentiles. Obviously what he started *was* eventually extended to Gentiles, but was this his intention, or was it just an accident of history caused by Paul and the other apostles?

Even some of the most conservative forms of Judaism incorporated a role for Gentiles: the God of the Jews was the God of all, even if the rest of the world was ignorant of the fact or refused to accept it. And there are hints that John the Baptist's message was not restricted to Jews. So even if Jesus *did* preach an essentially Jewish message to an essentially Jewish audience, it was still possible that technically at least he included Gentiles in his ultimate plan.

However, some stories suggest that whatever Jesus was up to, it was aimed at the Jews—or rather Israel—alone. The classic example is the episode in which he heals the daughter of a non-Jewish woman—a Syro-Phoenician in Mark, a Canaanite in Matthew. It is the only time in Mark when Jesus heals a Gentile, but although it might appear to be about his extending his message by implication to all non-Jews, in fact it is the opposite.

The event takes place "in the vicinity of Tyre," one of two coastal cities (the other being Sidon) under Philip's rule with a predominantly pagan Gentile population. Mark tells us:

> He entered a house and did not want anyone to know it; yet he could not keep his presence secret. In fact as soon as she heard about him, a woman whose little daughter was possessed by an evil spirit came and fell at his feet. The woman was a Greek, born in Syrian Phoenicia. She begged Jesus to drive the demon out of her daughter.
>
> "First let the children eat all they want," he told her, "for it is not right to take the children's bread and toss it to the dogs."
>
> "Lord," she replied, "even the dogs under the table eat the children's crumbs."
>
> Then he told her, "For such a reply, you may go; the demon has left your daughter."
>
> She went home and found her child lying on the bed, and the demon gone.[104]

As the Jews routinely called Gentiles "dogs," Jesus' brutally offensive response to the woman's request is that they will receive nothing from him until his mission to God's children, those of Israel, is completed. The woman's retort may impress him and even persuade him to change his mind, but what saves the day is not her quick-witted response to his analogy but her implicit acknowledgment that salvation belongs to Israel.[105] She acknowledges that the "crumb" she has accepted was the prerogative of a Jewish holy man to throw to her—a tacit admission of the superiority of the God of the Jews. *That* is what Jesus likes about it.

So the message of the story is not only very Jewish but also probably quite authentic, for two reasons. First, Gerd Theissen has demonstrated that it reveals a genuine familiarity with the situation around the border between Galilee and Tyre. This was a prosperous Hellenized area with a minority Jewish population, most of whom were farmers who supplied grain to the Gentiles at low prices because of Tyre's economic strength. So, in a sense, the Gentile "dogs" took food from the Jews' own children. Jesus' words therefore sharply remind the woman of the usual relationship between Jews and Gentiles in that area; they do not reflect early Christian debate about the inclusion of Gentiles. But crucially this situation no longer applied after the upheavals of the Jewish Revolt, so the source of this story must predate 66 CE.[106]

Secondly, the episode contradicts the Gospels in two ways. Jesus' behavior—described by Hooker as "almost churlish in his reluctance to help the Gentile woman, and erratic in the way in which he then changed his mind,"[107] though "churlish" is nowhere near strong enough to describe Jesus' casual racial insult—conflicts with his usual characterization in the Gospels. Not only that, but the woman scores a point over Jesus—another reason why a Christian would never have invented it.

Perhaps more important, Jesus' words and actions go completely against the Gospels' fundamental position that he was bringing salvation for all mankind. They must therefore have represented his known teaching—so well known that Mark could do nothing to change it. As Theissen asks, "why should an early Christian group attribute to Jesus an opinion it has rejected?"[108] It seems that this story was based on a genuine encounter with a pagan foreign woman in which something like the recorded exchange must really have happened.

So the evidence is that Jesus aimed his mission solely at the people of Israel, but how did he define them? Who did he include and exclude? For the moment let us say only that the evidence is that he and John the Baptist—unusually—included the Samaritans, which suggests an attempt to roll back history to a time when they were part of the kingdom, presumably in an attempt to gather as many of the lost tribes together as possible.

That may have been Jesus' raison d'être, but what exactly was his appeal for the crowds? He must have offered them some promise or hope that seized their imaginations and kept them coming to hear him. And as his core message was the imminent arrival of the Kingdom of God, he kept the semihysterical end-times expectations fueled, whether he was seen as the Messiah or another "agent of God." With his charisma and oratory, his miracle cures and exorcisms, Jesus would have seemed literally like an answer to their prayers.

Was there another element to Jesus' appeal? Was he, as many writers of recent years have argued, actually the claimant to the throne, as the descendant of the sacred line of David? The Gospels call him King of Israel or King of the Jews, a role that although related to the Messiah also implied a legal right to a historic inheritance. This question will be dealt with more fully when we come to his trial and execution, but let us say here that there is not the slightest suggestion that during the Galilee phase anyone was attracted to Jesus because they thought he was their rightful king, still less that he made any such claim about himself.

But one thing is very clear, that the people's perception of Jesus was colored by his former close association with John the Baptist. This begs some fundamental questions about the precise nature of the relationship between the two men during Jesus' Galilee mission following John's arrest, and between their respective groups of disciples. And it is time to begin to frame the great unasked question: who was really considered the greater of the two?

7

THE RIVAL CHRISTS

Despite the very different picture painted by the Christian churches, as we now know, Jesus began his career in John the Baptist's movement, later launching his own group, chosen from its ranks. But does this mean Jesus was John's chosen successor, furthering the cause with his former mentor's blessing, or was he a rival—or even a usurper?

The early Christian community was uncomfortable and ambivalent about the relationship between Jesus and the Baptist. Carl Kraeling says that for the gospel writers it was "a source of both joy and embarrassment,"[1] while Walter Wink poses a far-reaching question at the beginning of his classic study *John the Baptist in the Gospel Tradition* (1968): "Why did Jesus lavish on John words of such high praise that the church would later find them a source of profound embarrassment?"[2] However, as even the pages of the New Testament make abundantly clear, the evidence reveals that, at least during the early Galilee phase, Jesus was not only considered by others as John's successor, but that is how *he portrayed himself to the people.*

Whatever the background to Jesus' new role, the relationship between the two men seems to have suffered a major breakdown, although churchgoers are still routinely kept in ignorance of the fact. But almost unbelievably, there it is in the Gospels: while languishing in Herod's jail, John sends a message to Jesus expressing his doubts about his disciple's activities. Originally from Q, the astounding passage is found in Matthew and Luke, but not in Mark or John. This is Matthew's version:

> When John heard in prison what the Messiah was doing, he sent his disciples to ask him, "Are you the one who was to come, or should we expect someone else?"
>   Jesus replied, "Go back and report to John what you hear and see: the blind receive sight, the lame walk, those who have leprosy are cleansed, the deaf hear, the dead are raised, and the good news is proclaimed to the poor. Blessed is anyone who does not stumble on account of me." [3]

Could such a question really come from the same man who had so recently groveled at Jesus' feet, proclaiming him to be the Lamb of God? And as Wink points out, "The absence of a further response by John merely indicates what parties on both sides knew to be fact, that John did *not* accept Jesus as the Coming One." [4]

On purely logical grounds the story can hardly be a later fabrication, simply because it contradicts what the early Christians believed. As Robert L. Webb notes:

> . . . it is difficult to perceive the post-Easter Christian community creating this question from John which expresses doubt or even unbelief concerning Jesus' identity as John's expected figure, especially in light of their belief that John was Jesus' forerunner. . . . John is hardly a "witness" here; he is rather a questioning seeker (or possibly even a disillusioned sceptic!) whose expectations were in conflict with events. [5]

Webb also makes the point that later Christians are unlikely to have used the phrase "one who is coming" and would have had no problem with the term "Messiah."

The implications are truly seismic. For some tantalizingly unknown reason, John the Baptist began to doubt Jesus, and was worried enough while in prison to send a delegation to convey his concerns directly to him. Significantly, we do not learn John's response to Jesus' gnomic reply, but had it mollified him, we would certainly have been told. As it is, apparently John went to his death still doubting Jesus. The episode also implies that even though Jesus had his own following, John still considered himself to be in charge: why else would he feel he had the authority to question him?

As we have no clear idea what exactly John expected of Jesus, it is impossible to be sure what caused his doubts. Had he accepted and endorsed Jesus as the Coming One but now, because of his protégé's interpretation of the role, changed his mind? Or perhaps he had never proclaimed Jesus at all and refused to accept him now that he had a reputation and following in his own right.

Jesus' apparent non sequitur implies that healing, exorcising, and proclaiming the good news to the poor are not what John expected of him. His reply is actually a reference to a passage in the Book of Isaiah about God's coming judgment. However, much more relevantly, these parts of Isaiah had been blended into a prophecy of the Messiah: a Dead Sea text known as the *Messianic Apocalypse* had modified one line to read, "He will heal the wounded, resurrect the dead, proclaim glad tidings to the poor."[6] The crucial change was the addition of reviving the dead as a sign of the Messiah, which is not in Isaiah. This is the only text beside the Gospels where Isaiah has been changed in this way, and therefore there must be a connection. If Jesus was consciously using the modified version, then his reply to John the Baptist is effectively a declaration of messiahship.

This remarkably pivotal episode also reveals that at that time Jesus was still being thought of in terms of—even defined by—his relationship with John the Baptist. This is also clear elsewhere in the Gospels.

Exploiting John

Although the Baptist's question from his cell comes from Q and appears only in Matthew and Luke, the other two Gospels are by no means silent on the tensions between him and Jesus.

In Mark Jesus disputes with the unlikely combination of disciples of the Pharisees and the Baptist,[7] although the reference to Pharisees must be a later addition as they never had disciples. Scholars consider it much more likely that the passage originally referred solely to a dispute about the practices ordained by Jesus and John. The change served two purposes: it made the story more relevant to the situation of contemporary Christians, who were locked in an ongoing dispute with the Pharisees, and it obscured the fact that Jesus and John the Baptist disagreed about certain fundamental practices.

For example, John's disciples complained that Jesus' followers never had to undergo the rigors of fasting as they did. Although the average Jew was not usually required to fast regularly, the Pharisees fasted twice weekly. While it is implied here that the Baptist's disciples followed a similar practice, the important point is that it would have been odd to single out Jesus' disciples for criticism on this point *unless* they were considered to be members of a sect that *should* do it.

Jesus seems to have been struggling to free himself from his famous mentor's shadow, while at the same time relying on his connection with him to win people over. A similar situation occurs in the Fourth Gospel, where what was originally a reference to differences between Jesus and John has been disguised by another early change:

> An argument developed between some of John's disciples and a Jew over the matter of ceremonial washing. They came to John and said to him, "Rabbi, that man who was with you on the other side of the Jordan—the one you testified about—look, he is baptizing, and everyone is going to him." [8]

This passage has long been recognized as completely nonsensical. Why should John's disciples' debate with a Jew prompt them to ask their leader about his relative popularity with Jesus? And what connection does a dispute over "ceremonial washing" have with Jesus' baptizing?

As far back as the eighteenth century it was suggested that "Jew" (*Iaudaion*) originally read "Jesus" (*Iesoun*), an idea is still favored by many modern specialists in the Fourth Gospel.[9] And the issue had nothing to do with ceremonial washing: it was clearly about baptism. Exchange "Jew" for "Jesus" and "ceremonial washing" for "baptism" and the passage makes complete sense. It must have been changed because later Christians were uncomfortable with the idea that Jesus and John seriously disagreed at a personal level.

These examples highlight the paradoxical position that the gospel writers (and early Church) took about John the Baptist: they had to downplay his importance in his own right and the extent of his influence over Jesus, but at the same time had to marginalize any suggestion of personal disagreement or rift between the two. In terms of their message, the authors needed Jesus and John to be on the same side for certain purposes while, for other agendas, ensuring that their man appeared unequivocally far superior to John. This, we believe, reflects Jesus' own dilemma: he owed his own reputation to his association with the Baptist but also wanted to be seen as independent and uniquely glorious.

The Gospels themselves contain evidence that Jesus was considered as John's successor—and took pains to portray himself as such. This is even the subtext of the passage in which he contrasts his chosen lifestyle with his former master's: "For John came neither eating nor drinking, and they say, 'He has a demon.' The Son of Man came eating and drinking, and they say, 'Here is a glutton and a drunkard, a friend of tax collectors and sinners.'"[10]

Apart from the fascinating hint about Jesus' reputation for self-indulgence, again he is depicting himself as John's successor. He is implying that just because he lives a different, and less ascetic, lifestyle from John, that does not mean he is not still essentially a representative of what his former master began. And again it shows that the people continued to see him in terms of his association with John.

Another very telling episode occurs in Mark's Gospel. It happens late in Jesus' ministry, after John has been executed and when Jesus is preaching to crowds in the Jerusalem Temple. Members of the Sanhedrin lay a trap by demanding that he disclose the source of his authority—wanting him to say publicly that he is the Messiah or another divinely appointed agent (and giving themselves the golden opportunity of denouncing him as subversive to the Romans). Jesus replies that he will answer them if they will answer *him*: "John's baptism—was it from heaven, or of human origin? Tell me!" Their reason for refusing to reply is very significant: "They discussed it among themselves and said, 'If we say, "From heaven," he will ask, "Then why didn't you believe him?" But if we say, "Of human origin." . . .' (They feared the people, for everyone held that John was really a prophet.)"[11]

In other words, Jesus is using *John's* popularity, not his own, to threaten the Jerusalem authorities. That he should be doing this so late in his ministry shows that he is still, as far as the public is concerned, in John's shadow. But his words carry an even more significant implication: once again he is portraying himself as the Baptist's successor, the heir to his authority.

In Matthew and Luke (so again from Q), once the Baptist's emissaries have been sent back to deliver Jesus' reply to his doubts, in a reversal of the original situation Jesus tells them what he thinks of John, effectively endorsing his former master.

In Matthew (Luke is virtually identical)[12] Jesus begins with a series of questions to the crowd: "What did you go out into the wilderness to see? A reed swayed by the wind? If not, what did you go out to see? A man dressed in fine clothes? No, those who wear fine clothes are in kings' palaces." The opening words seem a little odd: why comment on John's famously humble attire and chosen lifestyle in the wilderness? Clearly Jesus is making a veiled comparison with somebody, but who was it? The meaning becomes quite clear once we know that the reed was the emblem of Herod Antipas, tetrarch of Galilee and Perea, which appeared on coins during his rule. Contrasting the Baptist and those living in king's palaces reinforces the association with Antipas and his family, without making what would have been the very unwise mistake of actually spelling it out. As the tetrarch was John's persecutor, Jesus was reminding the people it was John the Baptist they favored, not Antipas. Jesus was exploiting the people's hatred of the Herodians, but just as significantly, he was also reminding them that John the Baptist had stood up to the despised dynasty—and implying that he was continuing John's campaign.[13]

Jesus goes on: "Then what did you go out to see? A prophet? Yes, I tell you, and more than a prophet"—a term of exceptional honor, only otherwise accorded to Moses.[14] He then quotes a prophecy of Malachi about the Lord sending a messenger to prepare the way for him, explaining that it referred to John the Baptist. In Jesus' day there was a widespread belief that the venerable Old Testament figure of Malachi had been the last of the prophets, God having withdrawn the gift of prophecy after him, and that it would only be restored in order to herald in the last days. So essentially Jesus' message is that John the Baptist had ushered in the end-times.

He continues: "Truly I tell you, among those born of women there has not risen anyone greater than John the Baptist; yet whoever is least in the kingdom of heaven is greater than he." This is very odd. The exact meaning of these words has always been a hot topic among theologians and New Testament scholars—not to mention ourselves—because although the first part seems to praise John unequivocally, the second looks dangerously like some kind of insult. But Jesus himself said only the first part; scholars now agree that the second clause was a later addition, telling us what the early Church thought of the relationship between Jesus and John.[15] Carl Kraeling points out that both the phrases "more than a prophet" and "there has not risen anyone greater" "must be authentic because the early Church was scarcely in a mood with respect to the Baptist to have created them itself."[16]

However, the reason that the early Christian authors of Q felt compelled to add the second part, the "disclaimer" to Jesus' words, is enormously significant: *if they had not done so, their religion would have failed there and then.*

As Walter Wink observes, if the Church had allowed Jesus' original words to remain unchanged, "the church's claim that Jesus was the Christ would obviously be invalidated."[17] Jesus himself says that John the Baptist is (present tense as he was still alive at the time) the greatest person who ever lived—surely an astonishing and truly far-reaching statement. *On his own testimony Christ is admitting being subordinate to the Baptist.* As the whole point of the Church's interpretation of Jesus' incarnation was that he was above everyone who ever lived or ever would live, this was a time bomb waiting to go off and simply could not be left unchanged. And as early Christianity was faced with a rival movement that proclaimed John the Baptist as Messiah, it could easily have exploited Jesus' words as propaganda to win over Christians to that sect—as indeed they were. (Some have suggested that the phrase "born of women" was actually a slight on John, since it implied weakness. If so, this could be another later addition rather than Jesus' own words; otherwise it would undermine his basic message.)

Up to this point Matthew and Luke have been virtually identical, but then they diverge, Luke with the significant aside:

> (All the people, even the tax collectors, when they heard Jesus' words, acknowledged that God's way was right, because they had been baptized by John. But the Pharisees and the experts in the law rejected God's purpose for themselves, because they had not been baptized by John.) [18]

So it was *John* who determined whether someone was in or out of the movement. Matthew, however, continues Jesus' statement in a different way:

> From the days of John the Baptist until now, the kingdom of heaven has been subjected to violence, and violent people have been raiding it. For all the Prophets and the Law prophesied until John. And if you are willing to accept it, he is the Elijah who was to come. [19]

Although the meaning of the first sentence has long puzzled theologians, the significance of the whole statement is that Jesus is saying that John the Baptist was God's instrument for ushering in God's Kingdom—assuming a role for him that conflicts with his portrayal by the Church and the Gospels. As Wink points out, "It is unlikely that the church, engaged as it was in asserting Jesus' superiority over John, would have created a passage which credits John with the decisive act in the shift of the aeons, or that it would portray Jesus as merely John's successor." [20]

In other words, Jesus presented John the Baptist as the herald *not of himself but of the coming Kingdom of God*. But further—immensely significant—light is shed on this passage by the original Hebrew version of Matthew's Gospel, which gives the above saying as (in George Howard's translation):

> Truly I say to you, among all those born of women none has arisen greater than John the Baptizer.
> From his days until now the kingdom of heaven has been oppressed (and senseless persons) have been rending it.

For all the prophets and the law spoke concerning John.
If you wish to receive it, he is Elijah who is going to come.[21]

The first difference is that there is no "disclaimer" in the first sentence (confirming that it was a later addition). Secondly, its version of the attacks on the kingdom of heaven is much more intelligible than in the traditional Matthew: the "kingdom of heaven" movement has been under fire since John appeared.

But the truly telling difference is that where the episode conventionally has Jesus saying that the prophets and the Law prophesied *until* John the Baptist arrived (marking the momentous transition from the old days to the new era of Jesus), the Hebrew version has them prophesying *about* John. Everything in the Old Testament was geared toward the appearance of *John*—not Jesus!

In Mark's Gospel Jesus equates the Baptist with the prophet Elijah a second time, after John's death. Jesus has gone up a mountain with Peter, James, and John, where his face transfigures and his clothes become shining white before Moses and Elijah appear and speak to him. On the way down the mountain, when the disciples ask him, "Why do the teachers of the law say that Elijah must come first?" Jesus replies, "To be sure, Elijah does come first, and restores all things. Why then is it written that the Son of Man must suffer much and be rejected? But I tell you, Elijah has come, and they have done to him everything they wished, just as it is written about him."[22]

The disciples' question is prompted by the contemporary Jewish end-times belief that the last days would be heralded, or initiated, by the return of the prophet Elijah. In his answer Jesus is saying that Elijah has already returned, although "they" have in some way abused him. In fact the phrase "Son of Man"—by which Jesus usually means himself—is probably mistaken here for the more generic "son of man," in context referring to Elijah, so the whole statement about suffering and rejection applies to him.[23] Oddly, though, there are no known scriptural prophecies that this is how Elijah would be treated. In the context Jesus can be referring to only one person, as Matthew unequivocally confirms: "Then the disciples understood that he was talking to them about John the Baptist."[24] Jesus is, once again, depicting the Baptist as the herald of the end-times, beginning the process he himself is to complete.

However, once again, the Hebrew Matthew contains an enormously significant difference. While the traditional Greek version declares that Elijah "restores all things," in the original Hebrew he "will save all the world."[25] Here is Jesus himself proclaiming it is John the Baptist, the new Elijah, who was *the Savior of the world*.

Although most of the Hebrew Matthew is the same as the traditional version, tellingly all the major differences are found whenever Jesus talks about John the Baptist. And conversely, all those passages have been changed—but in the Hebrew every one enhanced the Baptist's status. The conclusion is inescapable: Matthew's Gospel *was rewritten by the early Church to downplay John the Baptist's importance and influence over Jesus*. If John was Jesus' Savior, they were determined that he would be no one else's. Even if it went against everything that Jesus stood for or ever sought, the Church would downgrade the Baptist in favor of their preferred Christ. And so it became.

It is quite obvious that, throughout his ministry, Jesus was judged in the light of his association with John the Baptist. When he first made an impact in Galilee, he was understood to be continuing John's work and he himself deliberately maintained the public's perception of his closeness to John, praising him and declaring that he, John, had inaugurated the end-times that he, Jesus, was now bringing to an apocalyptic climax. And even if Jesus managed to shift the focus onto himself in Galilee, in Jerusalem he still appealed to his association with the Baptist to win the people over and face down his opponents.

Old Skins, New Wine

Strangely, however, there are also passages in the Bible where Jesus appears to utter veiled slights against John, put-downs that suggest he was far more than just a onetime lieutenant who was devotedly and respectfully continuing his leader's unfinished work.

The synoptic Gospels include a passage, embedded in the response to John's disciples about the fasting controversy, in which Jesus uses various analogies contrasting old and new, involving imagery of wine, wineskins, and patched cloth. This only makes sense as a contrast between Jesus and John and their respective ways of doing things. A very similar passage appears in the Gospel of Thomas, although some of the imagery is a little different, and follows immediately after Jesus' "born of women" praise of John. The fact that it is in a different context *but is still associated with Jesus' comments about the Baptist* shows that all the earliest traditions recognized that this statement related to how Jesus compared himself to his former mentor. Thomas is sharper, beginning with a variation of the well-known saying (from Q): "A person cannot mount two horses or draw two bows. And a slave cannot serve two owners, but truly will honor the one and scoff at the other."[26]

As for the "old and new" analogies in both the synoptics and Thomas, there are two sets of imagery, the first apparently presenting some difficulties for the writers, presumably because being mere men they had no idea what they were talking about when it came to handling a needle and thread. Mark's original rendering is that no one sews a brand-new piece of cloth onto an old garment; it will only shrink later and make the tear worse.[27] The basic idea behind the imagery is that the old garment obviously represents John (who was not known for his fashion sense) and the new clothes Jesus. No point in grafting the new onto the old.

The wine imagery is in two parts: first Jesus observes that no one pours new wine into old wineskins, because they will burst, ruining the skin and—presumably more important to Jesus, given his bon vivant's reputation—losing the wine.[28] So it makes sense to pour new wine into new skins: once again it is not advisable to mix old and new. New will outperform old every time. It has been said that the "skins" image inevitably brings to mind John the Baptist with his animal-skin clothes, making this a deliberate dig. Jesus being the "new wine" could not be contained in the "old skin."[29]

Such sly slurs contrast greatly with Jesus' public praise of John and his keenness to associate himself with him in passages that are unlikely to have been invented by postresurrection Christians. But were the "wineskins" and "torn clothes" jibes invented by later Christians about the contemporary followers of the Baptist? Or did Jesus really say them?

It is obviously important that all Jesus' recorded praise of John takes place in public, whereas his implicit criticism appears to have been a private matter, either within his own circle or to a deputation of John's disciples—incidents that may reflect Jesus' private thoughts about John, although it is impossible to be sure. Again, though, we have to remember John the Baptist's skeptical question from prison, which implies at least some degree of uneasiness in the relationship between the former master and pupil.

The Two Messiahs

In the past couple of decades scholars have increasingly come to realize that John the Baptist was enormously important in his own right, not merely because of his connection with Jesus. This discovery directly challenges the two-millennia-old understanding that Jesus was a unique figure, the one and only Christ who needed *no one* to back him. One attempt to account for John's importance while retaining the traditional ideas of Jesus invokes the concept of a dual messiahship—that *both* Jesus and John the Baptist were Messiahs.

For most Jews, almost by definition, there could only be one Messiah, a concept that passed seamlessly into Christianity. However, in the two centuries before Jesus, when Jewish expectation of the imminent "agent of God" was building to a climax, there was much debate about the nature of the Chosen One, some even speculating that the scriptural prophecies referred to *two* divinely appointed deliverers. One, of King David's bloodline, would rule the nation, while the other, descended from the Israelites' first high priest, Aaron, would fill that time-hallowed role, as in the glory days under David and Solomon.

Exactly when this concept originated is unclear, although at that feverish time virtually every possible interpretation was explored. Some of the apparent contradictions between Old Testament texts foretelling the Messiah could be resolved by assuming that they referred to two figures. And given the original meaning of "Messiah," the concept could be adapted easily, since both would be *anointed* into their office, both men true Christs.

The idea surfaced in a few apocalyptic texts, notably the *Testaments of the Twelve Patriarchs*, generally placed in the second or first century BCE. But it was its appearance in the Dead Sea Scrolls that generated interest in the concept as a possible way of accommodating the new understanding of John the Baptist without also having to down-grade Christ. In the *Community Rule*, the two roles are the Messiahs of Aaron and Israel—the priestly Messiah being superior. Other Qumran texts include Old Testament messianic prophecies that were rewritten for two Messiahs.

The suggestion has been made—most recently by James D. Tabor in *The Jesus Dynasty*—that Jesus and John the Baptist consciously modeled their careers to conform with the dual Messiah idea, John as Messiah of Aaron and Jesus Messiah of David.[30] This would explain why John the Baptist was the more authoritative. However, in this scenario, after John's execution Jesus was left to combine both roles.

While the idea that Jesus and John were both Messiahs is relatively plausible, and even has a certain appeal, the actual evidence for it is thin and the supporting reasoning often circular: because the concept *might* have motivated Jesus and John, they *were* motivated by it. However, the evidence is that the Baptist never proclaimed Jesus as the Messiah (still less himself as the other one). And as a dual messiahship formed no overt part of Jesus' message, it has to be argued that both he and John kept it secret not only from the masses but also their own disciples. Some versions of the theory, such as Tabor's, also depend on Jesus and John the Baptist being related, as a dynastic element plays a large part in the dual Messiah belief, but as we have seen, the single item of evidence for their being cousins is tantalizingly ambiguous.

A key text for Tabor's overall argument is the Qumran *Messianic Apocalypse*, from which Jesus' reply to John's question from prison was apparently taken. Tabor uses it as evidence that Jesus and John were deliberately shaping their joint careers around such messianic ideas. However, the *Messianic Apocalypse* unequivocally concerns a *single* Messiah, not a dual messiahship, so if Jesus and John the Baptist approved of the text, it would suggest that they had in mind the conventional expectation of the Messiah.

However, the reason that the theory developed at all is highly significant: by having two Messiahs, the uncomfortable question of the relative statuses of Jesus and the Baptist can be avoided. But the fact that such a role for John has even been speculated is a huge change in the traditional Christian view that he was unworthy even to tie Jesus' shoelaces.

Herod's Horror

One episode reveals a great deal about the popular perceptions of the relationship between Jesus and John the Baptist. As Mark explains:

> King Herod [Antipas] heard about this [Jesus' healings and exorcisms], for Jesus' name had become well known. Some were saying, "John the Baptist has been raised from the dead, and that is why miraculous powers are at work in him" . . .
> But when Herod heard his, he said, "John, whom I beheaded, has been raised from the dead." [31]

(Many early manuscripts have in the first verse "He [i.e., Herod] was saying" instead of "Some were saying," which makes more sense.)

An implication of this is that Antipas knew nothing about John proclaiming the "greater one" who is to come; otherwise he would automatically assume they were talking about Jesus, not John returned. Once again this shows that this kind of announcement was never a major part of the Baptist's message.

But what did Antipas think had happened? Explanations based on reincarnation or the idea that the Baptist had risen from the grave and taken on Jesus' form are clearly untenable as the two men worked side by side. The puzzle is explained when we understand that this was a reference to a contemporary *magical* belief, that a person could acquire occult powers by taking control of the spirit of a dead person. This concept, first suggested by Carl Kraeling in 1940,[32] was developed by Morton Smith in *Jesus the Magician*, who explains:

> It was generally believed that the spirit of any human being who had come to an unjust, violent, or otherwise untimely end was of enormous power. If a magician could call up and get control of, or identify himself with, such a spirit, he could then control inferior spirits or powers.[33]

In other words, Antipas feared that Jesus had used black arts to raise John's spirit from the dead, and *this* was the source of his power.

However, the significance is not so much that Antipas had these fears, but that Mark thought it necessary to include them, even as examples of erroneous beliefs about Jesus. As Matthew Goulder points out (his emphasis):

> Mark will hardly have been concerned to tell his congregation wild ideas people had forty years before. It is much more likely that he gives the wrong ideas *because they are current in his own time*; especially when he gives them twice. There were Christians around in the 60s who thought these things.[34]

However, in our view it seems more likely that Mark had another group in mind: the John the Baptist sect. Did they believe that Jesus had in some way magically enslaved their master?

The Bad Samaritan

Certain, admittedly controversial, sources give more alleged information about John the Baptist—controversial both because academic opinion over their reliability differs, and because of their description of John and his relationship with Jesus.

The first is the early Church literature known collectively as the Clementina or, more accurately, the Pseudo-Clementines, allegedly by Clement of Rome (ca. 30–97), an early bishop of Rome (not to be confused with Clement of Alexandria), although there is no doubt that they were merely attributed to him to add a dash of authority. The collection consists of two major texts, the *Clementine Recognitions* and the *Clementine Homilies*—variations of the same work—together with some lesser writings. Both the *Recognitions* and the *Homilies* seem to have adapted a common, and now lost, source and purport to be Clement's account of how he became a Christian and one of Peter's assistants in the port of Caesarea in Samaria.

Most scholars date the original composition to between 150 and 200 CE. But, as with the Gospels, the important (and much more difficult) question is how old—and how reliable—their *information* was. In fact some scholars see them as depositories in which "ancient elements of primitive Jewish Christianity have been preserved."[35]

Robert Eisenman argues that not only are the Pseudo-Clementines drawn from many of the same sources as the Acts of the Apostles, but that they are more faithful, less edited and reworked.[36] Even the surviving versions are incomplete: the earliest version of the *Recognitions* is a Latin translation by Rufinus of Aquileia from about 410 CE, who states in his introduction that he left out certain parts.

Even what we have is something of a jaw-dropper, beginning with "Yea, some even of the disciples of John, who seemed to be great ones, have separated themselves from the people, and proclaimed their own master as the Christ."[37] In fact, the Clementina reveals that this John (or Johannite) sect was using the very argument that the early Christians feared, that Jesus himself had proclaimed John "greater than all men and all prophets."[38] (Significantly, they seem to have had no idea at that time of the "disclaimer" added to Jesus' statement in Matthew's Gospel.) They also argue that Jesus said that John "must be held to be greater than Moses, and than Jesus himself. But if he be the greatest of all, then must he be the Christ."[39]

As we already know that such a sect existed alongside the early Jesus cult, this passage merely confirms it. But the Pseudo-Clementines go on to make an incredible statement, identifying John the Baptist as the mentor of two of the most notorious heretics in Christian history, one of whom was the early Church's greatest adversary: the infamous Simon Magus and the less well known Dositheus.

This is quite astonishing. How could Christian writers have linked John the Baptist of all saints with such spiritual scum? And they mention them casually, as if everybody knew the connection.

Simon Magus (or Simon of Gitta) was a Samaritan and a contemporary of Jesus who was roundly condemned by the early Church as the first heretic and father and originator of all other possible heresies. He appears briefly in the Acts of the Apostles, during the evangelization of Samaria by Philip during the forties CE, so some ten years, probably less, after the crucifixion.[40] Philip found himself in competition with Simon, who "for some time" had been rather popular in the country. Although just called Simon, he is described by the verb *mageuon*, "practicing as a magus" and as performing *tais magiais*, "the works of a magus,"[41] hence his later name.

Although his Samaritan supporters proclaimed him "the divine power known as the Great Power"—neither they nor their hero was ever shy of hyperbole—Philip not only successfully converted the Samaritans, he also converted and baptized Simon himself. Or so the story goes.

And the story goes on: following Philip's success, Peter and the apostle John went to Samaria, in order to take the Holy Spirit to the Samaritans. Completely missing the point, Simon offered them money for the secret of the Holy Spirit, thereby creating the whole new mercenary sin of "simony." Rebuking him in the no-nonsense manner for which he was famous, Peter expelled Simon from the ministry, at which point the shamed Samaritan asked forgiveness. Unfortunately the story ends there, so we have no idea what happened to him. But that was certainly not the end of the extraordinarily colorful story of Simon Magus, the bad Samaritan.

Perhaps, though, Simon was not always so bad or so colorful. Even Acts acknowledges that he was for a time a member of the Christian community in Samaria, and though he is described as a "sorcerer" there is a tacit acknowledgment that what he did was very similar to what the Christians of that time were doing. Certainly he seems to come out of the same stable, but Acts never attempts to explain Simon's background, so this remains an intriguing hint—although a connection with John the Baptist, as in the Pseudo-Clementines, would explain the similarity.

However, it is very clear from other early Christian writings that Acts was extremely economical with the facts, as there was considerably more to say about Simon Magus. As if in the grip of a perverse fascination, the Church Fathers often refer to him, ingenuously supplying more information. Basically Simon Magus certainly did *not* repent (or if he did, he soon changed his mind) and continued to be a thorn in the early Church's side. He founded his own sect of the Simonians, which proudly continued his heresy.

Early Christianity boasted a whole genre of literature telling of magical/miraculous conflicts between Peter and Simon Magus—in a similar vein to modern battles between superheroes—such as the *Acts of Peter*, dating from ca. 190 CE. It reached its apogee in the tale of how Simon, in Rome, attempted to fly (inevitably with the aid of demons) and was sent crashing to his death by a prayer from Peter. This is all obviously fictitious, as it is very late and conflicts with earlier, slightly more mundane accounts of Simon's death. These described his rather more likely—but still predictably dramatic—end, when he had himself buried alive in order to rise again on the third day but unfortunately failed to do so. Perhaps even this tale was the gleeful Christians' propagandized version. He might simply have died and been buried.

However, while the individual stories can—disappointingly—be disregarded as early clerical fantasies, they do appear to have been based on a real memory of the antipathy between early Christians and Simon and/or his followers. The *Acts of Peter* was obviously written to show that the Christians, personified by Peter, with the blessing of God, easily bested the Magus.

The Pseudo-Clementine literature is a midway point between Acts and the more over-the-top tales, representing Peter as engaged in a series of public debates for the souls of the people of Palestine with Simon Magus. And as the more melodramatic stories were undoubtedly written between about 150 and 200 CE, the Clementina's sources were almost certainly earlier.

The Church Fathers had to attack Simon Magus because of the danger he and his movement posed to emerging Christianity. Clearly they were competing on the same ground, for the same hearts and minds, and people were attributing to him the identical magical abilities and charisma that the Church attributed to Jesus; in fact, *the Magus posed a threat because he was startlingly similar to Christ himself.* The Church Fathers never attempted to deny that Simon had done many of the things that Jesus was supposed to have done; instead they tried to show he could only do them because he was in league with the Devil, attempting to ape Jesus and mislead the people. One Father wrote of the "great havoc" that Simon had wreaked among Christians by confusing them.[42] Another, Hippolytus, had to spell it out as simply as possible: "he was not the Christ."[43] Obviously some people thought he *was.*

Simon was credited with a wide magical repertoire—shapeshifting into the appearance of others, or even animals, passing through solid objects, and so on. The Pseudo-Clementines claimed that he owed his abilities to his control of a dead boy's soul—the same magical practice that lay behind Herod Antipas' fears about Jesus controlling John the Baptist's spirit.

The earliest reference to Simon Magus outside Acts comes from a work of Justin Martyr—himself an inhabitant of Samaria—dating from the 150s CE, which identifies Gitta as his home town and claims that "nearly all the Samaritans confess him to be the first god and worship him."[44] Justin also says that Simon went to Rome during Claudius' rule (41–54 CE), where he performed miracles and was honored as a god, a statue of him being set up on an island in the Tiber. Unfortunately this was probably a misreading of an inscription on a statue to a Sabine deity, *Semoni Sanco Deo* and not *Simoni*,[45] although he probably did visit Rome. It is also from Justin that we first learn another key part of the Simon Magus legend, that he was accompanied on his travels by a former prostitute named Helen, his "first Thought" and "lost sheep."

The Church Fathers certainly attributed gnostic ideas to Simon Magus—indeed, making him their originator—but whether he was a gnostic in the sense we now understand it is hotly debated in academic circles. The consensus is that he was a "protognostic," advancing ideas from which "classic" gnosticism would develop.

A major difference between Simon Magus and Jesus is that the former wrote books setting out his spiritual philosophy, and although for obvious reasons they were suppressed in the earliest days, a few extracts have come down to us in rather unwise quotations by Church Fathers keen to supply counterarguments and show how they were the product of evil. The Magus' major work was the *Great Revelation* (*Apophasis Megale*), known only from paraphrased extracts in a work of Hippolytus of Rome, written around 230 CE. Hippolytus' work was itself only known from extracts until a mutilated copy, but with the section on the *Great Revelation* complete, was discovered in a Greek monastery in 1842, giving us the only substantial chunk of Simon's own words.

What comes across most clearly from Simon Magus' writing is the strange mix of conventional Judaism and paganism, particularly the emphasis on the Feminine and sexual mysticism. The *Great Revelation* has an obvious Judaic background, consisting largely of commentary on the Old Testament, such as the teachings of Moses, in terms of Simon's theology and cosmology, which is essentially gnostic, although without the later overt dualism. In fact Simon evidently found the material world a thing of great beauty rather than evil and corruption, and although he shared the classic gnostic concept that it was the creation of a lesser god, he found this quite encouraging.

Unexpectedly, Simon believed in the existence of many gods but only one supreme creator God, whose main power was his first-created being, the feminine entity "first conception (or Thought) of his Mind, the Mother of All."[46] According to the Magus, it was the First Thought, not God directly, who created the material world, initially by manifesting its ruling "powers and angels." However, in order to keep the First Thought on earth they had imprisoned her in human form, forcing her to continually reincarnate in female bodies. Although at first she became queens and other famous ladies—Helen of Troy, for example—she gradually descended further and further until she ended up as a prostitute in Tyre. It was here that Simon had found his "lost sheep," again known as Helen, and by purchasing her freedom he started the process of redeeming the material world. In other words, salvation.

The emphasis on a great female creative power, besides Helen's incarnation as a prostitute, led naturally to a form of sexual mysticism. Irenaeus fulminated that the Simonian priests "live immorally,"[47] while Hippolytus commented that "those who copy the vagabond magician Simon do like acts, and pretend that intercourse should be promiscuous. . . . For by purchasing the freedom of Helen, he (Simon) thus offered salvation to men by knowledge peculiar to himself."[48] According to Epiphanius, the Simonians used semen and menstrual blood in their "mysteries of obscenity,"[49] although as a hostile witness perhaps he overdid the giddy horror.

It must be said that at first glance Simon's fondness for sacred sex and reverence for more than one god sits awkwardly with the "Jewish" background of his teaching, but in fact this may not be as odd as it appears. Simon was not a Jew but a Samaritan, and Samaria was home to heretical forms of Judaism besides some surviving pagan religions, and our information about both is incomplete. Even so, although Simon Magus could have drawn on either to mingle with Jewish concepts, all these ideas seem remarkably at odds with the Clementina's image of him as the protégé of that apparently most puritanical of preachers, John the Baptist. But we must remember that relatively little is known about John, and there is that intriguing hint that he may have been at least more tolerant than is generally supposed; after all, didn't wicked prostitutes flock to him?

However, by far the most significant aspect of the Simon Magus story is the striking parallels between him and Jesus Christ, which proved so awkward for the early Church, both in Simon's alleged deeds and the fact that he could so easily be taken for a Christian: the Acts of the Apostles describes him as such, if only for a time. Epiphanius, in his major work against heresies, wrote that Simon Magus worked "under the cloak of Christ,"[50] and there is even a suggestion that he claimed to be the resurrected Jesus: Epiphanius fumed that Simon "told the Samaritans that he was the Father, and the Jews that he was the Son, and that in undergoing the passion he had not really done so but that it was only in appearance."[51]

Even the Church Fathers' depiction of Simon Magus as a demonic parody of Jesus is telling: after all, a parody has to be rather similar to what it parodies. They also vilified him as the originator of the "first heresy,"[52] but again, the terminology hides a clue. A heresy is a *variation* of a religion—believed by traditionalists to be a distorted or even perverted form, but nevertheless something that derives from the same root. And then there is the remarkable revelation that modern studies show that Jesus himself used the techniques of a magus, overturning centuries of denial of any similarity between him and Simon.

The fact that the Magus and the first Christian apostles in Samaria were basically competing from the same stance—and that he could switch, however briefly, to being a Christian—points in the same direction. But was Simon's teaching really a heretical form of Christianity? Strangely he had already established it in Samaria *before* the arrival of Jesus' first apostles within at most ten years of the crucifixion. What could have inspired Simon's own message? The Clementina suggests an answer arising from their shared teacher, John the Baptist.

Many Gods

However the writers of the Clementina chose to use their material about Simon Magus, the information matches what we know from other sources. There is, for example, the strange blend of Old

Testament Judaism and protognostic ideas: the *Clementine Homilies* state that, in his debate with Peter, Simon declared he believed in many gods under one God and that "[he] appeals to the Old Testament to show that there are many gods."[53] (The accuracy of this claim could only be judged after the extracts from his *Great Revelation* were found in 1842.)

In the *Homilies* Clement is told Simon's history by a Christian named Aquila, who declares that the Magus was one of the chief disciples of John the Baptist, a "Hemerobaptist" (literally "day-baptist"), but much more significantly, "the forerunner of Lord Jesus." John had even chosen Simon to succeed him, as the Theosophist G. R. S. Mead summarizes in his 1892 compilation of the ancient texts on the Magus:

> It was at Alexandria that Simon perfected his studies in magic, being an adherent of John, a Hemero-baptist, through whom he came to deal with religious doctrines. . . . Of all John's disciples, Simon was the favourite, but on the death of his master, he was absent in Alexandria, and so Dositheus, a co-disciple, was chosen head of the school.[54]

On his return, through his superior magical arts Simon eventually convinced even Dositheus that he was the true leader, known by the odd title of the Standing One.[55]

The term "Hemerobaptist" remains something of a mystery, although presumably it refers to a sect to which the ritual of baptism was a regular occurrence, rather than the one-off rite usually associated with John the Baptist. It is possible, however, that while the single initiatory rite may have characterized John's work with the masses, his inner circle—or the sect to which he and they belonged—could well have used it more frequently. This seems to be the case for the group that used the supposed Cave of John the Baptist at Suba, discussed in chapter 4, and is also suggested by the practices of the Mandaeans, as we will see shortly.

Another highly thought-provoking point is that the syntax of the original Greek of the *Homilies* specifically implies that Simon finished his magical training in Alexandria *because* he was a follower of John's, as if it should be obvious to the reader why this had to be.

Magic and the Baptist? And why the great Egyptian seaport of Alexandria? It is by no means obvious to us now: all the other sources only ever connect the Baptist with Palestine—Judea, Perea, and Samaria. The only other connection is in the Acts of the Apostles, where one Apollos, who preaches the "baptism of John," is said to have taken it to Ephesus from Alexandria.

According to the Pseudo-Clementines, John the Baptist had a circle of thirty disciples, representing the lunar calendar, just as Jesus' Twelve symbolized the months of the solar year. John's circle included Helen, who is named Luna (Latin for "Moon") in the *Recognitions*, although it has been suggested this was a misreading of Selene (the Moon goddess) for Helene. The interesting implication is that Helen was also originally one of John's closest disciples, and we recall that Jesus said John's message appealed to prostitutes.

Is there any other evidence of a connection between the notorious Gittite and John the Baptist? In the *Great Revelation* Simon wrote, "For now the axe is nigh to the roots of every tree: every tree that bringeth not forth good fruit, is cut down and cast into the fire."[56] Luke has the Baptist saying, immediately after the passage about God's being able to raise new "children of Israel" from stones (which possibly refers to non-Jews): "The axe has been laid to the root of the trees, and every tree that does not produce good fruit will be cut down and thrown into the fire."[57] Simon is either quoting John the Baptist or both are quoting from the same source.

The Shadowy Leader

While Simon Magus—the "Father of Heresies"—is well known, his fellow Samaritan Dositheus may not be so familiar, but he too founded a heretical sect: unsurprisingly, the Dositheans. It survived until at least the sixth century, after which it disappears from the historical record, usually presumed to have been eradicated (but see below). As with the Magus, and possibly Jesus, delusions of grandeur seem to have been the order of the day. Origen wrote not only that Dositheus had "said that he was the prophesied Christ" and "the Son of God," but also that the Dositheans believed he was still alive somewhere waiting to return, and that they had produced Dosithean "gospels."[58] Naturally none has survived.

What are we to make of this apparently bizarre association of John the Baptist with sex magicians and gnostic heretics? The least that can be said is that there were people living when the Pseudo-Clementines were written who obviously believed such things about him. Those texts were certainly composed by 250 CE, probably by 150, and others would argue that their sources are much closer to Jesus' time, but even so, why did these people believe those things about John, Simon, and Dositheus? Where on earth did they find such seemingly incongruous ideas? Had genuine information about the relationship between Jesus and the Baptist been passed down to the writers of the Clementina, or had someone in the intervening years just made it up?

It is difficult to imagine mainstream Christians, like the originators of the Clementina, inventing such things about an individual who was so intimately involved in Jesus' story. As the undoubted archvillain of the Pseudo-Clementines is Simon Magus, linking him to John the Baptist is hardly calculated to make the story appeal to a conventional Christ worshipper.

There is an obvious clue in the common theme of Samaria: Simon and Dositheus were Samaritans, and we know that John the Baptist's mission was linked with Samaria (as indeed was Jesus'). Wink speculates that "historically, Simonian gnosticism may have originated as a Samaritan wing of the Baptist movement."[59]

A connection with John would certainly explain a couple of enduring puzzles. First, why Simon Magus and Jesus seem to have had so much in common: if they had the same teacher, it was only to be expected. Second, how Simon had "evangelized" Samaria before the first Christian apostles got there.

It might also explain certain oddities in the Fourth Gospel, if, as we believe, it was written for the early Christian community in Samaria—presumably soon after the arrival of Jesus' apostles and during the struggle with Simon. It has been suggested that the "Samaritan" jibe at Jesus by the Jerusalem crowd in John's Gospel, which puzzled us earlier, was actually an allusion to Simon Magus, and would have been understandable to a Samaritan audience.[60]

But more significantly it might tie up another of our loose ends:

the conundrum of the sexual metaphors in the encounter between Jesus and the Samaritan woman at the well. If the Jesus movement in Samaria was in competition with an already established "Simonism," in which sexual practices and divinely appointed female partners played an all-important part, the writer of John's Gospel may have tried to subvert Simon's approach by appearing to go down the same avenue but twisting the story at the last moment. After all, had Simon been talking to the woman, no doubt it would have ended very differently.

Ultimately it is not what the Clementina reveals about Simon Magus or Dositheus but what it tells us about John the Baptist that is most intriguing. There are hints about people holding other fantastic beliefs about him. For example, there is a Syriac version of the *Clementine Recognitions*, significantly different from the Greek, that records the belief that John the Baptist was not really dead but concealed somewhere, ready to return.[61]

By itself the Clementina may be interesting, but what makes it really revelatory is its consistency with other sources, such as John's Gospel, which includes denials of the Baptist's messiahship— presumably aimed at those who saw him in a role that the writer believed should be reserved for Jesus. Also the Hebrew Matthew discussed above shows that in today's version of the Gospel, Jesus' own words about the importance of John the Baptist have been considerably watered down. As George Howard, the professor of religion who first published the significance of the Hebrew Matthew, notes:

> An interesting scenario emerges when the Gospel of John and the Pseudo-Clementine writings are compared with Shem-Tob's Matthew. The polemic against John the Baptist in the Fourth Gospel and the Pseudo-Clementines appears to be directed against the image of the Baptist portrayed in Shem-Tob's text.[62]

In other words, Matthew wrote that Jesus unequivocally extolled John the Baptist, yet the ideas on which those parts of Matthew were based are precisely those *condemned* in the Fourth Gospel and the Pseudo-Clementines. But those parts of Matthew's Gospel were rewritten *specifically* to cover up John's real status.

By describing Simon Magus, not Jesus, as John's true heir, the Pseudo-Clementines imply a great gulf and rivalry between the two spiritual leaders. But was it true? If there is even a glimmer of fact behind this, then the unthinkable has to be faced: much of what Christians believe about the origins of their religion is utterly and completely mistaken.

The Keepers of Secrets

The second controversial source about the vexed relationship between Jesus and John the Baptist comprises the sacred texts and traditions of the Mandaeans, a sect whose literature is collectively known as the Mandaica. Their homeland is, or rather was until recently, confined to southern Iraq, with a small presence over the border in Iran. (Since the 1991 Gulf War there are many expatriate or refugee communities scattered around the world, for example in London, Florida, and the Netherlands.) If for no other reason, they are uniquely fascinating as "the sole surviving remnant of ancient Gnosticism,"[63] which is reflected in their very name, from their word for "knowledge," *manda*.

Although known to Europeans only since first encountered in 1555 by Jesuit missionaries, who dubbed them "Christians of St. John"—a somewhat ironic and misleading term—the Mandaeans had put down roots in the region around what was Persia for many centuries. Not only do they appear in the Qu'ran as "Sabians," but tellingly, Arab writers of the eighth century link them to the Dositheans. They are still called *subba* by their Muslim neighbors, which probably derives from the Mandaeans' own word for baptism.[64]

The Mandaean associations become more and more intriguing: their priesthood is known as the *nasuraiia*, or Nasoreans, from *nasiruta*, or "secret knowledge," which in turn is derived from the Aramaic root *nsr*, "to keep or guard."[65] According to Mark Lidzbarski, the Polish-German scholar who was one of the first to study the sect in the late nineteenth and early twentieth century, *nasuraiia* should be interpreted as "keepers of secrets."[66]

Their rituals are unmistakable: as a modern specialist in the sect, the Turkish scholar Sinasi Gündüz, writes, "Among the Mandaean rituals baptism (*masbuta*) is the most important. Baptism can take place only in 'flowing (living) water,' i.e., in rivers of the Mandi pool. The flowing water of baptism is called 'jordan' (*iardna*)."[67] Baptism forms part of all their ceremonies and rites; it is not a one-off initiatory ritual as it is in Christianity and is assumed to have been in John the Baptist's movement. In that respect the Mandaeans are similar to the Hemerobaptists mentioned above.

Serious interest in the Mandaeans' holy books only began in the early part of the twentieth century, as it dawned on scholars that they might provide some vital clues to the origins of gnosticism—and even Christianity itself.

The Mandaeans' history, dislocated and confused though it is, nevertheless presents some intriguing possibilities. They claim a heritage that takes them back well beyond Jesus' day, originating much further to the west, in the region of Egypt and Palestine. But another historical claim is even more promising, as Gündüz explains (his emphasis):

> Although he does not play a central role in Mandaeism [i.e., in the practices of the religion], Yahia Yuhana, John the Baptist, *is* an important historical person in the Mandaean tradition. It is claimed for him that he was a great teacher, performing baptisms in the exercise of his function as priest. They believe that he was a Nazurai, and that he was skilled in the white magic of the priests and concerned largely with the healing of men's bodies as well as their souls.[68]

John appears in their literature under the names of Yuhana, which is Mandaean, and Yahia, derived from the Muslim Yahya. One of the most sacred Mandaean books is the *Drasia d-Yahia*, the *Teachings of John* or *Book of John*.

If true, anything the Mandaeans have to say about John will be uniquely fascinating. Could they really be the direct descendants of the John the Baptist sect that once competed with emerging Christianity? After all, Arab writers in the eighth century linked the Mandaeans to the Dositheans, who, according to the Pseudo-Clementines, were led by a disciple of the Baptist. But is this true?

The problem is that the Mandaeans' own account of their origins and history is a huge muddle, mainly because of their traumatic and lengthy history. Their traditions and sacred texts have absorbed a considerable amount of material from the various cultures with which they have coexisted (usually not very harmoniously), and while academics agree that their folktales are partly accurate, it is extremely hard to piece together a totally coherent and linear account. It has been said that one has not only to be a detective but a psychoanalyst to extract historical information from the Mandaean texts.[69]

Although, as their many references to Islamic practices and the use of the name Yahya for John shows, the Mandaean literature was formalized into a canon after the Muslim conquest of what is now Iraq in 640 CE, other texts—including parts of the Mandaean prayer book—can be traced back, on linguistic and paleographic grounds, to between 250 and 300 CE.[70] There are also distinct parallels between the Mandaica and the gnostic works in the Nag Hammadi collection, but the exact nature of their relationship—which influenced which, or whether both of them derived from a common source—has always been an academic minefield.[71]

The historical consensus about the sect has swung backwards and forwards. In the 1930s it was the done thing among scholars to see them as the genuine descendants of a sect that had been led, and perhaps even founded, by John the Baptist, even though it had changed a great deal in the intervening millennia. These far-reaching ideas received the invaluable support of no less a figure than Rudolf Bultmann, probably the twentieth century's most eminent and respected New Testament scholar, who argued in particular for a strong connection between the Mandaean sacred texts and the Gospel of John. Excitingly, parts of the Mandaica were discovered to echo precisely certain "protognostic" concepts that had always been considered unique to the Fourth Gospel. It was logical that there was some connection between the two, and as the Mandaean texts showed no sign of any awareness of John's Gospel, it seemed that either the Mandaica influenced the Gospel, or both derived from a common but now lost source, written by the Mandaeans' predecessors.

However, in the 1950s the academic consensus hit a wall of

skepticism, and by the beginning of the 1970s it had completely changed, owing entirely to the discovery of the Dead Sea Scrolls at Qumran. Some of them included parallels for the same concepts in John's Gospel, establishing that they were familiar to at least one Jewish sect before it was written, and providing a much more attractive source for those parts of the Gospel. As a result, the academic pendulum swung the other way. Not only was the significance of the Mandaean writings challenged, but it was argued that the sect itself dated from much later than previously thought, having not been founded until the seventh or eighth centuries, and not in Palestine at all. The deconstruction continued with the argument that the Mandaeans only adopted the Baptist as their prophet in Islamic times in order to qualify as a "people of the book"—as the Qu'ran specifies that all religions with a prophet and a holy book *should* (but rarely do) avoid persecution—and all their traditions about John were just so much fabrication.

However, following the publication of more Mandaean texts and the discovery of new historical evidence in the 1980s, the pendulum swung back again, and scholars began to accept once more that the Mandaeans *did* originate in Palestine some time around the time of Jesus and John the Baptist. For example, an analysis of the Mandaean script shows that it came from Nabataean and western Aramaic—current in the first century.[72]

Evidence in their legendary history pushes the story back even further. A key figure is "King Ardban," who gave them shelter when they fled from persecution by the Jews. Not only has this figure been positively identified as the Parthian king Artabanus III, who ruled between about 12 and 38 CE, but the Roman chronicler Pliny the Elder records the migration of the "Mandani" into Parthia during his reign.[73]

However, although scholarly opinion has now repatriated the Mandaeans to first-century Palestine, curiously the idea remains that the passages referring to John the Baptist came from Islamic sources. But the supporting arguments are riddled with questionable reasoning.

One of the main contentions is that John does not fulfill the expected role of the archetypal gnostic redeemer, nor is he said to have played any part in the founding of the Mandaean religion. However, if the Mandaeans had selected John to be their hero-prophet out of expediency, surely they would have turned him into their founder and at least a semidivine figure. If anything, the fact that they attributed no such role to him, simply making him one of their many leaders and teachers (albeit one of the most important), points to their image of John being based on a real man.

Critics of the authenticity of these traditions, such as the renowned German specialist in gnosticism Kurt Rudolph, seem to be revealing their own preconceptions: for example, Randolph observes that although baptism is the key ritual in the Mandaean religion, it includes no invocation to John—and since he thinks they *should* regard John as its instigator, this conspicuous absence "proves" that he was never of great consequence to them.[74] However, as we have seen, the evidence of recent years (such as the Cave of John the Baptist at Suba) suggests strongly that he was *not* the founder of a movement but the heir to one that had already existed for six or seven centuries. (The similarity of the name of the village closest to John the Baptist's cave, Suba, and the Arab name for the Mandaeans, *subba,* seems to be a genuine coincidence.)

The contradiction between the evidence that the Mandaeans existed in Palestine in the first century and a reluctance to admit that their traditions about John are based on anything substantial creates a wonderfully surreal scholastic paradox: the fact that a baptismal sect from first-century Palestine decided, many centuries later and thousands of miles from their original home, to pick as one of their folk heroes the leader of a baptismal sect in first-century Palestine is, we are told, pure coincidence.

Even Rudolph, however, widely regarded as the expert who demolished the case for a historical connection between the Mandaeans and John the Baptist, acknowledges that they possibly inherited certain traditions from earlier sects that *can* be traced back to him.[75] In other words, even if the Mandaeans are not the direct descendants of John's sect, they took their ideas from people who were—which makes one wonder what the argument was about all along. Nobody would suggest that the Mandaeans are the John the Baptist sect totally unchanged: obviously they have adopted a great deal from other sources and cultures during their long history.

But the very aspect of the Mandaean traditions that inspired

Rudolph to wonder about the possibility of an indirect link between the Mandaeans and the John sect is actually enormously significant. The crux lies in their claims about John the Baptist's relationship with Jesus. As we are about to see, the Mandaeans view the two men as *rivals*—although they are unequivocally on John's side—which is what Rudolph finds bewildering. This could hardly have been a fiction inspired by Muslim traditions (which accord great respect to Jesus as a prophet). It is hard not to agree with Yale professor of biblical studies Wayne A. Meeks' summary: "the Mandaeans must have taken over traditions in which John and Jesus were viewed as opponents."[76]

Jesus' Judas Role

It must be said that the Mandaeans' texts concerning John, like all their sacred books, are extremely difficult to see as a coherent story. In any case only a small portion of their holy books has been made available to outsiders: for obvious reasons, the Mandaeans have become reticent and insular, so it is impossible to have a complete picture. But the basic story is as follows.

Various portents preceded and attended John the Baptist's birth to an elderly couple in Jerusalem, Zakria and Nisbai (Zechariah and Elizabeth), said to be ninety-nine and eighty-eight, respectively. As the Jewish priests viewed his birth as disastrous, they sought to kill him, so the infant was taken by Enos-Uthra (Enoch, a "light being" or angel) into a hiding place in the mountains of Parwan, where he was taught until the age of twenty-two. John then returned to Jerusalem on a cloud to be reunited with his parents and began his preaching, which he continued until he was forty-two.

John is portrayed in the Mandaean literature as a prophet, ascetic, and, perhaps tellingly, a magician, who communicates directly with divine spirits while entranced. (The Mandaeans, like Simon Magus, believe in a system of many deities under the supreme God, known as the Great Life or the King of Light. Under him are creative entities called *uthria* and *malkia*, literally "riches" and "kings.") John is also said to have a wife, Anhar (Anna), with whom he had eight children, although the divine powers had to virtually force him into marrying, as he saw marriage as a distraction from his sacred calling.

Among those he baptizes is Jesus (Isu), although the version in the *Book of John* will shock mainstream Christians:

> Jesus Christ comes, moves about in humility, is baptised with the baptism of John, and becomes wise through John's wisdom. He then proceeds to pervert the word of John and change the baptism of Jordan, altering the words of kusta [the ritual greeting and handshake that forms an important part of Mandaean baptisms], and summoning wickedness and falsehood into the world.[77]

In the words of Gündüz, "The chief accusation against Jesus . . . is the falsity of his messiahship. Jesus . . . is always described as a 'false (or pseudo-) messiah' [and] 'a liar.'"[78] Indeed, "It is impossible to find one single positive pronouncement about Jesus in the whole Mandaean literature."[79] Despite the confusion of the Mandaeans' historical texts, what comes across loud and clear is that Jesus is the Judas of Mandaism, a very novel—in fact disturbing—idea for anyone brought up in the Christian West.

The men's rivalry is also implied in the Pseudo-Clementine literature, in which John's association with Simon Magus and Dositheus sets him squarely on the opposite side to Jesus and his apostles. But was this because of a rivalry that developed between their respective sects after the two masters were dead, or did they themselves begin the feud?

The evidence in the Gospels suggests the latter. Although Jesus praised John in public, he seems to have struck a rather different tone in private. And the two went their separate ways in their teaching, which invited comment and dissention—most damning being John's question from prison. So from the perspective of those who remained faithful to the Baptist, Jesus *did* "pervert" John's words. Just as the Mandaeans claim.

Death of John

Curiously, the Mandaean John stories say nothing about his arrest and execution. The only reference to his fate is in their book the

Ginza, in which he undergoes "a kind of celestial assumption,"[80] which is extremely odd if, as we are led to believe, the Mandaeans merely invented their connection with John the Baptist from Christian and Muslim sources. It is extremely odd anyway. Could it be that Mandaean beliefs about John's fate are kept secret as "deep doctrine," yet to be revealed to outsiders?

The story is rather more sensational in the Christian Gospels. The synoptics' narrative departs from its strictly linear course when it comes to John's death. The story is told in flashback in order to explain why Herod is afraid that Jesus is the Baptist returned, in some fashion, from the dead. Why is it done this way? Walter Wink makes the interesting suggestion that Mark tells of John's death at this point only because it has become unavoidable not to do so.[81] This implies that Mark would have preferred to leave it out entirely, which certainly seems so judging by what he omitted. As Wink puts it:

> He [John] is not portrayed as a martyr. Nothing is said of his courage in the face of suffering or his unswerving faith in the final triumph of his cause. In fact he scarcely manages to appear in his own death-scene at all! The emphasis is rather on what *they* do to him.[82]

To which we can add the conspicuous absence of any mention of Jesus' sorrow or anger at the news, despite his earlier praise for his former master. However, he does turn the treatment meted out to the "new Elijah" into a positive message for his own mission, claiming, for example, that John's death was intrinsically part of the prophesied pattern of the final days. But on the subject of his regret at the atrocity at the hands of Herod's men Jesus is utterly silent.

This is Mark's original account of John's end in prison:

> Herodias nursed a grudge against John and wanted to kill him. But she was not able to, because Herod feared John and protected him, knowing him to be a righteous and holy man. When Herod heard John, he was greatly puzzled; yet he liked to listen to him.
>
> Finally the opportune time came. On his birthday Herod gave a banquet for his high officials and military commanders and the leading men of Galilee. When the daughter of Herodias came in and danced, she pleased Herod and his dinner guests.

The king said to the girl, "Ask me for anything you want, and I'll give it to you." And he promised her with an oath, "Whatever you ask I will give you, up to half my kingdom."

She went out and said to her mother, "What shall I ask for?"

"The head of John the Baptist," she answered.

At once the girl hurried in to the king with the request: "I want you to give me right now the head of John the Baptist on a platter."

The king was greatly distressed, but because of his oaths and his dinner guests, he did not want to refuse her. So he immediately sent an executioner with orders to bring John's head. The man went, beheaded John in the prison, and brought back his head on a platter. He presented it to the girl, and she gave it to her mother. On hearing of this, John's disciples came and took his body and laid it in a tomb.[83]

(Why *didn't* the silly girl ask for half his kingdom?)

Matthew's account is shorn of much of the detail but adds that after burying their master, John's disciples went to tell Jesus.[84] Luke ignores the story completely, covering the Baptist's death by simply having Antipas say, "I beheaded John."[85] The Fourth Gospel says nothing about John the Baptist's fate.

Hardly a convincing story. Mark's insistence that Antipas admired and sought to protect the Baptist contradicts his emphasis two verses earlier that "Herod himself had given orders to have John arrested."[86] (What was it, protective custody?) Second, can we really believe that hard man Herod would rather risk stirring up a riot by killing the people's hero than break a casual promise to his stepdaughter? In any case, beheading was the penalty for treachery, subversion, or insurrection, suggesting Antipas instigated John's execution.[87]

Why does Mark want to exonerate Antipas and shift the blame onto his scheming wife? The characterization of Herodias as an archschemer who manipulated her husband seems to be accurate, though, judging by Josephus and other independent sources. When, in 39 CE, Caligula appointed Herod Agrippa I to rule some of the territories formerly held by Philip and made him king, Herodias rather unwisely—obviously in Lady Macbeth mode—nagged her husband to ask the emperor for a similar title. For his impertinence he was promptly stripped of his powers and exiled with her to Gaul, and his lands of Galilee and Perea were handed over to Agrippa.

But perhaps the biggest challenge to the legendary story is that not only does Mark fail to name the daughter who becomes Herodias' instrument of vengeance, but there is considerable doubt that she was the famous Salome. Quite how this traditional attribution first arose is unclear, although it could be because she became the best-known Herodian female of that generation. She was married first to Philip the tetrarch, who died in 34 or 35 CE, after which she remarried, again within the family, to one Aristobulus, to whom the emperor gave the kingdom of Lesser Armenia, which Aristobulus ruled with Salome as his queen. (Although her head is depicted on coins with her husband, from 64 Aristobulus appears alone, suggesting she had recently died.)[88]

As she is not a major historical figure, little is known about Salome, but she appears to have been too old for her role in the Gospel's tale. She had been married and so she must have been over thirteen, almost certainly a few years older, but the term Mark uses for Herodias' daughter generally means a girl of twelve or less. It is possible to think up scenarios to explain these discrepancies: Mark may have misunderstood her age, and between her marriages Salome may have returned to her mother. But then he never claims that the daughter was Salome. In fact, many early manuscripts of Mark's Gospel *do* give the daughter a name: also Herodias, which according to some scholars is the "best-attested" reading.[89] Of course Herodias might well have named one of her daughters after herself, the possibility of confusion explaining why some copyists ignored her offspring's name.

But is there any truth in Mark's scurrilous tale anyway? It is told in a very different style from the rest of his Gospel—a sudden intrusion of lurid intrigue into an otherwise dry narrative—suggesting he incorporated a separate story. And unfortunately there is no independent source: Josephus contents himself with merely saying that John the Baptist was executed on Antipas' orders.

Gerd Theissen argues that the story in the synoptic Gospels was a folktale that had grown up around the Baptist's death, just like the popular notion of a connection between his execution and Antipas' defeat in battle.[90] In the Hellenized world generally, the presence of women at banquets was always a sign of sexual license. The people considered the Herodian women immoral and licentious (probably with good reason), and this is why, Theissen suggests, the motif of the dancing girl was inserted to spice things up. But if he is right, and the story was essentially a folktale, then nothing about the Gospels' account of John the Baptist's execution is at all reliable.

On the other hand, if his death was a straightforward execution ordered by Antipas, why did it become such a lurid tale? Something must have made Antipas suddenly decide John had to die—even when he had more to lose by having him to put to death than by letting him rot in jail. But what really happened?

A way of approaching this question is to examine what the implications were for the movement John had started, and which was now centering on Jesus.

The Strangest Miracle

The immediate aftermath of the death of John the Baptist is the feeding of the multitude—providing enough to satisfy a huge crowd from a just a few loaves and a couple of fish. Although the Gospels present this purely as a miracle with symbolic overtones, clearly the event was far more significant, but its real message was either redundant by the time they were written or for some reason had been suppressed. And as the authors themselves had no idea what the story was all about, clearly they felt they had to explain it as a spectacular miracle.

Even so, the feeding of the crowd must have been one of Jesus' most important acts: together with the ensuing walking on water— with which it is linked in ways that are again far from clear—it is the only pre-Jerusalem episode that appears in all four canonical Gospels. Indeed the synoptic and Johannine descriptions agree more on this than any other event. Some of the detail is so precise that, for once, Mark and John must have drawn on the same very early source, which evidently was extremely important to the first Christians. But *why*? The Gospels' explanations make no sense even on their own logic.

The writers themselves imply heavily that there is something they are not telling us, either because they have no idea what it is or they want to keep it quiet. They relate that even at the time the disciples missed the point, and unusually, this time we are not even told what they failed to comprehend.

The first clue to the real significance of the feeding of the multitude is that it marks the end of the Galilee mission: in both Mark and John it is Jesus' last major act there, suggesting it was a transitional event that radically changed his direction. It also marks a decisive change in his relationship with the people. So far he has been an itinerant healer and preacher with a somewhat ambivalent attitude to the crowds: on the one hand enthusiastically gathering them to him but on the other often fleeing from their demands. But now something seems to click: he starts to proactively organize and lead them. Now, it seems, he has *authority*.

But did the "feeding" happen once or twice? Mark's Gospel has two separate episodes, one of five thousand and one of four, which also appear in Matthew. Luke and John have only the five thousand. In fact most scholars think that there was only one event, Mark doubling up the story because his sources included two slightly different accounts.[91] This seems the most likely explanation, but even if there were two separate incidents, then everything below applies equally to both. But first, the famous feeding of the five thousand, beginning with Mark's version.

Being pestered by the crowds, and having no time to themselves—not even a moment to grab a bite to eat—Jesus and the disciples withdraw to a "solitary place," but such is the people's enthusiasm that they follow, some even getting there first. Jesus has compassion on the crowd "because they were like sheep without a shepherd," and so "began teaching them many things." (While in Matthew this is "and healed those who were ill," which is also Luke's understanding, in John's Gospel Jesus has no interaction at all with them before the feeding.) It gets late and the people have had nothing to eat, but when the disciples ask him to send the crowd away so they can get some food, he insists that *they* should feed them. As they have only five loaves and two fish among them, this looks like a bit of a problem. But he offers a seemingly crazy solution:

Then Jesus directed them to have all the people sit down in groups on the green grass. So they sat down in groups of hundreds and fifties. Taking the five loaves and the two fish and looking up to heaven, he gave thanks and broke the loaves. Then he gave them to his disciples to set before the people. He also divided the two fish among them all. They all ate and were satisfied, and the disciples picked up twelve basketfuls of broken pieces of bread and fish. The number of the men who had eaten was five thousand.[92]

Nothing makes sense. First, although the people track down Jesus against his will, why was this such a problem? After all, he was supposed to have the ability to slip through crowds unnoticed: surely he of all people could have thrown them off. Second, as some of the crowd manage to arrive at the remote spot before Jesus himself, how did they know where he was going? This is especially odd as his party traveled by boat but the people followed on foot. Next, unless the entire five thousand were very disorganized, surely at least some of them would have thought to take a picnic. And even though the whole episode is based on the idea that Jesus is constantly besieged by crowds despite his wishes, it ends with his successfully dismissing them—so why didn't he just do that in the first place? In fact not only does he send them all away, but he then goes alone to a quiet spot to pray, although the whole rationale of the story is that he is unable to escape. Then, as Hooker points out, "One feature which is missing from the narrative is any expression of astonishment on the part of the crowd, nor does Jesus command secrecy," and Mark "emphasises later that, even though the disciples had witnessed the miracle, they did not understand it."[93] And finally there is the unique nature of this miracle: Jesus never does anything else like it.

Mark's second feeding is of four thousand with seven loaves and "a few small fish," with seven basketfuls of scraps picked up afterwards. Apart from that the details are virtually identical, although the account is briefer. Again it is emphasized that "About four thousand *men* were present."[94]

Matthew and Luke's accounts of the feeding of the five thousand are virtually identical, although Matthew explains, "The number of those who ate was about five thousand men, besides women and children."[95] Clearly Matthew finds Mark's statement that the crowd consisted solely of men rather unlikely, assuming they had their families with them—but this highlights the fact that his source was concerned only with the men. For Mark, either it was an all-male event or only the men were relevant.

The Fourth Gospel, as usual, adds a little circumstantial detail, such as the loaves' being made of barley. And as both John and Mark have the disciples give the same amount—two hundred denarii— that it would take to feed the crowd, they must have drawn from the same source. John's Gospel also has the strange emphasis on the crowd's being men: "and the men sat down, about five thousand of them." [96] But the most significant difference comes right at the end:

> And after the people saw the miraculous sign that Jesus did, they began to say, "Surely this is the Prophet who is to come into the world." Jesus, knowing that they intended to come and make him king by force, withdrew again to a mountain by himself. [97]

In this version the crowd *is* aware of the miraculous nature of the event, taking it as the definitive sign that he is "the Prophet who is to come into the world"—not, note, the Messiah. Although the crowd's reaction is quite different from the synoptics' version, it still makes little sense: why should being able to feed people convince them he is their king?

It is possible that there are Old Testament allusions in the story: some see a parallel with Moses' provision of manna to the Israelites in the wilderness, although this seems rather strained. The most specific analogy is with an episode in the Second Book of Kings, in which Elisha feeds a hundred men with twenty loaves. [98] The writer of John's Gospel seems to have had this in mind, because the loaves in the story are also made of barley.

But none of this really sheds much light on the meaning of the New Testament stories, and neither does it make much sense in terms of *Christians'* view of Jesus, since it has no relevance to any of their crucial beliefs, such as his divine status or role as humanity's Savior.

The puzzle deepens with the next event, Jesus' walking on water. Although it is made clear that the multiplication of food and the ability to walk on water are intimately linked, tantalizingly the reason is left unsaid. The walking on water—like the feeding, dissimilar to any other miracle that Jesus performs—appears almost identically in all four Gospels immediately after, and apparently somehow as a result of, the feeding of the five thousand.

Leaving the gathering in the wilderness, Jesus orders the disciples to travel ahead by boat while he goes alone up a mountain to pray, but in the night he terrifies them by appearing walking on the Sea of Galilee—they think he must be a ghost—and climbing into their vessel. Mark adds the magnificent non sequitur: "They were completely amazed, for they had not understood about the loaves; their hearts were hardened." [99]

Shortly after the second feeding and again in a boat, Jesus himself makes a reference to the disciples' missing the point about "the loaves":

> The disciples had forgotten to bring bread, except for one loaf they had with them in the boat. "Be careful," Jesus warned them. "Watch out for the yeast of the Pharisees and that of Herod."
>
> They discussed this with one another and said, "It is because we have no bread."
>
> Aware of their discussion, Jesus asked them: "Why are you talking about having no bread? Do you still not see or understand? Are your hearts hardened? Do you have eyes but fail to see, and ears but fail to hear? And don't you remember? When I broke the five loaves for the five thousand, how many basketfuls of pieces did you pick up?"
>
> "Twelve," they replied.
>
> "And when I broke the seven loaves for the four thousand, how many basketfuls of pieces did you pick up?"
>
> They answered, "Seven."
>
> He said to them, "Do you still not understand?" [100]

And that is the end of the story. What was all that about? Twice we are told the disciples had no idea of the significance of "the loaves," but although the writers hint heavily that there was a deeper meaning, clearly they have no intention of revealing it. Although it is unlikely that we will ever have a complete answer, all the clues point to the awesome nature of the meal being ritualistic rather than miraculous, and in some way relating to the Eucharist. Others have come to the same conclusion: Albert Schweitzer wrote, "The 'miracle of the loaves and fishes' was in reality the first Eucharist."[101]

In his First Letter to the Corinthians Paul implies that one of the major symbolic elements of the Eucharist was that the loaf had to be shared among all the worshippers because Jesus had only one body to share.[102] In the *Didache* the Eucharistic words liken the gathering of the faithful to the re-forming of the loaf from the crumbs scattered over the mountain.[103] Both reveal an association between the Eucharist and "the loaves," but it is impossible to go further than that.

A Military Maneuver

Despite the image of the feeding that Sunday schools and conventional Christians tend to paint—as a sort of jolly mass picnic with paranormal overtones—the passage is more specific, with the ordering of the men into *ranks*, having them sit "by hundreds and fifties." Andrew Lincoln, in his commentary on John's Gospel, notes that the men have been "grouped in military formation" in the wilderness, adding that "it is John's account that draws out these political dimensions of the feeding."[104]

Inevitably, at such an edgy time there would have been a political dimension to such a scene, whatever Jesus' own intentions. As Ernst Bammel, reader in early Christianity and Jewish studies, Cambridge University, points out, "The gathering of crowds in the desert as a starting point for messianic ventures is well-known from contemporary history."[105] Josephus describes several would-be Messiahs and freedom fighters who withdrew into the desert with a following, intending to march on Jerusalem. Whatever was going on, the feeding of the multitude would certainly have *looked* like the preliminaries to another uprising, but only John's Gospel addresses this issue, in its reference to the people wanting to make Jesus their king. As John Robinson says (his emphasis):

For behind this wilderness gathering was *not only* whatever physically this miracle of sharing involved, *not only* the mystical and sacramental truth which the Church came to see in it, but a highly charged political moment. For it very nearly turned into a para-military desert rising, leading to a messianic march on Jerusalem to overthrow the Romans.[106]

The political implication still stands whether Jesus wanted to be king or fled in horror. A large gathering of people massing before a leader in a remote place would have been perceived by the author-ities as at least a potential threat, as happened with John the Baptist. Raymond E. Brown argues that whatever Jesus intended by the feeding, it would have spelled danger, adding about the Fourth Gospel's version,

> The ministry of miracles in Galilee culminating in the multiplica-tion (which in John, as in Mark, is the last miracle of the Galilee ministry) aroused a popular fervour that created a danger of an up-rising which would give authorities, lay and religious, a chance to arrest Jesus legally.[107]

Clearly the meeting itself was the important aspect of the event, although the gathering of a large body of men in a deserted place suggests it was prearranged, not the spontaneous event of the Gospels. But there is another level, when seen in the light of the death of the Baptist.

In Mark's Gospel a connection with John's death and the feeding of the five thousand is implied by the fact that the feeding follows immediately after his execution. Today's version of Mark fails to make the association explicit, although Matthew does:

> John's disciples came and took his body and buried it. Then they went and told Jesus.
>
> When Jesus heard what had happened, he withdrew by boat privately to a solitary place. Hearing of this the crowds followed him on foot from the towns.[108]

In fact, there is overwhelming evidence that Mark's original ac-count also spelled this out, but this was deliberately obscured by early editors, as Ernst Bammel demonstrated in his 1984 analysis of the language and style of Mark's account. Bammel began with the observation that the term "apostles" in Mark's introduction to this episode—"The apostles gathered around Jesus and reported to him all they had done and taught"—seems to be a later editorial addition since it is a favorite term of the early Church but not of Mark. Moreover, in some early manuscripts it reads, "the *disciples* gathered around Jesus and reported to him all *he* had done and taught," although this has always been seen as a mistake: after all, why tell Jesus himself what he had been doing? But this assumes that the passage referred to *his* disciples.

There are also signs that the next sentence—"Then, because so many people were coming and going that they did not even have a chance to eat, he said to them, 'Come with me by yourselves to a quiet place and get some rest'"—was also a later addition to link to the feeding. If this sentence is taken out, Jesus' words make sense as advice to the disciples to withdraw into a place of privacy. But who was he talking to? Bammel concludes that the group was John the Baptist's disciples, and that as originally written by Mark, the text followed on directly from the previous passage about the Baptist's death:

> On hearing of this [John's death], John's disciples came and took his body and laid it in a tomb.
> And the disciples gathered around Jesus and reported to him all he [John] had done and taught. And he said to them, "Come with me by yourselves to a quiet place to get some rest." [109]

In other words, originally Mark, like Matthew, *did* link Jesus' retreat to the report of the Baptist's death by his disciples, but this Gospel was subsequently edited to obscure the connection between John's demise and the gathering in the wilderness. This alteration must have happened after Matthew had used it as a source. Bammel sums up:

> The disciples of John recount the execution of their master to Jesus and it is in consequence of this that Jesus *anekoresis* [withdrew]. The report can only mean that by taking this action the disciples recognise Jesus as the successor of John, that they adopt him as their own master. Jesus' reaction is characterised as well: *aneko-*

resis is a term that describes the refuge one takes from fiscal or some other form of oppression. It thereby establishes a bridge between Herod's punitive measure against John and the course of action taken by Jesus, a decision which may be seen as comprehensible on the assumption that the action taken by Herod is not necessarily limited to John but may be extended to other persons as well.[110]

It makes sense that Jesus would have been in danger after Herod Antipas' action against the Baptist. This idea is supported by the Gospel, although yet again it is not obvious because of the odd flashback sequence. First, we are informed about Antipas' fears that Jesus is John revived; second, the Baptist's death is told retrospectively; and last, we hear about the feeding of the five thousand as a consequence of or reaction to his death. So the proper *chronological* sequence of events should really be: John is executed, Jesus withdraws into the wilderness and feeds the five thousand, and Antipas gets scared. In other words, Herod's fears were a direct reaction to what Jesus had done in response to John's death—gathering a mass of men together in the wilderness.

Jesus' retreat also marked the moment when he truly came into his own, taking over the movement that had been John's, welcoming the Baptist's disciples into his own following, and emerging as the Baptist's successor in the eyes of the people. Ian Wilson, in *Jesus: The Evidence* (1984), writes of the feeding of the five thousand: "It seems clear that the popular following which John the Baptist had stirred up, the following so feared by Herod Antipas, had turned itself to Jesus, as John's star pupil, for its leadership."[111] However, not all of John's followers accepted Jesus as their new leader—otherwise the Baptist's sect would never have survived to threaten the early Church.

It is not too much of a leap to suggest that the crowd also reacted to the same news: it was those who had once been "excited to the utmost" by John the Baptist's teaching who now flocked to his former chief disciple. And Mark relates that Jesus "had compassion on them, because they were like sheep without a shepherd"—but why use such clear and specific imagery unless they *had* lost their leader?

It was certainly more than grief for their spiritual leader that united the men in the wilderness, sitting there in ranks so reminiscent of an army, with a strong implicit sense of purpose, organizing themselves in order to carry out some objective. They were turning to Jesus not just as John the Baptist's successor but as their leader, even their king. Was the uprising that Herod Antipas feared John the Baptist might inspire finally happening?

But why is the passage about the crowd's desire to make him king in John's Gospel but not the others? Did the writer of the Fourth Gospel invent it, or was it once in the synoptic source but removed? Bammel suggests that something *was* deleted from Mark that originally made the transition from the feeding of the multitude to the walking on water. Mark's account reads:

> They all ate and were satisfied, and the disciples picked up twelve basketfuls of broken pieces of bread and fish. The number of the men who had eaten was five thousand.
>
> Immediately Jesus made his disciples get into the boat and go on ahead of him to Bethsaida, while he dismissed the crowd. After leaving them, he went up on a mountainside to pray.[112]

The urgency implied by "immediately" is also, as Bammel points out, present in the verb *enagkases*, translated in the TNIV as "made" but more properly "forced." For some reason the disciples' departure and Jesus' retreat were a matter for haste. Since there is nothing in the preceding sentences about gathering scraps to explain this sudden urgency, Bammel concludes that something has been edited out. The only suggestion comes from the Fourth Gospel: the people wanted to make him king. The big question is whether Jesus actively sought this role or, as John's Gospel has it, recoiled from it.

Certainly there is an interesting connotation in the very fact that Jesus fed the people. The blessing and distribution of food was not only an intrinsic part of a priest's function but also an act that signified authority—as an important role of the head of a family at Passover, for example. So in providing food for the crowd, Jesus was essentially taking charge.

Although during his Galilee mission his behavior encouraged the speculation that he might be the Messiah, Jesus never made an explicit claim to that effect in public. In contrast, however, as we will see, when he entered Jerusalem he *overtly* associated himself with the role. This was a significant change between the Galilee and Jerusalem phases, and the pivotal moment was the feeding of the five thousand, which was itself caused by John the Baptist's death.

Two highly significant events take place immediately after "the loaves." In John's Gospel Jesus delivers his "bread of life" discourse, which precipitates a mass desertion of disciples—perhaps some of John the Baptist's followers, upset at Jesus' "new broom" actions. In Mark the feeding of the multitude is followed immediately by Peter's recognition of Jesus as the Messiah.

Was Christ a Killer?

The feeding of the five thousand marks the moment when Jesus took over John's movement. As Donovan Joyce sums up in *The Jesus Scroll*:

> The change in Jesus after the death of his cousin [*sic*] is remarkable. The aimless drifting about the country on a never-described and seemingly purposeless "mission" had gone. There is now purpose and resolution and a suddenly found weight of confidence and authority in all his utterances. It would be absurd not to imagine that this, in some way, was connected with John's death.[113]

And Shimon Gibson comments, "The career of Jesus only blooms . . . after the death of John the Baptist. But John the Baptist is clearly in command up to that point."[114]

The impact of John's death on Jesus' mission is undeniable, but what is less certain is the reason. Jesus could have been galvanized into action by the brutal execution of his master, spurred on to ensure that his mission was completed. Or perhaps the death finally allowed him to tear himself free of the Baptist's influence. Given the signs of tension and disagreement between the two men, and bearing in mind John the Baptist's skeptical question from his prison cell, the evidence supports the latter scenario.

Remember Joyce's suggestion that Jesus may actually have been responsible for John the Baptist's arrest—that he had informed on him to Herod Antipas in order to remove him, his greatest rival. In Joyce's scenario the reason Jesus fled to Galilee after John's arrest was that he was fleeing from *John's* followers. If so, then—even if indirectly—Jesus was responsible for John the Baptist's death. Direct evidence for Joyce's hypothesis is lacking, but it does highlight the fact that the person who gained most from the Baptist's removal was Jesus. (Certainly it was not Antipas.)

In *The Templar Revelation* we noted that the Gospels are distinctly evasive when describing the circumstances of John the Baptist's death, and there is no denying that his removal cleared the way for Jesus to take over his movement. But were we, as some took it, suggesting that Jesus was somehow personally responsible for John the Baptist's death—as one newspaper put it luridly, "Authors claim Christ may have been a Killer"?[115] After making his doubts about Jesus' fitness to lead public—by sending his disciples to question him—was John simply too much of an obstacle?

What we were proposing was not so much that Jesus initiated the crime, but that his *supporters* could have done so. Although we will examine this more fully in the next chapter, there was a network of supporters outside the immediate circle of disciples who worked to smooth Jesus' path. Perhaps they took it upon themselves to remove this obstacle to their Chosen One's elevation. There would have been no need to act under his instruction or even consult him. It is usually safer *not* to tell the individual whose career you are trying to further.

The exact circumstances of John the Baptist's death are suspicious, and all that can be said is that it was the result of some kind of palace intrigue into which Herod Antipas was either tricked or goaded against his wishes and all political sense. Curiously, it does seem that Jesus had his supporters within Antipas' household. We have seen that the wife of his steward was one of the women who traveled with Jesus, and Acts mentions in an aside that one of the first to join the new Christian sect after Jesus' crucifixion, Manaean, was Antipas' foster brother.[116] So there may have been a group of Jesus sympathizers in the palace that orchestrated John the Baptist's execution.

Whatever really happened, there is no doubt that the Baptist's death worked to Jesus' advantage, allowing him to take over John's movement—and marking a significant change in his own mission. Now he set his sights on Jerusalem, and his ultimate destiny.

8

ROAD TO THE CROSS

After Jesus took over John the Baptist's movement at the feeding of the five thousand, he entered the phase that took him to his terrible death in Jerusalem. The tension builds as his words and deeds take on a new, intense momentum—and also add to the great puzzle of his mission.

It is here that the synoptic Gospels and John's Gospel find themselves in substantial agreement for the first time, although they still differ over many often very important details. This—and the sheer space they all devote to the Passion—shows that, to the first Christians, Jesus' earlier career was only important in the light of its seismic finale.

There is no doubt that in the final phase Jesus was acting with a stronger sense of purpose, with a definite program in mind: Jerusalem was to be the climax of his mission. There is no doubt that he believed his destiny lay there; the only question is precisely what he believed it to be.

There are three views of his ultimate purpose. The traditional Christian belief is that it was to fulfill God's plan of the redeeming sacrifice: he had to suffer and die in Jerusalem in order for the resurrection to happen. The second explanation is that Jesus believed that by his being in Jerusalem at that particular time, *something* would happen that would bring about the Kingdom of God: Yahweh would intervene to fulfill the promises he had made through the prophets of old. The third is that Jesus went to Jerusalem intending to lead a popular uprising that would oust the Romans and establish him as the King-Messiah of the Jews.

All three have Jesus working to a definite plan and with a distinct end in sight, unlike in the Galilee mission. A major part of all three scenarios was making the great event happen at Passover. As Josephus explained, the major Jewish festivals were "the usual occasion for sedition to flare up,"[1] but Passover, which commemorated the Exodus, when the Israelites freed themselves from oppression in Egypt, was especially volatile. Robert Eisenman aptly describes it as "the Jewish National Liberation Festival."[2] Riots frequently broke out during the weeklong celebrations.

The population of Jerusalem of that time is estimated at twenty-five to thirty thousand, but at Passover it swelled to perhaps as many as 125,000.[3] Accommodation was at a premium, and most pilgrims had to stay in tents outside the city. Once it had been compulsory for Jews to spend the night in the holy city, but for practical reasons this rule had been relaxed so that they could sleep in its environs. Nevertheless, they had to eat the meal itself *within* the city.

One of the ways in which the "Passover plot" (to use Hugh J. Schonfield's evocative phrase) is revealed is in the hints of a group working from behind the scenes to facilitate Jesus' mission in the city. Although in Galilee he has supporters who give him food and shelter, there appears to be nothing more to it than that, while in the Jerusalem phase there are signs of a coordinated group who shelter him and facilitate his plans. Perhaps the most startling aspect of this cabal is that it manifestly did *not* include the disciples—even the closest, such as Peter—who seem to have been unaware that events were being orchestrated.

This issue has important implications for our understanding of what Jesus was about, as it suggests he was fitting into this mysterious group's preexisting agenda. This idea flies in the face of Christian thinking, in which he is quite simply God's Son, who needs nobody to pave the way or protect him. It also introduces an element of calculation and political savvy into his actions, which again sits uncomfortably with the conventional Christian view.

In his groundbreaking *The Passover Plot* (1965) Schonfield argued that the Gospels reveal clues about the existence of a shadowy group that smoothed the way and protected Jesus in the last phase of his mission. It arranges, for example, the provision of the colt on which he rides into Jerusalem in order to fulfill a messianic prophecy, and organizes the room for the Last Supper—employing passwords and secret signs. Schonfield identifies Bethany as the "base for his operations"[4] and its otherwise enigmatic residents, the family of Mary, Martha, and Lazarus, as the key members of this group. But was this network working for Jesus—or was he working for them?

The Bethany Family

Both gospel traditions agree that Jesus based himself in Bethany, on the Mount of Olives, from where he made the two-mile journey into Jerusalem every day before Passover. Not only was it conveniently close to the holy city but had he stayed in Jerusalem itself, he could be secretly taken at night by his enemies, whereas Bethany was handy for a quick dash into the desert at the first sign of trouble. Only Luke ignores Bethany as Jesus' base, saying he camped out on the Mount of Olives, and shows marked evasiveness about the village, consistently removing references to it from events that all the other Gospels agree took place in the locality.

Between his leaving Galilee and establishing himself in Bethany, both the synoptic and Johannine traditions have Jesus going to the place "across the Jordan" where John the Baptist first made his mark (i.e., Perea) for an unspecified time. This is particularly interesting if, as we believe, it was Jesus' taking over John's movement that turned his objectives toward Jerusalem. Visiting the Baptist's original base would be another potent demonstration that he was now the movement's leader.

The Fourth Gospel has Jesus moving backwards and forwards between Perea and Bethany during that period—most notably for the raising of Lazarus—before establishing himself in Bethany for Passover. This passage is not found in the synoptics but is in the Secret Gospel of Mark. Curiously, the place in Perea where we first heard of John the Baptist, and where Jesus goes at this stage of the story, was also called Bethany—"Bethany across the Jordan." Is this just a coincidence?

John's Gospel has Jesus moving, for safety, to another location during this period. After the raising of Lazarus, Jesus is told that the Jewish leaders now want him dead, and he withdraws with his disciples to the town of Ephraim, some twenty miles north of Jerusalem. The choice seems to have been more than just expediency, as Ephraim was "a city under Samaritan influence,"[5] as the name itself suggests, Ephraim being the most important of the two tribes from which the Samaritans were descended. The name was also given to the area—the bulk of Samaria—which it had once occupied. Yet again there is that intriguing Samaritan connection.

In Bethany the rather mysterious close friends of Jesus, the brother-and-sisters trio of Lazarus, Mary, and Martha, enter the spotlight. Many commentators have discerned a hint that the full story about them is being withheld, either because the gospel writers didn't know it or they were determined that no one else would.

The subject of the Bethany family is one of those about which Luke and John seem to be drawing on a source unknown to Mark or Matthew. Although Luke and John tell entirely different stories about the family, certain elements suggest a common source of information (probably oral rather than written). Luke tells us, as Jesus makes his way to Jerusalem, that

> he came to a village where a woman named Martha opened her home to him. She had a sister called Mary, who sat at the Lord's feet listening to what he said. But Martha was distracted by all the preparations that had to be made. She came to him and asked, "Lord, don't you care that my sister has left me to do the work by myself? Tell her to help me!"
>
> "Martha, Martha," the Lord answered, "you are worried and upset about many things, but only one thing is needed. Mary has chosen what is better, and it will not be taken away from her."[6]

As that is the full extent of an apparently inconsequential story—a sisterly tiff where Jesus comes across as rather ungrateful for Martha's effort to make him welcome—one wonders why Luke thought it worth including. Witherington observes:

> The use of the phrase "to sit at the feet of" in [Luke] 10.39 is significant since there is evidence that this is a technical formula

meaning "to be a disciple" of. If so, then Luke is intimating to his audience that Mary is a disciple and as such her behaviour is to be emulated.[7]

In fact Luke never actually says that Mary lived in the same house as her sister—he merely states that the house belongs to Martha, then adds that her sister Mary "sat at the Lord's feet." If the phrase means disciple, it implies that she was one of the women who traveled with Jesus, and that they were being put up at her sister's house. If she is also technically a guest, this might explain why she felt no pressure to roll up her sleeves and help with the chores, and also sheds some light on Jesus' words that she has "chosen what is better"—surely more fitting for one of his full-time followers than someone who is new to his message.

What prevents Luke's tale being simply some odd bit of gossip is that the same sisters also appear in John, although in a completely different and much more significant episode: the raising of Lazarus. In the Fourth Gospel the focus is on Lazarus, who is introduced as Martha and Mary's brother. A location is also specified: "Now a man named Lazarus was ill. He was from Bethany, the village of Mary and her sister Martha."[8] Significantly, while the writer feels he has to introduce Lazarus to his readers, he clearly feels no such necessity to introduce his sisters. In fact the situation is the opposite: he uses the sisters to identify Lazarus, as if confident his readers will already know who they are but less sure they will know him. He does, however, throw in a memory jogger: "This Mary, whose brother Lazarus now lay sick, was the same one who poured perfume on the Lord and wiped his feet with her hair."[9] This episode comes later, and the way this sentence is inserted makes it obvious that it *is* a reminder to the readers, who already know all about Mary and her anointing of Jesus.

Although we will deal with the raising of Lazarus later, what is significant here is the interaction between his two sisters and Jesus. They send word to him to come and help their ailing brother, and when Jesus arrives, Martha goes out to meet him, leaving Mary indoors. After a brief exchange with him—bordering on the reproachful, since she begins, "Lord, if you had been here, my brother would not have died"—Martha returns to the house and tells Mary that "the Teacher" has asked for her (although in the story as told in the Gospel he hasn't). Mary then goes out to Jesus and throws herself weeping at his feet.

The stories in Luke and John seem worlds apart, the only similarity being the names of the two sisters. But there is a definite parallel between the attitudes and characters of Martha and Mary. In both Martha is the active one who voices her complaints to Jesus, while Mary is more passive—or perhaps more relaxed, having a greater understanding of his purpose—and ends up at Jesus' feet. In fact the theme is repeated a third time during Jesus' anointing, as we will see, when Martha is specifically described as serving when Mary anoints his feet.

Such parallels in what are otherwise two completely different stories suggest that Luke and John are drawing on shared, if obscure, material. However, the passages in the two Gospels are enough to establish that Jesus had close friends and supporters, Martha and Mary, who lived in Bethany—with their brother, the highly significant Lazarus.

The Raising of Lazarus

As one of the most mysterious and sensational of all New Testament miracles, why is the raising of Lazarus only in John's Gospel? Didn't Mark and Q know about it? If they did, why leave it out? In the Fourth Gospel it is Jesus' key deed, which sealed his fate as far as the Jewish authorities were concerned: they decided to bring about his demise *because* he had brought Lazarus back from the dead, which converted many to his cause.

Perhaps the synoptics knew nothing about it because it never happened—the writer of John's Gospel either made it up or misunderstood a parable for a real event and let his imagination do the rest. However, Morton Smith's discovery of Mark's secret gospel undermined this only too attractive solution, but in doing so generated even more questions and confusion. If this text (or rather the tiny extracts that survive) is genuine—which we accept—then the Lazarus episode was in one of the other gospel traditions but was deleted because it related to teachings reserved for the higher initiates only. And this account suggests a symbolic, ritualistic interpretation of the event, rather than a literal miracle.

Secret Mark aside, there are clues—again in the odd interplay between the Gospels of John and Luke—that there is more to the Lazarus episode than we are allowed to know. This arises from the appearance in Luke of a character named Lazarus in the completely different context of a parable. While at first glance this seems like a coincidence—Lazarus is generally thought to be the Galilean version of Eleazar, which was quite a common name—certain features give pause for thought. John's is only one of two miracles in which the beneficiary is named. And Luke's parable is the only time in the New Testament where one of the characters in a parable is named—perhaps a slightly odd connection between the two Lazaruses, but an association of ideas nonetheless.

In the Fourth Gospel, Jesus is recalled from the other Bethany, in Perea, by Mary and Martha because their brother is sick. Mysteriously delaying until he somehow knows that Lazarus is actually dead, he eventually arrives when the youth has already been in his tomb for four days. It has been suggested that this is to make a specific point in terms of the Jewish belief that the soul leaves the body after three days: as Lazarus has been dead for four he is *seriously* dead.[10] After the exchanges with the two sisters discussed above, he goes to the tomb, weeps, and orders the boulder covering the entrance to be rolled away. Lazarus emerges, still in his grave clothes.

Witnessing this sensational miracle, some of the crowd are won over to Jesus' cause, but others denounce him to the Pharisees, resulting in an emergency meeting of the Sanhedrin. The basic complaint is that "If we let him go on like this, everyone will believe in him, and then the Romans will come and take away both our place [or "temple"] and our nation." The high priest Caiaphas argues that it is better that "one man die for the people" (a deliberately ironic echo of the Christian teaching about Jesus). The Sanhedrin therefore decide that Jesus must die.[11] Clearly the missing link between the two parts of the Sanhedrin's argument—the people will follow Jesus, and the Romans will take complete control of Judea—is the people's declaring him their leader. It was at this point that Jesus and the disciples withdrew for safety to the Samaritan town of Ephraim.

Comparing the familiar account of the raising of Lazarus with the parable in Luke, which contrasts the afterlife treatment of an unnamed rich man and a beggar named Lazarus, is particularly telling. Lazarus sits at the rich man's gate covered with sores that are licked by dogs. When both men die, angels carry him to Abraham's side while the rich man is taken to hell, where, seeing Lazarus' situation, he begs the venerable leader to send the ex-beggar to cool his thirst even with just a finger dipped in water. But Abraham tells him that he had his good things in life while Lazarus had it rough, and now that they are dead, their situations are reversed. The denouement is especially significant in terms of the raising of Lazarus. The rich man begs Abraham to send Lazarus to his (the rich man's) five brothers to warn them not to make the same mistake. Although Abraham replies that they already have their warning, from "Moses and the Prophets," the wealthy one insists that "if someone from the dead goes to them, they will repent." Abraham's final word is "If they do not listen to Moses and the Prophets, they will not be convinced even if someone rises from the dead."[12]

The common motifs between the two Lazarus tales are revealing: the return from the dead of a man named Lazarus, and the refusal of certain Jews to be won over to the truth. Andrew Lincoln makes the point that the punch line to Luke's parable "appears to be tailor-made for the fourth evangelist's theological perspective."[13]

Although the two stories are very different, as with the two Gospels' treatment of Martha and Mary the themes suggest that there must be *some* connection—a common source adapted differently by the authors of John and Luke. It seems that Luke picked the name for his parable from that source, showing he knew it and yet still chose not to include such a major event. Why not?

Secret Mark supplies the answer to all these questions: the raising of Lazarus was a *secret*. The account that, according to Clement of Alexandria, was omitted from the canonical Mark goes as follows:

And they came to Bethany, and a certain woman, whose brother had died, was there. And, coming, she prostrated herself before Jesus and says to him, "Son of David, have mercy on me." But the disciples rebuked her. And Jesus, being angered, went off with her into the garden where the tomb was, and straightaway a great cry was heard from the tomb. And going near Jesus rolled away the stone from the door of the tomb. And straightaway, going in where the youth was, he stretched forth his hand and raised him, seizing his hand. But the youth, looking upon him, loved him and began to beseech him that he might be with him. And going out of the tomb they came into the house of the youth, for he was rich. And after six days Jesus told him what to do and in the evening the youth comes to him, wearing a linen cloth over [his] naked [body]. And he remained with him that night, for Jesus taught him the mystery of the Kingdom of God. And thence, arising, he returned to the other side of the Jordan.[14]

The location is Bethany, but neither the dead youth nor his sister is named, although the timing and location make it obvious that it is Lazarus. Whether the sister is Martha or Mary is unclear. (Presumably it is Mary, as she ends up at Jesus' feet.)

Although the resurrection of the youth is depicted as a miracle, the sequel in which he comes to Jesus to be "taught the mystery of the Kingdom of God" seems to be a mystery-cult-type initiation, suggesting that the raising itself was merely symbolic.

Reading the exchange in John's Gospel between Martha and Jesus, it certainly looks like the "catechism"—formulaic questions and answers, and the declaration of the essential belief—that customarily accompanied such ceremonies. Martha's final affirmation, "I believe that you are the Christ, the Son of God, who was to come into the world," incorporates the same phrase "who was to come" (ho erchemonos) as used by John the Baptist when he first allegedly recognized Jesus as "the One." As so often with John's Gospel, the writer appears to have fleshed out the story to disguise the meaning.

Clearly there was a great deal about the Bethany group in general and Lazarus in particular that the early Christian sources did not want broadcast. Its omission from the "public" version of Mark, the Fourth Gospel's omission of the initiatory aspects of the raising of Lazarus, and Luke's hints, in the parable of the beggar Lazarus, that he too knew the story but chose not to include it, all point in this direction. Through Smith's discovery of Secret Mark and detective work based on it we can recover some of what was hidden, but by no means all of it.

However, this is extremely curious. It is hard to reconcile with the other image of Bethany, of a planned and concerted effort to have Jesus recognized as the Davidic Messiah. Performing secret initiations was not expected of the Messiah, but here there is a strong sense of the mystery schools, a gnostic—even pagan—atmosphere in the background. It would be tempting to assume that some muddle had crept into the Lazarus story by the time the Gospels were composed—were it not for the fact that Bethany was the location for not just one ritual with heavy mystical overtones, but two.

The "Christ-ening"

The other enigmatic event at Bethany is Jesus' anointing, while at supper, by a woman—beyond all but the smallest doubt Lazarus' sister Mary. It appears in all four canonical Gospels, although, like the raising episode, receiving wildly different treatments. The Gospels disagree on whether it happened just before or a few days after Jesus' entry into Jerusalem. In Mark it happens two days before Passover:[15]

> While Jesus was in Bethany, reclining at the table in the home of a man known as Simon the Leper, a woman came with an alabaster jar of very expensive perfume, made of pure [spike]nard. She broke the jar and poured the perfume on his head.

Some are outraged at this and rebuke the woman because of the waste of money—the perfume was worth three hundred denarii, and a laborer earned only one denarius a day—saying it should have been sold to help the poor. But Jesus defends the woman, saying:

> Leave her alone. Why are you bothering her? She has done a beautiful thing to me. The poor you will always have with you, and you can help them any time you want. But you will not always have me. She did what she could. She poured perfume on my body beforehand to prepare for my burial. I tell you the truth, wherever the gospel is preached throughout the world, what she has done will also be told, in memory of her.

For unexplained reasons this prompts Judas Iscariot to betray Jesus. He goes to the chief priests, who agree to pay him to hand over his master. The story then moves on to the Last Supper.

Matthew, as usual, repeats the story in his own words, but the essentials are the same. Before we turn to the third synoptic account, it is interesting to see how John tells this story, placing the event immediately before Jesus' entry into Jerusalem, six days before Passover, and also locating it at Bethany—but at the home of Lazarus, Martha, and Mary. Jesus reclines at table with Lazarus and Martha, while Mary performs the anointing. Mary's method of anointing is slightly different in John's Gospel: she anoints Jesus' feet—he is reclining at the table in the Greek style—and then wipes them with her hair.[16]

Could John's replacement of Mark's anonymous woman with Lazarus' sister simply be intended to create a rounded story? Apparently not: there appears to some solid fact behind the tale. Mark locates the event in Bethany, and since it is the home of Mary and her siblings, close friends of Jesus, it makes more sense for him to be there than with the otherwise unmentioned and unexplained Simon the Leper. More conclusively, as we saw above, John's Gospel assumes that his audience already knows who the sisters are, even using Mary's anointing role as a reminder when introducing the raising of Lazarus. So it seems as certain as we can be two thousand years after the event that the anointing woman was Mary, sister of Lazarus and Martha. And as Witherington points out, this means that "Mary is the only woman in the Gospels whom Jesus defends twice for her devotion and desire to serve her Master."[17] (Once here, and once in Luke's tale of Martha and Mary.)

Both traditions agree that the anointing was an integral and pivotal moment during Jesus' last days, but it is far less clear why. The event itself must have happened, as there was no point in inventing it: for once even Matthew ignores the temptation to crowbar a scriptural prophecy into his narrative, and neither does it add anything to the story of the Passion. The Gospels offer two explanations of its significance—that it relates to Jesus' coming death, and that apparently it inspires Judas to betray him—but both presuppose that Jesus knew he was going to die, and as we will see, the evidence is against it. The explanations must be later Christian attempts to find a meaning.

And why invent the bad feeling among the disciples? Something about the anointing certainly scandalized the men, although the Gospels' explanation—that they were outraged at the expense of the perfume—does seem rather unconvincing.

Luke may provide an answer in his own very strange version.[18] First he shifts the episode to much earlier—the Galilee phase, in fact, where it is sandwiched between Jesus' words about the Baptist that follow the latter's doubting question from prison and the introduction of Mary Magdalene and the other female disciples. Luke, too, sets it in the house of a Simon with whom Jesus is dining, but this one is a Pharisee.

Although some argue that there were two anointings by women during Jesus' ministry, this is just an attempt to reduce the glaring contradictions within the New Testament. The typically slapdash Luke probably just misplaced the incident. But it is the description of the woman—who, as in Mark, is unnamed—that is most different: she is "a woman who had lived a sinful life [literally 'who was a sinner'] in that town." The basic details of the anointing are the same as in the other accounts, with the extra detail that she first stands behind Jesus weeping.

Intriguingly, though, while Luke bases his narrative on Mark, he includes details—most conspicuously the woman wiping Jesus' feet with her hair—which are only found in *John*, showing once again that the two Gospels shared some common source. And it all relates to the ever-mysterious Bethany family.

The moral that Luke has Jesus delivering is different, too. (It would have to be, being in this version so far in advance of his death.) Simon the Pharisee is appalled that Jesus has allowed a sinful woman to touch him, but Jesus, reading his mind, responds with the parable about the moneylender who canceled two men's debts, one who owed a little and one who owed a lot, the moral being that he or she who is forgiven the most loves the forgiver the most. He then compares Simon's behavior with hers:

Do you see this woman? I came into your house. You did not give me any water for my feet, but she wet my feet with her tears and wiped them with her hair. You did not give me a kiss, but this woman, from the time I entered, has not stopped kissing my feet. Therefore, I tell you, her many sins have been forgiven—for she loved much. But he who has been forgiven little loves little.

Then he tells the woman that her sins are forgiven and that her faith has saved her, which sounds caring, even tender. Unfortunately this makes no sense: this woman *already* loves Jesus much, before he has forgiven her, so the moral of the parable is actually contradicted. (She has to love much to earn his forgiveness, not be forgiven to love him much.) It is very likely that Jesus' message was inserted separately into this episode: the story flows smoothly without it, and it is only in this part that the person Jesus addresses abruptly changes from "the Pharisee" to "Simon."

What exactly was the woman's sin? It is not spelled out, although one assumes that there were limited ways for a woman in that culture to gain such a reputation (one that allowed her to splash out on expensive perfumes, anyway). And the fact that, in order to wipe her hair on Jesus' feet, she must have let it loose would also be a sign that she was not entirely respectable.

The word that has always been translated as "sin" is the Greek *amartia*, which carries a less harsh connotation than the English suggests. Taken from archery, it means "to miss the mark" by failing to observe the letter of the Jewish Law. So whereas "sinner" implies a deliberate decision to do what is morally wrong, an *amartolos* was someone who tried to do the right thing by the Law but failed. The term covered not just Jews who failed to observe the Law but also individuals who were faced with no such demands for the simple reason that they were not Jewish.[19]

Admittedly it is hard to see how a woman could have gained such a reputation for nonobservance that it became her defining characteristic. Luke clearly has something more specific in mind, although not necessarily prostitution; she could have been a Samaritan or outside the Jewish Law in some other way.

However, the reason for Simon the Pharisee's outrage is more understandable than the line in the other Gospels that she has simply wasted expensive perfume. Submitting to such an act from a woman of dubious reputation—in fact submitting to it from *any* woman—would be exactly the kind of thing that would upset the male disciples (and might have caused Judas to doubt Jesus), but then again they must already have known she was a close friend of their leader.

In any case it is clear that Lazarus' sister Mary and Luke's "sinful woman" are the same person. But was she also, as Catholic tradition long maintained and many "alternative" theories still do, one and the same as Mary Magdalene? This—through the association with Luke's sinful woman—is the basis of her reputation as a prostitute, as well as her "maudlin" image as an inveterate, almost pathological, weeper and her traditional depiction with an alabaster jar.

Academics may throw their hands up in horror, but the identification of Mary of Bethany as Mary Magdalene is central to one of the most pervasive of all "fringe" theories of recent years, that of *The Holy Blood and the Holy Grail*, which fed into *The Da Vinci Code*. The equation of the Magdalene and the sister of Lazarus is used to support the hypothesis that she was Jesus' wife and the mother of his children, from whom the "sacred bloodline" is descended. However, the identification is by no means essential to that theory, or conversely, its being so does not automatically make the *Holy Blood* authors' extrapolations also correct. But leaving the whole bloodline issue out of the picture, is there any reason to connect the two women?

Although they were identified as one and the same in Western Christian tradition from at least the second century, the case is not entirely dependent on that; there is also an academic argument. One of its major advocates is American professor of religion and philosophy William E. Phipps, and although his conclusions were later adopted by the authors of *The Holy Blood and the Holy Grail* and used to support the "bloodline" idea, he was not advocating that particular concept.

The argument is straightforward. There are two women named Mary who enjoy a special relationship with Jesus and play important roles in the events at the end of his life: Mary Magdalene and Mary the sister of Lazarus. (Nowhere is the latter called "Mary of Bethany"; that is just the customary way of referring to her to avoid confusion with the various other Marys. John and Luke simply call her Mary.) Despite her importance to Jesus, Lazarus' sister Mary fails to appear in any of the events surrounding his crucifixion or burial (even though she lives nearby). Conversely, Mary Magdalene is the key woman in those events but does not appear previously (apart from one brief mention in Luke). Both anomalies are resolved, Phipps argues, if they are the same woman. And there is that possible implication in Luke that Bethany Mary traveled with Jesus, as did the Magdalene.

People were identified by where they were born, not where they lived later, so if "Magdalene" means "of Magdala"—which is by no means certain—she would have been known as such wherever she settled. (Just as with Simon of Cyrene and Joseph of Arimathea, both of whom lived in Jerusalem.) And there is evidence from Lazarus' name that the family came from Galilee.

Somewhat cheekily, Phipps appeals to Occam's razor—the principle usually wielded by defenders of the academic status quo, that when faced with a choice of several competing theories, one should choose the one that requires the least tweaking of the evidence—in arguing for the connection. He says that the razor should be used to "shave away the unnecessary multiplication of women whose special fondness for Jesus was reciprocated by him." [20]

There is other circumstantial evidence: in Luke, Mary Magdalene is introduced in the very next verse to the anointing by the sinful woman, perhaps suggesting an association of ideas (or even a hint for those in the know). Less persuasively, it has been suggested that the casting out of seven demons from her could be a reference to her previous sinful state and Jesus' forgiveness. Also, there is a telling association of ideas connected with Jesus' burial. Bethany Mary anoints his body beforehand, while Mary Magdalene visits his tomb to anoint his corpse, which turns out to be unnecessary because he has risen from the dead. So one Mary does what the other intends to do but never actually does. Finally, the association might have been sparked off by the fact that the town of Magdala was notorious for the immorality of its inhabitants, so Luke might have taken her name to suggest that she, too, was a bad woman. [21]

So, although the evidence is not strong enough to be absolutely certain that Mary Magdalene and Mary, sister of Lazarus, were the same person, it is a good deal stronger than many now maintain. (Ironically, because of its association with the *Da Vinci Code* phenomenon, those who would once have defended the Catholic teaching on the unity of the two women are now often the most strident in dismissing it.)

The identification of Bethany Mary with Mary Magdalene would only be of passing interest were it not for the role that the former played in the anointing of Jesus. But what *was* the significance of the act? Since "Messiah/Christ" meant "anointed one," at some point in his career Jesus must have been anointed, and yet the only such ritual in the whole story is this one. (Some claim that his baptism by John was the anointing, but quite clearly this is wrong: after all, the Baptist performed the rite on multitudes, and only one became Christ.)

The point is inadvertently driven home by Andrew Lincoln when he argues in relation to the Fourth Gospel's version: "That Jesus' feet and not his head are anointed indicates that it is a mistake to interpret the episode as a royal or messianic anointing."[22] But in Mark it *is* Jesus' head that is anointed, so by Lincoln's logic it *was* a royal or messianic anointing, or at least Mark understood it to be so.

It can be no coincidence that the act that transformed Jesus into the Christ was performed when he was consciously acting out the prophecies of the Messiah, and by one of the group that was orchestrating the drama. The major anomaly, however, is that the "christening" was performed by a woman, which makes no sense: traditionally it would have been the responsibility of a priest. But if this was indeed *the* anointing, having a woman in the priestly role would certainly explain the disciples' horror.

A clue about what was going on might be provided by Shimon Gibson's suggestion of a link between the foot wiping and the evidence of a foot-anointing ritual in the Cave of John the Baptist at Suba. Excavations turned up many thousands of fragments of jars, so many that smashing the oil and/or water jars must have been part of whatever rituals were carried out there, and Mark tells us quite specifically that the woman broke her jar. A link with the mysterious sect that used the Suba cave may be an intriguing clue about the ritual at Bethany.

Whatever the purpose of the anointing, we have another mysterious ritual involving the Bethany family, which only Jesus and the officiating woman—not the disciples—really understood. This repeats the pattern of the raising of Lazarus, which also took place at Bethany and involved the brother of the woman who anointed Jesus a few days later. That family seems to be closely involved in the profoundly symbolic ritual element of Jesus' elusive purpose.

The Entry into Jerusalem

Whatever the Bethany mysteries meant, they were essentially private acts for Jesus and his followers. But from this juncture the evidence begins to point to the deliberate orchestration of his *public* career, particularly the organization of the events that would enable him to fulfill the signs expected of the Messiah.

The idea that Jesus *consciously* modeled his career to fit the prophecies of the Messiah was first proposed in the 1930s, being advocated most famously by Hugh Schonfield in *The Passover Plot*. But why did it take two millennia for anyone to suggest this? After all, both Jesus and his backers knew the Old Testament prophecies essentially outlining how to qualify as the Messiah. All they had to do was make sure they were seen to be fulfilled.

In Mark's account Jesus and his group arrive on the outskirts of Jerusalem—"Bethphage and Bethany at the Mount of Olives"— then he sends two handpicked disciples ahead with the instruction "Go to the village ahead of you, and just as you enter it, you will find a colt tied there, which no one has ever ridden. Untie it and bring it here. If anyone asks you, 'Why are you doing this?' say, 'The Lord needs it and will send it back here shortly.'" They do so and take the colt back to Jesus, who rides it along the road to Jerusalem, where

> Many people spread their cloaks on the road, while others spread branches they had cut in the fields. Those who went ahead and those who followed shouted,
> "Hosanna!"
> "Blessed is he who comes in the name of the Lord!"

"Blessed is the coming kingdom of our father David!"
"Hosanna in the highest heaven!" [23]

Jesus enters Jerusalem and goes to the Temple's precincts, but as the day is well advanced, he returns to Bethany with the Twelve. Entering the city in this way was clearly connected with a prophecy made by Zechariah:

> Rejoice greatly, Daughter Zion!
>   Shout, Daughter Jerusalem!
> See your king comes to you,
>   righteous and having salvation,
> lowly and riding on a donkey,
>   on a colt, the foal of a donkey. [24]

This, as usual, is made explicit by Matthew (who because he mis-read the verse, has Jesus bizarrely riding both a colt and a donkey). [25] He builds up the whole event with the over-the-top description "When Jesus entered Jerusalem, the whole city was stirred and asked, 'Who is this?'" Luke has the same story of the colt (just one), but adds that Jesus wept as he came in sight of Jerusalem, declaring:

> If you, even you, had only known on this day what would bring you peace—but now it is hidden from your eyes. The days will come when your enemies will build an embankment against you and encircle you and hem you in on every side. They will dash you to the ground, you and the children within your walls. They will not leave one stone on another, because you did not recognize the time of God's coming to you. [26]

Anachronistically, this refers to long after Jesus' day, when the Romans did exactly that when besieging and eventually laying waste to the city in 70 CE—and it is transparently designed to show that the people of Jerusalem deserved it for rejecting him. As it is conspicuous by its absence from any other Gospel, it is obviously a post-Revolt invention. (It suited Luke's agenda of distancing Christians from the Jews who were so detested by Rome.)

The Fourth Gospel's account is shorter and omits how Jesus got the colt, merely saying he "found a young donkey and sat upon it." The writer does, however, have the crowd declaiming the same words and, even more significantly, relates this incident to the Zechariah prophecy—for once common ground of John's and Matthew's Gospels but no others.[27] If Matthew alone had linked his Lord's action to the prophecy it might not seem too impressive, but to find John invoking the same prophecy shows that the connection was understood right from the beginning.

Jesus' instructions reveal evidence of prearrangement. Even if we attribute his knowledge of the colt's location to psychic ability, that would hardly explain why its owner would immediately hand it over on hearing the words "The Lord needs it." If all donkey thieves did the same, no animal would ever have remained with its rightful owner.

Today most New Testament scholars acknowledge that the event was arranged well beforehand. A. R. C. Leaney observes that "The instructions seem to be founded on plans previously made, but we are left tantalisingly without a clue as to how or when,"[28] while John J. Kilgallen, author of a commentary on Matthew's Gospel, describes "The Lord needs it" as "a password."[29]

The donkey was not simply a convenient mode of transport but a deliberate move on Jesus' part: it is the only time in the Gospels that he travels any way other than walking or sailing. And it specifically allowed Jesus to fulfill Zechariah's prophecy, revealing that he—and his supporters—*wanted* the crowds to acknowledge him as their Messiah.

This is even more significant than most Christians realize. At Passover it was the custom to enter Jerusalem on foot as a sign of humility. The people should have been *offended* that he was riding into the holy city on the back of an animal. If they were happy with the arrangement, they must have recognized him as a special person to whom the usual customs no longer applied.

As kings customarily rode donkeys (horses being reserved for battle), clearly the crowds recognized Jesus as their rightful ruler, doing exactly what was prophesied of the great savior-king. John's Gospel underlines this by specifying that the people went out to meet (*upanteois*) Jesus with palm branches (the others leave the plant unspecified). *Upanteois* was used when the crowds flocked to greet a returning king, victorious leader, or visiting dignitaries, and palms were the symbol of both Israel and, since the days of the Maccabees, national liberation.[30]

The people's cries of "Hosanna! Blessed is he who comes in the name of the Lord!" come from Psalm 118, which also has the throng carrying branches in a procession.[31] Despite what generations of Christians have believed, "Hosanna" is not a cry of praise but means "Save us now!"; "in the first century AD it would presumably have been understood by Jews as an appeal to God to save his people from foreign domination."[32] Mark's misunderstanding is to blame for this time-honored bit of nonsense, "Save us now in the highest!" not making a great deal of sense.

Some argue that this whole episode was invented by later Christians specifically as "proof" that Jesus was the Messiah. However, there are powerful arguments against this. First, the Zechariah prophecy is primarily about a kingly warrior who will lead the people of Israel against their oppressors. Although it did not specifically use the term "Messiah," of course that iconic figure and the divinely sent warrior-king were one and the same in most Jewish messianic expectations—but not to even the earliest Christians. Even more damning for the fiction idea is the evidence of pre-arrangement. Why invent a story but include hints that the central event was contrived?

It seems that Jesus really did enter Jerusalem on a donkey to be seen as the Chosen One, intentionally proclaiming himself king, and the people—or at least some of them—fully understood the meaning of the drama.

The connection with the people wanting to proclaim Jesus king in John's version of the feeding of the five thousand is obvious, but although we are told Jesus refused the responsibility then, here he actively encourages the crowd. Perhaps it had been too soon, and too dangerous in Galilee. And his arrival was happening at Passover, magnifying both the symbolism and the troublemaking potential. (Also, significantly, it fits the description of him in the Slavonic version of Josephus' *The Jewish War*, which we will come to in due course.)

Not for the first time in the Jesus story there is a distinct feeling that something is being kept from us, and something curiously contradictory. The Bethany rituals—performed by his close friends but utterly baffling to the disciples—have a strong flavor of the mystery cults, even a pagan whiff to them. Yet the entry into Jerusalem (seemingly backed and orchestrated by the very same people) is hard-core Jewish-nationalist, and in this and other public events the disciples not only play an active part but get the plot immediately. The problem lies in attempting to reconcile the two apparently conflicting strands, trying to build up a picture of the true Jesus from both Jewish and pagan-flavored stories.

The End of the Temple

Having arrived—as king, in triumph—in Jerusalem as the Passover weekend approaches, Jesus goes into the city every day, preaching and verbally sparring with his adversaries. But his major act, in all four canonical Gospels, is decidedly proactive: the so-called "cleansing of the Temple." Although a crucial event in Jesus' mission, it is one of the most perplexing for New Testament scholars. The dilemma is that it is one of the few episodes that virtually all of them agree is based on a true event, while no explanation they offer of Jesus' motive and intentions is completely satisfactory. This is Mark's version:

> On reaching Jerusalem, Jesus entered the temple area and began driving out those who were buying and selling there. He overturned the tables of the money changers and the benches of those selling doves and would not allow anyone to carry merchandise through the courts. And as he taught them, he said, "Is it not written:
>
> My house will be called
> a house of prayer for all nations.
>
> But you have made it a 'den of robbers.'"[33]

Jesus' words conflate two Old Testament prophecies that we will examine in more depth shortly. In Mark it is because of his action that the Jewish leaders finally decide he has to die.

The other two synoptic Gospels follow Mark, although both condense the story, particularly downplaying the suggestion of violence (especially Luke, always keen to marginalize Jesus' subversive tendencies, who devotes just two sentences to it). Tellingly, both he and Matthew omit the words "for all nations" from the Isaiah quotation. John, on the other hand, plays *up* the violence:

> In the temple courts he found men selling cattle, sheep, and doves, and many others sitting at tables exchanging money. So he made a whip out of cords, and drove all from the temple area, both sheep and cattle; he scattered the coins of the money changers and overturned their tables. To those who sold doves he said, "Get these out of here! How dare you turn my Father's house into a market!"[34]

Jesus and his disciples certainly managed to cause a furor in the precincts of the Temple, targeting the people who sold animals for sacrifice and the money changers—who exchanged everyday, profane money for the special sacred shekels used only for religious purposes—as well as apparently blocking the entrances so it was impossible to bring in other merchandise. Most reconstructions have a couple of Jesus' larger minders—probably the Sons of Thunder—standing by the gates while he himself, having knocked over the tables, harangues the crowd.

The first question is the timing: while to the synoptics it is a climactic moment of Jesus' final days in Jerusalem, in John's Gospel it is at the very beginning of the story, during a visit to the holy city when he is still with the Baptist. Which is correct? The majority of scholars accept the synoptics, as such a major event fits the last days of Jesus' ministry better. Had he trashed the Temple precincts early on, he would probably not have survived as long as he did.[35] Moreover, when we come to understand Jesus' motivation, it will become apparent that only the synoptics' timing makes sense. It seems that the writer of John moved it to show that right from the outset Jesus intended to overturn the Jewish religion at a fundamental level, and that the Jews were always determined to destroy him.

So what was the "cleansing" all about? From the traditional Christian perspective—that Jesus came to supersede the old ways—there seems nothing untoward or inexplicable about his deed, but in the context of the time and culture there is a major problem: nothing the money changers and animal sellers were doing was remotely wrong. Indeed their practices had been established, it was believed, according to God's own word. So although Jesus' act is customarily referred to as the "cleansing" of the Temple, this creates entirely the wrong impression. The religion—the Law—required all Jews to sacrifice animals to God, and to ensure that they were ritually pure they had to be bought at the Temple. Moreover, they could not be paid for with everyday money but had to be exchanged for special sacred coins—as did the tax for the upkeep of the Temple payable by all Jews—which is why the money changers were there.

Faced with this problem, commentators usually assume that Jesus objected not to the sale of animals and exchange of money as such, but to the way these particular people were carrying out the business. The priests were corrupt, misusing the system for their own profit and self-aggrandizement, perhaps diverting the sacred funds into their own pockets instead of using them to maintain the Temple or help the poor and needy, and this was the true heart of Jesus' dramatic protest. Some go further and see it as an attack on the contemporary state of the whole Judaic religion, priests and worshippers alike having lost their understanding of the spirit, rather than the letter, of the Law. S. G. F. Brandon, for example, argues that "The attack must surely have been aimed at the high priest and other magnates who controlled the Temple and profited from its operations,"[36] while John J. Kilgallen suggests that Jesus was objecting to the fact that "the quest for money had overtaken the desire to pray."[37] But if that was Jesus' point, it is odd that none of the Gospels actually spells it out. We must assume that they present less than the complete picture, because no other explanation works if he was a conventional Second Temple Jew.

Even as a criticism of the priestly regime of the time, Jesus' actions simply fail to stand up. As an analogy, many traditionalist Catholic bishops have objected to the "liberal" ideas of certain popes, denouncing them in the most strident terms. But even they would stop short of leading an assault on St. Peter's, breaking open the collecting boxes, and pulling priests out of the confessionals.

Jesus' declaration that the Temple had become a "den of robbers" does superficially suggest that he was protesting against corruption.

But the phrase does not fit the situation at all. It is a reference to a prophecy of Jeremiah and therefore must be seen in the context of the prophet's overall message—an attack on the Judeans' hypocrisy and misuse of power. Jeremiah was criticizing the way that, in his day, the tribe of Judah used the Temple to control the other tribes of Israel, believing that they had the right to do what they liked provided they continued to worship in it. They were like robbers who made the Temple a base to which they retreated after committing crimes throughout the land. It is not the practices in the Temple that were the focus of his ire.[38]

Another hypothesis is that it was an attack on the whole sacrificial system, since he was not the first Jewish holy man to criticize the Temple and its sacrificial cult: certain prophets had done so before him. But there is, again, a crucial difference: they were attacking the notion that sacrifice *alone* was enough to keep within the Law, not agitating for the entire system to be abolished.[39] Morna Hooker puts her finger on the essential problem: "since the demand to offer sacrifice was included in a command of God, set out in the Torah, Jesus would hardly have challenged the whole system."[40]

However, Jesus' actions *were* a challenge to the whole system. Attacking the sacrifices meant attacking the whole basis of the religion, and of course preventing the exchange of coins would also bring worship to a halt. As the renowned American religious scholar John Dominic Crossan explains:

> There is not a single hint that anyone was doing anything financially or sacrificially inappropriate. Cleansing or purification are, therefore, very misleading terms for what Jesus was doing, namely, an attack on the Temple's very existence, a destruction—symbolic, to be sure, but none the less dangerous for that.[41]

And—a vital point made by Raymond E. Brown—even if any of the above *had* been what motivated Jesus, none of the people who witnessed his action would have understood.[42] They could only have seen it as sacrilege against the religion itself.

In fact there is no other way to see it: it *was* sacrilege.

But how could this be? Jesus' entry into Jerusalem was an explicit declaration that he was King of the Jews—so how could he then immediately attack his own people's proud religion? And how could he keep the support of Jewish nationalists such as the Zealots if he blasted their faith so sensationally and unambiguously? Could the standard Christian view, that he was tacitly declaring that God had changed the rules, and that the old ways were to be swept away in favor of a new covenant, be correct? Perhaps. But it would have been rather unfair to attack the Temple workers: after all, they were only obeying God's own orders. So what was it really all about?

The explanation offered by John's Gospel, that the money changers and animal sellers have turned "my Father's house into a market," can be discounted: it *had* to be a market, and if his Father had changed his mind, it was a ludicrously unfair way to announce it.

In fact, there is a way of reconciling Jesus' action with Judaism, once we understand that there were circumstances in which a prophet or other leader could attack the Temple without attacking the religion. And it is these circumstances to which Jesus refers through his use of the two prophecies.[43]

The synoptics have Jesus obliquely explaining by conflating two Old Testament texts—the first from chapter 56 of Isaiah, from which he quotes two lines. Through Isaiah the Lord promises he will not abandon even foreigners who accept and worship him:

> "these I will bring to my holy mountain
> and give them joy in my house of prayer.
> Their burnt offerings and sacrifices
> will be accepted on my altar;
> for my house will be called
> a house of prayer for all nations."
> The Sovereign Lord declares—
> he who gathers the exiles of Israel:
> "I will gather still others to them besides them already
> gathered."[44]

So Jesus—or Mark—is quoting a passage that refers to God not merely gathering together the scattered tribes of Israel, but even extending his covenant to non-Jews. Evidently God intends these people to observe the religion of Israel but will remove the ethnic exclusivity implied in his original covenant with Abraham.

In Isaiah's prophecy we have the perfect answer to the vital question of whom Jesus defined as Jewish: all those who accept the authority of Israel's God—even Samaritans, although they and the Jews hated each other and had major differences about religious practices.

But what of the second quotation? As we have seen, Jeremiah delivers God's rebuke to the backsliders, specifically among the tribe of Judah, who commit crimes and worship other gods but complacently believe that worshipping in the Temple automatically wipes the slate clean again: "Has this house, which bears my Name, become a den of robbers to you! But I have been watching! declares the Lord."[45] The Lord then proclaims that if they fail to mend their ways, the Temple will be removed from them, just as it was from the tribe of Ephraim: "Therefore, what I did to Shiloh I will now do to the house that bears my Name, the temple you trust in, the place I gave to you and your fathers. I will thrust you from my presence, just as I did all your brothers, the people of Ephraim."[46]

Jesus' actions clearly relate to this prophecy in some way. Criticism of the backsliding of "this generation" is a basic theme of his message (as it was of John the Baptist's), and the Jeremiah passage also essentially fits: the Temple authorities are only paying lip service to the religion while hypocritically pretending devotion, and using their position for their own profit and privilege. But for all its faults, few would accuse Second Temple Judaism of promoting pagan gods, or the Sanhedrin of sanctioning such a blasphemy. However, the passage could apply metaphorically: by accepting the rule of Rome, the Judeans are implicitly accepting the Romans' gods, including the cult of the emperor. So it is both a criticism of the Jerusalem authorities and an expression of Jewish nationalism, neither of which is very surprising.

What Jesus was saying was that the Temple *should* be a house of prayer for Yahweh worshippers from all nations, but since it has become a "den of robbers"—both by rejecting many of the perfectly legitimate worshippers and because those in charge have sold out to Rome—God, as threatened in Jeremiah, has withdrawn his sanction from it, and from the Judeans.

Effectively Jesus was declaring the *abolition* of the Jerusalem Temple, taking it on himself—as God's scourge—to remove power from the failed Jerusalem authorities. But why attack the money changers and animal sellers? Actually it is all of a piece, if understood not as an assault on those people but on what they stood for: the Temple itself. God could and would remove his favor from Jerusalem and Judah in certain circumstances—which Jesus clearly believed had arrived. But that did not mean that God had rejected the people of Israel as a whole.

The "cleansing" was nothing less than a call for total religious reformation—which, like most reformations, advocated a return to how things were believed to have been at the very beginning. Jesus wanted to hand over the leadership to different people entirely, who by implication would not necessarily even be based in Jerusalem. It was an act much more analogous to Martin Luther's nailing to the door of Wittenberg church his ninety-five theses calling for the removal of the regime in Rome that ruled the Church, but not for the abolition of the religion. Luther argued for a return to "first principles," to what Christianity was supposed to have been, rather than what it had become. And similarly Jesus wanted to revisit the first principles of the Israelite religion, as in the glory days of Moses and David.

When the event is seen in this way, its apparent incongruity with Jesus' de facto declaration of himself as King on his entry into Jerusalem also disappears. As King-Messiah he was claiming the right to abolish the Temple *according to God's wishes as expressed in the prophecies*. In fact *only* someone who claimed that authority could behave in such a way in the Temple and escape an immediate lynching, let alone retain any form of following. This also explains how Jesus could mount an assault on such a fundamental aspect of the Jewish religion while retaining the support of Zealots. If they accepted his unique status, they also accepted that he had the power to abolish even the Temple itself in the nation's interests. No wonder the authorities sought to destroy him.

But is there any way of telling whether this really was Jesus' motivation or merely Mark's interpretation? It is interesting that Mark made his point so obliquely: you have to look up the prophecies to work it out, but once you do, the meaning becomes clear. And the obliqueness must be intentional, otherwise he would have had Jesus spell it out. Matthew and Luke made the intention even harder to understand by removing the hugely important three words "for all nations." And John has come up with an even more nonsensical explanation.

All the gospel writers seem embarrassed by Jesus' real motivation. Mark gives the clearest explanation, but even he fails to make it explicit, suggesting that it is authentic. (Yet again, why invent something only to play it down?) This means that Jesus himself probably invoked the Isaiah and Jeremiah prophecies, if not during his action at the Temple then to his disciples at some point close to the event.

But if Jesus sought to remove the seat of power from Jerusalem, where would it go? There are a few possibilities. Perhaps he thought there should be no central authority or place of worship at all, as hinted in his words to the Samaritan woman in the Gospel of John, that the "true worshippers" would worship God in spirit and would not need *any* Temple. However, even if there was no one place to worship God, surely there would still need to be a central authority and organization. Another possibility is that, if Jesus thought that the world as they knew it was about to end—with the arrival of the Kingdom of God—then the issue of where Jews should worship was basically irrelevant. But in that case, why bother to trash the Temple?

If Jesus was envisaging another sanctuary, where might it have been? Could he have thought in terms of, for example, rebuilding the rival Temple on Mount Gerizim or elsewhere in Samaria? The Israelites' original center of worship had been the sanctuary at Shiloh, where the Ark of the Covenant was housed in the Tabernacle; that center had been under the guardianship of the tribe of Ephraim, ancestors of the Samaritans. (It did not shift to Jerusalem until David's day, when he took the Ark there.)

In that context the Jeremiah prophecy invoked by Jesus may have an extra significance, since it has God specifically warning the Judeans that if they fail to mend their ways, he will remove his favor from them, just he did with the tribe of Ephraim. Could Jesus have envisaged reversing the process by returning to Ephraim (i.e., the Samaritans) what God had taken from them and given to Judah?

There is a third possibility. There was no need to build a new temple outside Jerusalem: one already existed, even with the grudging sanction of the Jerusalem authorities. Largely forgotten today, it was in Egypt, at Leontopolis, in the *nome* (district) of Heliopolis. It was the only Jewish sanctuary apart from Jerusalem where sacrifices could be offered to God (the criterion for an "official" place of worship), which created a weird anomaly, since one of the basic principles of the religion at that time was that there could only be one sacred site where God could be approached.

The Leontopolis Temple had been in existence for some two hundred years before Jesus and would—only just—outlive the Jerusalem Temple. The precise circumstances of its origin are unclear, as there are contradictory accounts (even in Josephus), but it was founded around 170 BCE as a result of the repression in Jerusalem under the Seleucid ruler Antiochus Epiphanes, in what was history's first recorded attempt to eradicate the Jewish religion. There was a real fear that Jerusalem's days as the center of the religion were numbered. Many Jews fled into Egypt (where there was already a sizeable Jewish community); and someone, probably Onias, the son of the high priest who had been murdered by Antiochus, solicited the sanction of Egypt's ruler to construct a temple to replace the sacred building in Jerusalem. The refugee Jews were given a ruined temple formerly dedicated to the god Bubastis on which they built their new Temple.

After the depredations of Antiochus had been overcome by the Maccabean Revolt, and the threat of the end of Jewish worship in Jerusalem had passed, the Leontopolis Temple nevertheless stayed in business, with its own priesthood descended from Onias. For some reason its existence was tolerated, albeit grudgingly, by the leaders in Jerusalem. The Leontopolis Temple was closed down on the orders of the Roman governor of Egypt in 74 CE, four years after the destruction of the Jerusalem Temple.

If Jesus was declaring that God's authority should be removed from Jerusalem and from Judah, did he think it should be transferred to Egypt's Leontopolis?

The Uprising

Although dealing with events in Jesus' day, Josephus' *The Jewish War* notoriously has one glaring omission—there is no mention of him. However, there was a version of the book that passed down an entirely different line of transmission—and therefore of copying and editing—from the familiar version. In the Middle Ages it was translated into Slavonic, the language spoken throughout eastern Europe in the ninth century and from which modern languages such as Russian are descended, and the text remained unknown in western Europe until a German scholar, Alexander Berendts, published it in 1906.

The Slavonic *Jewish War* is very different from the standard version: substantial parts are omitted, long passages added, and the sections that are the same in both appear in a "more primitive form" in the Slavonic.[47] And it does have references to a figure who is clearly Jesus—although it simply calls him "the miracle worker." Controversy reigns over the authenticity of these passages: were they deleted from Josephus' original, or are they fabrications inserted at some point in the long history of copying? The translator of *The Jewish War*, G. A. Williamson, defends the Slavonic version:

> These records, like the famous allusions in *Antiquities*, are condemned as spurious by critics who, victims of their own wishful thinking and bent on destruction, are prepared without a trace of MS authority to bracket or reverse the meaning of any passage that conflicts with their pet theories. Such a proceeding is in the last degree unscientific. It is to be observed also that the forging of these passages for propaganda purposes could not have rendered the least service to a Christian apologist; they could never influence anyone not already convinced by the Gospels; they are in many important points irreconcilable with Christian tradition; and they clearly reveal their author not as a believer but as a doubting, if curious, onlooker.[48]

Williamson certainly has a point. If someone in later centuries deleted, added, or amended the text, what was his motive? When a passage is changed because it appeared blasphemous to a later Christian, the reason is obvious. But when a supposed alteration makes no sense even in Christian terms, then there is no clear motive, suggesting the passage must be original.

What adds weight to the case for the authenticity of the Slavonic edition is that from a reading of the *standard* version of *The Jewish War* it is very apparent that something has been missed out. The chronicle moves far too quickly over Pilate's governorship, his eleven years taking up less than a page in the modern paperback edition—very uncharacteristic of Josephus' verbose style. We are told of Pilate's appointment (in 26 CE) and given some brief details of the serious problems he had with the Judeans because of his highhanded attitude, but then abruptly the discussion shifts to the repercussions for the Jews of the death of Tiberius and the succession of Caligula in 37 CE. Precisely the most interesting years from the point of view of Christian history are over in a moment. And in the Slavonic version this is exactly where the account of Jesus comes, right in the middle of the discussion of other flash points between the Jews and Pilate.

In many ways the debate about the authenticity of the Slavonic edition is purely academic, since the version tells us nothing new about Jesus himself—except for the possible implications of one part. Because of his wonder-working many of the "common people" ask him to become their king and lead them in expelling the Romans from Judea. As a result he is arrested by the Jewish authorities and crucified on Pilate's authority.

Also intriguing is the reaction of the Jewish authorities when they hear of the people's request to Jesus:

> When the suggestion came to the ears of the Jewish authorities, they met under the chairmanship of the high priest and exclaimed: "We are utterly incapable of resisting the Romans; but as the blow is about to fall [i.e., the rebellion is starting and Jesus is going to lead it] we'd better go and tell Pilate what we've heard, and steer clear of trouble, in case he gets to know from someone else and confiscates our property, puts us to death, and turns our children adrift." So they went and told Pilate, who sent his troops and butchered many of the common people.[49]

The biggest clash with the Gospel picture is the statement that, as a result of the Sanhedrin's warnings, Pilate did not merely arrest Jesus but also sent troops who "butchered many of the common people." And yet this account does receive some confirmation from the Gospels, which make it clear that some form of bloodshed had occurred shortly before Jesus' arrest.

In the famous scene in which Pilate gives the crowd the choice of releasing Jesus or the criminal Barabbas, the latter is introduced as being "in prison with the rebels who had committed murder in the uprising."[50] What uprising? Mark says nothing about such an event, and yet refers to it here as if it was familiar to his readers. Some kind of violent action—on what scale it is impossible to tell—must have taken place around that time.

Logic demands that there *must* have been at least an indirect connection between Jesus' actions and the bloodshed. The cumulative evidence—from John's account of the feeding of the five thousand, the Slavonic *Jewish War*, and, above all, Jesus' mode of entry into Jerusalem—is that Jesus was consciously and publicly claiming the role of king. His very presence would inevitably have exacerbated the climate of unrest. You could hardly walk into that seething cauldron—especially at that time of year—proclaim yourself king, and start altercations in the Temple without stirring up at least the first rumblings of a much wider insurrection. Some people—Barabbas perhaps—could well have jumped the gun because they had heard that the king had finally come and expected him to order the revolt at any moment. There would have been no necessity to issue direct instructions; Jesus' presence was enough. It was inevitable that some Jews would start pushing their luck with Roman soldiers. And being told that the people wanted to make someone out there into a king who would lead a rebellion against him would have been enough for Pilate to order his men to throw their not inconsiderable weight around.

Jesus might not have said anything. He might even have urged his followers to do nothing to provoke the Romans. But he must have known that simply by being there—after the way he had entered the holy city and his actions in the Temple—he was potentially igniting a rebellion. Jesus might not have *ordered* acts of violence, but he certainly *caused* them.

Undoubtedly, Jesus encouraged the people to think that he was their divinely mandated leader. And, as we will see, he was certainly tried and executed specifically because he posed a political threat. But from the beginning Christians have always believed that this was an unavoidable misunderstanding, that while he was indeed the Davidic Messiah, God's plan had changed and Jesus' kingdom "was not of this world," although nobody—neither his opponents nor his followers—could understand this until he had risen after being crucified.

None of that works. If Jesus had no earthly, royal ambitions, why choose to enter the sacred city in precisely the manner that was expected of the King-Messiah? Arriving on a donkey after that blatant password-and-plotting scenario hardly makes the choice a coincidence. From this circumstance, and his violence in the Temple, we might agree with the likes of S. G. F. Brandon that Jesus' agenda was first and foremost political.

But an unavoidable paradox runs through Jesus' story from the very beginning, most glaringly during his last days in Jerusalem. If he had set out to claim the throne of Jerusalem and make himself king of the Jews, what was all the Bethany business about? The raising of Lazarus and the anointing by his sister seem more fitting as a purely spiritual scenario, and this element, with its mystery-cult atmosphere, is hard to reconcile with the conventional Judaism that the King-Messiah was supposed to represent and protect.

However, the evidence is equally strong that both these—apparently contradictory—aspects of the Jesus story are based on something real, and the evidence is that the family of Bethany who were at the center of all the peculiar, semipagan rituals also organized the campaign to have Jesus acclaimed as the Messiah.

Now the story reaches a climax, with the blood-soaked drama of the crucifixion and its extraordinary aftermath. This is where the king of the Jews becomes Lord of the Christians. But first a ritual meal of unique significance.

The Very Last Supper

The story usually goes: In a simple, perhaps even stark, upper room in a Jerusalem side street, the great Christian drama truly begins. As dusk falls, the disciples gather round Jesus to celebrate Passover, and as the evening advances, he quietly instigates the powerful rite of the Eucharist, explaining that the broken bread will remind them of his physical sacrifice and the wine represent his blood, spilled for all mankind. Then he announces to the astounded men that one of them will betray him.

However, as we saw earlier, the evidence shows that the communal meal in which Jesus' body was symbolically eaten in the form of bread and his blood drunk as wine had been a practice of the inner discipleship for some time—at least from the immediate aftermath of the feeding of the five thousand. It assumed a special significance at the Last Supper because it was the *last* time that Jesus presided over the rite, not the first.

As with the provision of the colt on which Jesus rode into Jerusalem, the synoptic accounts of the arrangements for the Last Supper contain evidence of advance, secret planning. There is even a clear and conscious association with the earlier event: in Mark's Gospel eleven consecutive words are the same in both sets of instructions given by Jesus.

On the first day of the Feast of the Unleavened Bread, when it was customary to sacrifice the Passover lamb, Jesus' disciples asked him, "Where do you want us to go and make preparations for you to eat the Passover?"

So he sent two of his disciples, telling them, "Go into the city, and a man carrying a jar of water will meet you. Follow him. Say to the owner of the house he enters, 'The Teacher asks: where is my guest room, where I may eat the Passover with my disciples?' He will show you a large room upstairs, furnished and ready. Make preparations for us there."[51]

Some fellow traveler in Jerusalem has made a room ready for Jesus and his group, but its location is kept secret from the disciples until the last moment. It requires a middleman, a cutout: instead of simply giving the two disciples the address, they have to meet a man with a water jar who will take them to the house. Carrying water jars was something that only women normally did, so a man would have really stood out in a crowd.[52] Then there is a recognition phrase to prove to the owner of the house that they are genuinely Jesus' men: "The Teacher asks: where is my guest room, where I may eat the Passover with my disciples?"

These elements must be authentic. A man carrying a water jug has no symbolic meaning and relates to no scriptural prophecy. So, as with the provision of the colt, somebody has organized it—and not one of the immediate circle of the Twelve. Back to the Bethany family.

What would be the reason for such prearrangement and secrecy just to find a room where Jesus and his disciples can eat dinner? It only really makes sense in terms of security, that he was determined that no word would leak out to the authorities about his location that night. Only a few trusted people knew of the arrangement until the last moment, and Jesus was aware of the danger he was in, and on guard against betrayal. Was this a simple and sensible precaution, or did he already know about Judas?

Although all the sources agree that the meal took place around Passover, the synoptics claim it was the Passover meal (seder) itself, while John has it happening a day or so before. Knowing which is correct has certain implications for the ensuing events, Jesus' trial and crucifixion; for example, there is controversy over whether the Sanhedrin, the ruling council which also served as a "supreme court" in religious matters, was permitted to meet on a holy day (which the synoptic chronology requires). It might also shed some light on the year of Jesus' death, depending on which day of the week Passover fell. There are all kinds of contradictions, not only between but also within the Gospels. For example, Mark's claim that it took place "On the first day of the Feast of Unleavened Bread, when it was customary to sacrifice the Passover lamb" makes no sense, since the lambs were slaughtered the day *before* the festival started.

On balance, however it probably *was* the seder, because it was a requirement that the meal be eaten in Jerusalem itself, and in the case of the Last Supper special arrangements were made to ensure that it was (whereas on the other days Jesus had returned to Bethany each evening).

With God on His Side?

The Last Supper makes the perfect dramatic setting for the betrayal of Jesus by Judas Iscariot. But this crucial event also poses one of the key questions of Jesus' final days: did he actually expect to die?

Christians believe that everything was divinely ordained: the whole purpose of Jesus' life was that he would sacrifice himself for the sins of all mankind. He went to Jerusalem knowing how it would end (and even repeatedly tried to explain this to the disciples, with little success). On the other hand, if it can be proven that Jesus did not want or expect to die, then not only would this help our understanding of the meaning of his mission, but the whole Christian position would begin to crumble. Discovering exactly what Judas did (if anything) will obviously be important in deciding between these two alternatives.

Jesus' betrayal was part of the earliest Christian belief. Even Paul, in one of the rare allusions to his Lord's earthly life, states that he was betrayed, although providing no details. Most—but by no means all—commentators agree on the fact of Judas' treachery, because admitting that one of the Twelve whom Jesus had personally appointed was a traitor was too embarrassing for the early Christian community to have invented. But there is less agreement on the detail, since the whole scenario seems to have been contrived to provide a rationalization and theological justification for that embarrassing fact, and indeed to turn it to the Church's advantage by claiming that Jesus knew about Judas but needed his treachery to facilitate his own destiny. This idea reached its apogee in the recently discovered Gospel of Judas.

Although discovered in a cave on the banks of the Nile in the 1970s, its existence was "kept under wraps . . . to maximize its financial gain for its Swiss owners"[53] until announced on July 1, 2004. A translation was published, along with various tie-in books and a major National Geographic Channel documentary, in time for Easter 2006. Unusually, fragments of the book were sacrificed to carbon dating, which came up with a date of between 220 and 340 CE, but of course this only reveals the age of that particular copy. References by the Church Fathers show that it existed in about 180 CE, and it is generally thought to have been composed in the mid–second century, perhaps as early as 130 CE.

The Gospel was the product of a gnostic sect that believed that Judas Iscariot had done God's will, "betraying" Jesus on his own orders; Judas was the one disciple who truly understood what Jesus was about. Without the betrayal there would have been no atoning death and resurrection. It is a thought that occurs to most intelligent New Testament readers: since the whole point of Jesus' incarnation was his sacrificial end and subsequent triumph over death, was Judas really doing the *right* thing? Does he really deserve to be the most reviled man in history?

But can this Gospel be trusted? Is there any connection with the real Judas Iscariot? Almost certainly not. It appears to be based on nothing more than theological speculation on the paradox of Judas' role as the traitor without whom God's plan could never have been fulfilled.

That is not to say that the canonical Gospels present any more authentic information. There are screaming absurdities in the stories of Jesus' announcement of the imminent betrayal at the Last Supper, beginning with Mark:

> While they were reclining at the table eating, he [Jesus] said, "Truly I tell you, one of you will betray me—one who is eating with me."
>
> They were saddened, and one by one they said to him, "Surely not I?"
>
> "It is one of the Twelve," he replied, "one who dips bread in the bowl with me. The Son of Man will go just as it is written about him. But woe to that man who betrays the Son of Man! It would be better for him if he had not been born." [54]

Jesus then concentrates on the sacred bread and wine ritual, and nothing is said about Judas' treacherously slipping away. The disciples sing a hymn, then leave for the Mount of Olives.

Predictably, John's Gospel is far more elaborate. First Jesus quotes an appropriate line from Psalm 41, "He who has shared my bread has lifted up his heel against me," [55] explaining the betrayal as scriptural fulfillment. It goes on:

> After he had said this, Jesus was troubled in spirit and testified, "Very truly I tell you, one of you is going to betray me."
>
> His disciples stared at one another, at a loss to know which of them he meant. One of them, the disciple whom Jesus loved, was reclining next to him. Simon Peter motioned to this disciple and said, "Ask him which one he means."

Leaning back against Jesus, he asked him, "Lord, who is it?"

Jesus answered, "It is the one to whom I will give this piece of bread when I have dipped it in the dish." Then, dipping the piece of bread, he gave it to Judas, the son of Simon Iscariot. As soon as Judas took the bread, Satan entered into him.

So Jesus told him, "What you are about to do, do quickly." But no one at the meal understood why Jesus said this to him. Since Judas had charge of the money, some thought Jesus was telling him to buy what was needed for the Feast, or to give something to the poor. As soon as Judas had taken the bread, he went out. And it was night.[56]

The embroidery of the tale with added layers of detail and interpretation comes across clear and strong. The dipping into the communal dish has been elaborated into Jesus' handing Judas a piece of bread (his symbolic body, remember—the eucharistic symbolism is still there in John's account even though he never deals directly with the rite itself). The fact that he does this as a sign to the beloved disciple—who fails to share this information with Peter—emphasizes that his alleged source was more trusted by Jesus than was Peter. But most important of all, the Fourth Gospel's version fits its overall image of Jesus as the divine transcendental being who retains control at all times, even initiating his own betrayal. So John's version makes unreliable history. But is Mark's any better?

Hardly, because of one glaring logical problem: if Jesus knew that one of his companions was going to betray him, why announce it to the disciples? Although it makes a compelling story, what good would it have done? They would find out soon enough anyway, and spelling it out was more likely to prevent its happening: it might have scared Judas off, or some of the men with the shortest fuse might have inflicted their own summary justice. (Discovering the traitor's identity was not exactly difficult: watch out for the one who slips away early and doesn't accompany them to the Mount of Olives.) And if the Gospel of Judas is correct to say that Judas willingly played his role in accordance with Jesus' wishes, then Jesus' announcement makes even less sense. Jesus' objective could just have easily been achieved without a traitor. If the authorities were out to arrest him, all he had to do was show himself. Clearly his announcement of the enemy within and the imminence of his betrayal was simply a device to preempt awkward questions about the all-knowing Christ's allowing a traitor in his inner circle and not seeing it coming.

In fact common sense says that Jesus' security precautions to prevent his enemies from finding out where he was celebrating Passover prove he wanted to *evade* capture. Other details, such as his posting guards in the garden of Gethsemane, also show that was trying to avoid arrest. Finally, Judas' role fits too neatly: from the beginning Christians saw Jesus' death as a sacrifice, and in all the best myths sacrifice requires a betrayer.

For these reasons we can discount all the New Testament references to Judas at the Last Supper as something of a theological pantomime. That does not necessarily mean that he did not betray Jesus, just that the first the disciples would have known about it—assuming the Gospels' description of Jesus' arrest is reliable—is when Judas turned up with the arrest party and pointed him out.

Mark provides persuasive evidence that the very earliest descriptions of the Passion began with Jesus' arrest: there is linguistic and grammatical evidence of a break in the narrative between the Last Supper and the arrest. And tellingly, when he describes Jesus being seized, Mark introduces Judas as if it is the first time he has appeared in the story. This suggests that the earliest traditions about the last day of Jesus' life began with his arrest, not with the Last Supper, indicating that nothing particularly significant happened during the meal—it assumed significance just because it was the last time his disciples were with him—and that the first the group knew about any form of treachery was when Judas arrived with the arrest squad.

All this assumes that the Judas episodes are even halfway true. Some argue that not only the fact of Jesus' betrayal is invention but so is Judas Iscariot himself. The foremost advocate of this view is Hyam Maccoby in *Judas Iscariot and the Myth of Jewish Evil* (1992), who sums up his conclusions: "Judas Iscariot appears in it [the Gospel story] not because there actually was such a person, but because such a person is needed for the story to have its maximum psychological impact . . . the story of Judas Iscariot is almost entirely fictional." [57]

Maccoby believes that the logic of the Gospels demanded a traitor, so one had to be invented, and argues that Judas was chosen

simply because of his name—from the tribe of Judah and therefore
symbolizing the Jews as a people. This fitted the anti-Jewish agenda
of the early Christians, keen to highlight the Jews' role in Jesus'
death while downplaying the Romans.' Making the betrayer one
who bore the very name of the people was, for Maccoby, psycho-
logically rather too neat: he argues that its tragic outcome was the
anti-Semitism of Christian history.

The accounts of Judas' ultimate fate *are* clearly fiction. The
Gospels of Mark and John say nothing about it. In Matthew, when
he heard Jesus had been condemned to death, he was overcome
with guilt, threw the money back at the chief priests, and hanged
himself.[58] According to Luke, Judas used the money to buy a field,
in which, for some unexplained reason, "he fell headlong, his body
burst open, and all his intestines spilled out."[59] Obviously Judas, of
all people, could never be allowed to die peacefully in his bed.

When accounts diverge so much, we are firmly in the realm of
rumor, if not actual fantasy. In fact it is obvious that the Judas story
has been concocted from various Old Testament verses. Zechariah
talks about throwing thirty pieces of silver into the Temple (as Judas
does in Matthew). Jeremiah had a field that was bought for silver, as
the priests buy one with the "blood money" Judas returns. In the
Second Book of Samuel a traitor who conspires against David,
Ahithophel, hangs himself.[60] It is safe to say that nobody knew what
happened to Judas Iscariot. His fate remains a mystery.

But none of this means that Judas' betrayal was necessarily *total*
fiction. All the earliest traditions maintained that Jesus had been fatally betrayed, and just because his followers chose to cite scriptural
and prophetic references to try to make sense of it does not mean
that the betrayal itself was invented just to fit the references. Had
Jesus met his end through some other circumstances, the scriptures
and prophets would have been scoured for quotations that fitted that
scenario.

Neither does it necessarily follow that, because Judas' very name
conveniently connected Jesus' persecutors with the Jews as a race,
the character was invented with that purpose in mind. After all, it
was a very common name: there were even two Judases among the
Twelve. (So on Maccoby's logic, why not pick the *other* Judas rather
than invent a new one?)

Taking the evidence as a whole, Judas Iscariot probably did betray Jesus, but all the reasons—and especially the curiously unconvincing business at the Last Supper—are fiction. But what was his reason?

Mark supplies no motive at all: although the chief priests give Judas money, it is only after the evil deed is done. Matthew, obviously seeking a plausible motive, has him negotiating a price with the priests, while Luke takes this idea even further. But these additions merely highlight Mark's failure to provide a motive: as C. H. Dodd asked, "Is it not possible that the earliest tradition of all knew nothing about the motive of Judas' treachery?"[61]

Logically, unless Judas was debriefed after the event, none of his former companions could have known what made him betray his master. Most modern researchers assume he had become fatally disillusioned, having devoted himself to a leader who had failed to live up to his expectations. However, we find it significant that both gospel traditions link Judas' betrayal with the blood/wine rite. Such pagan teaching is exactly what would have scandalized a fiery Jewish nationalist—assuming the *sicarius* derivation of his surname is correct—as John's Gospel tells us it did a number of his other disciples. On this reasoning it was Jesus' inner teaching that Judas betrayed to the chief priests.

However, with or without the shadowy Judas, the Jesus story now reaches its terrible climax, with a torn and twisted body nailed to a cross—the end of a common rebel. Yet out of such a shameful death rose one of the world's greatest and most enduring religions.

9

FROM JESUS TO CHRIST

Christians see Christ's torment and death on the cross as an un-complicated narrative which may be nightmarish but which also has the most exalted ending possible: his resurrection and triumph over death on behalf of all those who believe in him. Yet once again there are glaring anomalies and inconsistencies across the Gospels, and sometimes within them, showing that the story is not so simple.

There is compelling evidence that the earliest written account of Jesus' deeds told of the Passion, beginning with his arrest in the Garden of Gethsemane, and detailing his trial, condemnation, crucifixion, and burial. It ended with the discovery of the empty tomb.[1] (This was still the basic format of Mel Gibson's 2004 film *The Passion of the Christ*.) This Passion narrative was incorporated virtually wholesale into Mark's Gospel as its ending. Part of the evidence for this is that the synoptic and Johannine accounts start to agree closely from Gethsemane through to the discovery of the empty tomb, then diverge again—wildly—after that.

Because of the sequence of scenes and interplay of characters—two thousand years later it still lends itself perfectly to cinematic dramatization—some have argued that the Passion was first written as a play. It even conforms to the conventions of a certain genre of Greek and Roman drama that presents the death (and often resurrection) of a hero or god, which is thought to derive from mystery cults enacting the myth of their hero.[2]

Does this mean that those who believe Jesus himself was just a myth are right? Not at all: events in the lives of real people were dramatized too. But if the original Passion narrative was written from a dramatic perspective—whether to be read aloud or performed—it probably does mean that only the bare bones of the story are even halfway reliable.

This is particularly frustrating, as knowing exactly why Jesus was condemned should shed some light on his essential message. Even if we only discovered how his opponents perceived him, it would still be an important clue. But in fact the information just confuses matters.

The early sources offer three different reasons for Jesus' execution. Although the *position* of the evangelists is that Jesus was put to death for the religious crime of blasphemy, for claiming to be the Messiah and the Son of God, the *information* they provide indicates that he was crucified for the political crime of sedition. (The synoptic Gospels acknowledge that was the official reason but maintain that the Jewish leadership framed Jesus, wishing him dead as a blasphemer.) Finally, the earliest Jewish traditions about Jesus were unanimous that he was condemned for practicing pagan magic. As the Mishnah (ca. 200 CE but based on earlier writings) says, "On the Sabbath of the Passover festival Jesus was hung [on the cross] . . . because he has practiced sorcery and seduced Israel and estranged them from God."[3] Unhelpfully, the three explanations reflect the three main categories of modern theory about Jesus: he was a religious reformer, nationalist rebel leader, or magician. But is there any way to reconcile them, or at least be confident we can reject the wrong ones?

The nearest thing we have to an independent account is the brief and controversial reference in Josephus' *Antiquities of the Jews* (which we believe to be an embroidered version of his original). This merely states that Pilate condemned Jesus to be crucified "at the suggestion of the principal men amongst us,"[4] which of course agrees with the essentials of the Gospel stories—the initiative was that of the Jewish leadership but the sentence was passed by Pilate— but fails to cast much light on the matter. Tacitus, in a passage on the "deadly superstition" of Christianity in his *Annals*, written around 115 CE, also states that their founder, "Christus," had been executed by Pilate but gives no more detail.[5]

The way the Gospels deal with Jesus' trial, condemnation, and death has been the subject of endless analysis, debate—and of course controversy. It was, for the first Christians, the vitally important part of the whole story, Jesus' death having become the core of their faith, and—a point that is often missed—also for purely practical reasons. In terms of persuading people of the truth of their religion, they had to convince others that their leader could have been horribly put to death and yet still be worth following. Every means of doing so was pressed into service, every line of scripture that could be used to justify a claim that went so far against normal conceptions of success and failure was brought into play, and every memory (real or imagined) of what Jesus had said was sifted for evidence that he had *wanted* his story to end that way. And it all found its way into the Gospels.

The key question is how much the process of theologizing and justification has changed the story, and the degree to which scriptural prophecies were not only projected back onto the historical events but how much the details were altered to fit them.

Agony in the Garden

The story of Jesus' Passion begins in the Garden of Gethsemane on the Mount of Olives, where he undergoes his "Agony"—his last-minute doubts and terror about the climax that is now unavoidable. He knows it has to happen. He is arrested, and it begins.

After the Last Supper Jesus leads the disciples to the Mount of Olives, where they seek out "a place called Gethsemane" (olive oil press). He tells them to keep watch, going off with his favorites—Peter, James, and John—saying, "My soul is overwhelmed with sorrow to the point of death," then wanders off alone. Instead of keeping a lookout, however, they fall asleep. When alone Jesus prays to his Father to "Take this cup from me," while submitting himself to his will, wherever it might lead. Each time he goes off, he returns to discover his three main disciples asleep, and berates them.[6]

(Luke has an angel coming down to comfort Jesus—he is very fond of angels—and having Jesus literally sweat blood in his anguish.[7] John, who always portrays Jesus as transcendentally superhuman, chooses not to depict the Agony at all.)

The "Take this cup from me" passage can be discounted simply on the grounds of common sense. The Gospels report that Jesus said this when alone, his companions not only elsewhere but asleep, so how can anyone possibly know what happened? The detail about the three disciples falling asleep does have the ring of authenticity, though. It hardly burnishes their image, nor does it make Jesus seem very astute for picking such dopes to stand guard, and it is a peculiar thing for a devotee to make up.

In Mark, as Jesus is remonstrating with his dozing disciples for the third time, he looks up and sees the arrest squad approaching, declaring, "The hour has come. Look, the Son of Man is delivered into the hands of sinners." The party, led by Judas Iscariot, comprises "a crowd armed with swords and clubs, sent from the chief priests, the teachers of the law, and the elders." The traitor has arranged a sign by which he will point out Jesus to them: "The one I kiss is the man; arrest him and lead him away under guard." The "Judas kiss" is absurd. Surely the chief priests would have thought to send someone who knew what Jesus looked like—after all, he had been preaching in the Temple daily—and Judas could have just said, "That's him!" The kiss might make a good story, but it lacks verisimilitude.

As Jesus is being arrested, one of the disciples draws a sword and attacks "the servant of the high priest," cutting off his ear. In Mark this act is presented without comment, while Matthew deals with this example of violence, albeit justified, by one of Jesus' disciples by having him admonish the swordsman:

> Put your sword back in its place, for all who draw the sword will die by the sword. Do you think I cannot call on my Father, and he will at once put at my disposal more than twelve legions of angels? But how then would the Scriptures be fulfilled that say it must happen in this way?[8]

Matthew uses this passage to cover the apparent contradiction in Mark's account of Jesus as a man of peace having armed men in his entourage, and the embarrassment of mere mortals' being able to take him so easily. Luke goes further and has Jesus heal the man's ear.

In Mark Jesus confronts the arrest party, asking, "Am I leading a rebellion that you have come out with swords and clubs to capture me? Every day I was with you, teaching in the temple courts, and you did not arrest me. But the Scriptures must be fulfilled."[9] At that, all the disciples flee (together with the youth wearing nothing but a linen cloth).

John's Gospel transparently rewrites the story. It has the arrest party consisting not of an armed crowd but a "cohort" of soldiers—by implication Romans—that is, *six hundred* men. And when Jesus goes out to meet them, "knowing all that was going to happen"—there is no Judas kiss, for how could *this* Jesus fall for such a trick?—declaring, "I am he," all six hundred fall to the ground. He then commands them to let the disciples go and voluntarily goes with them, none of which seems remotely probable.[10]

However, the core of this story does make sense in terms of how the Temple authorities would have arranged the arrest. They take Jesus as stealthily as possible, at night when there are no crowds to cause trouble. And they go straight for the leader, avoiding the disciples and the risk of starting an affray. It is a snatch squad, exactly what one would expect.

If we discount Jesus' announcement of his betrayal at the Last Supper and the transparent elaborations of Matthew, Luke, and (especially) John, and concentrate on other details that are much more unlikely to be inventions—such as Jesus' posting lookouts and the relaxed state of the disciples—it seems he was not expecting to be arrested. Therefore the pervasive sense of impending destiny and supernatural transcendence is entirely a retrospective imposition. Jesus was as unaware of what was coming as anyone else in a similar position, which perhaps makes the subsequent terror and agony all the more wretched and poignant.

The Trial

The Gospels have the arrest being ordered and organized by the "chief priests, teachers of the law, and the elders," the Jerusalem "establishment"—the Sanhedrin that had civil authority in Jerusalem, within the limits imposed by the Roman prefect. (Only John's Gospel implies that the Romans, through the supply of the cohort, were involved at that stage.) Jesus is taken before the Sanhedrin, presided over by the high priest Caiaphas, who then hand him over to Pontius Pilate for judgment and sentencing.

(Luke also has a hearing of sorts before Herod Antipas, who is in town for Passover, but if it had happened, undoubtedly the other Gospels would have included it. Wherever possible Luke draws parallels between the trial of Jesus and that of Paul as described in his other work, Acts, and tellingly, Paul was tried in Caesarea before the then Roman prefect and Herod Agrippa I.[11] Similarly, John's Gospel has Jesus first being taken to the house of Annas, Caiaphas' father-in-law, for questioning, after which Annas sends him to Caiaphas. There was a calculated reason for spuriously introducing Annas into this story, as he was reviled by Christians because a later member of his family, which held a virtual monopoly on the high priesthood for decades, was responsible for the martyrdom of James the Just in 62 CE.)

Oceans of ink have been spilled over the authenticity of the Gospels' description of the trial in terms of Jewish and Roman legal customs and practices, the results of which can be summarized very briefly: nobody knows one way or the other.[12] Some have argued that it was impossible for the trial before the Sanhedrin to have happened as described, as assemblies were forbidden at night and on holy days (in this case, if the synoptic version of events is correct, Passover itself). Others counter that it was an informal trial, more of an interrogation in order to prepare a charge to lay before Pilate. Even so, the legitimacy of the proceedings and the points of law have been challenged: for example, had Jesus really criminally blasphemed? Could the Sanhedrin at that time pass a death penalty for certain crimes? (Its powerlessness to do so is the Gospels' reason for involving Pilate.) But in truth no one knows enough about the way such trials were conducted: the process has to be reconstructed from the Old Testament decrees about how things should be done, and what we know of later, post-Revolt, Jewish legal practices. And in any case, even if we knew everything there was to know about the theory of first-century Jewish jurisprudence, the Sanhedrin might not have stuck to normal practice: who would argue if they flouted the law? Pilate and Caiaphas could well have had an agreement that, in order to preempt any potential unrest at Passover, troublemakers would be handed over for summary judgment and immediate punishment. In the end, all we can be sure of is that Jesus was arrested and condemned to die by crucifixion. Everything that happened in between is uncertain.

However, there is no reason to doubt the basic story, that Jesus was arrested by the Jewish leaders and sentenced by the Roman prefect. The big question—way beyond mere academic or theological interest—is the balance of responsibility between them. The Gospels unequivocally have the Jewish leaders bearing the brunt of the blame: Jesus is arrested on their initiative and they dragoon a reluctant Pilate into passing a death sentence, a scenario that laid the foundation for generations of the most horrific anti-Jewish hatred by Christians. Scholars have taken many views about the balance of responsibility, at one extreme basically agreeing with the Gospels, that it was the Jewish leaders' initiative and they connived to persuade Pilate to have Jesus killed, and at the other having Pilate pressuring the Sanhedrin to find some way to rid himself of this nuisance. (As he had appointed the high priest, their interests coincided anyway.)

Of course, even if it was agreed that the Sanhedrin was entirely to blame, that would do nothing to justify Christianity's anti-Semitism, since it meant that only the Temple leaders of that time (who were disliked by most of the people in any case) were responsible. The gospel writers' unforgivable crime against humanity was to extend the blame to all Jews by having the crowd agree with them. (At least Mark has them being whipped up into hysterical demands for Jesus' death by the duplicitous chief priests.)

But why, exactly, was Jesus condemned? Clearly the outcome was a Roman penalty for a crime against Rome: crucifixion was the punishment set down throughout the Empire for those who challenged its authority, either slaves who rebelled or subject peoples who organized revolt or spread sedition.

According to the New Testament, when Jesus was handed over by the Sanhedrin, Pilate was concerned with just one question: "Are you the king of the Jews?" Making such a claim would be by definition rebellion against Rome (irrespective of whether it was backed with force) since it denied the sovereignty of the emperor. In Mark Jesus' reply is gnomic: "You have said so."[13] But how would Mark know what he said? None of Jesus' followers was present.

(Predictably John has a longer and even more obscure question-and-answer session between Pilate and Jesus, in which Jesus' answer to the key question is "My kingdom is not of this world. If it were, my servants would fight to prevent my arrest by the Jewish leaders."[14] However, a would-be Messiah could never have said that; possessing a kingdom in this world was the whole point.)

As A. N. Sherwin-White, a specialist in Roman law, points out, whatever the veracity of the Gospel accounts of the Sanhedrin trial, they all agree that the only or main charge put before Pilate was political.[15] Since the outcome was a sentence reserved for political crimes, this must be right. As Hyam Maccoby remarks:

> Claiming to be the Messiah meant claiming to be King of the Jews. If it had meant that Jesus regarded himself as God, the High Priest would have regarded Jesus as merely a harmless lunatic; but it meant something much more urgent and practical than that—it signalled revolt.[16]

So that appears to settle that. Except that, as Maccoby points out, according to the Gospels Jesus was *framed* by the Jewish leadership, who had actually found him guilty of blasphemy but had no power to execute him, and so concocted a charge that would persuade Pilate to do it for them. But was it the evangelists who were guilty of framing—by falsely accusing the Jews?

According to Mark, Caiaphas calls witnesses against Jesus, but they have been put up to it and commit perjury. Their main allegation is that Jesus had threatened to destroy the Temple and build another within three days. Even this attempt to frame him fails because their testimony disagrees. Thwarted by the witnesses' incompetence, Caiaphas instead asks Jesus, "Are you the Messiah, the Son of the Blessed One?" When he replies, "I am," and adds, "And you will see the Son of Man sitting at the right hand of the Mighty One and coming on the clouds of heaven," the high priest declares that he has blasphemed and so condemned himself. The rest also declare him "worthy of death." They beat him up, then drag him off to Pilate.[17] Caiaphas' use of the phrase "Messiah, the Son of the Blessed One" must be a fabrication, since the high priest is assuming the Christian redefinition of the role of the Messiah: the traditional Jewish Messiah was never expected to be the Son of God. (Mark's account is followed by the other synoptics, with a few embellishments. John's Gospel, by contrast, leaves the accusations against Jesus somewhat mysterious, as the members of the Sanhedrin merely question him "about his disciples and his teaching" before handing him over to Pilate as a "criminal.")[18]

What is odd is that Jesus' fracas in the Temple a few days earlier furnished the perfect charge against him on both religious and political grounds, yet according to the Gospels it was not used against him. Although the Temple is mentioned in the synoptic accounts, it appears in the false testimony of witnesses who claim to have heard him say, "I will destroy this temple made with human hands and in three days will build another, not made with hands." To the synoptics this is a false charge because, although Jesus predicted the Temple's downfall, he said nothing about having a part in it himself.

In our reconstruction Jesus' scene in the Temple was effectively a declaration of its abolition and the removal of God's blessing. Could this "false" testimony be a garbled or evasive acknowledgment that the main charge against him was that he had called for an end to the Jerusalem Temple and the building of (or transfer of authority to) another? As an attack on the Temple it was blasphemy, and as a claim of authority—not recognized by Rome or the Temple establishment—it was sedition. So Caiaphas and Pilate could at least agree on that.

So why didn't the gospel writers—for whom the "cleansing" was the key event as far as Jewish opposition is concerned—make it the crucial aspect of the trial? The obvious answer is that in Christian terms it was nowhere near enough: indeed it was irrelevant. Jesus was the divine hero, the Son of God himself, who had sacrificed himself on humanity's behalf. To have him done to death simply for declaring the abolition of a place of worship that, by the time most if not all of the Gospels had been written no longer even existed, lacked the storyteller's all-important awe and wonder. Who would have cared?

In fact the Temple incident is there in the trial, if only just, but its emphasis has been changed to serve Christian theology. The over-turning of the money changers' tables as symbolizing the end of the Temple's authority has been turned into a threat to destroy the building (which Mark can genuinely claim was a false charge). The sacrilege has become the charge of blasphemy, but now the point is not simply that Jesus attacked a fundamental part of Second Temple Judaism (which would have left later Christians distinctly under-whelmed) but what was, to the early Church, the essential aspect of their Lord, his special relationship with God. And the political element—the implicit claim to messianic authority—has become the concern about Christ pretending to be King of the Jews.

It could only have been Jesus' violent demonstration of author-ity in the Temple that got him arrested and executed. Not only is it his sole reported action that could possibly have justified a Roman death warrant, but it would have screamed out for such a sentence.

The Mob's Choice

All four Gospels are adamant that Pilate found Jesus innocent but had him executed because the crowd demanded it.

First he gives them the choice between Jesus and the rebel Barab-bas. According to Mark, giving the populace such a choice was a Passover custom. As we noted, Mark's tone implies he expected his audience to be familiar with Barabbas and the incident that led to his imprisonment—leading an insurrection that caused many deaths.

Barabbas means "son of the father," a seemingly pointless name: is it really so unique to have a male parent? But the alternative spelling in some early manuscripts—Barrabbas—if correct, might mean "son of our teacher" (*bar rabban*); according to Saint Jerome (who produced the official Latin translation of the Bible around the turn of the fifth century), the now-lost Gospel of the Hebrews in-terpreted the name in that way.[19] Intriguingly, some early manu-scripts of Matthew, besides other early Christian texts, give his full name as Jesus Barabbas.[20]

Donovan Joyce proposed that Barabbas may even have been Jesus' own son—which works with both the "son of the father" and the "son of our teacher" derivation, although there is not much more to the argument.[21] Against it is the disparity between Mark's manifest expectation that his readers already knew this character and the absence of any other mention of children of Jesus, which, if they existed, can only be explained by a cover-up by the first Christians, who for one reason or another wanted to keep them secret. If this was the case, Barabbas would hardly have been mentioned so casually (if at all).

However, the "custom of the Feast" described by Mark, where the governor gave the people the opportunity to release a prisoner, is complete fiction. There is no historical record of such a custom, even in the writings of Josephus, who scrupulously and proudly emphasized every legal concession the Romans accorded his people—and neither does it make any sense. Freeing a criminal is unlikely to impress the people with the implacable authority of Rome, especially when the prefect allows them to have a convicted rebel released in place of someone whom he has declared innocent.

Clearly the purpose of inventing the custom is part of the process of shifting the blame for Jesus' death firmly onto the Jews. But does this mean that the whole Barabbas story was shamelessly made up? It is difficult to be certain, although Raymond E. Brown's suggestion, that Barabbas' release was an unconnected event that happened to take place at about the same time (not everything that happened in Jerusalem in those days was about Jesus) but was subsequently assumed to be connected, is quite persuasive.[22] After all, the episode must have been a very early tradition to turn up in all four Gospels. Had Mark or his source completely invented Barabbas, no doubt they would have introduced him in a flurry of spurious detail.

Having agreed to release Barabbas, Pilate allegedly then asks the crowd what he should do with Jesus—an act which S. G. F. Brandon uncompromisingly brands as "ludicrous in the extreme" and "preposterous."[23] Indeed! This is tantamount to a Nazi overlord asking Russian peasants what he should do with a criminal. The crowd call for Jesus to be crucified, and even though Pilate continues to demand of them, "Why? What crime has he committed?" eventually he gives in and orders Jesus to be crucified to death. (Matthew also describes him washing his hands to show he bears no responsibility, and has the crowd proclaiming, "His blood is on us and on our children!"[24] Surely no crowd in history—apart from the extras in *The Passion of the Christ*—would ever say that, especially to a hated oppressor.) Clearly the reactions of the masses are a nonsensical fiction. A Roman governor would never have let the crowd have their way, especially not an infamously hard man like Pilate.

There is also the evidence of the *titulus*, the notice that read, "The King of the Jews," which, according to all four Gospels, was fixed to Jesus' cross. After a thorough review of the evidence, Ernst Bammel concluded that the title referred to the crime of *laesa majestas*, essentially a challenge to the emperor's authority.[25] The notice seems to have been a straight statement of the crime for which Jesus was being executed, not the sick mockery it is usually thought—which of course means that Pilate *had* found him guilty, whatever the Gospels say.

The Climax

At least when Jesus was led out to crucifixion he was back in the public eye, but although the gospel writers no longer had to use their imaginations about what happened, the New Testament's version of events is still a mix of real memories and theological elucidation. While the detail of Simon of Cyrene being forced to carry Jesus' cross seems, as we have seen, to be based on a genuine memory passed down within the Christian community in Rome by his sons, other details seem to conform too neatly with the scriptures. For example, the soldiers casting lots for Jesus' clothes seems contrived to fit Psalm 22, as cited in John's Gospel: "They divide my clothes among them/and cast lots for my garments."[26]

One thing was terribly, horribly sure. Crucifixion was one of the most traumatic ways to die ever devised by mankind. A very common punishment throughout the Empire—the slave leader Spartacus and thousands of his fellow rebels were crucified along the main road into Rome as a dire warning—it was frequently employed to stamp out insurrection by the Jews. As a result of the riots that followed Herod the Great's death in 4 BCE, two thousand people had been crucified in Jerusalem alone.[27] Crucifixion was specifically designed by highly efficient sadists to be an extremely nasty and degrading way to die—long-drawn-out, agonizing, public, and humiliating (victims would lose control of their bladder and bowels after just a short time). It was totally irreconcilable with the age-hallowed expectations of the Messiah.

At nine in the morning (according to the synoptics; the Fourth Gospel gives no specific timings) they nail him to the cross (Luke adds Jesus saying, "Father, forgive them, for they do not know what they are doing,"[28] although as this is absent from many early manuscripts, it may well be a much later creation).

According to Mark (followed by Matthew), Jesus was crucified along with two rebels (*lestai*), who join the bystanders in yelling insults at him for claiming to be the Messiah.[29] Luke, as transparent as ever, changes them to "criminals"—even associating Jesus with rebels in this way would be too much of a reminder to his correspondent Theophilus about the reason people were usually crucified. And just in case he does remember, Luke has the two criminals argue between themselves so that one has the chance to say, "We are punished justly, for we are getting what our deeds deserve. But this man has done nothing wrong."[30] Apart from the near impossibility of crucified men being able to spit out such coherent statements, Luke's desperation to distance both himself and Jesus from the whole subject of sedition has become rather embarrassing. John's Gospel just has Jesus being crucified with two "others." In any event, we can accept that he was crucified with men who had rebelled against Rome's authority, perhaps in the Barabbas uprising a few days earlier.

The women followers from Galilee, who appear to come out of nowhere, watch Jesus being crucified. Mark names them as Mary Magdalene, Mary the mother of James the Younger and Joseph, and Salome. Matthew replaces the last with "the mother of Zebedee's sons," but it is unclear whether she and Salome are the same woman. Luke names none of them, but only John's Gospel has Jesus' mother present:

Near the cross of Jesus stood his mother, his mother's sister, Mary the wife of Clopas, and Mary Magdalene. When Jesus saw his mother there, and the disciple whom he loved standing near by, he said to her, "Woman, here is your son," and to the disciple,

"Here is your mother." From that time on, this disciple took her into his home.[31]

If Jesus' mother was there, why didn't the synoptics know? Perhaps the writer of the Fourth Gospel wanted to counter the idea that Jesus and Mary were not on the best terms, appealing to his anonymous authority, the beloved disciple, as his source so that nobody would object. (But would one of the disciples dare attend the crucifixion, when all the others were in hiding?) Some have argued that the synoptics' "other Mary," the mother of James the Younger and Joseph (who otherwise plays no part in the story), is really Jesus' mother, her identity obscured because of the Gospels' anti-family agenda.[32] On the other hand, others, such as Ben Witherington III, think the passage in John's Gospel is implausible, asking where the beloved disciple, who is absent from the opening list of those present, came from.[33]

In the synoptic version, at noon a three-hour darkness descends on the land, at the end of which Jesus dies. His last words vary between the Gospels, and one imagines they must have presented the authors with a golden opportunity for propagandizing. Yet Mark and Matthew have him crying out in Aramaic, "My God, my God, why have you forsaken me?"—the opening line of Psalm 22. ("*Eloi*"—"God"—is, we are told, mistaken for "Elijah" by some of the bystanders, who think he must be calling for Elijah to rescue him. Or perhaps they thought he was calling upon Elijah come again, John the Baptist, for help that never came.) "Someone" offers him a spongeful of wine vinegar on the end of a stick to drink. (John, always wanting Jesus in control, has him ask for it.) Then, with a loud cry, Jesus dies.[34]

Since Jesus' words come from a psalm, did he actually say it—or something like it—or was it another example of retrospectively fulfilling prophecy? It is not the most obvious Old Testament line to put into Jesus' mouth, as it rather goes against the spirit of the story; if a devoted follower invented the shout, he would surely have had Jesus say something more edifying (as Luke did, changing it to a quote from Psalm 31: "Father, into your hands I commit my spirit").[35] The memory of his specific Aramaic words and the detail that some people misheard them also has the ring of authenticity; it is hard to imagine Mark making them up. Perhaps Jesus did call out these words; or if the line from the psalm was added, perhaps it was because it was the nearest scriptural quote to Jesus' actual cry. If so, then Jesus' last words reflected a heart-wrenching sense of abandonment, spiritual desolation, and failure. In contrast, John's Gospel has the simple "It is finished," said with a dignified bowing of the head.[36]

Various portents are said to occur at the moment of Jesus' death. In Mark and Luke the curtain or veil in the Temple is torn in two, but Matthew improves on this, adding, "The earth shook, the rocks split, and the tombs broke open. The bodies of many holy people who had died were raised to life. They came out of the tombs after Jesus' resurrection and went into the holy city and appeared to many people."[37] Call us skeptics, but this scene from a zombie B movie seems to have escaped the chroniclers—indeed *everyone*—of the time.

John's Gospel downplays the supernatural set dressing, even ignoring the veil rending, although, more persuasively, he does add the detail:

> Because the Jewish leaders did not want the bodies left on the crosses during the Sabbath, they asked Pilate to have the legs broken and the bodies taken down. The soldiers therefore came and broke the legs of the first man who had been crucified with Jesus, and then those of the other. But when they came to Jesus and found that he was already dead, they did not break his legs. Instead, one of the soldiers pierced Jesus' side with a spear, bringing a sudden flow of blood and water. The man who saw it has given testimony, and his testimony is true. He knows that he tells the truth, and he testifies so that you also may believe. These things happened so that the scripture would be fulfilled: "Not one of his bones will be broken," and, as another scripture says, "They will look on the one they have pierced."[38]

Breaking the legs curtailed the long-drawn-out agonies of crucifixion, so was actually an act of mercy, although it hardly sounds like it. Crucifixion was supposed to last as long as possible, death being caused by a mixture of exposure to the elements (Golgotha being on the edge of a desert), shock, and thirst. Breaking the victim's legs, however, meant that with his arms nailed outwards and upwards and with nothing to support his weight, he would asphyxiate, dying perhaps not immediately but considerably sooner than otherwise.

Does the mention of leg breaking demonstrate that the writer of John had access to inside information, or have the details been contrived to fit the prophecies, that Jesus' bones had to remain unbroken and he had to be pierced in some way? Even the detail of the "blood and water" issuing from the chest wound has been much debated. Some have suggested possible medical explanations, while others argue instead for symbolic interpretations based on the scriptures.[39]

One suspect detail is the intervention with the spear, allegedly because of the approaching Sabbath. In fact the prohibition was only that the bodies of those who had *died* on the cross should not be left there (at nightfall on any day, not just the Sabbath).[40] There was no such rule about those still alive on the cross, and the whole point of crucifixion was that it took a long time—preferably days. So the Jewish leaders' seeking the hastening of the three men's death makes no sense, and neither does Pilate's agreement to their request.

However, hastening the *burial* because sunset was approaching (again on any day) makes sense—if it was allowed. As crucifixion was almost as much a deterrent as a punishment, the bodies would be left there to rot and for the birds to mutilate, and usually were *not* buried (in all cultures of the time, not just the Jewish, the ultimate degradation). Had this element been relaxed in Judea to soothe Jewish sensibilities, and were the bodies given back to relatives for burial?

From a thorough survey of the historical record, Crossan established that the Romans seldom made any concessions to the Jewish Law.[41] There are references to bodies being handed over as a special act of magnanimity for those crucified on the eve of the emperor's birthday—although the mercy did not extend to releasing the living man—but there is no evidence for a similar practice at Jewish festivals. On the other hand, that it did happen occasionally is shown by the discovery in 1968 of bones of one first-century crucifixion victim in a family tomb in Jerusalem, although this was the only one ever found of all the tens, maybe hundreds of thousands of victims. Presumably, though, burial required a special dispensation from the governor, or an exceptionally impressive bribe from the family concerned.

It is the day before the Sabbath, which begins at nightfall, and haste is needed to ensure Jesus' body is interred before it begins. The somewhat mysterious sympathizer, the wealthy Joseph of Arimathea, goes to Pilate to ask for Jesus' body. Pilate agrees, although Mark tells us he was surprised that Jesus had died so quickly and checks with the centurion left guarding the victims.

According to Mark, Joseph of Arimathea was a council member who was "waiting for the Kingdom of God."[42] Luke describes him as a member of the Sanhedrin but *not* a follower of Jesus; he acts simply because he thought Jesus had been treated unjustly.[43] Matthew drops the connection with the Sanhedrin, simply describing him as a "rich man" who had "become a disciple of Jesus."[44] In John's Gospel he is "a disciple of Jesus, but secretly because he feared the Jewish leaders"[45] (again, there is nothing about his membership in the Sanhedrin). But disappointingly for lovers of legend, new thinking casts doubt on Joseph of Arimathea's identity and role. He may not have been one of Jesus' followers at all but simply a member of the Sanhedrin charged with burial of the bodies.

In John there is a major contradiction: the Jewish leaders ask for the bodies to be "taken away" because a special Sabbath is approaching, but then Joseph of Arimathea requests Jesus' body from Pilate.[46] Even more oddly, Acts states that Jesus was taken down from the cross and buried by the same Jewish leaders who were behind his death—quaint, to say the least, for Luke, who tells the "standard" version of Jesus' burial in his Gospel.[47]

A very persuasive explanation of these anomalies was put forward by Gerd Lüdemann, director of the Institute of Early Christian Studies at Göttingen University, whose *The Resurrection of Jesus* (1994), incredibly, provoked calls for his prosecution in his native Germany. (Undeterred, the following year he produced a more mainstream version, *What Really Happened to Jesus*, cowritten with Alf Özen.) Lüdemann argues that it *was* the Jewish leaders who had Jesus taken down and buried—Joseph of Arimathea being the Sanhedrin member given the task—but this account became unacceptable to later Christians, so they made it more faith-friendly by turning Joseph into a secret follower of Jesus.[48]

Looking Back at Golgotha

The conventional Christian interpretation of the crucifixion is that it was quite simply what Jesus came to earth for and, even though he might have gone through the Agony of doubt and fear, he accepted his fate as an inevitable part of God's plan. A more academic view is that through his familiarity with the scriptures Jesus had come to identify with the role of the suffering Servant that he equated with the Messiah and so went willingly to his death but expected God to step in and save him at the last minute. That would account for his anguished and desolate cry from the cross: "My God, my God! Why have you forsaken me?" This, famously, was the conclusion of Hugh Schonfield in *The Passover Plot* and has been championed recently by James Tabor, who writes in *The Jesus Dynasty*:

> If Jesus did come to anticipate his suffering at the hands of his enemies, I am convinced that he expected that he would be *saved* from death, delivered from the "mouth of the lion" as the Psalmist had predicted (Psalm 22:21). In text after text that deals with the suffering of God's righteous servants they are always rescued from the "gates of death" at the last moment.[49]

However, both interpretations assume that being crucified was part of Jesus' plan, but the evidence simply does not back this up. All the New Testament passages where Jesus reveals foreknowledge of his fate—such as the announcement of his betrayal—can be shown to be retrospective justification, precisely in order to show that Christ had never been caught out by this unexpected turn of events. The security precautions he employed also indicate that he had absolutely no intention of being captured. Another vital point is that although the "sacrificial death to bring salvation" theme is central to all early Christian writings, including those of Paul and three of the four canonical Gospels, it is conspicuously absent from Mark, the first Gospel to be written. True, Mark includes scenes in which Jesus tries to explain to the uncomprehending disciples that he must suffer, die, and rise again, but nowhere does he explain *why* this has to happen.

All this, however, is not remotely relevant if he didn't die on the cross at all. Notoriously there are widely held theories that Jesus' "death" was a carefully orchestrated sham, and that the post-resurrection appearances were of a man who simply hadn't risen from the tomb at all.

The Empty Tomb

For Christianity, everything in the story up to this point—even the most sensational miracles—was merely a preliminary. As Paul said, "if Christ has not been raised, our preaching is useless and so is your faith . . . if Christ has not been raised your faith is futile." [50]

Before trying to decide what exactly happened—whether it was the greatest miracle or the most shameless deception of all time—we need to take a close look at the information the Gospels choose to present.

One of the few brave enough to wrestle with the historical reality of the resurrection is Gerd Lüdemann, who objects in the most strident terms to the Church's assertion that the resurrection is a matter for faith that can never be understood like other factual, historical events:

> This argument is out of this world. Everything ends up in "I believe in order to understand," a statement which cannot be left unquestioned in the context of modern scholarship. As long as absurdity is not to be made the criterion of the truth of theological statements, academic theologians (*and* preachers in church) must be concerned for their remarks to be comprehensible. [51]

The Jews believed in resurrection in a physical sense rather than an emergence into an ethereal or spiritual existence: the flesh-and-blood body would literally be reanimated, fully capable of all its previous activities, just like Lazarus and the holy people that Matthew has ambling out of the tombs when Jesus dies. Yet the Gospel accounts want it both ways. We are assured that Jesus *had* physically resurrected in the Jewish way, being seen and touched by his disciples—even seen to eat—but then he ascended into heaven and disappeared from sight forever. The next step was the idea of a mystical communion between earthly Christians and spiritual Jesus.

The Gospel stories of the resurrection consist of the discovery of Jesus' empty tomb and the subsequent appearances of the risen man-god to his disciples and others. These two parts are entirely different in character and need to be examined separately.

Jesus' body was placed in the tomb on the Friday, with a heavy stone blocking the entrance to keep out scavenging animals. It was left there for the Sabbath, which ended at sunset on the Saturday, and during the hours of darkness of the night of Saturday/Sunday. All four Gospels begin with the discovery early on the Sunday morning that the tomb was mysteriously empty, and all associate this discovery with Mary Magdalene, and in three cases other female disciples.

Mark's explanation, which makes perfect sense, is that Mary Magdalene and the other women went to the tomb at first light on the Sunday to complete the required anointing of the body, which they had had to abandon on the Friday because there was no time. Mark's version is that Mary Magdalene, Mary the mother of James, and Salome go to the tomb to perform the anointing, but when they arrive, the stone has been rolled away. They go inside and find a young man in a white robe sitting there, who tells them, "Don't be alarmed. You are looking for Jesus the Nazarene, who was crucified. He has risen! He is not here. See the place where they laid him. But go, tell the disciples and Peter, 'He is going ahead of you into Galilee. There you will see him, just as he told you.'" But the women flee, too scared to tell anyone.[52]

The original of Mark's Gospel ended there, with no risen Jesus appearing to the disciples. This part was added later—being based on Luke—specifically because it was such an embarrassing omission. But was Mark's original ending lost, or could it have been suppressed for some reason?

The women's *not* telling anyone what happened makes a very strange ending. Surely there should be some explanation of how the news spread, if not some actual evidence that Jesus has risen. On the other hand, a casual loss of the original ending is not very convincing either. If it happened, it must have been when there was just the one copy of the manuscript in existence, but the community would have ensured it was copied immediately, precisely because of the risk of loss or damage. So presumably, sometime between the original composition and the first surviving manuscripts some three centuries later, it had been decided that Mark's ending was unacceptable. (As Schonfield notes wryly, "Some suspicion is created that the lost end of Mark was not necessarily accidental."[53]) Alternatively, it has been speculated that the ending was part of the "inner doctrine" removed from Mark's original version.[54] Whatever the explanation, though, clearly Mark *believed* that Jesus had risen, although we will probably never know whether he originally described Jesus' postresurrection appearances, and if so what he said about them.

There is another clue: while the two Gospels based on Mark merely embellish his tale of the empty tomb, their descriptions of Jesus' postresurrection appearances are wildly different, revealing that in Mark they found no inspiration even for flights of fancy, and showing that the end had been lost even by the time they came to use it.

Matthew develops the empty tomb scenario into a fantasy in which when Mary Magdalene and the "other Mary" arrive at the tomb there is an earthquake, then an angel whose "appearance was like lightning and . . . clothes were as white as snow" descends, rolls away the stone to show that the tomb is empty, then delivers basically the same message as the young man in Mark. In this account, however, rather than being scared out of their wits, the women are "filled with joy" and run off to tell the disciples the good news—and then collide with Jesus himself. They seize his feet in adoration, and he tells them to let the men know he will see them in Galilee. Perhaps we should take at least the earthquake and angel with a generous pinch of salt.[55]

Matthew, alone of the four, also informs us about the story that Christianity's enemies were spreading about the empty tomb: that Jesus' disciples simply stole his body and pretended he had risen from the dead. Matthew's lavish embellishments of Mark's basic tale were obviously designed to scotch this slander. First Matthew has

Pilate, at the insistence of the Jewish leaders, posting guards outside the tomb to prevent the body from being stolen. Then he has the women—and Roman soldiers—actually seeing the stone being rolled away by the angel. Matthew is adamant that the soldiers saw it all too but were bribed by the chief priests to say Jesus' body had been taken while they were asleep, which is not very convincing.

Significantly, as this Gospel was aimed at a predominantly Jewish-Christian audience, Matthew clearly felt he had to address this issue, although the other gospel writers either had no idea of the story or knew it would be news to their audience. Having the women actually meet Jesus—again not taken from Mark—also seems designed to head off skeptical questioners. In fact the two verses telling of Jesus' appearance were clearly inserted into the original account, presumably some time after Matthew wrote it. The narrative runs perfectly smoothly without them, and Jesus' appearance is oddly superfluous for such an amazing phenomenon, as he only tells the Marys what the angel has already told them to do, which they are already doing. So Matthew's version is completely worthless.

Luke has essentially the same story as Mark—this time with Mary Magdalene, Mary the mother of James, and Joanna—but with two men "in clothes that gleamed like lightning" in the tomb. They deliver the message that Jesus has risen to the Eleven, who react with skepticism. Peter, though, goes to the tomb and confirms that it is open and empty, with Jesus' linen burial clothes lying there. (The presence of the burial clothes—also in John's Gospel—seems to be a more subtle attempt than Matthew's to counter the claim that Jesus' body was simply stolen, since whoever did it was unlikely to unwrap it first.) [56]

Predictably, John's story is somewhat self-indulgent. Mary Magdalene goes alone to the tomb in the dark and sees it has been opened, so goes to fetch Peter and the beloved disciple. They go in, see the grave clothes, and leave, baffled (as usual). Mary Magdalene remains by the tomb weeping (as usual), then sees two angels in white in the tomb, who ask her the reason for her tears. She replies, "They have taken my Lord away and I don't know where they have put him." Then she turns around and sees Jesus but fails to recognize him. Through her tears she mistakes him for the gardener, asking him if he has moved the body and to tell her where he has taken it. (Encountering two angels must have been a bit of a clue that something a trifle unusual was going on.) But when he says simply, "Mary," she instantly recognizes him. "Do not hold on to me, for I have not yet ascended to the Father," he says, then instructs her to go and tell the men, which she does.[57]

Although traditionally rendered as "Don't touch me," the Greek "*me mou aptou*" literally means "Stop touching me."[58] *Aptou* can mean anything "from making contact with a garment to having intercourse with a partner."[59] The innuendo might not be unintentional in John (the only Gospel to use this verb), possibly as another example of his verbal game playing. Yet again this writer has used certain non-Jewish literary forms in his very unique telling of the encounter between Mary Magdalene and the risen Jesus. Andrew Lincoln explains:

> The focus on one woman at the empty tomb, together with a number of its other emphases, means that this account is reminiscent of conventions in ancient Greek romances . . . where a lover distractedly seeks the body of the beloved in a tomb, finds the tomb empty, believes it has been robbed, later meets the beloved, who was not dead after all, but fails to recognize him or her until the beloved's voice triggers recognition, and they finally embrace each other before falling to the ground together.[60]

That customary—and rather startling—ending may be why the gospel writer chose the wide-ranging *aptou*. But as with the tale of Jesus and the Samaritan woman, the writer has subverted the payoff; rather than the expected falling to the ground, Jesus tells the Magdalene to get off him—another example of John's use of erotic traditions, but abruptly switching the ending.

Besides these romances, in Mary's words to the angels and "gardener" there is a striking echo of the Egyptian mystery plays of Isis and Osiris, a further example of John's characteristic devices—drawing a parallel between Jesus and pagan gods. As with the erotica, the writer's motive is unfortunately lost on us today, but unexpected fun though it might be, there is no reason to take the details of John's account of the discovery of the empty tomb any more seriously than Matthew's.

The common features of the resurrection story are that Mary Magdalene is involved (with other female followers), the tomb is already open, and there is at least one person available to deliver Jesus' message (and even his presence is dependent on the women's word). Sadly we can discount Matthew and John's claim that Jesus himself put in an appearance: after all, Mark and Luke would certainly have included it if it had featured in the early tradition.

On this basis the "empty tomb" stories are unimpressive: all that happens is that Jesus' body is found to be gone. But of course this discovery takes on a whole new complexion in the light of the claims that in the following days the risen Jesus was seen by his disciples.

However, before turning our attention to the miraculous element, we should stress that when the Jesus movement began to establish itself on the central claim that Jesus had risen from the dead, its opponents were unable to prove them wrong. Had there been an identifiable tomb, it would have been easy enough. Yet nobody even tried to use this argument against the first Christians, suggesting that whatever really happened, Jesus had been placed in a tomb and his body had indeed totally disappeared.

Flagrant Contradictions

The Gospel accounts of the postresurrection exacerbate the underlying problem, being not just different but literally irreconcilable. Matthew, for example, has the risen Jesus instructing the disciples to return to Galilee, where they meet him. Conversely, Luke has Jesus instructing the *same* disciples to remain in Jerusalem and has him appear there. It would be difficult to come up with two more blatantly contradictory accounts.

The synoptics tell very different stories. Mark has no postresurrection appearances at all. Matthew describes a very brief scene in which the eleven remaining disciples travel to the appointed mountain in Galilee, where Jesus appears and gives them the most peremptory instructions to go to "all nations," spreading his message and baptizing. The Gospel ends, "And surely I am with you always, to the very end of the age." Nothing is said about the manner of his departing, or even that he does depart.[61]

Luke has the lengthy story of how a man appears and walks with two disciples on the road to Emmaus, a village seven miles from

Jerusalem, but they fail to recognize him. They tell him about Jesus' crucifixion and the empty tomb, and the stranger explains how all this was prefigured in the scriptures. When they arrive at Emmaus, they invite him to stay the night, but as he breaks bread they suddenly realize the man is their Lord himself. The pair return immediately to Jerusalem to find the Eleven, but just as they are passing on the amazing news, Jesus appears, proving he is no ghost by inviting them to touch him and eating a piece of fish. He instructs them to preach "repentance for the forgiveness of sins" to all the nations. He then leads them to nearby Bethany, where he is "taken up into heaven." By implication this is either the same day as he disappeared from the tomb or the following day.[62] Weirdly, however, at the beginning of his sequel, the Acts of the Apostles, Luke completely contradicts himself by having Jesus appear and teach the disciples "over a period of forty days."[63]

John's Gospel describes Jesus appearing among the disciples on the Sunday evening, even though they have locked themselves in the house for fear of the Jewish authorities. He breathes on them to bestow the Holy Spirit, passing on the power to forgive sins. But Thomas, who had not been present, refuses to believe it, so a week later Jesus reappears and invites him to touch his wounds so that he can believe.[64] This is where John's Gospel originally ended. The whole of what is now chapter 21, describing Jesus' appearance to Peter and other disciples while fishing on the Sea of Galilee (giving Jesus the opportunity to forgive Peter for his cowardly denials), and with the beloved disciple's testimonial, was tacked on later.[65]

So, unlike the story of the Passion, there was no agreement among the early traditions about what exactly happened after Jesus rose from the grave. Everybody believed it had happened, but nobody was sure of the details, which suggests we are dealing with rumor, folklore, and/or fantasy.

However, there is another early Christian text that touches very briefly on Jesus' postresurrection appearances: Paul's First Letter to the Corinthians, which almost certainly predates the Gospels (except perhaps for Mark). Despite its brevity it still reveals how the risen Jesus was perceived at the very beginning of the religion. Paul states that after rising on the third day,

he appeared to Cephas [Peter], and then to the Twelve. After that, he appeared to more than five hundred of the brothers and sisters at the same time, most of whom are still living, though some have fallen asleep. Then he appeared to James, then to all the Apostles, and last of all he appeared to me also, as to one abnormally born ["runt of the litter"].[66]

This is intriguing for several reasons. First, there is no mention of Mary Magdalene or any women; the first person to whom Jesus chooses to appear is Peter, which of course matches none of the Gospels. An appearance to more than five hundred followers, most of whom were still alive when Paul wrote, is similarly unrecorded. He then mentions Jesus appearing to James the Just, his brother, which also is not in any of the Gospels.[67] And finally Paul includes himself in the list.

The fact that Paul alludes to witnesses of postrising appearances by Jesus who are still around—lots of them—is significant, since, unlike the Gospels' authors, he was writing as one believer to others about matters on which they already agreed. The presence of so many in the Christian community who had witnessed that appearance must have been common knowledge, and so they must have really existed. But if there was such a mass witnessing of the risen Lord so early, why didn't the gospel writers know about it?

Gerd Lüdemann has provided a very plausible explanation for the discrepancies between Paul's summary and the Gospels: they are describing an entirely different kind of experience.[68] Paul's revelation on the road to Damascus clearly bore little resemblance to, for example, the Doubting Thomas episode. It was an inner experience of the ascended Jesus some time after the ascension—similar to the modern "born again" personal epiphany, not an encounter with someone who can eat fish. As Lüdemann pointed out, this distinction implies that the other appearances on Paul's list are similar revelations. And the appearance to the five hundred, he suggests, is actually a reference to the Pentecost experience in Acts, when the Holy Spirit comes upon a large group of believers who begin to speak in tongues. The physical Jesus does not materialize in their midst; they have an *inner* experience of him. Indeed in Paul's list of people to whom Jesus "appeared," as Crossan notes, a more accurate translation of the Greek is "revealed to."[69]

On this reasoning the "appearances" to Peter and James the Just were of a similar nature. Lüdemann's case is compelling and carries major implications. If in Paul's day the Christian community considered personal visionary experiences of Jesus as proof of his rising from the dead, and given the deeply unconvincing later accounts in the Gospels of the physical resurrection, then clearly the early Church knew nothing about the latter. All it knew was that the tomb where his body had been laid was found to be inexplicably empty just a couple of days later, and that some of his followers—his principal disciples at first, but at least one large group of more ordinary devotees—had the inner vision of him. However we might explain those visions, there were no corporeal, flesh-and-blood appearances.

The Christians had a very strong motive to concoct such tales. Similar stories had spread about their first great persecutor, the Roman emperor Nero—who may even have been responsible for the deaths of Peter and Paul. Nero died in 68 CE, but within a year there were widespread rumors that he had either not died or had returned from the dead. It was even said he had been seen alive. As with Jesus, there were many tales of where and by whom he had been seen, all different. He even became known as Nero *redivivus*—the Resurrected Nero—and there was a common belief that he had gone into hiding in Parthia, where he would raise an army and return to conquer Rome. Indeed, between his death and the late eighties CE, three impostors in Parthia claimed to be Nero. (Presumably they *were* all fakes.)[70] So Christians had a major incentive to outresurrect their most sadistic persecutor.

Lüdemann himself opts for a psychological explanation for the visions, pointing out that there is essentially no difference between the disciples' experience, in which they felt the presence of Jesus, and those of many bereaved people who feel their loved ones' continued presence. Jesus' disciples were clearly bereft and in deep mourning. Lüdemann's conclusion—which probably explains why German Christians sought his prosecution—is (emphasis his) "the assumption of a resurrection of Jesus is completely unnecessary as a presupposition to explain these phenomena. *A consistent modern view must say farewell to the resurrection of Jesus as a historical event.*"[71]

As with Jesus' healings, it hardly matters for our purposes whether the postcrucifixion appearances were paranormal phenomena or hallucinations induced by deep grief. What is important is that they are not unique. But whatever lay behind them, such early Christian belief in Jesus' continued existence could only work if his tomb had genuinely been found empty and nobody knew the location of his body. So how can we explain the empty tomb? Where did Jesus' body go?

Once we discount the resurrection as a real event—there is no way around that—there are only two possibilities: either somebody moved the body, or Jesus was not dead.

Did Jesus Survive?

There are two basic variants of the theory that Jesus was still alive when taken down from the cross. The first is that he regained consciousness naturally in the tomb. The second is that his death was deliberately faked.

Even the first, however, required collusion by his followers, since he could not have got out of the tomb by himself when the entrance was blocked by a large boulder. The first to visit the tomb, therefore, would have found him alive and spirited him away (not necessarily to convince people he had risen, but to protect him from the Romans: obviously, as a condemned man, he had to stay "dead").

The idea that Jesus might literally have survived the cross, being taken down in the belief that he was dead but subsequently recovering, has been suggested many times in both fact and fiction, beginning as far back as the 1770s by the colorful German theologian Karl Friedrich Bahrdt. The idea has proved irresistible to novelists—witness *The Brook Kerith* by George Moore in 1916 and D. H. Lawrence's novella *The Man Who Died* (originally *The Escaped Cock*) in 1931. In nonfiction its most famous proponent was Schonfield in *The Passover Plot*, but others include Donovan Joyce in *The Jesus Scroll* and of course Baigent, Leigh, and Lincoln with *The Holy Blood and the Holy Grail*. The last three books all take the line that Jesus' survival was the result of a plot by his supporters.

The idea that Jesus did not die on the cross, at least in the sense that we understand it, began quite early. One gnostic teacher, Basilides, who flourished in the 120s and 130s CE, believed that

Simon of Cyrene had been crucified in Jesus' place. Variations of this concept (such as a completely illusory Jesus, a kind of holographic doppelgänger, being crucified—which is also found in the Qu'ran) surface in several gnostic texts. However, this idea was not based on any inside information about the crucifixion but on gnostic theology: as Jesus had merely taken on a man's form while remaining the divine being who had existed alongside the creator since the beginning of time, he could neither suffer nor die.

However, the modern theories have some valid points. If the Gospels' timing is to be believed, Jesus died unexpectedly quickly, after only about three hours on the cross. This is acknowledged in Mark, when Pilate expresses surprise at Joseph of Arimathea's request, seeking confirmation that Jesus is really dead before agreeing to release the body. On the other hand, we have no way of knowing Jesus' physical condition and general state of health: he could have suffered a heart attack because of the remorseless stress.

We know from Josephus that it was possible to survive the rigors of crucifixion. In his autobiography he describes how, during the siege of Jerusalem, he came across three men he knew among the mass being crucified outside the city, and successfully persuaded Titus to let them down. However, only one of them survived.[72]

In those times confirming death was not an exact science, and still today people declared dead revive on mortuary slabs and sometimes even during their own funeral. So it could easily have happened in those less sophisticated times, and to Jesus, but is there any *positive* evidence? Perhaps, but what proponents of the survival story tend to cite as proof are some of the more suspicious details of the story.

It is often pointed out that in Mark's Gospel the word Joseph of Arimathea uses when he asks Pilate for Jesus' "body" is *soma*, which means a living body, though when Pilate replies he uses *ptoma*, corpse. However, as we have seen, the story of Joseph's meeting with Pilate was probably contrived, so it is pointless to read anything into the linguistic subtleties. (And in any case, asking Pilate for Jesus' "living body" might be a bit of a giveaway.) Instead, perhaps Mark's hidden message is that Jesus' followers knew him to be living for time and all eternity.

Schonfield suggested that Jesus had arranged to be given a narcotic to induce the semblance of death, and it was this—not wine vinegar—that was on the sponge lifted up to him on the stick. As he points out, if anything vinegar should have had a stimulating effect, but if the Gospel is accurate Jesus immediately slumped as if dead after drinking it. But can we really trust such fine detail, especially as the Gospels have demonstrably altered the facts to conform to Old Testament prophecies (for example, gambling for Jesus' clothes)? Crossan links the vinegary sponge (as well as the wine and myrrh drink offered to Jesus at the beginning of his ordeal) with the end with Psalm 69: "They put gall [poison] in my food/and gave me vinegar for my thirst."[73] If Crossan is correct, then Schonfield's argument is built on very shaky foundations.

All this is arguable, but it is nowhere near proof. Some positive evidence of Jesus' survival is needed, such as a reliable report of his being seen later—which ironically, the Gospels' accounts totally fail to supply. First, they can easily be shown to be later mythmaking, and second, if he came round from a coma or narcotic-induced un-consciousness, he would have been in no condition to walk around, still less talk not just coherently but triumphantly, later that day (certainly not attempting the seven-mile walk to Emmaus and back) or indeed for at least many days, if not weeks, afterwards.

Not to be put off, researchers cite other controversial claims—that records exist of Jesus' life after the crucifixion. Donovan Joyce's book *The Jesus Scroll* (1973) was the result of a strange experience in 1964 when he was waiting in Tel Aviv airport for his flight home. He was approached by an Israeli, who claimed to be an archaeolo-gist but admitted using an assumed name, who offered him $5,000 to smuggle out of the country an ancient scroll he alleged had been stolen from the current excavations at the fortress of Masada, the scene of the Jews' last stand after the end of the first Jewish Revolt, in 73 CE. (Researching the excavations for a novel had taken Joyce to Israel in the first place.)

The mystery man took Joyce into an airport lavatory and hur-riedly told him about the scroll: it had been written during the siege of Masada by one "Jesus son of Jacob of Gennesareth," who said he was eighty years old, the legitimate heir to the line of Maccabean kings, and that he had a son. The implication is that this was proof that Jesus was still alive in 73 CE—and that he had been married and had at least one child. Although intrigued, Joyce declined the offer of the scroll, fearing the consequences if he was caught, and never heard of it again.[74]

Although the document is sometimes cited as evidence of Jesus' survival—for example in *The Holy Blood and the Holy Grail*—the evidence is far too slender. It amounts to no more than a brief glimpse of an ancient scroll in an unintelligible language and a whispered conversation in an airport bathroom with a man who refused to give his identity. And even the scroll seems not to be by *the* Jesus anyway: after all, who was Jacob of Gennesareth? And can we really believe that Jesus continued to live among the Jews of Judea without anyone's noticing (or informing on him to the Romans)? To be fair to Joyce, the experience only provided the incentive to kick off his research into the historical Jesus; he never claimed it proved anything.

There is also a recurring claim that Jesus traveled to India after the crucifixion, where he was revered as a holy man, eventually being buried in Kashmir. The foremost champions of this theory are Aziz Kashmiri (*Christ in Kashmir*, 1973) and Holger Kersten (*Jesus Lived in India*, 1986), both citing a sacred Hindu text, the Bhavishya Maha Purana, and its story of the celebrated first-century maharaja Shalivahana, the patron of a certain holy man. At their first encounter this individual gives his name as Isha-Masihah (Jesus Messiah) and says that he is "the Son of God" and was "born of a virgin." Since the Puranas, Sanskrit texts narrating Hindu mythology, supposedly date from ca. 3000 BCE, this is widely regarded as a prophecy of Jesus' coming, although advocates of the "Jesus in India" theory argue that this part was actually composed in or shortly after Shalivahana's lifetime.

However, while Jesus might conceivably have called himself "Son of God," he would never have identified himself in the other two ways: the belief in his virgin birth was not current in his lifetime and using "Messiah" in the way Christians redefined the title is nonsense. (Proclaiming himself Messiah in anything other than a Jewish context would have been a hopeless anachronism.) In fact there is a good case that this part of the text was actually the invention of Christian missionaries of the late eighteenth or early nineteenth century, as a ploy to convince Hindus that their sacred texts prophesied Jesus.[75]

Most of the rest of the argument relies on the identification of

Jesus with a holy man called Yuz Asaf (Persian for "Leader of those Cured of Sores"), known from a number of texts and legends, who appeared from a distant land and traveled throughout what is now Afghanistan, Pakistan, and India soon after Jesus' day, and whose tomb is in a temple in the Kashmiri town of Srinagar. The equation of Yuz Asaf with Jesus—the origins of which cannot be pinpointed with certainty, although it appears to go back to at least the tenth century—depends mainly on perceived similarities between their deeds, chiefly miraculous cures, and teachings, and is a cornerstone of the unorthodox Muslim Ahmadiyya or Ahmadi sect. However, all the hard evidence in terms of inscriptions and carvings cited as "proof" that Yuz Asaf was Jesus is later than the tenth century, so only proves that the people who made them believed it.

And then there is Rennes-le-Château.

An Esoteric Cliché

Almost every alternative historian worth his or her salt will eventually feel compelled to cast an eye over the mysteries of the tiny village of Rennes-le-Château in remote and rugged southern France, virtually in the foothills of the Pyrenees.

There seems to be a fascination, if not an obsession, with finding Jesus' burial place in or around Rennes-le-Château, for reasons that are far from obvious. Researchers keep making the connection, taking a variety of routes, often contradictory, to get there. Opinions are divided on whether the living Jesus went to France after surviving the crucifixion or only his body was carried there, and if the latter, whether it was taken there by Mary Magdalene soon after his death, or later by a secret group such as the Knights Templar that retrieved it from its original burial place in the Holy Land. Some of the many books on the subject include *L'Or du Temple et le tombeau du Christ* by S. P. Simon (1990); *The Tomb of God* (1996) by Richard Andrews and Paul Schellenberger; *The Arcadian Cipher* (2000) by Peter Blake and Paul S. Blezard; and *Jesus After the Crucifixion: From Jerusalem to Rennes-le-Château* (2007) by Graham Simmans. Each argues for a completely different location for Jesus' tomb.

The core tale is of Abbé Bérenger Saunière, the village priest between 1885 and 1917, who came into a mysterious—and huge—source of wealth. We have written about this story extensively elsewhere,[76] but it is important to underline here that, while there certainly is a genuine mystery connected with Saunière and the village, the leap to a link with Jesus is truly stupendous—not to mention a mystery in its own right.

The whole business really stems from the book that took the Rennes-le-Château mystery to the English-speaking world in 1982, *The Holy Blood and the Holy Grail* by Michael Baigent, Richard Leigh, and Henry Lincoln, which connected the Saunière story to the theory that the bloodline of Jesus and Mary Magdalene was established in France and secretly survives to this day, protected by the elusive secret society the Priory of Sion. (The three authors themselves, however, never claimed that Jesus might be buried in the locality; the central issue for them was that his offspring settled in France. Bringing Jesus himself into the story has, however, proved irresistible to many who were inspired by their book.) Although the bloodline theory itself is demonstrably very shaky, the argument that establishes a connection between the mysteries of the Languedoc and Jesus' life in Palestine—the legends of Mary Magdalene traveling to southern France after the crucifixion and living out the remainder of her life there—does seem to be more persuasive.

A measure of the degree to which a speculative connection between the Saunière affair of the turn of the twentieth century and the life of Jesus nearly two thousand years earlier has, despite any solid evidence, hardened to the point that it is virtually taken for granted is shown by events of the early 2000s. A survey using ground-penetrating radar discovered the presence of a large, square object buried beneath the enigmatic building built by Saunière, the Tour Magdala, prompting the idea that the priest might have buried it and that it might provide the solution to the mystery. In the end it turned out to be a large stone, but during the two years of anticipation between the discovery and the excavation, most of the speculation centered on what the object might tell us about the origins of Christianity. (But why should it?) The driving force behind the project was the leading New Testament scholar Robert Eisenman, and the survey team itself—like the American foundation that provided the funding—was more at home with biblical archaeology, having just finished a similar survey at Qumran. Experts assembled for the excavation work made statements to the press about the possibility of finding "items relating to the foundation myth of the Church."[77]

As we show in *The Sion Revelation* (2006), the Rennes-le-Château mystery has been the subject of much convoluted postwar myth-making and manipulation, with various themes and concepts from French esotericism being woven into the story. One major motif of this embellishment is that the mystery somehow concerns a tomb: most obviously through the inclusion of Nicolas Poussin's painting *The Shepherds of Arcadia* in the myth. (Allegedly it was Saunière's purchase of a copy that enabled him to discover the "secret.") Many who have attempted to unscramble the riddles have reasoned that if the secret involves a tomb, it must be that of someone important—and they don't come much more important than Jesus.

Most theories use clues, usually maps and other signs "encoded" in works of art, to calculate a specific location where, we are proudly told, they will find Jesus' body—if only they had permission to dig. But all such theses are open to the same objections. Symbols that could be variously interpreted are seen only with the tunnel vision of the researcher's pet theory, while medieval and Renaissance painters are assumed to have modern surveying and cartographic skills in order to hide such precise maps in their works. And simply arriving at the X that marks the spot isn't good enough; the proof of the theory is what lies under X. (The rationale is usually, if this is a map and you follow it, you arrive somewhere; therefore the somewhere is where you're supposed to be.)

Unless hard evidence emerges, Rennes-le-Château must be dismissed as the last resting place of Jesus. So we are back to the conundrum of the empty tomb: if Christ never emerged alive, then his body must have been moved. But where?

Jesus' Grave(s)

As we mentioned in the opening chapter, in February 2007 it was claimed that an ossuary containing Jesus' bones had been found, attracting worldwide attention (especially because it was fervently championed by Oscar-winning film director James Cameron).

The ossuary in question, measuring two feet by ten inches by five inches (60 by 25 by 30 centimeters) and inscribed with the name "Yeshua bar Yoseph" (Jesus son of Joseph) was one of ten, certainly dating from the first century, found in a family tomb that was uncovered in Talpiot, a suburb of Jerusalem, during building work in 1980. The ossuaries were placed in storage and it was only in 1996 that a BBC team making a documentary about the Easter story chanced upon them.[78] As noted in chapter 1, finding a Jesus who was the son of a Joseph is hardly remarkable, but what made this artifact particularly intriguing was that the five other inscribed ossuaries found with it bore names with a special resonance for Christians. (The remaining four had no inscriptions.) There were a Joseph (Yose), two Marys (Marya and Mariamenou, the second being a Greek rendering), a Matthew (Matya), and a Juda (Yehuda), son of Jesus. Had Jesus been buried with his parents and other members of his family? Could the second Mary have been Mary Magdalene—perhaps Jesus' wife? And was Juda their son? In 1996 the conclusion was that this was unlikely to be *the* Jesus' family: all the names were very common (Mary being the most common female name, the second Mary probably being her daughter). Finding them all together was not too unlikely statistically. That is where the story stopped for a decade.

Then in 2007 the Talpiot ossuaries returned to international attention, with the claim that further study had strengthened the case for a connection with Christ. The driving force behind this claim was Israeli researcher Simcha Jacobovici, who directed a Discovery Channel documentary, *The Lost Tomb of Jesus* (with Cameron as executive producer), and cowrote *The Jesus Family Tomb* with Charles Pellegrino. The "discovery" was unveiled to great media fanfare at a press conference in New York, the Israeli Antiquities Commission loaning them the ossuaries for the event.

Further examination had shown that the second Mary was actually "Mariamne called Mara" (*Mariamenou e Mara*), Jacobovici claiming that Mariamne was equivalent to Magdalene. While the others were all common names, Magdalene is unique; finding a Jesus buried alongside her stretched coincidence too far. (As James

Cameron put it, "If you find a John, a Paul, and a George, you're not going to leap to any conclusions . . . unless you find a Ringo.")[79] Jacobovici also declared that "Mara" meant "master," so the inscription should read "Magdalene called the Master," reflecting her high status among early Christians.

Moreover, analysis of the DNA of fragments of bone in the Jesus and Mariamne ossuaries showed that they had different mothers (only the mitochondrial DNA, inherited from the female line, was analyzed), so, being in the same family tomb, they were assumed to be married. If so, then "Juda, son of Jesus" was the child of Jesus and the Magdalene.

All very impressive and exciting. But Jacobovici's case soon began to crumble under expert scrutiny—especially that of theologian Ronald V. Huggins of the Salt Lake Theological Seminary. Sadly the key equation of "Mariamne" and "Magdalene" was based on a very basic misunderstanding. Mariamne is just one of several Greek variants of the Jewish Mariam, translated as Mary. In the fourth-century *Acts of Philip*, a female apostle named Mariamne appears whom most historians take to be Mary Magdalene. Jacobovici misunderstood them to mean that Mariamne was a variant of Magdalene, but it is only a variant of Mary—so Cameron's "Ringo" analogy breaks down. Besides, specialists dispute Jacobovici's interpretation of "Mara" as "Master"; although it is certainly a nickname, probably based on the similarity to Mariamne, its exact meaning is obscure.

As for the DNA, the lack of a shared mother hardly means this particular pair must be husband and wife; they could equally well be father and daughter, or represent a number of other relationships. And it was admitted that Jacobovici had submitted only the "Jesus" and "Magdalene" bones for DNA analysis, and none of the others. If the other men in the tomb, Matthew and Joseph, also failed to match Mariamne, then she could just as well have been married to one of them. And why was neither compared with the DNA of Mary, assumed to be the mother? Neither was the DNA of the son of Jesus, Jude, compared with that of Mariamne to establish that she was his mother. (Jacobovici says that the bones from this ossuary have been lost.)[80]

Unfortunately, then, the case of the Talpiot ossuaries is considerably less watertight than the hype implied. In any case how could Jesus' followers possibly have got away with claiming he had been taken bodily up to heaven when his corpse was lying in an easily identifiable family vault in the vicinity of Jerusalem?

Curiously, a Jewish tradition not only claims that Jesus was buried in Galilee but also identifies his grave, which can still be seen today on a hillside near Tsfat, north of Capernaum, where several respected holy men from close to Jesus' time were buried (although about a century later, after the Revolt).[81] Only one source alleges that the Tsfat grave belongs to Jesus—a sixteenth-century work by the Kabbalist Rabbi Isaac ben Solomon Luria. But where did he learn this? And why did no one else mention it in the intervening millennium and a half? James Tabor, who champions the grave, says that neither Jew nor Christian would want to know: Christians for obvious reasons and Jews because it would reveal Jesus to have been conventionally Jewish, whereas they claim he was an apostate. (Rabbi Isaac, unusually, considered Jesus as one of the "righteous.") But surely, if the information existed to be passed down to Isaac, somewhere between the first and sixteenth century *somebody* would have mentioned it. As evidence it is simply too thin.

And the whole point of Jesus' burial—if there was one—was that it had to remain secret. The greatest secret.

Damage Limitation

There is no persuasive evidence that Jesus physically survived the cross or that he lived out the rest of his life in some remote place. As for his death being faked, *why*? The most obvious motive is an escape plan hastily devised by his followers, but could they have organized it so quickly? And if Jesus' leadership was deemed so important that he had to be saved, why did he disappear but not continue to lead? Could it be that he continued to direct operations from a hiding place and that the instructions received "mystically" by his followers had a more prosaic origin? Possibly, but there is no specific evidence, and as we will see, his disciples' disarray and confusion continued for some time after his disappearance.

Because of the logistical difficulties of organizing a rescue in such circumstances, most "survival" theories assume it had been plotted in advance, involving a sham crucifixion. Schonfield argues that Jesus wanted to enact the role of the "suffering servant of God," believing this would be the trigger for God to reveal himself to the world, but he had a backup plan in case God failed to oblige by a specific time. Or possibly, by enduring a dying-and-rising experience (essentially a magnified version of the mystery of the Kingdom of God ritual played out in the real world), he believed he would become godlike. However, both of those ideas require absolute belief that what is expected to happen *will* happen. There was no room for hazardous plots and backup plans, and being half-crucified would be nowhere near enough.

In the end it seems that Jesus did not survive the cross, either by chance or design. But there is still the silent witness of the empty tomb. Presumably, and all too prosaically, Jesus' body was simply removed—and the Jews' explanation right from the start, which Matthew was so desperate to counter, is essentially correct.

But why move his dead body? Perhaps for a secret reburial, for fear of desecration by the Romans, or to return it to his family in Galilee. Another possibility is that if he was not, strictly speaking, Jewish, those closest to him—presumably the Bethany group—would want to bury him with the appropriate rites. Given the pagan air that clings to Bethany, this should not be discounted.

Perhaps, though, the body was removed to create precisely the effect Christians take to be proof of Jesus' divine triumph over death and the grave, creating a mix of hope for his followers and fear for his opponents. (Herod Antipas was deeply disturbed by the thought that John the Baptist might have come back to haunt him, so how would he react to Jesus' apparent rising from the grave?) Given the stakes he was playing for, Jesus—and his backers—could not have been unaware of the possibility that he might end up on a Roman cross. Maybe the group of which he was part had (with or without his knowledge) devised a "plan B" to salvage what they could if the worst happened, or even turn it to their advantage.

Lüdemann makes the point that, because of the disarray among the disciples after Jesus' arrest, they were in no position to organize the theft of his body. However, the Eleven were not his only

devotees—the other "fixers," at Bethany, could have organized it.
(And if Mary Magdalene was Lazarus' sister, then it was one of the
Bethany group who first brought news of the empty tomb.)

It is a long way from that essentially simple subterfuge to the rise
of a major international religion based on the idea that Jesus rose
from the dead.

10

THE FINAL REVELATION

The final mystery of Jesus' life is what happened between the resurrection and the start of Christianity. Even if he *had* resurrected and ascended as Christians believe, his immediate followers might have been impressed, but how did they convince noneyewitnesses that it was a reality? If, as we believe the evidence shows, the original experience of the risen Jesus was strictly spiritual, the same question applies: how did those who had that experience persuade others to sign up? It is not the first but the second generation of Christians that needs explaining.

The Cult Leader

The immediate reason for the disciples' refusal to let go is easily identified: whatever Jesus was, and whatever his objectives, he clearly possessed a unique and potent charisma. To his followers he was an exceptional individual who could never be defeated by mere mortal powers, even the mighty Roman Empire.

However, being charismatic and inspirational is no guarantee of either great wisdom or impeccable ethics: many cult leaders are astoundingly magnetic personalities with enormous power over their followers, for good or evil, but all too often the latter. The fact remains, however, that Jesus' initial attraction, whatever it was based on, led to the most successful religion the world has ever seen.

There is a huge irony that Jesus as an individual conforms best to the image of the cult leader that is so derided by modern "cult buster" organizations, almost exclusively run by Christians. According to them, the key telltale signs of a cult leader are a charismatic individual who claims a special relationship with and direct guidance by God, and who preaches an imminent apocalyptic event and instructs his followers to cut all ties with family to follow him, to be prepared to suffer and if necessary die for him.

So the main reason that his immediate followers continued to believe in him after he had failed to do what they expected can be explained simply by the "cult leader" hypothesis. But this solution still fails to account for the movement's continuation and emergence as a religion.

The eventual success of Christianity in establishing itself as a world religion could simply be attributed to an accident of history, Christianity's winning the favor of the Emperor Constantine in the mid–fourth century. He could have picked one of its rivals—the worship of Mithras, for example, or the even greater competitor, the religion of Isis and Osiris[1]—and *that* would have prevailed for two millennia. But we still need to explain how the faith survived for the previous three centuries, because, on the face of it, Christianity had little obvious attraction.

Not only did the Jesus movement grow after Jesus' disappearance, but it took on many different—and often contradictory—forms, such as the two main streams, the "Jewish Christianity" of the Jerusalem Church and the "Gentile"—or pagan—Christianity of Paul. How could two such radically different groups have been inspired by the veneration of the same man? There were even variations within the Gentile form, although Paul's version was eventually to triumph. If we accept that gnostic Christianity, which began to make an impact less than a hundred years after Jesus, was a development of certain strands of his teaching that remained outside both the Jewish and Pauline versions, we have a third major stream. And when we add into the mix the movement that upheld John the Baptist—and arguably related sects such as those of Simon Magus and Dositheus—then the situation becomes an even greater muddle.

Discussing the diversity of forms that the early religion took, Bentley Layton draws attention to "the coexistence of essentially different theological opinions and traditions about the significance of Jesus, some of which seem to be as old as Christianity itself."[2]

If Jesus had presented a clear and definitive message, how could so many different "opinions and traditions" have grown up about him so quickly? Islam split after Muhammad's death, but about leadership, not a difference of opinion about the source of his revelation or the core set of beliefs that defined the new religion: everyone knew where they stood about Islam.

Yet another sign of this divergence is that, once established, the Church had to expend so much energy battling heresies—Christian groups with fundamentally different ideas about the nature of the religion, particularly of Jesus himself. In the 370s CE Epiphanius, the Bishop of Salamis (in Cyprus), compiled a vast work defending Church orthodoxy, the *Panarion* (*Medicine Chest*), in which he condemned no fewer than eighty heresies. Although some of these were in fact not Christian at all but pagan religions that predated Jesus, the remainder still demonstrates the huge variety of belief among Christians. Christianity, almost by definition, is a religion that is open to many interpretations.

The Return

The big problem was that Jesus had conspicuously failed to fulfill the specific role expected of the Messiah: unite the people of Israel and lead them to victory over their oppressors. Instead, as we have repeatedly emphasized, he had been captured, tried, and put to death in a particularly horrific and shameful manner. His immediate followers—especially when faced with the disappearance of his body—seem to have coped by clinging to the belief that he would return to complete his messianic mission almost immediately, with the benefit of even greater superpowers. Not only that, but in the immediate aftermath of the crucifixion it seemed that Jesus' predictions about the coming of the Kingdom of God were indeed about to be fulfilled, which would have encouraged belief in his imminent return.

The whole of Mark's chapter 13 is devoted to Jesus' giving his "inner circle" of Peter, James, John, and Andrew darkly apocalyptic warnings of the signs that will precede the coming of God's kingdom on earth so they will know how to respond. Because of its stylistic and linguistic differences from the rest of the Gospel, since the nineteenth century this section—the "Little Apocalypse"—has been recognized as a separate piece of apocalyptic writing that Mark turned into Jesus' prediction. And although from the contents it is obvious that it dates from after Jesus' lifetime, it is still important for its insights into the mind-set of his followers in the years immediately after the crucifixion.

The first sign, according to Jesus, is that "Many will come in my name, claiming 'I am he,'" in order to deceive his followers. Interestingly—in the light of the belief that he *did* rise from the dead and appear to people—he is saying not that men will falsely claim to speak with his authority, but that they will actually claim to *be* him. (Could the author have Simon Magus in mind?) Then Jesus moves on to more specific signs—the wars and rumors of wars, earthquakes and famines, also warning that his disciples will be persecuted by both religious and secular authorities. These are portents that the end is approaching, but his followers are to hold their nerve: these are the "birth-pains" of the kingdom and as such are to be welcomed. The *real* sign is when they see "the 'abomination that causes desolation' standing where it does not belong." This will bring about great suffering that only the "elect" will survive. Even Jesus himself had no inkling of the exact timing of this event.

This section includes the statement "this generation will certainly not pass away until all these things have happened," which presented a major embarrassment for second- and third-generation Christians, since Jesus meant it would happen in the lifetime of those around him. But it never did. Attempts have been made to interpret "this generation" in some other way, perhaps as "this race"—i.e., the Jewish people—but none works, and they only serve to highlight the problem.

It is often assumed that the Little Apocalypse referred to the cataclysms of the Jewish Revolt of 66–70 CE, at least thirty years after the crucifixion. However, many scholars—most prominently Gerd Theissen—have argued that it more closely fits an earlier period, in which alarm was created among the people of Palestine but, because it blew over, had less of an impact on history.[3]

First, the events said to signpost the *approach* of the last days fit the circumstances of the years 36–37 CE—the year after the crucifixion—particularly the war with Nabataea. We recall that two years earlier its king, Aretas IV, had annexed Herodian territory, inflicting a great defeat on Herod Antipas' army; now the Romans were about to send their legions against Aretas. At the time this conflict threatened to destabilize the region and have grave implications for the Jews. Nabataea was a rich and powerful kingdom, and if the war escalated the Jewish lands would have been caught between two mighty armies: the terror of this threat would have been a forcing ground for all kinds of apocalyptic fears. And there were other hostilities in the region at the time, for example in Parthia and Armenia, hence "wars" plural. The Nabataean war was broken off in March 37 CE when the Roman commander heard of the death of Tiberius. The war stopped and an uneasy period of "rumors of war" began. A severe earthquake hit the region in April 37 CE, about a month after Tiberius' death, prompting fears that the Parthians would take advantage of the devastation to invade (more rumors of war).

The wars of which Jesus speaks mark the approach of God's judgment, and, as we know, the people linked the Nabataean war to the execution of John the Baptist, who had famously proclaimed the imminence of God's judgment. So it makes sense that the writer of the Little Apocalypse had that war in mind.

So Theissen argues that Jesus' discourse best fits the circumstances of the year 36–37 (certainly better than 66–70, when there was no earthquake, for example) and speculates that the people would ask, "How often do so many things happen in such a short time: war with Parthians and Nabataeans, the death of an emperor, earthquake, God's visible intervention on behalf of a prophet who had announced the impending end?"[4] It was this undiluted sequence of traumas that created the apocalyptic mood—the feeling that God's judgment was about to fall—from which the discourse, or its source, emerged.

In a specifically Christian context there was another event—which Theissen failed to notice—that fits the Little Apocalypse:

the persecution ordered by the Sanhedrin which began with the stoning of the first martyr, Stephen. This event panicked large numbers of the new sect into fleeing—the persecution that Paul, as Saul, took part in with such gusto. It must have coincided with all the other events listed above (since Paul's conversion happened in 37 at the latest).

But what about the sign that the end *had* arrived: what was the "abomination that causes desolation" standing where it did not belong? How does it fit into that timescale? And does it confirm or refute Theissen's theory? The Greek *to bdelugma tes eremoseos* more accurately means "desolating sacrilege"[5] and is the literal translation of the Hebrew *shiqquz meshomem*, which refers to the conversion of the Temple altar into a pagan altar. But as it does not refer to the *destruction* of the Temple but its desecration, again it fails to work in terms of the Jewish Revolt. (Neither can it have been written afterwards, since there was no longer any Temple to desecrate.)

The phrase is very specific and comes from the Book of Daniel, where it refers to a terrible blasphemy of two hundred years before Jesus' day.[6] In 167 BCE Antiochus Epiphanes, as part of his campaign to eradicate Judaism, took control of the Temple and had a statue of Zeus erected over the high altar. It was this that sparked off the Maccabean Revolt. So it was a sacrilegious act by a foreign power that, paradoxically, resulted in the Jews' freeing themselves. Jesus drives the parallel home, declaring that when his followers see this they must immediately flee to the hills, which was precisely the Maccabees' response. Clearly something similar is referred to here—but what?

Many argue that it best fits the critical events of 40–41 CE, when Tiberius' successor Caligula ordered the conversion of the Temple to the imperial cult, complete with a huge statue of himself as Jupiter—such an abomination that the Jews would have no choice but to resist.[7] Caligula ordered that it be carried out by force and dispatched two divisions of his army, twelve thousand troops. A bloody catastrophe seemed imminent. The showdown was only averted by Caligula's assassination in the spring of 41; his successor Claudius countermanded the order. As the crisis still had to be resolved, the Little Apocalypse must have been composed when it still seemed that events would usher in the last days, so before the spring of 41.

Both Matthew and Luke changed the passage to reflect the Christians' situation at a later stage. Matthew expands the sufferings Jesus says his disciples will endure between the first of the signs and the "desolating sacrilege"—which in Mark clearly related to persecutions in Jerusalem and the lands of Palestine—into those in other nations (so at least after Nero's first persecution in 64).[8] He also sets the crucial sign of the desolating sacrilege after the Gospel has first been proclaimed in all nations. While keeping Jesus' words about the signs from his source, Matthew adapted them to a changed situation—effectively highlighting the specific place and time of Mark's original. Luke has amended the passage even more to fit the circumstances of the year 70, the most telling change being replacing the key sign of the desolating sacrilege with "Jerusalem being surrounded by armies"[9]—incidentally highlighting even more the irrelevance of Mark's original version to that situation.

So this section of Mark was written about the Caligula crisis, an impending desecration of the Temple that seemed inevitably would lead to a war with Rome, and with the Nabataean war, earthquake, the first persecutions by the Jews, and other horrors fresh in the memory. However, it could hardly be a prediction of Jesus," since the crisis failed to turn into an apocalypse.

Jesus may well have issued apocalyptic warnings—proclaiming the imminence of the Kingdom of God implied an initial period of conflict and confusion—but whatever he said had been embroidered in the light of the situation in 41. It makes sense that he would have cited the Nabataean war—if our chronology is right, just brewing at the time of his last visit to Jerusalem—since it was linked with the death of John the Baptist. But Jesus' followers, seeing the horrors unfold, associated them with his crucifixion, sustaining the belief that he would soon be vindicated and return in glory.

Ecstasy

But here we hit what should have been a major obstacle: Jesus never returned. "This generation" did pass away without seeing him. So why did they continue to believe? Why did the movement not just wither and die as soon as it was obvious there would be no Second Coming? And the same question hangs over Paul's certainty that the world would end within his lifetime.

. How did they persuade other Jews that it was worth following someone who had so conspicuously failed to fulfil messianic expectations? On the other hand, Gentiles would be singularly unimpressed by the claim that the proof of Jesus' message was that he had died and risen again—a routine ability of their own gods, who also took on human form and walked among humanity. As we have seen, many even believed that resurrection happened to the likes of Nero.

Could it have been Jesus' moral and ethical teaching—either his own or Paul's version—that pulled in new converts? It seems not. There was nothing unique or special about that. In the Jewish world the message "be nice to other people," originally from the Old Testament, was already part of Judaism. To the Gentiles, many of the pagan religions (again such as the Isis cult) and philosophical schools made the same points. So the puzzle deepens: just what was the attraction of Christianity?

Probably the most important factor, at least to Gentiles, was the ecstasies experienced by the early Christians. Paul's writings—our only source on their actual practices—make it clear that the two related "inspired" phenomena, speaking in tongues and prophecy, played an important part in worship in the early Church. In fact some of his letters attempt to impose order on what must have been chaotic and cacophonous assemblies, more menagerie than holy meeting.

This phenomenon began at Pentecost—fifty days after Passover— when the disciples gathered together and were suddenly "filled with the Holy Spirit and began to speak in other tongues as the Spirit enabled them."[10] In a kind of reversal of the Tower of Babel curse, Acts has the diverse assembly being able to comprehend one another in their own language, but these verses were certainly introduced later.[11] The original clearly described the unintelligible babblings that characterize "speaking in tongues"—which came to embarrass the early Church as it started to impose some structure on worship, hence the alteration to Acts. And as Paul shows, this mass gabbling continued to be part of Christian worship—presumably what impressed newcomers. Ordinary people seemed to be in the grip of some supernatural force, explained to them as the Holy Spirit.

This sense of being possessed by something greater than oneself is by no means unique to Christianity now and certainly wasn't then. Paul himself writes of pagan prophetesses who were given to "inspired" rantings. What does seem unusual, though, is the scale and regularity with which it happened among Christians gathered together to worship Jesus. However, there have always been, and still are, sects who actively encourage and even expect mass ecstatic experiences. In that sense the modern charismatic Christian movement is closer than mainstream churches to the original form of Christianity that caught on in the Gentile world. The irony is that mainstream Christians still tend to consider this as a rather embarrassing form of mass hysteria, while making an exception at least for the original Pentecost, if not for Paul's version of worship.

The Martyr and the Brother

That may be why Christianity attracted Gentile converts, but why did it continue behind so many different masks?

The prevailing (though by no means unchallenged) academic view sees the story as simple: Jesus' religious and interwoven political agendas were solely and fundamentally Jewish. Although there is disagreement about whether his main concern was religious reformation or political as the legitimate king of the Jews, either way it was entirely and exclusively Judaic. The Jerusalem Church headed by his brother James the Just was the true continuation of Jesus' movement, and Paul's Gentile version a radical departure that would have shocked Jesus. But the Jerusalem Church was either wiped out during the Roman suppression of the Jewish Revolt or so badly damaged that it lost its authority, leaving the field clear for Paul's version to triumph. However, the historical evidence shows that this simple and straightforward picture is plainly and utterly wrong.

As we have seen, it is impossible to dismiss all the non-Jewish elements in the Gospels as later inventions. Throughout there is that strange interplay between Jewish nationalism and elements that seem to have been at least inspired by mystery-cult practices and pagan magic.

Then there is the puzzle about James the Just's emergence as the head of the Jerusalem Church, having appeared nowhere in the Gospels' story. Some have tried to show that he *was* one of the disciples but this fact was deliberately obscured by the gospel writers because of the split between Paul and the Jerusalem Church. Those who advocate the dynastic hypothesis, such as James Tabor and Hyam Maccoby, explain James' leadership simply as his due, since he was literally next in line to the throne. Maccoby even explains Peter's being given the "keys to the kingdom" by Jesus as meaning that he was chosen as his chief minister, a role that he continued under James; he could not become leader himself, not being one of the family.[12]

The major problem for all these views (particularly Maccoby's) is that they ignore the evidence that Peter *did* initially take over the helm and was only later displaced by James. Paul writes after his three-year sojourn in Arabia and Damascus: "I went up to Jerusalem to get acquainted with Cephas and stayed with him fifteen days. I saw none of the other apostles—only James, the Lord's brother."[13]

Clearly at that time—three or four years after the crucifixion—Peter, not James, was the top man in Jerusalem: Paul goes to see him and only mentions James in passing. So although James did become leader of the community, it was no overnight promotion. By the time of Paul's return to Jerusalem fourteen years later, however, James was firmly in charge—and remained so until his martyrdom in 62 CE—and Peter had been demoted. But the reason for Peter's eclipse is highly significant. As Gerd Lüdemann writes:

Peter had declined very rapidly in importance in the earliest community. For in the controversy over the question whether the strict Jewish law still has any significance for Christians, the main part of the earliest community which was more faithful to the law, under the leadership of James, won the day over the Peter party, which was freer of the law.[14]

In his Letter to the Galatians, Paul boasts of rebuking Peter at a meeting in Antioch for his "hypocrisy" in siding with James' faction: "I said to Cephas in front of them all, 'You are a Jew, yet you live like a Gentile and not like a Jew. How is it then that you force

Gentiles to follow Jewish customs?' " [15] So Peter is halfway between the Jewish and Gentile Christians, neatly reflecting the ambivalence of Jesus' teaching—and remember, this is a man who knew him personally.

Even so, the early Gentile faction manifestly downplayed the influence of James and the family: he just floats into the Acts of the Apostles, never being introduced and with nothing being said about his kinship with Jesus. He is first mentioned when Peter escapes from prison and instructs other disciples to tell James what has happened. (Since Peter was arrested on the orders of Herod Agrippa, this event must have been after Herod's accession in 41.) It is only because we have already been told that the disciple James, the son of Zebedee, had been killed that we know it is not him. This new James then appears in the rest of the story as leader of the Jerusalem Church, although the narrative still focuses on Peter and Paul. It is only from Paul's Letters and other early writings that we learn that this James was Jesus' brother.

However, this evasiveness does not imply that James was erased from the earlier story or that he walked unchallenged into the leadership. And why should we assume that, just because he was family, he understood Jesus better than those who had traveled with him? Brothers often fail to see eye to eye on religion or politics, and during his mission relations between Jesus and his family were strained. Robert Eisenman's contention that "Who and whatever James was, so was Jesus" [16]—i.e., by understanding what James was about we can identify the historical Jesus—is not necessarily so.

The major division in the early Christian sect was between those who saw it in exclusively Jewish terms and others who wanted to make it more Gentile-friendly. The two positions were represented respectively by James and Paul (with Peter wavering somewhere in between). They were adopted by the two earliest Christian communities in Jerusalem and Antioch in Syria, effectively leading to Christianity's first general council, in Jerusalem in 48 or 49, in order to iron out their differences, specifically because the Antioch community ignored the Jewish Law.

Paul and Barnabas, as Antioch's leaders, argued their case to James, with the result that he agreed that non-Jews who became Christians did not have to convert to Judaism. (Jews who became

Christians, however, were expected to remain true to the Law.) This was Christianity's first major step toward becoming a separate religion rather than a sect within Judaism. However, it is very clear that far from abandoning the Jewish elements in the dozen or so years of its existence, the Antioch Church had a markedly non-Judaic character from the very beginning—even owing its origins to dissidents who had fled from Jerusalem.

Acts tells of the stoning of the first Christian martyr, Stephen, for blasphemy, within a year or two of the crucifixion—when Saul/Paul makes his first entrance. Stephen appears when there is a dispute between the "Hebraic Jews" and "Greek Jews" within the Jerusalem Church, the latter complaining that they were being discriminated against in the distribution of alms. The Twelve appointed Stephen and six others under him to take charge of administration. All of the appointees had Greek names, which suggests that, rather than being a simple administrative appointment, the seven represented the leadership of the "Greek Jews" in the movement.[17]

The specific charge against Stephen by his Jewish opponents is that he had spoken "blasphemous words against Moses and against God"—i.e., he disagreed with at least aspects of Mosaic Law—and (like Jesus) against the Temple, saying that Christ would return to destroy it. However, these charges, again as with Jesus, are said to have been trumped up and bolstered by false witnesses, which begs the question why, if Stephen's opponents had to invent them, they were opposed to him in the first place.

Weirdly, though, Stephen's defense in Acts ends by confirming the charge. After a long speech he declares "the Most High does not live in houses made by human hands" and berates the Sanhedrin for having Jesus put to death.[18] Even as it stands, Stephen's speech reveals what one scholar called "heterodox Judaism."[19]

This history seriously undermines the concept of James the Just as Jesus' true successor. The one certain thing about Jesus is that he not merely criticized but actively opposed Temple worship. We believe that he was calling for the Temple to be abolished, but even if he was only condemning the current regime as corrupt, he was still questioning the Temple's legitimacy—and Stephen seems to be echoing the same idea. Jesus himself was ultimately condemned to death for his passionate outburst against the Temple; Stephen seems to represent a faction that was more faithful to Jesus' teachings on the issue than James, and he, too, paid the price. Yet one of the few specific pieces of information we have about James is that he not only advocated that Jesus' followers worship at the Temple but did so himself *daily*. Not only did he want to do so, he was actually allowed to. The contrast between the two brothers on this fundamental subject could hardly be greater.

According to Acts, Stephen's execution started a persecution that scattered the fledgling Christian sect, some fleeing into Samaria. (It was then that Philip encountered Simon Magus. In fact there is a tradition that Stephen himself was a Samaritan.[20]) Others fled further, to Phoenicia, Cyprus, and Antioch.[21] The scattering was hugely important, being the true start of the Christian mission.

But James, when he became head of the sect, not only escaped persecution but was allowed to worship at the Temple, unmolested, for at least twenty-six years (if our date of 36 CE for the crucifixion is correct, but even longer if it was earlier). True, when he was eventually killed it was by the Sanhedrin, but why did it take them so long? Why wasn't he set up like Stephen?

The most logical explanation is that the persecution that began with Stephen's execution affected only one part of the Jesus sect, whose unorthodox views about the Temple were unacceptable to the Jewish authorities. Members who accepted Temple worship were allowed to continue in Jerusalem, but they were the ones who were *unfaithful* to Jesus' teaching. They took the safer route.

The difference over this fundamental issue shows that James was not continuing Jesus' agenda and was actively appeasing the priesthood. This, and the fact that he had never been a disciple or in any way involved with Jesus' mission, strongly suggest that he opportunistically took over the movement his brother had founded, exploiting his kinship.

But why did James want to take over his brother's movement? It seems that, rather than having a genuine desire to continue Jesus' work, he took the helm because he *disagreed* with what Jesus had done. He wanted to restore the movement to something closer to his own religious convictions, something more Jewish. This would explain how one of the brothers who had disagreed with Jesus during his lifetime emerged as his successor. If his family considered

Jesus mad or possessed because they strongly disagreed with what he was preaching, then an attempt to subvert the movement he had created would make perfect sense. James really was appeasing the Jewish leaders in the modern sense of the word. Indeed he would probably have welcomed their action against Stephen and the "Greek" faction, as it purged the sect of an undesirable element. It is significant that he became head of the sect only after their persecution, suggesting he took control specifically to counter the non-Jewish element. (Could it even be that the Jewish element in the sect informed on Stephen to the Sanhedrin? Acts has certain Jews who oppose his teaching being behind the alleged frame-up and not, as in Jesus' case, the Jewish leaders themselves.)

Eisenman, among others, views James as the leader who continued the "true" form of Christianity and Paul as a kind of "neutralizer" who deliberately set out to draw the teeth of the new movement and make it more acceptable to the very forces it opposed: the Roman Empire and the Herodians. However, it can be argued—we would say more plausibly—that it was *James* who attempted to "neutralize" the new movement and re-create it in a form more acceptable to the Jewish leaders.

In fact there has always been a school of thought—though not as popular as it once was—that rather than Paul's "Hellenizing" Jesus' Jewish message, James "Judaized" it, turning away from what his brother taught. This school sees Stephen as a representative of the "Hellenists" who kept the true version.[22]

So who were the "Hellenists"?

The Pagan Christians

The group within Jesus' immediate postcrucifixion following that was labeled "Greeks" (*Elleniston*) in Acts and "Hellenists" by New Testament scholars were far more than just Jews who spoke Greek or adopted a Greek lifestyle: they also adopted certain "Greek"—non-Jewish or, more pointedly, pagan—religious ideas. Oscar Cullmann defines them as "Jews who differed from the official Judaism, showing tendencies more or less of a hellenistic character and possibly a syncretistic origin."[23] "Hellenists," with its connotations of an intellectual affinity with Greek culture and philosophy, is nowhere near strong enough: "paganizers" would be better.

Although he did not found the Hellenists' center at Antioch, Paul became its leader. There was no need for him to persuade them to adopt his "pagan" form of Christianity; they already had it.[24] If anything it was the other way round: he was influenced by the paganizers in Antioch.

Another major center for the Hellenists was Samaria, and it seems that some of those who fled the persecution after Stephen's martyrdom founded the Samaritan Christian community for which John's Gospel was written. As Cullmann wrote (his emphasis), "We have more than general considerations to indicate a very close connection, if not a complete identity, between the *Hellenists in Jerusalem and the Johannine group*,"[25] pointing to "common roots" between Stephen's defense speech in Acts and the theology of John's Gospel (including its view of Jesus), both of which derive from Samaritan beliefs. But were the Hellenists who fled to Samaria really taking Jesus' teaching back to its roots?

Compared with many religions, Judaism has always been remarkably tolerant toward internal divergence of ideas, provided certain core beliefs are retained. There has never been the kind of persecution of heresies that make the history of Christianity so ugly—i.e., attacking a particular sect simply because it fails to agree with every point of doctrine. However, two things were not tolerated: direct blasphemy and attempts to mix Judaism with other religions (itself a form of blasphemy). Therefore, for the Jewish leaders to have ordered a persecution on religious grounds, they must have considered that the Jesus sect had committed one of those sins.

All the evidence suggests that the reason for the persecution of part, not all, of the sect was that it included elements from foreign, pagan religions. As John Dominic Crossan muses:

> I suspect that it was their opening of Judaism to paganism and their
> willingness to abandon any ritual tradition standing in their way
> that had caused his [Paul's] initial persecution of Christianity, and
> it was precisely what he had persecuted them for that he now accepted as his destiny.[26]

Crossan makes a major point. If Paul was persecuting the first Christians—as part of the clampdown sparked by Stephen's arrest—he must have known why. To suddenly see the error of his ways and join the sect he was trying to destroy *and then want to change it into something else* makes no sense. Surely as an apostle Paul would have advocated the very things that offended him as a zealous Jew. And, significantly, after his conversion, he settled not in Jerusalem but in Antioch—an unashamed center of the pagan element he had persecuted. In other words, he never persecuted the whole sect, just the "pagan" part—and it was to *that* he converted.

But did the Jewish or pagan Hellenist side represent Jesus' true teaching? The answer is probably both (partly) and neither (completely): they simply separated out the two strands that he had somehow woven together. But none of this resolves the contradiction inherent in Jesus' own mission. How can we reconcile the pagan and Jewish elements in his message?

The answer may lie in the vexed connection with the much-maligned land of Samaria.

More Gods Than One

John the Baptist took his mission into the heart of Samaria and Jesus appears to have followed in his footsteps, or at least John's Gospel—which claims he did—was written for an early community of his Samaritan followers. It was to there that the "Hellenists" among Jesus' postcrucifixion community fled, and where they effectively took over Simon Magus' following. And, if we read between the lines of Acts, they themselves were taken over: Acts implies that the work of Philip—named as one of the Hellenists—was taken over by Peter and John on behalf of the Jerusalem Church, and it was this mix that produced John's Gospel.

Indeed a good starting point in resolving the paradox of Jesus is with the Magus, who, as we discussed in chapter 7, was not only too like him for the early Church's comfort but also appears to have shared John the Baptist as master. Simon, too, easily although apparently more overtly mixed conventional "Jewish" ideas—really "Israelite," since he was a Samaritan—with a kind of semipaganism, teaching that one God presided over a pantheon of many lesser deities, justifying this idea by referring to the books of Moses. This was said of him in the *Clementine Homilies* but it was not until the nineteenth century that extracts of his works surfaced that confirmed it in his own words.

Oddly enough, John's Gospel hints that Jesus may have shared this apparently heretical theology. In the episode where a crowd of Jews attempts to stone him for the blasphemy of claiming to be God, Jesus responds:

> Is it not written in your Law, "I have said you are 'gods'?" If he called them "gods," to whom the word of God came—and Scripture cannot be broken—what about the one whom the Father set apart as his very own and sent into the world? Why then do you accuse me of blasphemy because I said, "I am God's Son"?[27]

By "gods" Jesus seems to be referring to the prophets, although such terminology is decidedly odd. What makes his argument especially strange is that there is no such statement in the Old Testament books in which the Law is set down, but there is, however, something very similar in Psalm 82, and it seems to be this that Jesus (or the writer of John's Gospel) had in mind. The psalm begins, "God presides over the great assembly; he gives judgment among the 'gods.'" God goes on to condemn the "gods" for not defending the weak and needy against the wicked, before ending:

> I said, "You are 'gods';
>   you are all sons of the Most High;
> But you will die like mere mortals,
>   you will fall like every other ruler."[28]

It is usually assumed that, as in the Jesus quotation, the "gods" are the prophets, which is why it is within quotation marks in the English translation. But without the context, this short psalm would read quite naturally as a supreme God addressing the assembly of the lesser gods, a notion that would sit happily with other Middle Eastern or Greek religions.

The writer of the psalm, like the composer of John's Gospel—

and Simon Magus—seems to be under the impression that some-where in scripture God spoke of other gods. There is nothing like that in the Old Testament as we know it, but John's Gospel was written for a Samaritan audience, to whom Simon Magus preached, and their scriptures and traditions were different from—and al-legedly more authentic than—those of the Jews. If their version of the Books of Moses included such a passage about the "gods," then presumably that was how Simon Magus justified his argument. It seems likely that the very reason this episode was included in John's Gospel was to counter Simon's teaching.

But we should also bear in mind that the original religion of the Israelites was also more polytheistic than is generally believed, with other lesser deities—and astonishingly, the great goddess, Asherah—being worshiped alongside Yahweh. The Jewish anthropologist and Orientalist Raphael Patai, in his classic study *The Hebrew Goddess* (1967, revised 1990), writes:

> For about six centuries [after the Israelites arrival in Canaan] . . . that is to say, down to the destruction of Jerusalem by Nebuchad-nezzar in 586 BCE, the Hebrews worshiped Asherah (and next to her also other, originally Canaanite, gods and goddesses) in most places and times. Only intermittently, although with gradually in-creasing intensity and frequency, did the prophetic demand for the worship of Yahweh as the one and only god make itself be heard and was it heeded by the people and their leaders.[29]

Even the Jewish scriptures acknowledge that Solomon—renowned for his wisdom and the builder of Yahweh's first Tem-ple—"was not fully devoted to the Lord his God" and sacrificed to other deities, male and female.[30]

We explained this practice in chapter 2 by the prevalence in the ancient world—classically in Egypt—of the concept that there was one supreme creator-god who created the lesser deities, essentially his various aspects who depended on him for their continuing power. It would hardly be surprising if the Israelites originally held such a view—and would certainly explain some of the anomalies in their scriptures (such as the origins of the "sons of God" who in Genesis father heroes on mortal women).[31]

This belief was explicitly what Simon Magus taught. But had he dreamed it up independently in the first century, or was he aware that it was what the original Israelites believed? And had he learned it from a particular sect or tradition?

Another (in)famous aspect of Simon's teaching harks back to the ancient days of Israel. This is his declaration that Helen, the prostitute he had freed in Tyre, was God's "First Thought," Yahweh's first-created being, to whom he had assigned the power to create worlds. This idea is based on the venerable Jewish concept of Hokmah or Wisdom, a creative female power who worked in partnership with Yahweh. As Raphael Patai explains, "In the Book of Job, Wisdom is described as a personage whose way is understood and place known only by God himself, while the Book of Proverbs asserts that Wisdom was the earliest creation of God, and that ever since those primeval days she (Wisdom) has been God's playmate."[32] (She sounds rather like Peter Pan's Tinker Bell.)

Again, Simon's teaching reveals an understanding of an earlier, more fluid form of the Israelite religion that also has parallels in the New Testament. The famous opening words of John's Gospel (believed by some to come from a hymn composed by the followers of John the Baptist) are "In the beginning was the Word, and the Word was with God, and the Word was God. He was with God in the beginning. Through him all things were made; without him nothing was made that has been made."[33]

Even though the TNIV uses "he" to describe this first-created entity through whom God makes everything manifest, and John's Gospel identifies this being with Jesus, it seems the Word was originally *feminine*, like Hokmah. The phrase "the Word was with God" is a bad translation, the Greek meaning literally "the Word went towards God," but even that fails to convey all its implications. The American scholar George Witterschein writes (his emphasis), "we can even use the word *erotic* to describe a yearning for unity to overcome separation," before relating how his Jesuit mentor had been haunted throughout his life by the full significance of the phrase:

He felt that Christianity had made a grave error . . . in failing to understand this "movement towards." The key to it all, he said, was the attraction between man and woman, which parallels (has the same source as) the attraction between the Word and God, and between the created universe and its origin in the separation between the Word and God.[34]

So the Word must be female. And it is significant that this passage opens the Gospel that was competing for the same hearts and minds as Simon Magus.

Hokmah also surfaces in the other canonical Gospels—appearing under her Greek name of Sophia—and is even fundamental to Q, which is not just a "wisdom book" but a book *about* Wisdom. As Crossan puts it, "In the Q Gospel's vision, divine Wisdom came down to earth and spoke through the prophets of old, spoke through John the Baptist and Jesus recently, and continues to do so today through the Q community."[35]

Burton L. Mack writes that, in the Jewish tradition from which Q derived, "wisdom was personified as a woman (drawing on the mythologies of the Egyptian goddesses Maat and Isis)."[36] But again she is effectively disguised because of flaws in the translation. In Q everything that happens does so through the Wisdom of God (*e sophia tou theou*), which the TNIV translates as "God in his wisdom"—for example in Luke: "God in his wisdom said, 'I will send them prophets and Apostles, some of whom they will kill and others they will persecute.'"[37] As it stands, this seems vague enough—a mere turn of phrase—but the *literal* meaning is much more specific: "the Wisdom of God said . . ." The Wisdom of God is the *female* entity attached to God, and she is at the core of Q. (In fact there is evidence that the Holy Spirit was derived from Hokmah and so was originally feminine, and therefore the Christian Trinity of Father, Son, and Holy Spirit is not quite the all-male power base we have been led to believe.)

So again we find common ground between Jesus and Simon Magus, which simply confirms what the Church Fathers made such a fuss about. Indeed several commentators have seen a parallel between the Simon Magus/Helen partnership and Jesus and Mary Magdalene's relationship as consistently presented in the gnostic texts.[38] There are two possible reasons for this. Either later gnostics created a fantasy of the Jesus/Magdalene relationship to conform to the historical model of Simon and Helen, or the two couples genuinely worked and behaved in a similar way.

Significantly, some academics have argued that Simon Magus was trying to reintroduce to the Israelite religion the feminine aspect once embodied in Yahweh's consort Asherah and his "playmate" Wisdom.[39] This would fit what we know about Simon perfectly, reconciling the apparent contradiction between his blend of sexual mysticism and polytheism (of sorts), which he justified by appealing to the Old Testament.

Astoundingly, given the startling similarities between Simon Magus and Jesus, we find here a perfect solution to the contradictions also surrounding Jesus. We have argued that he targeted his messianic mission at all the "people of Israel," aiming to restore their original worship. But how did he define "Israel"? He would have had to include the Samaritans, despite opposition from the Jews. This underlines the similarities between Jesus and Simon Magus— and the key to their apparently incongruous bond lies not only in Samaritanism but also in John the Baptist.

The Samaritan Connection

The Jews claimed that when the Assyrians conquered the northern kingdom in the eighth century BCE they deported the indigenous tribes, making the Samaritans of Jesus' day the descendants of foreigners who only superficially incorporated Yahweh into their distasteful pagan worship. However, the Assyrian records declare that their conqueror, Sargon, although taking many thousands of captives from the capital city, let the rest "keep their property."[40] In fact even the Old Testament books—such as Second Chronicles, Isaiah, and Jeremiah—contradict the Judean slur by describing Samaria as inhabited by descendants of the tribes long after the conquest.[41] The Samaritans had just as much of a claim to be descended from the original tribes as the Judeans.

Amazingly, the Samaritans are still with us—if only just. There are some seven hundred in twenty-first-century Israel and Palestine, most still clinging to the area around Mount Gerizim (now an Israeli artillery outpost) and in a suburb of Tel Aviv. They are a very closed community, rarely accepting converts, who in any case are not thick on the ground. And unfortunately today's Samaritans have little en-

lightenment to offer about their religion in the days of Jesus and
Simon Magus. Samaritanism underwent its own root-and-branch reform in the fourth century CE, which established a strict doctrine and
purged any deviations. Ironically, the reform was influenced by Christian ideas—being particularly inspired by John's Gospel.[42]

In fact, they became fanatically monotheistic—even changing the
awkward plural *elohim* ("gods") in the Old Testament to the singular,
and modifying terms such as "sons of God" (in Genesis) to "sons of
rulers" and "angels" to "kings." They made over six hundred revisions
to their version of the Pentateuch, removing any suggestion that God
was anything other than the one all-powerful being.[43] However, what
the Samaritans believed before the reforms of the fourth century CE
is not certain, although their obsession with rewriting "the gods" suggests they may have been protesting too much, and that at least some
Samaritans did share Simon Magus' belief in many gods.

Because of the Jewish Revolt, there is no longer much information
to go on. But there is some. John MacDonald, in *The Theology of the
Samaritans* (1964), explains that in the third to first centuries BCE:

> one great system of thought (really a related series of similar sys-
> tems) . . . certainly influenced the Samaritans. This was Gnosti-
> cism, particularly in its so-called Judaist form. The Samaritans were
> at this time scattered throughout the great cities of Egypt, Samaria,
> Asia Minor and Asia Major. They had a synagogue in Antioch;
> there was a large community in Alexandria, and there were com-
> munities large and small in many other places.[44]

Antioch again. So there was a Samaritan influence there, where
the "Hellenist" Christians settled (besides Samaria itself).

And, despite the Judeans' denials, the Samaritans had preserved a
form of the Israelite religion from before the reforms in Judea that
followed the return from the Babylonian captivity. In the words of
Andrew Lincoln, Samaritanism was the "heir to the religion of ancient Israel over against mainstream Judaism."[45]

We also recall that the Samaritans were descended from the tribes
of Ephraim and Manesseh, the former once being the dominant
tribe, on whose land was originally located the focus of the religion,
the Tabernacle housing the Ark of the Covenant. And according to

some, it was only those tribes (plus Benjamin) that had entered the region from Egypt, the other nine being native Canaanites. So if anything *was* still to be found from those very earliest days, and even from the Israelite religion as practiced in Egypt—possibly even influenced by its religion—Samaria was the place to find it.

In *The Templar Revelation* we linked Jesus and his associates to aspects of the ancient Egyptian religion but could only speculate about the origins of the connection and how it could be reconciled with the undeniably Jewish elements of his mission. We suggested that Jesus, John the Baptist, Mary Magdalene, and Simon Magus were somehow aware that Israel's original religion had incorporated much more of the spiritual ideas of Egypt, particularly the sacred feminine, than did Judaism in Jesus' own day. Now, the history of the Samaritans has provided a highly plausible route for those long-forgotten ideas to be transmitted down to the first century, within the people of Israel but outside the mainstream of Judaism.

As we have seen, unlikely as it sounds, the Essenes' "cousins" in Egypt, the Therapeutae, adopted practices from the cult of the orgiastic wine god Dionysus. Similar eclecticism—maybe even directly linked to the Therapeutae—produced the "Jewish Egyptian" text *The Book of Joseph and Asenath*, incorporating what appears to have been some kind of precursor to Jesus' form of the Eucharist, which we have argued is more likely to be *Samaritan* Egyptian.

These connections may supply the answer to the long-acknowledged mysteries surrounding early Christianity in Egypt: how it got there, and the ease with which it was integrated with the local pagan religions.

Frustratingly, it is impossible to be certain about the exact nature of the earliest form of Christianity in Egypt, although it is known that it arrived in Alexandria very early—probably even before its advent in Rome itself. In fact, the curious absence of references to such a major city as Alexandria in any of the New Testament books has often been remarked upon; the single mention, in Acts, links it to John the Baptist's movement, not Jesus' (when Paul encountered John the Baptist's apostle Apollos from Alexandria).

We know virtually nothing about early Christianity in Egypt. As Bruce Metzger notes, "The origins of the Church in Egypt are enveloped in deep mystery. When it was that Christianity was first introduced into Egypt, and by whom, is totally unknown."[46] S. G. F.

Brandon adds, "Christianity must have arrived early in Egypt and . . . the silence preserved in the Christian tradition about its origins must be considered strange."[47]

However, perhaps the silence is not so strange after all. Although it is acknowledged that the Jesus/John movement reached Egypt very early, as Helmut Koester points out, "The beginnings of Christianity in Egypt were 'heretical' and therefore Christian writings composed in this early period were not preserved."[48] It is not too difficult to extrapolate the nature of the "heresy": tellingly, the Egyptian Christians seemed to have blended in perfectly well with the established pagan mystery cults, particularly that of Serapis (a Hellenized reworking of the Osiris and Isis cult).

That this was a major feature is startlingly plain from the Emperor Hadrian's writings in 134 CE during a visit to Egypt: "There are Christians who worship Serapis, and devoted to Serapis are those who call themselves bishops of Christ."[49]

So clearly the "Christianity" of the Baptist, and Jesus himself, was seen as virtually inseparable from the Serapis religion of Egypt, itself a contemporary revision of the ancient and much-loved worship of Isis and Osiris, to which mystery—and sexual—rituals were central.

Jesus the Nazorean

Early in our quest to find the historical Jesus we encountered the question of whether "Nazarene" really meant "of Nazareth" or had an entirely different root. The two main claimants are *nazir*, meaning "branch" (from an association of the Messiah with the "branch of Jesse"), and *nazr* (plural *nozrim*), "guardian/keeper."

A particularly intriguing sect once existed in northern Israel—in Galilee and Samaria—called the *Nasaraioi* (Nasarenes), whom early Church writers tended to muddle with the heretical Christian *Nazoraioi* (Nazorenes), although fortunately Epiphanius, who had personal experience of the former, provided the necessary clarification. He described the Nasarenes in ways that suggest they had affinities with both the Samaritans and Dositheans, the sect founded by Dositheus, who, according to the Pseudo-Clementine works, was a disciple of John the Baptist and an associate of Simon Magus.

Indeed some scholars have identified these Nasarenes as the ancestors of the Mandaeans, being "adherents of the Baptism of John."[50] Hugh Schonfield agrees: "There is good reason to believe that the heirs of these Nazareans [sic], though time and circumstances have wrought many changes, are the present Nazoreans (also known as Mandaeans) of the Lower Euphrates."[51] Most researchers—even the normally skeptical Kurt Rudolph—accept some kind of connection between the Nasarenes and the Mandaeans, although its extent remains controversial.

The fact that the Mandaeans call their priests *nasuraiia*, from *nasiruta*, "secret knowledge," surely confirms the connection. But more significantly, the Nasarenes were around *before* John the Baptist, making him—as indeed the Mandaeans insist—not their founder but a leader of the movement.

The name of this sect clearly derives from the Hebrew *nozrim*, "guardians." In Schonfield's words, it "relates to a community whose members regarded themselves as the 'maintainers' or 'preservers' of the true faith of Israel."[52] And as the name is used of themselves by groups connected with John the Baptist, it is surely perverse to deny that *Nazoraios* meant the same when applied to John's most famous follower, Jesus.

But *"Nasarene" and "Samaritan" mean exactly the same.* Although the Jews traced the name Samaria to an ancestor of the people named Shemer, the Samaritans themselves insisted it came from *shamar,* "to guard" or "to keep," indicating, in British academic Matthew Black's words, that they regarded themselves as " 'keepers' or 'guardians' of the true Law and inheritance of Israel."[53] Black suggests that the Nasarene sect was a "survival into New Testament times of the old pre-Ezra type of Hebrew religion" and that it originated with the "Samaritan schism" (i.e., the split that began with the division of Israel into the northern and southern kingdoms, reaching its climax after the return of the Jews from Babylon).[54]

Finally, in our quest for a sect that existed in Jesus' and John the Baptist's day but had kept itself secret long enough to preserve elements of the original Israelite religion, we must remember the Cave of John the Baptist at Suba. Although associated with John, and certainly used for baptismal rites in his day, the cave itself was constructed many centuries before. Could it have been built by the Nasarenes?

Now the apparently disparate strands—Samaria; the John the Baptist sect; Simon Magus; Jesus' peculiar Judaism tinged with a flavor of pagan mysteries, gnosticism, and the sacred feminine; and the true meaning of messiahship—can be seen not as individual subjects or puzzles but as intrinsic keys to a great secret.

One that reveals that, of all the Church's many cover-ups, one stands head and shoulders above them all, and which once known, changes everything.

The Deadly Disclaimer

Since the very beginning of their religion, Christians have been trying to suppress the truth about the extent of the influence that John the Baptist had over Jesus. The reason for this age-old conspiracy is obvious—but nonetheless shocking: the claims about Jesus on which first their faith and later their power structure was built would fall apart if they admitted the truth.

Their first act of censorship was adding a qualification to Jesus' statement "Among those born of women there has not risen anyone greater than John the Baptist," thereby distorting his own words. The unpleasant rider was "yet whoever is least in the kingdom of heaven is greater than he." As we have seen, this qualification was added because Jesus' own words undermined the very image of him that Christians were trying to promote. Their claims that Jesus was the One would simply have been invalidated.

We had always assumed that the all-important phrase was added very early. However, the discovery of the "Hebrew Matthew" shows that it originally had no such disclaimer. The Pseudo-Clementine literature also reveals that the unedited words of Jesus were still being used against Christians by the devotees of John the Baptist at least until the middle of the second century. The first Christians' fear, which underpinned the addition of the disclaimer, was in fact justified: the John sect was using Jesus' own words to prove its case. Therefore the change of the "born of women" passage to the form in which Christians have always known it must have happened later, showing that the censorship must have been more systematic, involving the alteration of more manuscripts.

The Hebrew Matthew also reveals other examples of editing of Jesus' original praise for John the Baptist. Sometimes it took just one word: Jesus was originally reported as saying that the Law and all the prophets had spoken *about* John—making him the culmination of all things—but this was changed to *until* John, implying that Jesus had superseded everything. More radically, Jesus' original identification of the Baptist with Elijah—momentously including the revelation that John had come to "save the world"—in their hands became the rather more ambiguous "restore all things." From being declared Savior of the world *by Jesus himself*, John was suddenly demoted to herald of the Christ.

This is all the more outrageous when it is recognized that Jesus owed his own status and following to his association with John, promoting himself as his successor, the one who continued the Baptist's work. This, too, had to be ruthlessly downplayed by the early Church: how could Christ have chosen to act according to someone else's program?

The survival of various sects that upheld the primacy of John the Baptist—the most long-lived being the Mandaeans—always threatened to reveal the truth. Indeed, as we argued in *The Templar Revelation*, the Johannite secret has raised its head from time to time, only to be ruthlessly suppressed each time.[55] The deadly "Johannite secret" has always been there, lurking just under the surface, threatening to haunt the Roman Church. And there are signs that efforts to stop its leaking out—moves as old as the religion itself—continue to this day.

"Theological Dynamite"

Most people are now aware of the peculiar events surrounding the Dead Sea Scrolls, and the fact that for decades a scholarly "cartel" (the term of leading scroll expert Geza Vermes)[56] controlled and restricted access to the texts in ways that went well beyond academic protectiveness. The full story was told in Baigent and Leigh's *The Dead Sea Scrolls Deception* (1991), but the crux is that, as soon as the existence of the scrolls became known, the Vatican, through the Catholic École Biblique, took control of both the documents themselves and the excavations at Qumran.

The first scrolls were found in a cave near Qumran, then in Jordan, in late 1946 or early 1947. Archaeologists discovered more caves between 1951 and 1956, and a little under a mile away the remains of a settlement were found. It has always been assumed that the community had hidden the scrolls in the caves in the cliffs above during the Roman suppression of the First Jewish Revolt. An academic "closed shop" was set up almost immediately, and the whole project—of deciphering, translating, and analyzing the texts and excavating the site—became the École Biblique's responsibility, which continued even after Qumran became Israeli territory after the Six-Day War of 1967.

For decades study of the scrolls was controlled by French Dominican priests, first Father Roland de Vaux, then after his death in 1971 Pierre Benoît, who kept a tight grip on the project until his death in 1987. In 1990—after the brief reign of John Strugnell, who had to resign after his anti-Jewish rant in a press interview—a new team was set up under Emanuel Tov of the Hebrew University, but even he failed to overcome, in Vermes' uncompromising words, "the secrecy rule imposed on the Scrolls by de Vaux and his academic-imperialist heirs."[57]

The bulk of the texts and fragments had been identified, deciphered, and catalogued by 1960, when a concordance of the words appeared. And yet even that was not made available to the academic team that was supposed to be studying the documents until the late 1980s—and even then it was on a strictly private basis.[58]

It was only in 1991, a few months after the publication of *The Dead Sea Scrolls Deception*, that the conspiracy began to unravel. In September two American scholars included a previously unpublished text in a paper, sparking threats of legal action. In response Los Angeles' Huntington Library made publicly available the photographs of the complete collection it had been given on conditions of confidentiality. In November the U.S. Biblical Archaeology Society, with the assistance of Robert Eisenman, also a key source for Baigent and Leigh, published a two-volume collection of illustrations of nearly the whole collection. The forty-year embargo was finally broken.

It is usually assumed that the Vatican was so determined to keep the Dead Sea Scrolls from both independent scholars and the public in case they contained information that challenged or undermined its teachings about Jesus or its version of the origins of Christianity. But why should the discovery of a cache of documents that had belonged to an isolated Jewish sect—assumed to be Essenes—cause the Catholic authorities to go into quite such a tailspin? Had Qumran been an early Christian settlement the reaction might have been more understandable, but why assume that Jewish apocalyptic texts would contain anything of importance for Christianity?

Those who believed in a conspiracy had to assume not that the Vatican was anxious about possible discoveries, but that it had already found something deeply damaging and was attempting to suppress it. However, the problem, as highlighted by Vermes in his 2005 criticisms of Baigent and Leigh's theory, is that, since the embargo was broken, nothing concerning Jesus that might have justified such an effort has come to light—none of what Vermes called the "theological dynamite" that the theory required.[59]

But if we consider the issue from the perspective of potential revelations not about Jesus, but about John the Baptist, then suddenly we have very good reasons for Rome's immediate anxiety.

The Great Secret

A potential disaster for the equilibrium of the Church began with the discovery of almost two hundred thousand Jewish manuscripts, from various periods, in the *geniza* (storeroom) of a ninth-century synagogue in Old Cairo in the nineteenth century. One of these— comprising two incomplete copies—was particularly exciting not only because it dated from around 100 BCE, but it also because it was the product of a previously unknown sect.

This "Book of Commandments" told how the group had been founded around the time of the Maccabean revolt by a divinely inspired man identified only as the "Teacher of Righteousness," "Only Teacher," or "Only One," the Messiah of both Aaron and Israel and the "star out of Jacob" prophesied in the Book of Numbers. When he was rejected, the sect had withdrawn to Damascus, where he died, although he was expected to rise again in triumph "at the end of the days."

A striking feature of the text was its antipathy to the tribe of Judah and the line of David: clearly the Teacher hailed from another tribe. For this sect, the Davidic messianic bloodline had been replaced by one originating with Zadok, David's high priest, hence their description of themselves as "the sons of Zadok," from which scholars coined "Zadokites."

A major study of what was then known as the Zadokite Book of Commandments was published in 1910 by Solomon Schechter, president of the Jewish Theological Seminary of America, who argued that this previously unknown sect most closely matched what little was known of the Dositheans, founded by the man who, as we know, the Pseudo-Clementine literature associated with John the Baptist and Simon Magus. Not only did certain features of their beliefs match, but the new text revealed they used the same thirty-day calendar, and Arab writers described the Dositheans using two of the Teacher of Righteousness' titles, the Only One and the Star, of their own founder. In the light of this, Schechter proposed that the Dositheans were an offshoot of the Zadokites, rising from the time of schism and apostasy that the Book of Commandments describes following the Teacher's death.[60]

There was more. The text offered an explanation for one of the weirder aspects of the Pseudo-Clementine literature when it told that the first major split in the series of schisms that produced the followings of John the Baptist, Simon Magus, and Dositheus was that of the Sadducees. Surely there could be nothing further from that heterodox trio than the ultraconservative priestly aristocracy at the core of the Temple establishment. Not surprisingly, this had always been regarded as evidence that the Pseudo-Clementines were unreliable, to say the least. However, "Sadducee" is the Greek rendering of the Hebrew *Zadokim*. Both they and the "sons of Zadok" claimed descent from Zadok, although the latter fiercely contested the Sadducees' claims, believing themselves to be his legitimate heirs. Either group could be called Zadokites or Sadducees, depending on the language, so unexpectedly the Cairo discovery showed that the writers of the Pseudo-Clementines *did* know what they were talking about: there was a link between "Sadducees" and Dositheans.[61]

Schechter also argued that the Zadokites/Dositheans had made "special missionary efforts" to the Jewish Temple founded by Onias in Egypt's Leontopolis, writing:

> The severance of the Egyptian Jews from the Palestinian influ-
> ence . . . prepared the ground for the doctrines of such a Sect as the
> Zadokites in which an allegiance to Judah and Jerusalem was re-
> jected, and in which the descendants of the House of Zadok (of
> whom indeed Onias himself was one) represented both the Priest
> and the Messiah.[62]

However, Schechter's conclusions were to be revised following the discovery of the Dead Sea Scrolls. The Zadokite Book of Commandments, and the sect behind it, are now considerably better known, since a number of copies—none complete, but enough to reconstruct the entire work—were found at Qumran. Now known as the Damascus Rule (or Damascus Document), it is thought to concern the origins and the statutes of the Qumran sect, now believed to be Essenes, rather than the Dositheans.

As we saw in chapter 7, the discovery of the Dead Sea Scrolls had caused a rethinking of another example of academic orthodoxy, which—by a fortuitous turn of events—also relates to the John the Baptist sect. This was the question of Mandaean origins. Before the scrolls were discovered, the accepted line was that the Mandaeans were genuinely the descendants of his followers, but afterwards, from the end of the 1950s until the 1980s, they were regarded as a later creation with no connection with him or his time. Now they have been repatriated to first-century Palestine—albeit with some reservations about the extent of their historical connection with the Baptist.

The pre–Dead Sea Scrolls position was largely due to the influence of academics such as Richard Reitzenstein and, particularly, Rudolf Bultmann, who demonstrated parallels between the Mandaeans' sacred texts and certain concepts in the Gospel of John. Obviously there was a link between them and the community that produced the Gospel. As the Dead Sea Scrolls changed attitudes to the Mandaeans because they provided another parallel, much closer geographically and historically to the writing of John's Gospel, the consensus shifted away from a Mandaean origin for John's Gospel to one that pointed to a Jewish sectarian connection (and as a result Mandaean studies fell into disrepute for a few decades).

Weirdly, the new generation saw the Dead Sea Scrolls as proving Bultmann wrong, whereas they had actually proved him right. He never argued that the Mandaeans had existed in exactly the same form we know today before John's Gospel was written, but that *a sect from which the Mandaeans were to descend*, whose writings were lost to history, had been around at that time, and had influenced the gospel writer and his community. In fact the discoveries at Qumran revealed the existence of exactly the sect, and exactly the writings, that Bultmann had predicted. As Charles H. H. Scobie of the Presbyterian College, Montreal, said in his 1964 study of John the Baptist, "On the Mandaean hypothesis, the Scrolls are the very place where we would expect to find the ideas which entered Christianity via a 'pre-Mandaean' John the Baptist."[63] One of the few who seems to have noticed that the Scrolls vindicated rather than undermined Bultmann, Wayne A. Meeks, wrote in 1967 of the advocates of the new position, "Perhaps it is not too much to say that, if they could prove their case, they would thereby only succeed in bringing the Qumran ideology under the umbrella of Bultmann's 'gnostic myth.'"[64]

This implies the existence of a connection between the Qumran sect and the Mandaeans, precisely what some researchers, such as the German Otto Huth, have argued.[65] In fact, specific links between the Qumran literature and the Mandaica were noted from the very beginning, for example in 1957, when Theodor H. Gaster, in the first popular book about the Dead Sea Scrolls, discussed the early excitement that they might finally solve some of the mysteries of Christian origins:

In order to get the whole question in the right perspective, it should be observed that just as many things in the Dead Sea Scrolls as can be paralleled from the New Testament can be paralleled equally well from the Apocrypha and Pseudepigrapha of the Old Testament . . . and from the earlier strata of the Talmud. Moreover, many of them find a place also in the ancient doctrines of such sects as the Mandaeans of Iraq and Iran and the Samaritans, so that even if they have not come down to us through Jewish channels, we can still recognize in them part of the common Palestinian thought and folklore of the time.[66]

Gaster went on to demonstrate how many of the specific expressions used by the writers of the scrolls about their community are exactly the same as the ones Mandaeans use of themselves. But more significantly, Gaster connected the scrolls with the "ancient doctrines" of the Mandaeans *and* the Samaritans, drawing the strands together even more tightly.

There is more. The Qumran sect seems to have used the Samaritans' version of the Pentateuch: there are additions and omissions, particularly in their version of Exodus, and quotations in the Dead Sea Scrolls reveal the same idiosyncrasies. Besides, French New Testament scholar Annie Jaubert has established connections between the Qumran and Samaritan calendars, both of which differ from the standard Jewish one of that time.[67]

As with the Mandaeans and the Samaritans, there are both similarities and differences between the material in the Dead Sea Scrolls and what we know of John the Baptist's teaching and objectives. There is a widely held theory that he—if not Jesus himself—was a member of the Qumran sect, but with both John and Jesus the differences are as glaring between what they taught and the material in the scrolls as the similarities are obvious. In John the Baptist's case at least there seems to have been an *awareness* of some of the scrolls' material, although perhaps little more.[68]

There is no absolute one-to-one correspondence between the ideas and concepts in the Dead Sea Scrolls and, respectively, those of the Mandaeans, the Samaritans, and John the Baptist. But there are enough specific similarities to show they were all part of the same complex of sects. And while it is not accurate to say that the Qumran community was Mandaean, there is a stronger connection than is generally recognized.

Into this mix we have to add the Zadokites, who, before the discovery of the scrolls, academics had linked to the Dositheans. This, too, implies a connection between the Qumran sect and the family of sects that included the Baptist's group. Indeed, some continued to see the link even after the Dead Sea discovery. The eminent specialist in gnostic origins, Robert McLachlan Wilson, and Jean

Daniélou (the French Jesuit professor of Christian origins who became a cardinal) both argued that the Qumran sect was actually Dositheans,[69] the latter drawing the strands even closer together by musing that Dositheus "seems to represent a Samaritan Messianism combined with ascetic ideals, a sort of Samaritan Essenism."[70]

Surely, though, the Dead Sea Scrolls mean we must be firmly, even fiercely, in traditional Jewish territory, with a community that cut itself off from the Gentile world to study its sacred texts, and with none of the awkward "pagan mystery" material that we find with Simon Magus and Jesus? But unexpectedly, even here there are tantalizing signs of outside influence. Few discuss Qumran's "cave 7," discovered in 1955 and filled with documents—now reduced to thousands of small, mostly unreadable scraps—all in Greek, one of which is from a comedy by Menander. Hardly compatible with the Dead Sea sect's puritanical image.[71] Some of their scrolls (e.g., the *Manual of Discipline*) use "terminology similar to that of the mysteries,"[72] suggesting that the Qumran sect was familiar with their practices.

Another sign that the Qumran community was more complex than is generally believed comes from the work of metallurgist and historian Robert Feather on the famous Copper Scroll. This huge artifact, about eighty feet (24 meters) long, is made out of thin copper incised with writing that supposedly reveals the locations of hidden deposits of treasure and other valuables. Various clues in the lettering and writing style show that although the Copper Scroll was created in the first or second century BCE, it was a copy of a document that went back perhaps another six hundred years.

Feather established that the copper's chemical composition is almost identical to that of similar scrolls used in Egypt (the only place where writing on copper scrolls was practiced, the one at Qumran being the *sole* other example). He also demonstrated that the lists of quantities of precious metals and other luxury commodities used Egyptian weights and measures. But why should a Roman-period Jewish sect possess something that not only made a link with Israel's ancient past but also with Egypt? At the very least it shows that ancient secrets were being preserved by sects such as those at Qumran.

Despite popular belief, it has still not been conclusively proven that the Qumran community was part of the Essene sect, as was suggested very soon after the discovery of the scrolls. But if not, it was one of a group of related sects that sprung up in those apocalyptic times that explored various ways of grappling with the problem of what the future held by trying to rediscover the past. If, for example, they knew that their ancestors had venerated a goddess, they might have been inspired to investigate the contemporary Egyptian Isis cult.

So when the Dead Sea documents came to light in 1947, it seemed they might well provide proof of two theories relating to the John the Baptist sect. There were Solomon Schechter's hypothesis of a connection between the Damascus Rule and the Dositheans, and Rudolf Bultmann's prediction of the existence of a sect bridging the gap between the community for which John's Gospel was written (which seems to have been Samaritan) and the Mandaeans. The potential for lifting the lid on the long-suppressed truth about John the Baptist provides a much more solid reason for the Catholic damage-limitation machine to have leapt into overdrive, for them to be afraid that their two-thousand-year-old secret might be about to break.

That this was the Vatican's fear receives some confirmation from an odd story that recently emerged through Robert Feather, the expert on the Copper Scroll.[73] With his deep interest in biblical archaeology and Christian origins, Feather won the confidence of one of the key members of the École Biblique's original archaeological team at Qumran, the reclusive Józef T. Milik, a Polish former Catholic priest who settled in France. In 1999 Feather learned from Milik that one discovery had been suppressed—not a scroll, but human remains in the community's burial ground: a headless body, which Milik was convinced belonged to John the Baptist.

Agog with curiosity, as fascinatingly related in his *The Secret Initiation of Jesus at Qumran* (2005), Feather confirmed that such a body had indeed been found but the discovery covered up. The team from the École Biblique had excavated several bodies between 1949 and 1956, and while most had been passed on to other institutions in the United States and Europe, it had kept a few back—but had consistently denied the fact until 2000. During the course of these transfers some of the remains went "missing" and are now impossible to trace. And the records for one of them mention nothing about a skull. Ultimately, however, despite much dogged detective work, Feather was unable to trace those remains.

So it does seem that a headless body was found at Qumran during the early excavations but for some reason the information was suppressed for some half a century. Why? It could hardly be because the Catholic authorities *knew* the body was John the Baptist's—how could they?—but because they were afraid it *might* be, and that it could establish a connection between him and Qumran and the Dead Sea Scrolls. If nothing else, it might have inspired the kind of close interest in the Baptist they have always been so keen to avoid. If it was thought—or even speculated—that John's disciples had taken his body to Qumran, then it would inspire greater interest in the link between the Dead Sea Scrolls, the Dositheans, and, most significantly, the Mandaeans, which has been so successfully downplayed.

The Greatest Challenge

In recent years the Catholic Church—like other branches of Christianity—has found itself in the novel position of having to defend its age-old dogma, as millions of people around the world have been inspired to question certain central ideas about Jesus. Although the Vatican was pushed onto the ropes by the global debate about whether Christ was married to Mary Magdalene—a controversy it could certainly have done without—some of its members must have been in a way rather relieved. After all, that debate accidentally served as a distraction from the scandal with the gravest potential threat to the Church's authority and power.

If the Magdalene marriage debate has rocked the Catholic Church to its very foundations—and it still has a long way to go—then the revelation that Christ himself named John the Baptist as Savior of the world threatens to blow those foundations apart once and for all. Even knowing that John the Baptist's status was such that some regarded him as the Christ, let alone that Jesus himself seemed to be one of them—that he apparently even subordinated himself to another holy man—changes everything. If Jesus was neither unique nor superior, why follow him?

For two thousand years Jesus' own words have been deliberately distorted and ignored so that the priesthood could control its flock unmolested. It seems that even Jesus himself would once have agreed that Christians have been worshipping the wrong Christ for two millennia.

NOTES AND REFERENCES

Introduction

1. Geoffrey Ashe, *The Virgin: Mary's Cult and the Re-emergence of the Goddess*, rev. ed. (London: Arkana, 1988), 43.
2. Karl Weidel, quoted in Robert Eisler, *The Messiah Jesus and John the Baptist According to Flavius Josephus' Recently Discovered "Capture of Jerusalem" and Other Jewish and Christian Sources* (London: Methuen & Co., 1931), 417.

1: Between the Lines

1. See Carsten Peter Thiede, *The Cosmopolitan World of Jesus: New Findings from Archaeology* (London: SPCK, 2004), 50; Ronald V. Huggins, "The Devil's in the Details: A Review of *The Jesus Family Tomb* and *The Lost Tomb of Jesus*" (Institute for Religious Research Web site, www.irr.org/Huggins-Jesus-tomb.pdf, 2007), 5.
2. Jean-Yves Leloup, *The Gospel of Philip: Jesus, Mary Magdalene, and the Gnosis of Sacred Union* (Rochester, VT: Inner Traditions, 2004), 7.
3. Eusebius, trans. G. A. Williamson, rev. and ed. Andrew Louth, *The History of the Church from Christ to Constantine* (London: Penguin, 1989), 66.
4. Galatians 1:16.
5. E. P. Sanders, *Paul, the Law, and the Jewish People* (London: S. C. M. Press, 1983), 5.
6. Galatians 1:11–12.
7. 1 Corinthians 15:3–8.
8. For example, 2 Corinthians 11:26.
9. Romans 15:20.
10. Michael Goulder, *A Tale of Two Missions* (London: S. C. M. Press, 1994), ix–x.
11. 2 Corinthians 11:4.
12. See Sanders, *Paul, the Law, and the Jewish People*, 207; A. N. Wilson, *Paul, the Mind of the Apostle* (London: Sinclair-Stevenson, 1997), 113–18; Goulder, 1–5.
13. S. G. F. Brandon, *Jesus and the Zealots: A Study in the Political Factor in Primitive Christianity* (Manchester, England: Manchester University Press, 1967), 285.
14. Mark 9:40; Matthew 12:30.
15. C. H. Dodd, *The Interpretation of the Fourth Gospel* (Cambridge, England: Cambridge University Press, 1953), 447.
16. Andy Gaus, trans., *The Unvarnished New Testament* (Grand Rapids, MI: Phanes Press, 1991), 23.

17. Bruce Metzger, quoted in Ian Wilson, *Jesus: The Evidence* (London: Weidenfeld and Nicolson, 1984), 30.

18. Robert W. Funk, Roy W. Hoover, and the Jesus Seminar, *The Five Gospels: The Search for the Authentic Words of Jesus* (New York: Scribner, 1996), 6.

19. Although the story appears in a Syrian Christian treatise of the third century, the earliest reference to it as a *Gospel* story dates from 1118.

20. David Marshall, *The Battle for the Book* (Grantham, England: Autumn House, 1991), 29.

21. Nothing is ever 100 percent agreed in New Testament scholarship, and there is still a minority that holds that Mark is a summary version of Matthew and Luke. However, for the reasons we are about to discuss, this argument does not stand up.

22. Eusebius, 103–4.

23. Gerd Theissen, *The Gospels in Context: Social and Political History in the Synoptic Tradition* (Edinburgh: T. & T. Clark, 1992), 119–20.

24. Thiede, *The Cosmopolitan World of Jesus,* 82–83.

25. Romans 16:13.

26. For example, John A. T. Robinson, *Redating the New Testament* (London: S. C. M. Press, 1976), 106; A. R. C. Leaney, *A Commentary on the Gospel According to St. Luke* (London: Adam & Charles Black, 1966), 283.

27. Morton Smith, *Clement of Alexandria and a Secret Gospel of Mark* (Cambridge, MA: Harvard University Press, 1973), 446.

28. Quoted in Scott G. Brown, *Mark's Other Gospel: Rethinking Morton Smith's Controversial Discovery* (Waterloo, Ontario: Wilfred Laurier University Press, 2005), xvii–xix.

29. Ibid., xi.

30. Ibid., 21.

31. Ibid., 9–10.

32. Ibid., 35.

33. Ibid., 13.

34. Ron Cameron, ed., *The Other Gospels: Non-Canonical Gospel Texts* (Guildford, England: Lutterworth Press, 1983), 68. Others who took this view included Helmut Koester and Hans-Martin Schenke.

35. Ibid.

36. S. G. F. Brandon, *The Fall of Jerusalem and the Christian Church: A Study of the Effects of the Jewish Overthrow of A.D. 70 on Christianity* (London: SPCK, 1978), 227.

37. Eusebius, 104. The translator of this edition, G. A. Williamson, assuming that Papias made an error, has changed "Hebrew" to "Aramaic," but we have returned it to the original.

38. See Floyd A. Filson, *A Commentary on the Gospel According to St. Matthew* (London: Adam & Charles Black, 1971), 17; and F. F. Bruce, *The New Testament Documents: Are They Reliable?,* rev. ed. (Leicester, England: InterVarsity Press, 2000), 47.

39. Matthew 11:11.

40. George Howard, *Hebrew Gospel of Matthew* (Macon, GA: Mercer University Press, 1995), 234.

41. Burton L. Mack, *The Lost Gospel: The Book of Q and Christian Origins* (Shaftesbury, England: Element, 1994), 186.

42. Leaney, 5.

43. Luke 9:9, Gaus translation, 133.

44. See chapter 8, 293–94, and chapter 10, 362.

45. John 21:24.

46. C. H. Dodd, *Historical Tradition in the Fourth Gospel* (Cambridge, England: Cambridge University Press, 1963), 12.

47. Andrew T. Lincoln, *The Gospel According to Saint John* (New York: Continuum, 2005), 18–19.

48. Ibid., 22.

49. John 21:22–24.

50. Lincoln, 521.

51. The theory was argued by Aileen Guilding in 1960 in *The Fourth Gospel and Jewish Worship: A Study of the Relation of St. John's Gospel to the Ancient Jewish Lectionary System* (Oxford: Clarendon Press, 1960).

52. Dodd, *Historical Tradition,* 10.

53. Lincoln, 27.

54. C. F. D. Moule, *The Birth of the New Testament,* rev. ed. (London: Adam and Charles Black, 1981), 134; Dodd, *Interpretation,* 9; Matthew Black, *An Aramaic Approach to the Gospels and Acts,* rev. ed. (Oxford: Clarendon Press, 1967), 149–50.

55. See chapter 6, 203–204, and chapter 9, 339.

56. Ian Wilson, *Are These the Words of Jesus?: Dramatic Evidence from Beyond the New Testament* (Oxford: Lennard Publishing, 1990), 80.

57. Raymond E. Brown, *The Gospel According to John* (London: Geoffrey Chapman, 1971), vol. I, 175.

58. G. R. S. Mead, *The Gnostic John the Baptizer: Selections from the Mandaean John-Book, Together with Studies on John and Christian Origins, the Slavonic Josephus' Account of John and Jesus, and John and the Fourth Gospel Proem* (London: John Watkins, 1924), 20.

59. Oscar Cullmann, *The Johannine Circle—Its Place in Judaism, Among the Disciples of Jesus, and in Early Christianity: A Study in the Origin of the Gospel of John* (London: S. C. M. Press, 1976), 37.

60. E. Hennecke, ed., rev. Wilhelm Schneemelcher, *New Testament Apocrypha* (London: James Clarke & Co./Louisville, KY: Westminster John Knox Press, 1991–92), vol. 1, 98.

61. Luke 12:27; Matthew 6:28; Bentley Layton, *The Gnostic Scriptures: A New Translation with Annotations and Introductions* (London: S. C. M. Press, 1987), 386 (Gospel of Thomas saying 36). The "do not card" reference is not found in the Coptic Nag Hammadi copy, but is from the Greek Oxyrhynchus fragments.

62. Jean-Yves Leloup, *The Gospel of Mary Magdalene* (Rochester, VT: Inner Traditions, 2002), 6.

63. James M. Robinson, ed., *The Nag Hammadi Library in English,* rev. ed. (New York: E. J. Brill, 1996), 524.

64. Layton, *The Gnostic Scriptures,* xxii.

65. Stephen J. Patterson, James M. Robinson, and Hans-Gebhard Bethge, *The Fifth Gospel: The Gospel of Thomas Comes of Age* (Harrisburg, PA: Trinity Press International, 1998), 68.

66. Wilson, *Are These the Words of Jesus,* 58.

67. John A. T. Robinson, *Can We Trust the New Testament?* (London: Mowbrays, 1977), 56.
68. Lincoln, 534.

2: The Man Who Never Was and the Christ Who Shouldn't Have Been

1. Josephus, trans. William Whiston, *The Antiquities of the Jews* (London: George Routledge & Sons, 1898), 530.
2. Ibid., 596.
3. In Excursus II in Vermes' and Millar's revision of Schürer's *The History of the Jewish People in the Age of Christ.* See especially p. 437 for their reconstruction of Josephus' original words.
4. There is the added complication of a version of Josephus' earlier *Jewish War* written in Slavonic that includes some even more controversial references to Jesus. We will discuss this in chapter 8.
5. Geoffrey Ashe, *The Virgin: Mary's Cult and the Re-emergence of the Goddess,* rev. ed. (London: Arkana, 1988), 41.
6. Burton L. Mack, *The Lost Gospel: The Book of Q and Christian Origins* (Shaftesbury, England: Element, 1994), 57–58; Carsten Peter Thiede, *The Cosmopolitan World of Jesus: New Findings from Archaeology* (London: SPCK, 2004), 47.
7. Mack, *The Lost Gospel,* 47.
8. Mark 1:1.
9. R. J. Condon, *Our Pagan Christmas* (London: National Secular Society, 1995), 12.
10. Thiede, *The Cosmopolitan World of Jesus,* 52.
11. See chapter 9, p. 343.
12. Mark 1:12–13; Matthew 4:1–11; Luke 4:1–13.
13. Deuteronomy 8:3 and 6:13.
14. Ashe, 108.
15. For example, ibid., 107–8.
16. Desmond Stewart, *The Foreigner: A Search for the First-Century Jesus* (London: Hamish Hamilton, 1981), chapter 8.
17. Gerd Theissen, *The Gospels in Context: Social and Political History in the Synoptic Tradition* (Edinburgh: T. & T. Clark, 1992), 219.
18. Ibid., 206–20.
19. Luke 4:5–8. Jesus quotes from Deuteronomy 6:16.
20. As with the uncertainty about the emperor, it is also possible that the king intended here is Agrippa I's son, Agrippa II. As he was a child at the time of his father's death, Rome again took direct rule, but he was given parts of Palestine by Nero in 53 CE and ruled until the Jewish Revolt. The comparison in Luke's temptation scene may therefore have been to Nero/Agrippa II rather than Caligula/Agrippa I. Either way it originated after Jesus' lifetime but before 66.
21. See, for example, Matthew Black and H. H. Rowley, eds., *Peake's Commentary on the Bible* (London: Thomas Nelson and Sons, 1962), 198.
22. See Raphael Patai, *The Hebrew Goddess,* rev. ed. (Detroit: Wayne State University Press, 1990), chapter 1.
23. Exodus 20:3.

24. *Encyclopaedia Judaica,* 2nd ed. (Detroit: Thomson Gale, 2007), vol. 11, 144.
25. Romans 13:1–7
26. Josephus, trans. G. A. Williamson, *The Jewish War,* rev. ed. (Harmondsworth, England: Penguin, 1970), 74.
27. Thiede, *The Cosmopolitan World of Jesus,* 91–94.
28. Mack, *The Lost Gospel,* 59.
29. Malachi 4:5.
30. 1 Samuel 10:1; Isaiah 45:1.
31. Joseph Klausner, *The Messianic Ideal in Israel: From Its Beginning to the Completion of the Mishnah* (London: George Allen & Unwin, 1956), 241.
32. Ibid., 483. See also chapter 9.
33. Ashe, 35.
34. Alan Richardson, *The Political Christ* (London: S. C. M. Press, 1973), 35–36.
35. Deuteronomy 21:23.
36. 1 Corinthians 1:21 (Gaus, 310).
37. Isaiah 53:4–5.

3: Born of a Virgin?

1. Robin Lane Fox, *The Unauthorized Version: Truth and Fiction in the Bible* (London: Penguin, 1992), 31.
2. For example, David Marshall, *The Battle for the Book* (Grantham, England: Autumn House, 1991), 229–30; Geoffrey Ashe, *The Virgin: Mary's Cult and the Re-emergence of the Goddess,* rev. ed. (London: Arkana, 1988), 78.
3. A. N. Sherwin-White, *Roman Society and Roman Law in the New Testament* (Oxford: Clarendon Press, 1963), 163–64.
4. For example, James D. Tabor, *The Jesus Dynasty: Stunning New Evidence about the Hidden History of Jesus* (London: HarperElement, 2006), 55–56; Ashe, 62–63. Ashe writes that the basis of his reasoning is "If the New Testament is not to be self-contradictory." Why make such an assumption?
5. Jeremiah 22:30.
6. Tabor, 66.
7. Ibid., 52.
8. Mark 10:46–48.
9. Mark 12:35–37.
10. Mark 6:3.
11. Matthew 13:55.
12. Luke 4:22.
13. Morna D. Hooker, *A Commentary on the Gospel According to St. Mark* (New York: Continuum, 1992), 153.
14. Ashe, 80–84.
15. Luke 1:32–33.
16. Luke 1:46–47.
17. A. R. C. Leaney, *A Commentary on the Gospel According to St. Luke* (London: Adam & Charles Black, 1966), 23.
18. This theory was first proposed by F. C. Burkitt in the early years of the twentieth century.
19. Carl H. Kraeling, *John the Baptist* (New York: Charles Scribner's Sons, 1951), 17.

20. Ibid., 18.
21. Isaiah 7:14.
22. We are indebted to Keith Prince for his detailed study on our behalf of the use of *parthenos.*
23. Ashe, 24–26.
24. Ibid., 59–61.
25. Ibid., 30–31.
26. Origen, trans. and ed. Henry Chadwick, *Contra Celsum,* rev. ed. (Cambridge, England: Cambridge University Press, 1965), 28 and 31.
27. John 8:41; Ian Wilson, *Are These the Words of Jesus?: Dramatic Evidence from Beyond the New Testament* (Oxford: Lennard Publishing, 1990), 107.
28. Tabor, 75; Robert Eisler, *The Messiah Jesus and John the Baptist According to Flavius Josephus' Recently Discovered "Capture of Jerusalem" and Other Jewish and Christian Sources* (London: Methuen & Co., 1931), 407, citing a 1906 study by Adolf Deissmann.
29. Micah 5:2.
30. Fox, 30–31.
31. John 7:42.
32. Josephus, trans. G. A. Williamson, *The Jewish War,* rev. ed. (Harmondsworth, England: Penguin, 1970), 348.
33. Numbers 24:17.
34. Dio Cassius, trans. Earnest Cary, *Dio's Roman History* (London: William Heineman/Cambridge, MA: Harvard University Press, 1914–27), vol. 8, 143.
35. Ibid., 147. Cassius wrote his chronicle in the first quarter of the third century, but his account was drawn from contemporary records.
36. Matthew 2:12.
37. Luke 2:49–50.
38. Geza Vermes, *Jesus the Jew: A Historian's Reading of the Gospels* (London: William Collins, 1973), 21.
39. For the "Buddhist Jesus" theory, see Elmar R. Gruber and Holger Kersten, *The Original Jesus: The Buddhist Sources of Charistianity* (Shaftesbury, England: Element, 1995).
40. Eusebius, trans. G. A. Williamson, rev. and ed. Andrew Louth, *The History of the Church from Christ to Constantine* (London: Penguin, 1989), 81.
41. W. E. Phipps, *Was Jesus Married? The Distortion of Sexuality in the Christian Tradition* (Lanham, MD: University Press of America, 1986), 8.
42. Ben Witherington III, *Women in the Ministry of Jesus: A Study of Jesus' Attitudes to Women and Their Roles as Reflected in His Earthly Life* (New York: Cambridge University Press, 1984), 30.
43. Phipps, *Was Jesus Married?*, 26.
44. Vermes, *Jesus the Jew,* 102.
45. Phipps, *Was Jesus Married?*, 68.
46. Robert Feather, *The Secret Initiation of Jesus at Qumran: The Essene Mysteries of John the Baptist* (Rochester, VT: Bear & Co., 2005), 46.
47. For example, Isaiah 11:1.
48. Hugh J. Schonfield, *The Pentecost Revolution* (London: Hutchinson, 1974), 278.

4: "Excited to the Utmost"

1. Morna D. Hooker, *A Commentary on the Gospel According to St. Mark* (New York: Continuum, 1992), 36.
2. Robert L. Webb, *John the Baptizer and Prophet: A Socio-Historical Study* (Sheffield, England: JSOT Press, 1991), 363.
3. Hooker, 37.
4. Mark 1:5.
5. 2 Kings 1:8.
6. Mark 1:7.
7. Hooker, 38; Webb, 284.
8. Matthew 21:32.
9. Raymond E. Brown, *The Gospel According to John* (London: Geoffrey Chapman, 1971), vol. 1, 49.
10. Ibid., lxviii.
11. Rudolf Bultmann, *The Gospel of John: A Commentary* (Oxford: Basil Blackwell, 1971), 18–19.
12. Webb, 32.
13. Ibid., 269.
14. See ibid., 203–5.
15. Mark 1:11.
16. Hooker, 45.
17. Matthew 3:15.
18. Webb, 83.
19. Luke 3:1–22.
20. John 1:29–34.
21. Mark 6:17–18.
22. Mark 1:14.
23. Matthew 4:12.
24. John 3:24.
25. Some, such as Shimon Gibson, *The Cave of John the Baptist: The First Archaeological Evidence of the Truth of the Gospel Story* (London: Arrow, 2005), 132–34, assign the Baptist's execution to 28 or 29 on the basis of Luke's dating of his first appearance to those years and the assumption that his preaching provoked a swift response from Antipas. However, it seems more likely that John built up his mission for some time before it became large enough to attract Antipas' attention (and he could hardly have made the provocative condemnation of Antipas' divorce before it had happened). The earlier date would not explain why people associated John's death with a military defeat seven or eight years later, nor why Aretas took so long to avenge the insult to his daughter.
26. Hugh J. Schonfield, *The Essene Odyssey* (Shaftesbury, England: Element, 1984), 40.
27. Quoted in Charles H. H. Scobie, *John the Baptist* (London: S. C. M. Press, 1964), 195.
28. Interviewed in the documentary *The Secret Family of Jesus,* presented by Dr. Robert Beckford, produced and directed by David Batty, CTVC for Channel 4, 2006.
29. Maurice Goguel, *Au seuil de l'Évangile Jean-Baptiste: La tradition sur Jean-*

Baptiste—Le baptême de Jésus—Jésus et Jean-Baptiste—Histoire de Jean-Baptiste (Paris: Payot, 1928), 236.

30. C. H. Dodd, *Historical Tradition in the Fourth Gospel* (Cambridge, England: Cambridge University Press, 1963), 272–74; Webb, 283.
31. Walter Wink, *John the Baptist in the Gospel Tradition* (London: Cambridge University Press, 1968), 38.
32. Gibson, 182–83.
33. Webb, 283–88.
34. The significance of this is explored in depth in chapter 7.
35. Webb, 172.
36. See Lynn Picknett and Clive Prince, *The Templar Revelation: Secret Guardians of the True Identity of Christ*, rev. ed. (London: Corgi, 2007), chapter 13.
37. W. H. Brownlee, "John the Baptist in the New Light of the Ancient World," in Krister Stendahl, with James H. Charlesworth, eds., *The Scrolls and the New Testament* (New York: Crossroad Publishing, 1992), 36.
38. Webb, 36.
39. Matthew 3:9–10.
40. James D. Tabor, *The Jesus Dynasty: Stunning New Evidence about the Hidden History of Jesus* (London: HarperElement, 2006), 285.
41. John 3:22.
42. Wink, 93; Scobie, 163–64.
43. Gibson, 194.
44. Ibid., 213.
45. Ibid., 163–66.
46. Ibid., 207.
47. Ibid., 192.
48. Ibid., 207–8.

5: The Man Behind the Mission

1. Robert Eisler, *The Messiah Jesus and John the Baptist According to Flavius Josephus' Recently Discovered "Capture of Jerusalem" and Other Jewish and Christian Sources* (London: Methuen & Co., 1931), 414–15, citing a 1926 study by Rendell Harris.
2. Hugh J. Schonfield, *The Passover Plot: New Light on the History of Jesus* (London: MacDonald/Futura, 1977), 99.
3. Bruce M. Metzger, *The New Testament: Its Background, Growth, and Content*, rev. ed. (Nashville, TN: Abingdon Press, 2003), 109.
4. Morna D. Hooker, *A Commentary on the Gospel According to St. Mark* (New York: Continuum, 1992), 81.
5. Ibid.
6. Andrew T. Lincoln, *The Gospel According to Saint John* (New York: Continuum, 2005), 326.
7. C. H. Dodd, *Historical Tradition in the Fourth Gospel* (Cambridge, England: Cambridge University Press, 1963), 226.
8. Matthew 11:19.
9. Hooker, 54.
10. See Jean Daniélou, *A History of Early Christian Doctrine before the Council of Nicaea*, vol. 1 (London: Darton, Longman and Todd/Philadelphia: Westminster Press, 1973), 71.

11. Josephus, trans. G. A. Williamson, *The Jewish War,* rev. ed. (Harmondsworth, England: Penguin, 1970), 183.
12. Burton L. Mack, *The Lost Gospel: The Book of Q and Christian Origins* (Shaftesbury, England: Element, 1994), 61–62.
13. Robert Eisenman, *James the Brother of Jesus: The Key to Understanding the Secrets of Early Christianity and the Dead Sea Scrolls* (London: Watkins, 2002), xxii–xxiii.
14. Mark 3:8.
15. Luke 9:52–56.
16. Luke 10:25–37.
17. Luke 17:11–19.
18. Matthew 10:5.
19. John 8:48.
20. John 4:4–42.
21. Genesis, chapters 29 and 24, respectively.
22. Lincoln, 172.
23. Ibid., 173.
24. Ibid., 181.
25. Ben Witherington III, *Women in the Ministry of Jesus: A Study of Jesus' Attitudes to Women and Their Roles as Reflected in His Earthly Life* (New York: Cambridge University Press, 1984), 3–4.
26. Lincoln, 124.
27. Michael Baigent, Richard Leigh, and Henry Lincoln, *The Messianic Legacy* (London: Corgi, 1987), 72.
28. A. R. C. Leaney, *A Commentary on the Gospel According to St. Luke* (London: Adam & Charles Black, 1966), 132.
29. S. G. F. Brandon, *Jesus and the Zealots: A Study in the Political Factor in Primitive Christianity* (Manchester, England: Manchester University Press, 1967), 204.
30. Hooker, 157.
31. Mark 15:40–41.
32. Luke 8:1–3.
33. Witherington, 117. See also W. E. Phipps, *The Sexuality of Jesus: Theological and Literary Perspectives* (New York: Harper and Row, 1973), 53.
34. Leaney, 150.
35. Mark's account of the postresurrection appearances also states that Jesus had driven seven demons out of Mary Magdalene, but this is a later addition that is probably based on Luke.
36. James M. Robinson, ed., *The Nag Hammadi Library in English,* rev. ed. (New York: E. J. Brill, 1996), 222. On the Sophia's dating, see 221.
37. Ibid., 244. The text we have is from the second century, but clues point to its being based on an original written before the year 100.
38. Jean-Yves Leloup, *The Gospel of Philip: Jesus, Mary Magdalene, and the Gnosis of Sacred Union* (Rochester, VT: Inner Traditions, 2004), 5.
39. Robinson, *The Nag Hammadi Library in English,* 145.
40. The Coptic borrowing of *Koinonos* from Greek sometimes generates confusion, as in Greek the *-os* ending would make it a masculine noun. However, Coptic did not follow the same grammatical rules.

41. W. E. Phipps, *Was Jesus Married? The Distortion of Sexuality in the Christian Tradition* (Lanham, MD: University Press of America, 1986), 136.
42. Robinson, *The Nag Hammadi Library in English*, 148.
43. Ibid.
44. Jean-Yves Leloup, *The Gospel of Mary Magdalene* (Rochester, VT: Inner Traditions, 2002), 6.
45. Michel Tardieu, quoted in ibid., 9.
46. Michel Tardieu, quoted in ibid.
47. *Pistis Sophia,* 135. This is discussed in more detail in Lynn Picknett, *Mary Magdalene: Christianity's Hidden Goddess,* rev. ed. (London: Constable, 2004), chapter 4.
48. John 21:15.
49. Hooker, 204.
50. Mark 8:27–30.
51. Hooker, 203, referring to Luke 9:21.
52. Mark 10:35–45.
53. Hooker, 246.
54. Mark 3:20–34.
55. Luke 11:27–28.
56. John 7:5.
57. For example, S. G. F. Brandon, *The Fall of Jerusalem and the Christian Church: A Study of the Effects of the Jewish Overthrow of* A.D. *70 on Christianity* (London: SPCK, 1978), 194–97.
58. For example, Geoffrey Ashe, *The Virgin: Mary's Cult and the Re-emergence of the Goddess,* rev. ed. (London: Arkana, 1988), 103–10; and Graham Phillips, *The Marian Conspiracy: The Hidden Truth about the Holy Grail, the Real Father of Jesus, and the Tomb of the Virgin Mary* (London: Pan Books, 2001), 130–35.
59. James D. Tabor, *The Jesus Dynasty: Stunning New Evidence about the Hidden History of Jesus* (London: HarperElement, 2006), 5.
60. Eisenman, *James the Brother of Jesus,* xxii.

6: Signs and Wonders

1. Gerd Theissen, *The Gospels in Context: Social and Political History in the Synoptic Tradition* (Edinburgh: T. & T. Clark, 1992), 97–120.
2. Ibid., 115.
3. Matthew 7:12.
4. Quoted in Ian Wilson, *Are These the Words of Jesus?* (London: Weidenfeld and Nicolson, 1984), 38 and 177.
5. Leviticus 19:18.
6. Mark 9:42.
7. For example, Luke 10:21, John 13:33. Note that although the TNIV translates the latter as "my children," the Greek word literally meant "little children."
8. Matthew 18:1–6.
9. Matthew 10:42.
10. Luke 17:1–3.
11. Matthew 10:37.
12. Luke 14:26.

13. Luke 12:51–53.
14. Matthew 10:34; Gospel of Thomas saying 16, in Jean-Yves Leloup, *The Gospel of Thomas: The Gnostic Wisdom of Jesus* (Rochester, VT: Inner Traditions, 2005), 15.
15. Hugh J. Schonfield, *The Passover Plot: New Light on the History of Jesus* (London: MacDonald/Futura, 1977), 81–82.
16. Matthew 5:17–18.
17. See Helmut Merkel, "The Opposition between Jesus and Judaism," in Ernst Bammel and C. F. D. Moule, eds., *Jesus and the Politics of His Day* (Cambridge, England: Cambridge University Press, 1984).
18. Burton L. Mack, *The Lost Gospel: The Book of Q and Christian Origins* (Shaftesbury, England: Element, 1994), 111.
19. Ibid., 111–12.
20. Morna D. Hooker, *A Commentary on the Gospel According to St. Mark* (New York: Continuum, 1992), 120.
21. Mark 4:33–34.
22. Matthew 5:1–2.
23. Wilson, *Are These the Words of Jesus?*, 77.
24. Ron Cameron, ed., *The Other Gospels: Non-Canonical Gospel Texts* (Guildford, England: Lutterworth Press, 1983), 49.
25. Wilson, *Are These the Words of Jesus?*, 130–31.
26. Morton Smith, *Clement of Alexandria and a Secret Gospel of Mark* (Cambridge, MA: Harvard University Press, 1973), 89–90.
27. Mark 1:15.
28. Hooker, 55.
29. Mark 9:1.
30. Hooker, 211.
31. Ellis Rivkin, *What Crucified Jesus?* (London: S. C. M. Press, 1986), 64.
32. For example, 2 Samuel 7:14 and Psalm 2:7.
33. See Carsten Peter Thiede, *The Cosmopolitan World of Jesus: New Findings from Archaeology* (London: SPCK, 2004), 52.
34. Daniel 7:13–14.
35. Confusingly, though, the Gospels sometimes use the term just to mean "man." So when Jesus says "the Son of man is lord of the Sabbath," does he mean that he is greater than the Sabbath, or that everybody is?
36. Josephus, trans. William Whiston, *The Antiquities of the Jews* (London: George Routledge & Sons, 1898), 218–19.
37. Hooker, 65.
38. Mark 7:31–37.
39. Andrew T. Lincoln, *The Gospel According to Saint John* (New York: Continuum, 2005), 281. For other examples of the use of spittle in cures, see John M. Hull, *Hellenistic Magic and the Synoptic Tradition* (London: S. C. M. Press, 1974), 76–78.
40. Tacitus, trans. W. H. Fyfe, rev. and ed. D. S. Levene, *The Histories* (New York: Oxford University Press, 1997), 81–82.
41. W. E. Phipps, *The Sexuality of Jesus: Theological and Literary Perspectives* (New York: Harper and Row, 1973), 47.
42. Hooker, 85.
43. 2 Kings 4:18–36.

44. Luke 7:11–16.
45. Mark 5:35–43; Matthew 9:23–26; Luke 8:49–56.
46. Ian Wilson, *Jesus: The Evidence* (London: Weidenfeld and Nicolson, 1984), 99–113.
47. For example, Morton Smith, *The Secret Gospel: The Discovery and Interpretation of the Secret Gospel According to Mark,* updated ed. (Wellingborough, England: Aquarian Press, 1985), 101–2.
48. Hull, 1.
49. John 2:1–12.
50. Michael Baigent, Richard Leigh, and Henry Lincoln, *The Holy Blood and the Holy Grail,* updated ed. (London: Arrow, 1996), 348–49.
51. Morton Smith, *Jesus the Magician* (London: Victor Gollanz, 1978), 120.
52. E.g., C. H. Dodd, *Historical Tradition in the Fourth Gospel* (Cambridge, England: Cambridge University Press, 1963), 224–26; Raymond E. Brown, *The Gospel According to John* (London: Geoffrey Chapman, 1971), vol. 1, 101; Lincoln, 132–33.
53. Lincoln, 132.
54. Marvin W. Meyer, ed., *The Ancient Mysteries—A Sourcebook: Sacred Texts of the Mystery Religions of the Ancient World* (San Francisco: Harper and Row, 1987), 227.
55. Ben Witherington III, *Women in the Ministry of Jesus: A Study of Jesus' Attitudes to Women and Their Roles as Reflected in His Earthly Life* (New York: Cambridge University Press, 1984), 80.
56. Brown, vol. 1, 101.
57. Dodd, *Historical Tradition,* 226–27.
58. Mark 4:35–41; Matthew 8:25–27; Luke 8:22–25.
59. See chapter 7, 264–74.
60. The prayer is in Matthew 6:9–13.
61. Luke 11:2–4.
62. Andy Gaus, trans., *The Unvarnished New Testament* (Grand Rapids, MI: Phanes Press, 1991), 138.
63. James D. Tabor, *The Jesus Dynasty: Stunning New Evidence about the Hidden History of Jesus* (London: HarperElement, 2006), 152–53.
64. John 4:1–2.
65. Smith, *The Secret Gospel,* 78.
66. Mark 14:51–52.
67. See A. N. Wilson, *Paul: The Mind of the Apostle* (London: Sinclair-Stevenson, 1997), 25–26, and H. J. Schoeps, *Paul: The Theology of the Apostle in the Light of Jewish Religious History* (London: Lutterworth Press, 1961), 115.
68. Hyam Maccoby, *Paul and Hellenism* (London: S. C. M. Press/Philadelphia: Trinity Press International, 1991), 90. He devotes chapter 4 of his book to this argument.
69. 1 Corinthians 10:16.
70. 1 Corinthians 11:23–25.
71. Albert Schweitzer, *Paul and His Interpreters: A Critical History* (London: Adam and Charles Black, 1912), 199.
72. Ibid.
73. Mark 14:22–25.
74. John 6:45–56.

75. Joachim Jeremias, *The Eucharistic Words of Jesus* (London: S. C. M. Press, 1966), 108.
76. Lincoln, 232.
77. Hyam Maccoby, *Judas Iscariot and the Myth of Jewish Evil* (London: Peter Halban, 1992), 65.
78. John 6:70–71.
79. Jeremias, 125.
80. A. R. C. Leaney, *A Commentary on the Gospel According to St. Luke* (London: Adam & Charles Black, 1966), 72.
81. Jeremias, 170.
82. Ibid., 186–87.
83. Ibid., 203.
84. Maccoby, *Judas Iscariot,* 66.
85. Johannes Betz, "The Eucharist in the *Didache,*" in Jonathan A. Draper, ed., *The Didache in Modern Research* (New York: E. J. Brill, 1996), 245.
86. Quoted in ibid., 246.
87. See ibid.
88. Draper, 29; Jeremias, 134.
89. Hooker, 342.
90. Tabor, 229.
91. Smith, *Jesus the Magician,* 122.
92. Meyer, 227.
93. See the extract from Philo in ibid., 229–31.
94. See Karl Georg Kuhn, "The Lord's Supper and the Communal Meal at Qumran," in Krister Stendahl, with James H. Charlesworth, eds., *The Scrolls and the New Testament* (New York: Crossroad Publishing, 1992), 74–77.
95. Genesis 41:45.
96. E. W. Brooks, *Joseph and Asenath: The Confession and Prayer of Asenath, Daughter of Pentephres the Priest* (London: S. C. M. Press, 1918), 52.
97. John MacDonald, *The Theology of the Samaritans* (London: S. C. M. Press), 1964), 30.
98. Hull, 1.
99. The two quotes are in Heinrich Laible's introductory essay, "Jesus Christ in the Talmud," in Gustaf Dalman, *Jesus Christ in the Talmud, Midrash, Zohar, and in the Liturgy of the Synagogue: Texts and Translations* (London: Deighton, Bell & Co., 1893), 47 and 52.
100. Origen, trans. and ed. Henry Chadwick, *Contra Celsum,* rev. ed. (Cambridge, England: Cambridge University Press, 1965), 28 and 31.
101. Smith, *The Secret Gospel,* 105–6.
102. Smith, *Jesus the Magician,* 125–26.
103. Hooker, 182.
104. Mark 7:24–30.
105. Hooker, 182.
106. Theissen, 63–79.
107. Hooker, 182.
108. Theissen, 63.

7: The Rival Christs

1. Carl H. Kraeling, *John the Baptist* (New York: Charles Scribner's Sons, 1951), 123.

2. Walter Wink, *John the Baptist in the Gospel Tradition* (London: Cambridge University Press, 1968), x.
3. Matthew 11:2–6.
4. Wink, 24.
5. Robert L. Webb, *John the Baptizer and Prophet: A Socio-Historical Study* (Sheffield, England: JSOT Press, 1991), 281.
6. James D. Tabor and Michael O. Wise, "4Q521 'On Resurrection' and the Synoptic Gospel Tradition: A Preliminary Study," in James H. Charlesworth, *Qumran Questions* (Sheffield, England: Sheffield Academic Press, 1995), 153.
7. Mark 2:18–22.
8. John 3:25–26. The TNIV gives this as "certain Jew," although the "certain" was not in the original Greek.
9. For example, John A. T. Robinson, *Can We Trust the New Testament?* (London: Mowbrays, 1977), 38; Charles H. H. Scobie, *John the Baptist* (London: S. C. M. Press, 1964), 154; and Andrew T. Lincoln, *The Gospel According to Saint John* (New York: Continuum, 2005), 157.
10. Matthew 11:18–19.
11. Mark 11:27–33.
12. Matthew 11:7–18; Luke 7:24–35.
13. See Gerd Theissen, *The Gospels in Context: Social and Political History in the Synoptic Tradition* (Edinburgh: T. & T. Clark, 1992), 26–42.
14. James Tabor, interviewed in *The Secret Family of Jesus* documentary (see p. 399, note 28).
15. For example, James D. Tabor, *The Jesus Dynasty: Stunning New Evidence about the Hidden History of Jesus* (London: HarperElement, 2006), 152. There is disagreement over whom Jesus meant by "least in the kingdom of heaven," some taking it to mean his followers (i.e., even the least of them are better than John), while others argue that is a circumlocution, meaning "I am greater" (which we accepted when writing *The Templar Revelation*). However, a clue that the former is correct comes from Matthew (5:19), when, during the Sermon on the Mount, Jesus says that anyone who sets aside any of the Law's commands "will be called least in the kingdom of heaven" (whereas those who keep them will be "called great in the kingdom of heaven"): in other words, they will make it into the kingdom but will be rather low down in the pecking order. Clearly the phrase does not mean "I" in this passage.
16. Kraeling, 137.
17. Wink, 24.
18. Luke 7:29–30.
19. Matthew 11:12–14.
20. Wink, 21–22.
21. George Howard, *Hebrew Gospel of Matthew* (Macon, GA: Mercer University Press, 1995), 49.
22. Mark 9:2–13.
23. See Wink, 14–15.
24. Matthew 17:12–13.
25. Howard, 219.
26. Bentley Layton, *The Gnostic Scriptures: A New Translation with Annotations and Introductions* (London: S. C. M. Press, 1987), 388.

27. Mark 2:21.

28. Mark 2:22.

29. Owen St. Victor, *Epiphany: The New Age and Its Mysteries from the Time of the Jordan Prophets* (Leuven, Belgium: Sancta Sophia, 1991), 19.

30. See especially Tabor, 163–68.

31. Mark 6:14, 16.

32. Kraeling, 160.

33. Morton Smith, *Jesus the Magician* (London: Victor Gollanz, 1978), 34.

34. Michael Goulder, *A Tale of Two Missions* (London: S. C. M. Press, 1994), 128.

35. Matthew Black, *The Scrolls and Christian Origins: Studies in the Jewish Background of the New Testament* (Chico, CA: Scholars Press, 1981), 75, summarizing the conclusions of Oscar Cullmann.

36. Robert Eisenman, *James the Brother of Jesus: The Key to Understanding the Secrets of Early Christianity and the Dead Sea Scrolls* (London: Watkins, 2002), 603.

37. Alexander Roberts and James Donaldson, eds., *Ante-Nicene Christian Library: Translations of the Writings of the Fathers down to AD 325*, 25 vols. (Edinburgh: T. & T. Clark, 1867–97), vol. 3, 179.

38. Ibid., 182.

39. Ibid.

40. Acts 8:4–24.

41. Edwin M. Yamauchi, *Pre-Christian Gnosticism: A Survey of the Proposed Evidence* (London: Tyndale Press, 1973), 58.

42. Epiphanius, quoted in G. R. S. Mead, *Simon Magus: An Essay* (London: Theosophical Publishing Society, 1892), 24.

43. Quoted in ibid., 13.

44. Quoted in ibid., 8.

45. Yamauchi, *Pre-Christian Gnosticism,* 59.

46. From Irenaeus' *Contra Haereses,* quoted in Mead, 9.

47. Quoted in ibid., 10.

48. Quoted in ibid., 21.

49. See ibid., 26.

50. Quoted in ibid., 24–25.

51. Quoted in ibid., 24.

52. Epiphanius, quoted in ibid., 24.

53. Ibid., 35.

54. Ibid., 31.

55. In the later *Recognitions* Dositheus is said to be the *founder* of a sect and Simon Magus a disciple who usurped him, and there is no explicit connection with John the Baptist. However, the passage opens with the apparent non sequitur "For after that John the Baptist was killed . . . Dositheus broached his heresy," (Roberts and Donaldson, eds., vol. 3, 197) showing that the passage was rewritten to downplay the connection between John and Dositheus and that the version in the Homilies is the more faithful to the original source.

56. Quoted in Mead, *Simon Magus,* 18.

57. Luke 3:9.

58. Origen, trans. and ed. Henry Chadwick, *Contra Celsum,* rev. ed. (Cambridge, England: Cambridge University Press, 1965), 325.

59. Wink, 85.
60. Smith, *Jesus the Magician*, 81–82.
61. Raymond E. Brown, *The Gospel According to John* (London: Geoffrey Chapman, 1971), vol. 1, 48.
62. Howard, 219.
63. Edwin M. Yamauchi, *Gnostic Ethics and Mandaean Origins* (Cambridge, MA: Harvard University Press, 1970), 1.
64. Sinasi Gündüz, *The Knowledge of Life: The Origins and Early History of the Mandaeans and Their Relation to the Sabians of the Qur'an and to the Harranians* (Oxford, England: Oxford University Press, 1994), 20.
65. Yamauchi, *Gnostic Ethics and Mandaean Origins*, 60.
66. Quoted in Robert Eisler, *The Messiah Jesus and John the Baptist According to Flavius Josephus' Recently Discovered "Capture of Jerusalem" and Other Jewish and Christian Sources* (London: Methuen & Co., 1931), 232.
67. Gündüz, 3.
68. Ibid., 223.
69. R. Macuch, cited in Yamauchi, *Gnostic Ethics and Mandaean Origins*, 70.
70. Yamauchi, *Gnostic Ethics and Mandaean Origins*, 5.
71. See ibid., chapter 3.
72. Yamauchi, *Pre-Christian Gnosticism*, 129.
73. See Gündüz, 66.
74. See Yamauchi, *Pre-Christian Gnosticism*, 124.
75. Wayne A. Meeks, *The Prophet-King: Moses Traditions and the Johannine Christology* (Leiden: E. J. Brill, 1967), 13.
76. Ibid., 13.
77. Quoted in Gündüz, 104.
78. Ibid., 103.
79. Ibid., 104.
80. Maurice Goguel, *Au seuil de l'Évangile Jean-Baptiste: La tradition sur Jean-Baptiste—Le baptême de Jésus—Jésus et Jean-Baptiste—Histoire de Jean-Baptiste* (Paris: Payot, 1928), 123.
81. Wink, 11.
82. Ibid., 13.
83. Mark 6:19–29.
84. Matthew 14:6–12.
85. Luke 9:9.
86. Mark 6:17.
87. Eisenman, *James the Brother of Jesus*, 110.
88. Theissen, 90–91.
89. For example, ibid., 89.
90. Ibid., 81–97.
91. For example, Morna D. Hooker, *A Commentary on the Gospel According to St. Mark* (New York: Continuum, 1992), 163 and 187.
92. Mark 6:39–44.
93. Hooker, 168.
94. Mark 8:1–10.
95. Matthew 14:21.
96. John 6:10.

97. John 6:14–15.
98. 2 Kings 4:42–44.
99. Mark 6:51–52.
100. Mark 8:14–21.
101. Albert Schweitzer, *The Mysticism of Paul the Apostle* (London: A. & C. Black, 1931), 107.
102. 1 Corinthians 10:17.
103. Johannes Betz, "The Eucharist in the Didache," in Jonathan A. Draper, ed., *The Didache in Modern Research* (New York: E. J. Brill, 1996), 246.
104. Lincoln, 214.
105. Ernst Bammel, "The Feeding of the Multitude," in Ernst Bammel and C. F. D. Moule, eds., *Jesus and the Politics of His Day* (Cambridge, England: Cambridge University Press, 1984), 222.
106. John A. T. Robinson, *Can We Trust the New Testament?*, 93.
107. Brown, vol. 1, 249–50.
108. Matthew 14:12–13.
109. Bammel, "The Feeding of the Multitude," in *Jesus and the Politics of His Day*, 212–15.
110. Ibid., 215.
111. Ian Wilson, *Jesus: The Evidence* (London: Weidenfeld and Nicolson, 1984), 88.
112. Mark 6:42–46.
113. Donovan Joyce, *The Jesus Scroll* (London: Sphere, 1975), 85.
114. In *The Secret Family of Jesus* documentary (see p. 399, note 28).
115. *Edinburgh Evening News,* August 22, 1998.
116. Acts 13:1.

8: Road to the Cross

1. Josephus, trans. G. A. Williamson, *The Jewish War,* rev. ed. (Harmondsworth, England: Penguin, 1970), 34.
2. Robert Eisenman, *James the Brother of Jesus: The Key to Understanding the Secrets of Early Christianity and the Dead Sea Scrolls* (London: Watkins, 2002), 417.
3. Joachim Jeremias, *The Eucharistic Words of Jesus* (London: S. C. M. Press, 1966), 42.
4. Hugh J. Schonfield, *The Passover Plot: New Light on the History of Jesus* (London: MacDonald/Futura, 1977), 109.
5. Oscar Cullmann, *The Johannine Circle—Its Place in Judaism, Among the Disciples of Jesus, and in Early Christianity: A Study in the Origin of the Gospel of John* (London: S. C. M. Press, 1976), 90.
6. Luke 10:38–42.
7. Ben Witherington III, *Women in the Ministry of Jesus: A Study of Jesus' Attitudes to Women and Their Roles as Reflected in His Earthly Life* (New York: Cambridge University Press, 1984), 101.
8. John 11:1.
9. John 11:2.
10. Andrew T. Lincoln, *The Gospel According to Saint John* (New York: Continuum, 2005), 322.
11. John 11:45–52.

12. Luke 16:19–31.
13. Lincoln, 332.
14. Morton Smith, *Clement of Alexandria and a Secret Gospel of Mark* (Cambridge, MA: Harvard University Press, 1973), 447.
15. Mark 14:1–10.
16. John 12:1–11.
17. Witherington, *Women in the Ministry of Jesus*, 115.
18. Luke 7:36–50.
19. George Witterschein, introduction to Andy Gaus, trans., *The Unvarnished New Testament* (Grand Rapids, MI: Phanes Press, 1991), 13.
20. W. E. Phipps, *Was Jesus Married? The Distortion of Sexuality in the Christian Tradition* (Lanham, MD: University Press of America, 1986), 66.
21. Ibid., 64.
22. Lincoln, 337.
23. Mark 11:1–11.
24. Zechariah 9:9.
25. Matthew 21:1–11.
26. Luke 19:42–44.
27. John 12:12–21.
28. A. R. C. Leaney, *A Commentary on the Gospel According to St. Luke* (London: Adam & Charles Black, 1966), 245.
29. John J. Kilgallen, *A Brief Commentary on the Gospel of Matthew* (Lewiston, NY: Mellen Biblical Press, 1992), 165.
30. Lincoln, 343.
31. Psalm 118:25–27.
32. Morna D. Hooker, *A Commentary on the Gospel According to St. Mark* (New York: Continuum, 1992), 259.
33. Mark 11:15–17.
34. John 2:14–16.
35. Lincoln, 141–44; Raymond E. Brown, *The Gospel According to John* (London: Geoffrey Chapman, 1971), vol. 1, xxxvii.
36. S. G. F. Brandon, *Jesus and the Zealots: A Study in the Political Factor in Primitive Christianity* (Manchester, England: Manchester University Press, 1967), 332.
37. Kilgallen, 168.
38. Lincoln, 143.
39. See Matthew Black, *The Scrolls and Christian Origins: Studies in the Jewish Background of the New Testament* (Chico, CA: Scholars Press, 1981), 39; and Hooker, 264.
40. Hooker, 263.
41. John Dominic Crossan, *Who Killed Jesus? Exposing the Roots of Anti-Semitism in the Gospel Story of the Death of Jesus* (New York: HarperCollins, 1995), 64.
42. Raymond Brown, vol. 1, 121.
43. Some seeking a way out of this dilemma, such as Andrew Lincoln (138) and James Tabor (220), have cited another Old Testament prophecy, the closing words of the book of Zechariah (14:21): "And on that day there will no longer be a merchant in the house of the Lord Almighty." The wording is uncertain, however, and most translations have "Canaanite" for

"merchant." The full text relates to a wave of Jewish conquest that will convert the whole world to the worship of their God. However, this prophecy is conspicuous by its absence in the Gospel accounts of the "cleansing," so clearly the writers made no connection between it and Jesus' motives. Moreover, the people Jesus attacked in the Temple were not merchants in the proper sense. In any case, in Zechariah the absence of traders in the Temple (if they, not Canaanites, were intended) will happen only *after* God's kingdom on earth has been established, whereas the other two prophecies from which Jesus quotes refer to events that will happen as *part of the process* of establishing the kingdom, and are therefore more relevant to his own situation.

44. Isaiah 56:6–8.
45. Jeremiah 7:11.
46. Jeremiah 7:14–15.
47. See G. A. Williamson's appendix to his translation of Josephus, *The Jewish War.*
48. Ibid., 396.
49. Ibid., 399.
50. Mark 15:7.
51. Mark 14:12–31.
52. Schonfield, *The Passover Plot,* 138–39.
53. James M. Robinson, *The Secrets of Judas: The Story of the Misunderstood Disciple and His Lost Gospel* (New York: HarperCollins, 2006), vii.
54. Mark 14:18–21.
55. Psalm 41:9.
56. John 13:21–30.
57. Hyam Maccoby, *Judas Iscariot and the Myth of Jewish Evil* (London: Peter Halban, 1992), 1–2.
58. Matthew 27:3–5.
59. Acts 1:18.
60. Zechariah 11:11–13; Jeremiah 32:9; 2 Samuel 17:23.
61. C. H. Dodd, *Historical Tradition in the Fourth Gospel* (Cambridge, England: Cambridge University Press, 1963), 27.

9: From Jesus to Christ

1. See John Dominic Crossan, *The Cross That Spoke* (San Francisco: Harper & Row, 1988), especially chapter 3.
2. See Gilbert Murray, "Excursus on the Ritual Forms Preserved in Greek Tragedy," in Jane Ellen Harrison, *Themis: A Study of the Social Origins of Greek Religion* (Cambridge, England: Cambridge University Press, 1912).
3. Quoted in Heinrich Laible, "Jesus Christ in the Talmud," in Gustaf Dalman, *Jesus Christ in the Talmud, Midrash, Zohar, and in the Liturgy of the Synagogue: Texts and Translations* (London: Deighton, Bell & Co., 1893), 88.
4. Josephus, trans. William Whiston, *The Antiquities of the Jews* (London: George Routledge & Sons, 1898), 530.
5. Tacitus, trans. and ed. Michael Grant, *The Annals of Imperial Rome,* rev. ed. (London: Penguin, 1996), 365.
6. Mark 14:32–41.

7. Luke 22:39–46.
8. Matthew 26:52–54.
9. Luke 22:52–53.
10. John 18:1–11.
11. John Dominic Crossan, *Who Killed Jesus? Exposing the Roots of Anti-Semitism in the Gospel Story of the Death of Jesus* (New York: HarperCollins, 1995), 113.
12. See Ernst Bammel, ed., *The Trial of Jesus* (London: S. C. M. Press, 1970); Ellis Rivkin, *What Crucified Jesus?* (London: S. C. M. Press, 1986); S. G. F. Brandon, *The Trial of Jesus of Nazareth* (London: B. T. Batsford, 1968); A. N. Sherwin-White, "The Trial of Christ," in D. E. Nineham et al., *Historicity and Chronology in the New Testament* (London: SPCK, 1965).
13. Mark 15:2.
14. John 18:36.
15. A. N. Sherwin-White, "The Trial of Christ" in Nineham, 111.
16. Hyam Maccoby, *The Mythmaker: Paul and the Invention of Christianity* (London: Weidenfeld & Nicolson, 1986), 48.
17. Mark 14:55–65.
18. John 18:19–24.
19. E. Hennecke, ed., rev. Wilhelm Schneemelcher, *New Testament Apocrypha* (London: James Clarke & Co./Louisville, KY: Westminster John Knox Press, 1991–92), vol. 1, 162.
20. Raymond E. Brown, *The Gospel According to John* (London: Geoffrey Chapman, 1971), vol. 2, 856.
21. Donovan Joyce, *The Jesus Scroll* (London: Sphere, 1975), 106.
22. Brown, vol. 2, 871–72.
23. Brandon, 100.
24. Matthew 27:25.
25. E. Bammel, "The *Titulus*," in Ernst Bammel and C. F. D. Moule, eds., *Jesus and the Politics of His Day* (Cambridge, England: Cambridge University Press, 1984).
26. Psalm 22:18.
27. See Martin Hengel, *Crucifixion: In the Ancient World and the Folly of the Message of the Cross* (London: S. C. M. Press, 1977), especially chapters 5–7.
28. Luke 23:34.
29. Mark 15:32; Matthew 27:44.
30. Luke 23:41.
31. John 19:25–27.
32. For example, James D. Tabor, *The Jesus Dynasty: Stunning New Evidence about the Hidden History of Jesus* (London: HarperElement, 2006), 87.
33. Ben Witherington III, *Women in the Ministry of Jesus: A Study of Jesus' Attitudes to Women and Their Roles as Reflected in His Earthly Life* (New York: Cambridge University Press, 1984), 92–93.
34. Mark 15:33–37; Matthew 27:45–50.
35. Luke 23:46.
36. John 19:30.
37. Matthew 27:51–53.
38. John 19:31–37.

39. See Brown, vol. 2, 946–48.
40. Crossan, *Who Killed Jesus?*, 163–64.
41. Ibid., chapter 6.
42. Mark 15:43.
43. Luke 23:50–51.
44. Matthew 27:57.
45. John 19:38.
46. John 19:31.
47. Acts 13:29.
48. Gerd Lüdemann with Alf Özen, *What Really Happened to Jesus: A Historical Approach to the Resurrection* (London: S. C. M. Press, 1995), 22–24.
49. Tabor, 204–5.
50. 1 Corinthians 15:14, 17.
51. Lüdemann and Özen, 5.
52. Mark 16:1–8.
53. Hugh J. Schonfield, *The Passover Plot: New Light on the History of Jesus* (London: MacDonald/Futura, 1977), 159.
54. Ian Wilson, *Are These the Words of Jesus?: Dramatic Evidence from Beyond the New Testament* (Oxford: Lennard Publishing, 1990), 89.
55. Matthew 28:1–10.
56. Luke 24:1–12.
57. John 20:1–18.
58. Brown, vol. 2, 992.
59. W. E. Phipps, *The Sexuality of Jesus: Theological and Literary Perspectives* (New York: Harper and Row, 1973), 67.
60. Andrew T. Lincoln, *The Gospel According to Saint John* (New York: Continuum, 2005), 496.
61. Matthew 28:16–20.
62. Luke 24:13–51.
63. Acts 1:3.
64. John 20:19–29.
65. C. H. Dodd, *The Interpretation of the Fourth Gospel* (Cambridge, England: Cambridge University Press, 1953), 9.
66. 1 Corinthians 15:3–8.
67. Jesus' appearance to James was, according to Jerome, in the now-lost Gospel of the Hebrews. Jerome quoted the passage, in which the risen Jesus shares bread and wine with his brother, but few take it seriously. It seems to have been created by the Jewish Christians in order to put their founder, James, on the same level as Peter and the other apostles.
68. Lüdemann and Özen, 102–29.
69. Crossan, *Who Killed Jesus?*, 204.
70. For example, Tacitus, trans. W. H. Fyfe, rev. and ed. D. S. Levene, *The Histories* (New York: Oxford University Press, 1997), 63–64; and Gaius Suetonius Tranquillus, trans. Robert Graves, rev. Michael Grant, *The Twelve Caesars* (London: Penguin, 2006), 247–48. Nero's alleged return was also recorded by Dio Chrysostom, in the Sybilline Oracles, and by Saint Augustine of Hippo.
71. Lüdemann and Özen, 130.

72. Josephus, trans. H. St. J. Thackeray, *The Life/Against Apion* (London: William Heinemann/New York: G. P. Putnam's Sons, 1926), 155.
73. Crossan, *Who Killed Jesus?*, 143–47.
74. Joyce, chapter 1.
75. See the discussion on the Hindu Universe Web site, www.hindunet.com /forum.
76. See our *The Sion Revelation: Inside the Shadowy World of Europe's Secret Masters* (London: Time Warner, 2006), chapters 3 and 4.
77. Theologian Dr. Serena Tajé, quoted in Léopold Sanchez, "Rennes-le-Château—Vrai ou faux? Le trésor du curé," *Le Figaro,* July 7, 2001.
78. Joan Bakewell, "The Tomb That Dare Not Speak Its Name," *Sunday Times News Review,* March 31, 1996.
79. Reported in, for example, David van Biema, "Is This Jesus's Tomb?" *Time,* February 26, 2007.
80. Ronald V. Huggins, "The Devil's in the Details: A Review of *The Jesus Family Tomb* and *The Lost Tomb of Jesus*" (Institute for Religious Research Web site, www.irr.org/Huggins-Jesus-tomb.pdf, 2007), 11–5; Simcha Jacobovici and Charles Pellegrino, *The Jesus Family Tomb: The Discovery, the Investigation, and the Evidence That Could Change History* (New York: HarperCollins, 2007), 174.
81. Tabor, 268–70.

10: The Final Revelation

1. The rivalry between Christianity and the Isis cult—and the unexpected similarities between them—is examined in more detail in our *The Templar Revelation: Secret Guardians of the True Identity of Christ,* rev. ed. (London: Corgi, 2007), 393–97.
2. Bentley Layton, *The Gnostic Scriptures: A New Translation with Annotations and Introductions* (London: S. C. M. Press, 1987), xviii.
3. For example, Gerd Theissen, *The Gospels in Context: Social and Political History in the Synoptic Tradition* (Edinburgh: T. & T. Clark, 1992), 157–61.
4. Ibid., 156.
5. Morna D. Hooker, *A Commentary on the Gospel According to St. Mark* (New York: Continuum, 1992), 313–14.
6. Daniel 12:11.
7. For example, Hooker, 313–18; S. G. F. Brandon, *The Fall of Jerusalem and the Christian Church: A Study of the Effects of the Jewish Overthrow of A.D. 70 on Christianity* (London: SPCK, 1978), 107–9.
8. Matthew 24:1–35.
9. Luke 21:5–36.
10. Acts 2:4.
11. Gerd Lüdemann, with Alf Özen, *What Really Happened to Jesus: A Historical Approach to the Resurrection* (London: S. C. M. Press, 1995), 95–98.
12. Hyam Maccoby, *Judas Iscariot and the Myth of Jewish Evil* (London: Peter Halban, 1992), 152–53.
13. Galatians 1:18–19.
14. Lüdemann and Özen, 83.
15. Galatians, 2:14.

16. Robert Eisenman, *James the Brother of Jesus: The Key to Understanding the Secrets of Early Christianity and the Dead Sea Scrolls* (London: Watkins, 2002), 963.

17. Acts 6:1–6.

18. Acts 6:11–7:53.

19. Oscar Cullmann, *The Johannine Circle—Its Place in Judaism, Among the Disciples of Jesus, and in Early Christianity: A Study in the Origin of the Gospel of John* (London: S. C. M. Press, 1976), 43.

20. Ibid., 50.

21. Acts 8:1, 11:19.

22. For a discussion, see Matrin Hengel, *Between Jesus and Paul: Studies in the Earliest History of Christianity* (London: S. C. M. Press, 1987), chapter 1.

23. Quoted in Matthew Black, *The Scrolls and Christian Origins: Studies in the Jewish Background of the New Testament* (Chico, CA: Scholars Press, 1981), 76. See Oscar Cullman, "The Significance of the Qumran Texts for Research into the Beginnings of Christianity," in *The Scrolls and the New Testament,* ed. Krister Stendahl with James H. Charlesworth (New York: Harper Bros., 1957).

24. Brandon, *The Fall of Jerusalem and the Christian Church,* 218–19.

25. Cullmann, *The Johannine Circle,* 43.

26. John Dominic Crossan, *Who Killed Jesus? Exposing the Roots of Anti-Semitism in the Gospel Story of the Death of Jesus* (New York: HarperCollins, 1995), 204.

27. John 10:34–36.

28. Psalm 82:6–7.

29. Raphael Patai, *The Hebrew Goddess,* rev. ed. (Detroit: Wayne State University Press, 1990), 34.

30. 1 Kings 11:4–8.

31. Genesis 6:4.

32. Patai, 97–98.

33. John 1:1–3.

34. Introduction to Andy Gaus, trans., *The Unvarnished New Testament* (Grand Rapids, MI: Phanes Press, 1991), 15–16.

35. Crossan, *Who Killed Jesus?,* 26.

36. Burton L. Mack, *The Lost Gospel: The Book of Q and Christian Origins* (Shaftesbury, England: Element, 1994), 150.

37. Luke 11:49.

38. For example, John Romer, *Testament: The Bible and History* (London: Michael O'Mara, 1996), 205.

39. For example, Karl W. Luckert, *Egyptian Light and Hebrew Fire: Theological and Philosophical Roots of Christendom in Evolutionary Perspective* (New York: State University of New York Press, 1991), 299–308.

40. James Alan Montgomery, *The Samaritans—The Earliest Jewish Sect: Their History, Theology, and Literature* (Eugene, OR: Wipf and Stock, 2006), 49–50.

41. See John MacDonald, *The Theology of the Samaritans* (London: S. C. M. Press), 1964), 22–23.

42. Ibid., 33.

43. Ibid., 69.

44. Ibid., 30.
45. Andrew T. Lincoln, *The Gospel According to Saint John* (New York: Continuum, 2005), 176–77.
46. Bruce M Metzger, *The Early Versions of the New Testament: Their Origin, Transmission, and Limitations* (Oxford: Clarendon Press, 1977), 99.
47. Brandon, *The Fall of Jerusalem and the Christian Church*, 222.
48. Quoted in Luckert, 294.
49. Rev. Dr. Giles, *Hebrew and Christian Records: An Historical Enquiry Concerning the Age and Authorship of the Old and New Testaments* (London: Trübner and Co., 1877), vol. I, 86.
50. See Black, *The Scrolls and Christian Origins,* 66–68.
51. Hugh J. Schonfield, *The Passover Plot: New Light on the History of Jesus* (London: MacDonald/Futura, 1977), 208.
52. Ibid., 207.
53. Black, *The Scrolls and Christian Origins,* 69.
54. Ibid., 74.
55. See Picknett and Prince, *The Templar Revelation,* especially chapter 17.
56. Geza Vermes, *Scrolls, Scriptures, and Early Christianity* (New York: T. & T. International, 2005), 5.
57. Ibid.
58. Ibid., 4.
59. Ibid., 1–2.
60. S. Schechter, *Documents of Jewish Sectaries* (Cambridge, England: Cambridge University Press, 1910), vol. 2, xxi–xxii.
61. Stanley Jerome Isser, *The Dositheans: A Samaritan Sect in Late Antiquity* (Leiden: E. J. Brill, 1976), 119.
62. Ibid., xxvi.
63. Charles H. H. Scobie, *John the Baptist* (London: S. C. M. Press, 1964), 28.
64. Wayne A. Meeks, *The Prophet-King: Moses Traditions and the Johannine Christology* (Leiden: E. J. Brill, 1967), 12.
65. See Edwin M. Yamauchi, *Pre-Christian Gnosticism: A Survey of the Proposed Evidence* (London: Tyndale Press, 1973), 123–24.
66. Theodor H. Gaster, *The Scriptures of the Dead Sea Sect* (London: Secker and Warburg, 1957), 30.
67. Scobie, 171.
68. Hooker, 41–42.
69. Isser, 119.
70. Jean Daniélou, *A History of Early Christian Doctrine before the Council of Nicaea,* (London: Darton, Longman and Todd/Philadelphia: Westminster Press, 1973), vol. 1, 72.
71. Carsten Peter Thiede, *The Earliest Gospel Manuscript? The Qumran Papyrus 7Q5 and Its Significance for New Testament Studies* (Carlisle, England: Paternoster Press, 1992), 43.
72. Marvin W. Meyer, ed., *The Ancient Mysteries—A Sourcebook: Sacred Texts of the Mystery Religions of the Ancient World* (San Francisco: Harper and Row, 1987), 227.
73. Robert Feather, *The Secret Initiation of Jesus at Qumran: The Essene Mysteries of John the Baptist* (Rochester, VT: Bear & Co., 2005), chapters 27–33.

SELECT BIBLIOGRAPHY

Main details are for the editions cited. Where this is not the first edition, details of the original publication follow (where known).

Allegro, John M. *The Sacred Mushroom and the Cross: A Study of the Nature and Origins of Christianity within the Fertility Cults of the Ancient Near East.* Revised edition. London: Abacus, 1973 (London: Hodder and Stoughton, 1970).

Andrews, Richard, and Paul Schellenberger. *The Tomb of God: The Body of Jesus and the Solution to a 2000-Year-Old Mystery.* London: Little, Brown & Co., 1996.

Ashe, Geoffrey. *The Virgin: Mary's Cult and the Re-emergence of the Goddess.* Revised edition. London: Arkana, 1988 (London: Routledge and Kegan Paul, 1976).

Baigent, Michael. *The Jesus Papers: Exposing the Greatest Cover-up in History.* New York: HarperCollins, 2006.

Baigent, Michael, Richard Leigh, and Henry Lincoln. *The Holy Blood and the Holy Grail.* Updated edition. London: Arrow, 1996 (London: Jonathan Cape, 1982).

———. *The Messianic Legacy.* London: Corgi, 1987 (London: Jonathan Cape, 1986).

Baigent, Michael, and Richard Leigh. *The Dead Sea Scrolls Deception.* London: Jonathan Cape, 1991.

Bakewell, Joan. "The Tomb That Dare Not Speak Its Name," *Sunday Times News Review,* March 31, 1996.

Bammel, Ernst, ed. *The Trial of Jesus.* London: S. C. M. Press, 1970.

Bammel, Ernst, and C. F. D. Moule, eds. *Jesus and the Politics of His Day.* Cambridge, England: Cambridge University Press, 1984.

Barnstone, Willis, and Marvin Meyer, eds. *The Gnostic Bible.* Boston: Shambala, 2003.

Beasley-Murray, G. R. *Baptism in the New Testament.* Carlisle, England: Paternoster Press, 1972.

Black, Matthew. *An Aramaic Approach to the Gospels and Acts.* Revised edition. Oxford: Clarendon Press, 1967 (first edition 1946).

———. *The Scrolls and Christian Origins: Studies in the Jewish Background of the New Testament.* Chico, CA: Scholars Press, 1981 (New York: Charles Scribner's Sons, 1961).

Black, Matthew, and H. H. Rowley, eds. *Peake's Commentary on the Bible.* London: Thomas Nelson and Sons, 1962.

Blake, Peter, and Paul S. Blezard. *The Arcadian Cipher: The Quest to Crack the Code of Christianity's Greatest Secret.* London: Sidgwick and Jackson, 2000.

Bornkamm, Günther. *Paul.* London: Hodder and Stoughton, 1975. (*Paulus.* Stuttgart: W. Kohlhammer, 1969.)

Brandon, S. G. F. *The Fall of Jerusalem and the Christian Church: A Study of the Effects of the Jewish Overthrow of A.D. 70 on Christianity.* London: S. P. C. K., 1978 (first edition 1951).

———. *Jesus and the Zealots: A Study in the Political Factor in Primitive Christianity.* Manchester, England: Manchester University Press, 1967.

———. *The Trial of Jesus of Nazareth.* London: B. T. Batsford, 1968.

Brooks, E. W. *Joseph and Asenath: The Confession and Prayer of Asenath, Daughter of Pentephres the Priest.* London: S. P. C. K., 1918.

Brown, Dan. *The Da Vinci Code: A Novel.* New York: Doubleday, 2003.

Brown, Raymond E. *The Gospel According to John,* 2 vols. London: Geoffrey Chapman, 1971.

Brown, Scott G. *Mark's Other Gospel: Rethinking Morton Smith's Controversial Discovery.* Waterloo, Ontario: Wilfred Laurier University Press, 2005.

Bruce, F. F. *The Books and the Parchments.* Revised edition. London: Marshall Pickering, 1991 (London: Pickering and Inglis, 1950).

———. *The New Testament Documents: Are They Reliable?* Revised edition. Leicester, England: Inter-Varsity Press, 2000. (*Are the New Testament Documents Reliable?* London: Inter-Varsity Fellowship of Evangelical Unions, 1943.)

Bultmann, Rudolf. *The Gospel of John: A Commentary.* Oxford: Basil Blackwell, 1971 (*Das Evangelium des Johannes.* Göttingen: Vandenhoeck and Ruprecht, 1964).

Burney, C. F. *The Aramaic Origin of the Fourth Gospel.* Oxford: Clarendon Press, 1922.

Caldwell, Thomas. "Dositheos Samaritanus," *Kairos: Zeitschrift für Religionswissenschaft und Theologie* 4 (1962).

Cameron, Ron, ed. *The Other Gospels: Non-Canonical Gospel Texts.* Guildford, England: Lutterworth Press, 1983.

Carlson, Stephen C. *The Gospel Hoax: Morton Smith's Invention of Secret Mark.* Waco, TX: Baylor University Press, 2005.

Charlesworth, James H. *Qumran Questions.* Sheffield, England: Sheffield Academic Press, 1995.

Condon, R. J. *Our Pagan Christmas.* London: National Secular Society, 1974.

Crossan, John Dominic. *The Cross That Spoke.* San Francisco: Harper & Row, 1988.

———. *Who Killed Jesus? Exposing the Roots of Anti-Semitism in the Gospel Story of the Death of Jesus.* New York: HarperCollins, 1995.

Cullmann, Oscar. *Jésus et les révolutionnaires de son temps: Culte, société, politique.* Neuchâtel: Delachaux et Niestlé, 1970.

———. *The Johannine Circle—Its Place in Judaism, Among the Disciples of Jesus, and in Early Christianity: A Study in the Origin of the Gospel of John.* London: S. C. M. Press, 1976 (*Der johanneische Kreis, sein Platz im Spätjudentum, im der Jüngerschaft Jesu und im Urchristentum,* Tübingen: J. C. B. Mohr, 1975).

Dalman, Gustaf. *Jesus Christ in the Talmud, Midrash, Zohar, and in the Liturgy of the Synagogue: Texts and Translations.* London: Deighton, Bell & Co., 1893.

Daniélou, Jean. *A History of Early Christian Doctrine before the Council of Nicaea*, 3 vols. London: Darton, Longman and Todd/Philadelphia: Westminster Press, 1964, 1973, 1977. (Translated revision of *Histoire des doctrines chrétiennes avant Nicée*. Paris: Desclée et Cie, 1958, 1961, Tournai/Éditions du Cerf, 1978).

Dio Cassius. Trans. Earnest Cary. *Dio's Roman History*, 9 vols. London: William Heinemann / Cambridge, MA: Harvard University Press, 1914–27.

Dodd, C. H. *Historical Tradition in the Fourth Gospel*. Cambridge, England: Cambridge University Press, 1963.

———. *The Interpretation of the Fourth Gospel*. Cambridge, England: Cambridge University Press, 1953.

Draper, Jonathan A., ed. *The Didache in Modern Research*. New York: E. J. Brill, 1996.

Ehrman, Bart D. *The Apostolic Fathers*, 2 vols. Cambridge, MA: Harvard University Press, 2003.

———. *Misquoting Jesus: The Story Behind Who Changed the Bible and Why*. New York: HarperCollins, 2005.

Ehrman, Bart D., and Michael W. Holmes. *The Text of the New Testament in Contemporary Research: Essays on the Status Quaestionis*. Grand Rapids, MI: William B. Eerdmans, 1995.

Eisenman, Robert. *James the Brother of Jesus: The Key to Understanding the Secrets of Early Christianity and the Dead Sea Scrolls*. London: Watkins, 2002. (London: Faber and Faber, 1997).

———. *The New Testament Code: The Cup of the Lord, the Damascus Covenant, and the Blood of Christ*. London: Watkins, 2007.

Eisler, Robert. *The Messiah Jesus and John the Baptist According to Flavius Josephus' Recently Discovered "Capture of Jerusalem" and Other Jewish and Christian Sources*. London: Methuen & Co., 1931 (original German 1928).

Encyclopaedia Judaica. 2nd edition, 22 vols. Detroit: Thomson Gale, 2007.

Eusebius. Trans. G. A. Williamson. Rev. and ed. Andrew Louth. *The History of the Church from Christ to Constantine*. London: Penguin, 1989 (first edition 1965).

Feather, Robert. *The Copper Scroll Decoded: One Man's Search for the Fabulous Treasures of Ancient Egypt*. London: Thorsons, 1999.

———. *The Secret Initiation of Jesus at Qumran: The Essene Mysteries of John the Baptist*. Rochester, VT: Bear & Co., 2005.

Filson, Floyd V. *A Commentary on the Gospel According to St. Matthew*. London: Adam & Charles Black, 1971 (first edition 1960).

Fox, Robin Lane. *The Unauthorized Version: Truth and Fiction in the Bible*. London: Penguin, 1992 (London: Viking, 1991).

Freke, Timothy, and Peter Gandy. *Jesus and the Goddess: The Secret Teachings of the Original Christians*. London: Thorsons, 2001.

———. *The Jesus Mysteries: Was the "Original Jesus" a Pagan God?* London: Thorsons, 1999.

———. *The Laughing Jesus: Religious Lies and Gnostic Wisdom*. New York: Harmony Books, 2005.

Funk, Robert W., Roy W. Hoover, and the Jesus Seminar. *The Five Gospels: The Search for the Authentic Words of Jesus*. New York: Scribner, 1996.

Gaster, Theodor H. *The Scriptures of the Dead Sea Sect*. London: Secker and Warburg, 1957.

Gaus, Andy, trans. *The Unvarnished New Testament*. Grand Rapids, MI: Phanes Press, 1991.

Gibson, Shimon. *The Cave of John the Baptist: The First Archaeological Evidence of the Truth of the Gospel Story*. London: Arrow, 2005 (London: Century, 2005).

Giles, Dr. Rev. [J. A.] *Hebrew and Christian Records: An Historical Enquiry Concerning the Age and Authorship of the Old and New Testaments*, 2 vols. London: Trübner and Co., 1877.

Goguel, Maurice. *Au seuil de l'Évangile Jean-Baptiste: La tradition sur Jean-Baptiste—Le baptême de Jésus—Jésus et Jean-Baptiste—Histoire de Jean-Baptiste*. Paris: Payot, 1928.

Goulder, Michael. *A Tale of Two Missions*. London: S. C. M. Press, 1994.

Gruber, Elmar R., and Holger Kersten. *The Original Jesus: The Buddhist Sources of Christianity*. Shaftesbury, England: Element, 1995. (*Der Ur-Jesus: Die buddhistischen Quellen des Christentums*. Munich: Langen Müller, 1994.)

Guilding, Aileen. *The Fourth Gospel and Jewish Worship: A Study of the Relation of St John's Gospel to the Ancient Jewish Lectionary System*. Oxford: Clarendon Press, 1960.

Gündüz, Sinasi. *The Knowledge of Life: The Origins and Early History of the Mandaeans and Their Relation to the Sabians of the Qur'an and to the Harranians*. Oxford, England: Oxford University Press, 1994.

Harrison, Jane Ellen. *Themis: A Study of the Social Origins of Greek Religion*. Cambridge, England: Cambridge University Press, 1912.

Hengel, Martin. *Between Jesus and Paul: Studies in the Earliest History of Christianity*. London: S. C. M. Press, 1983 (translations of essays from various German publications, 1971–83).

————. *Crucifixion in the Ancient World and the Folly of the Message of the Cross*. London: S. C. M. Press, 1977. (Translated revision of "*Mors turpissima crucis*: Die Kreuzigung in der antiken Welt und die 'Torheit' des 'Wortes vom Krenz.'" In J. Friedrich, W. Pöhlmann, and P. Stuhlmacher, eds. *Rechtfertigung*. Tübingen: J. C. B. Mohr/Göttingen: Vandenhoeck & Ruprecht, 1976.)

Hennecke, E., ed. Rev. Wilhelm Schneemelcher. *New Testament Apocrypha*, 2 vols. London: James Clarke & Co./Louisville, KY: Westminster John Knox Press, 1991–92. (*Neutestamentliche Apokryphen*, Tübingen: J. C. B. Mohr, 1923–24.)

Hooker, Morna D. *A Commentary on the Gospel According to St. Mark*. New York: Continuum, 1992 (London: A. & C. Black, 1981).

Howard, George. *Hebrew Gospel of Matthew*. Macon, GA: Mercer University Press, 1995. (Revised edition of *The Gospel of Matthew According to a Primitive Hebrew Text*. Macon, GA: Mercer University Press, 1987.)

Huggins, Ronald V. "The Devil's in the Details: A Review of *The Jesus Family Tomb* and *The Lost Tomb of Jesus*," Institute for Religious Research Web site, www.irr.org/Huggins-Jesus-tomb.pdf, 2007.

Hull, John M. *Hellenistic Magic and the Synoptic Tradition*. London: S. C. M. Press, 1974.

Isser, Stanley Jerome. *The Dositheans: A Samaritan Sect in Late Antiquity*. Leiden: E. J. Brill, 1976.

Jacobovici, Simcha, and Charles Pellegrino. *The Jesus Family Tomb: The Discovery, the Investigation, and the Evidence That Could Change History*. New York: HarperCollins, 2007.

James, Montague Rhodes. *The Apocryphal New Testament*. Oxford: Clarendon Press, 1924.

Jeremias, Joachim. *The Eucharistic Words of Jesus*. London: S. C. M. Press, 1966. (Translated revision of *Die Abendmahlsworte Jesu*. Göttingen: Vandenhoeck and Ruprecht, 1960.)

Josephus. Trans. William Whiston. *The Antiquities of the Jews*. London: George Routledge & Sons, 1898.

————. Trans. G. A. Williamson. *The Jewish War*. Revised edition. Harmondsworth, England: Penguin, 1970. (first edition 1959).

————. Trans. H. St. J. Thackeray. *The Life/Against Apion*. London: William Heinemann/New York: G. P. Putnam's Sons, 1926.

Joyce, Donovan. *The Jesus Scroll*. London: Sphere, 1975 (London: Angus and Robertson, 1973).

Kashmiri, Aziz. *Christ in Kashmir*. Srinagar, India: Roshni, 1973.

Kasser, Rodolphe, Marvin Meyer, and Gregor Wurst, eds. *The Gospel of Judas: From Codex Tchacos*. Washington, DC: National Geographic, 2006.

Keener, Craig S. *A Commentary on the Gospel of Matthew*. Grand Rapids, MI: William B. Eerdmans, 1999.

Kenyon, Frederic G. *The Chester Beatty Biblical Papyri: Descriptions and Texts of Twelve Manuscripts on Papyrus of the Greek Bible*. London: Emery Walker, 1933.

Kersten, Holger. *Jesus Lived in India: His Unknown Life Before and After the Crucifixion*. Shaftesbury, England: Element, 1986.

Kilgallen, John J. *A Brief Commentary on the Gospel of Matthew*. Lewiston, NY: Mellen Biblical Press, 1992.

Klassen, William. *Judas: Betrayer or Friend of Jesus?* London: S. C. M. Press, 1996.

Klausner, Joseph. *The Messianic Idea in Israel: From Its Beginning to the Completion of the Mishnah*. London: George Allen & Unwin, 1956.

Kraeling, Carl H. *John the Baptist*. New York: Charles Scribner's Sons, 1951.

Krosney, Herbert. *The Lost Gospel: The Quest for the Gospel of Judas Iscariot*. Washington, DC: National Geographic, 2006.

Lawrence, D. H. *The Man Who Died*. London: Martin Secker, 1931.

Layton, Bentley. *The Gnostic Scriptures: A New Translation with Annotations and Introductions*. London: S. C. M. Press, 1987.

————, ed. *Nag Hammadi Codex II, 2–7*, 2 vols. Leiden: E. J. Brill, 1989.

Leaney, A. R. C. *A Commentary on the Gospel According to St. Luke*. London: Adam & Charles Black, 1966 (first edition 1958).

Leloup, Jean-Yves. *The Gospel of Mary Magdalene*. Rochester, VT: Inner Traditions, 2002. (*L'Évangile de Marie: Myriam de Magdala*. Paris: Albin Michel, 1997.)

————. *The Gospel of Philip: Jesus, Mary Magdalene, and the Gnosis of Sacred Union*. Rochester, VT: Inner Traditions, 2004. (*L'Évangile de Philippe*. Paris: Albin Michel, 2003.)

————. *The Gospel of Thomas: The Gnostic Wisdom of Jesus*. Rochester, VT: Inner Traditions, 2005. (*L'Évangile de Thomas*. Paris: Albin Michel, 1986.)

Lincoln, Andrew T. *The Gospel According to Saint John*. New York: Continuum, 2005.

Luckert, Karl W. *Egyptian Light and Hebrew Fire: Theological and Philosophical*

Roots of Christendom in Evolutionary Perspective. New York: State University of New York Press, 1991.

Lüdemann, Gerd. *The Resurrection of Jesus: History, Experience, Theology.* London: S. C. M. Press, 1994. (*Die Auferstehung Jesu: Historie, Erfahrung, Theologie.* Stuttgart: Radius-Verlag, 1994.)

Lüdemann, Gerd, with Alf Özen. *What Really Happened to Jesus: A Historical Approach to the Resurrection.* London: S. C. M. Press, 1995. (*Was mit Jesus wirklich geschah: Die Auferstehung historisch betrachtet.* Stuttgart: Radius-Verlag, 1995.)

Lupieri, Edmondo. *The Mandaeans: The Last Gnostics.* Grand Rapids, MI: William B. Eerdmanns, 2002. (*I Mandei: Gli ultimi gnostici.* Brescia, Italy: Paideia, 1993.)

Maccoby, Hyam. *Judas Iscariot and the Myth of Jewish Evil.* London: Peter Halban, 1992.

———. *The Mythmaker: Paul and the Invention of Christianity.* London: Weidenfeld & Nicolson, 1986.

———. *Paul and Hellenism.* London: S. C. M. Press/Philadelphia: Trinity Press International, 1991.

MacDonald, John. *The Theology of the Samaritans.* London: S. C. M. Press, 1964.

Mack, Burton L. *The Lost Gospel: The Book of Q and Christian Origins.* Shaftesbury, England: Element, 1994. (New York: HarperCollins, 1993.)

———. *A Myth of Innocence: Mark and Christian Origins.* Philadelphia: Fortress Press, 1988.

———. *Who Wrote the New Testament?: The Making of the Christian Myth.* New York: HarperCollins, 1995.

Marshall, David. *The Battle for the Book.* Grantham, England: Autumn House, 1991.

Mead, G. R. S. *The Gnostic John the Baptizer: Selections from the Mandaean John-Book, Together with Studies on John and Christian Origins, the Slavonic Josephus' Account of John and Jesus, and John and the Fourth Gospel Proem.* London: John Watkins, 1924.

———. *Simon Magus: An Essay.* London: Theosophical Publishing Society, 1892.

Meeks, Wayne A. *The Prophet-King: Moses Traditions and the Johannine Christology.* Leiden: E. J. Brill, 1967.

Metzger, Bruce M. *The Early Versions of the New Testament: Their Origin, Transmission, and Limitations.* Oxford: Clarendon Press, 1977.

———. *The New Testament: Its Background, Growth, and Content.* Revised edition. Nashville, TN: Abingdon Press, 2003 (London: Lutterworth Press, 1969).

———. *The Text of the New Testament: Its Transmission, Corruption, and Restoration.* Revised edition. Oxford: Clarendon Press, 1968 (first edition 1964).

Meyer, Marvin W., ed. *The Ancient Mysteries—A Sourcebook: Sacred Texts of the Mystery Religions of the Ancient World.* San Francisco: Harper and Row, 1987.

Meyer, Marvin, and Richard Smith, eds. *Ancient Christian Magic: Coptic Texts of Ritual Power.* New York: HarperCollins, 1994.

Montgomery, James Alan. *The Samaritans—The Earliest Jewish Sect: Their History, Theology, and Literature.* Eugene OR: Wipf and Stock, 2006 (Philadelphia: John C. Winston Co., 1907).

Moore, George. *The Brook Kerith: A Syrian Story*. Edinburgh: T. Werner Laurie, 1916.

Moule, C. F. D. *The Birth of the New Testament*. Revised edition. London: Adam and Charles Black, 1981 (first edition 1962).

Mowinckel, S. *He That Cometh*. Oxford: Basil Blackwell, 1956.

Neill, Stephen, and Tom Wright. *The Interpretation of the New Testament 1861–1986*. Revised edition. New York: Oxford University Press, 1988 (first edition 1964).

Nineham, D. E., et al. *Historicity and Chronology in the New Testament*. London: SPCK, 1965.

Origen. Trans. and ed. Henry Chadwick. *Contra Celsum*. Revised edition. Cambridge, England: Cambridge University Press, 1965 (first edition 1953).

Osman, Ahmed. *The House of the Messiah: Controversial Revelations on the Historical Jesus*. London: HarperCollins, 1992.

Patai, Raphael. *The Hebrew Goddess*. Revised edition. Detroit: Wayne State University Press, 1990 (New York: KTAV Publishing, 1967).

Patterson, Stephen J., James M. Robinson, and Hans-Gebhard Bethge. *The Fifth Gospel: The Gospel of Thomas Comes of Age*. Harrisburg, PA: Trinity Press International, 1998.

Phillips, Graham. *The Marian Conspiracy: The Hidden Truth about the Holy Grail, the Real Father of Jesus, and the Tomb of the Virgin Mary*. London: Pan Books, 2001 (London: Sidgwick and Jackson, 2000).

Phipps, W. E. *The Sexuality of Jesus: Theological and Literary Perspectives*. New York: Harper and Row, 1973.

———. *Was Jesus Married? The Distortion of Sexuality in the Christian Tradition*. Lanham, MD: University Press of America, 1986 (New York: Harper and Row, 1970).

Picknett, Lynn. *Mary Magdalene: Christianity's Hidden Goddess*. Revised edition. London: Constable, 2004 (first edition 2003).

Picknett, Lynn, and Clive Prince. *The Sion Revelation: Inside the Shadowy World of Europe's Secret Masters*. London: Time Warner, 2006.

———. *The Templar Revelation: Secret Guardians of the True Identity of Christ*. Revised edition. London: Corgi, 2007 (London: Bantam Press, 1997).

———. *The Turin Shroud: How Leonardo da Vinci Fooled History*. Revised edition. London: Little, Brown, 2006. (*Turin Shroud—In Whose Image?* London: Bloomsbury, 1994.)

Pistis Sophia. Trans. G. R. S. Mead. Revised edition. London: J. M. Watkins, 1921 (London: Theosophical Publishing Society, 1896).

Raskin, Jay. *The Evolution of Christs and Christianities*. Philadelphia: Xlibris, 2006.

Richardson, Alan. *The Political Christ*. London: S. C. M. Press, 1973.

Rivkin, Ellis. *What Crucified Jesus?* London: S. C. M. Press, 1986 (Nashville, TN: Abingdon Press, 1984).

Roberts, Alexander, and James Donaldson, eds. *Ante-Nicene Christian Library: Translations of the Writings of the Fathers down to AD 325*, 25 vols. Edinburgh: T. & T. Clark, 1867–97.

Roberts, C. H., ed. *An Unpublished Fragment of the Fourth Gospel in the John Rylands Library*. Manchester, England: Manchester University Press, 1935.

Robertson, J. M. *Christianity and Mythology*. Revised edition. London: Watts & Co., 1910 (first edition 1900).

————. *Pagan Christs: Studies in Comparative Hierology.* Revised edition. London: Watts & Co., 1911 (first edition 1903).

Robinson, James M., ed. *The Nag Hammadi Library in English.* Revised edition. New York: E. J. Brill, 1996 (first edition 1977).

————. *The Secrets of Judas: The Story of the Misunderstood Disciple and His Lost Gospel.* New York: HarperCollins, 2006.

Robinson, John A. T. *Can We Trust the New Testament?* London: Mowbrays, 1977.

————. *Redating the New Testament.* London: S. C. M. Press, 1976.

Romer, John. *Testament: The Bible and History.* London: Michael O'Mara, 1996 (first edition 1988).

Rowley, H. H. *The Servant of the Lord and Other Essays on the Old Testament.* Revised edition. Oxford: Basil Blackwell, 1965 (London: Lutterworth Press, 1952).

Rudolph, Kurt. *Mandaeism.* Leiden: E. J. Brill, 1978.

S., Acharya. *The Christ Conspiracy: The Greatest Story Ever Sold.* Kempton, IL: Adventures Unlimited Press, 1999.

St. Victor, Owen. *Epiphany: The New Age and Its Mysteries from the Time of the Jordan Prophets.* Leuven, Belgium: Sancta Sophia, 1991.

Sanchez, Léopold. "Rennes-le-Château—vrai ou faux? Le trésor du curé," *Le Figaro,* July 7, 2001.

Sanders, E. P. *The Historical Figure of Jesus.* London: Allen Lane, 1993.

————. *Jesus and Judaism.* London: S. C. M. Press, 1985.

————. *Paul and Palestinian Judaism: A Comparison of Patterns of Religion.* London: S. C. M. Press, 1977.

————. *Paul, the Law, and the Jewish People.* London: S. C. M. Press, 1983.

Schechter, S. *Documents of Jewish Sectaries,* 2 vols. Cambridge, England: Cambridge University Press, 1910.

Schoeps, H. J. *Paul: The Theology of the Apostle in the Light of Jewish Religious History.* London: Lutterworth Press, 1961. (*Paulus: Die Theologie des Apostels im Lichte der jüdischen Religionsgeschichte.* Tübingen: J. C. B. Mohr, 1959.)

Schonfield, Hugh J. *The Essene Odyssey.* Shaftesbury, England: Element, 1984.

————. *The Passover Plot: New Light on the History of Jesus.* London: Macdonald/Futura, 1977 (London: Hutchinson, 1965).

————. *The Pentecost Revolution.* London: Hutchinson, 1974.

Schürer, Emil, rev. Geza Vermes and Fergus Millar. *The History of the Jewish People in the Age of Christ (175 BC–AD 135),* 2 vols. Edinburgh: T. & T. Clark, 1973, 1979. (*Geschichte des jüdischen Volkes im Zeitalter Jesu Christi.* Leipzig: Hinrichs, 1886.)

Schweitzer, Albert. *The Mysticism of Paul the Apostle.* London: A. & C. Black, 1931. (*Die Mystik des Apostels Paulus.* Tübingen: J. C. B. Mohr, 1930.)

————. *Paul and His Interpreters: A Critical History.* London: Adam and Charles Black, 1912. (*Geschichte der paulinischen Forschung.* Tübingen: J. C. B. Mohr, 1911.)

————. *The Quest of the Historical Jesus: A Critical Study of Its Progress from Reimarus to Wrede.* Baltimore: Johns Hopkins University Press, 1998. (*Von Reimarus zu Wrede: Eine Geschichte der Leben-Jesu-Forschung.* Tübingen: J. C. B. Mohr, 1906.)

Scobie, Charles H. H. *John the Baptist*. London: S. C. M. Press, 1964.

Sherwin-White, A. N. *Roman Society and Roman Law in the New Testament*. Oxford: Clarendon Press, 1963.

Simmans, Graham. *Jesus After the Crucifixion: From Jerusalem to Rennes-le-Château*. Rochester, VT: Bear and Co., 2007.

Simon, S. P. *L'Or du Temple et le tombeau du Christ: L'Enigme de Rennes-le-Château revelée*. Voreppe, France: Éditions Curandera, 1990.

Smith, Morton. *Clement of Alexandria and a Secret Gospel of Mark*. Cambridge, MA: Harvard University Press, 1973.

————. *Jesus the Magician*. London: Victor Gollancz, 1978.

————. *The Secret Gospel: The Discovery and Interpretation of the Secret Gospel According to Mark*. Updated edition. Wellingborough, England: Aquarian Press, 1985 (New York: Harper and Row, 1973).

Stendahl, Krister, with James H. Charlesworth, eds. *The Scrolls and the New Testament*. New York: Crossroad Publishing, 1992 (New York: Harper and Bros., 1957).

Stewart, Desmond. *The Foreigner: A Search for the First-Century Jesus*. London: Hamish Hamilton, 1981.

Suetonius Tranquillus, Gaius. Trans. Robert Graves, rev. Michael Grant. *The Twelve Caesars*. London: Penguin, 2006 (first edition 1957).

Tabor, James D. *The Jesus Dynasty: Stunning New Evidence about the Hidden History of Jesus*. London: HarperElement, 2006.

Tacitus. Trans. and ed. Michael Grant. *The Annals of Imperial Rome*. Revised edition. London: Penguin, 1996 (first edition 1956).

————. Trans. W. H. Fyfe, rev. and ed. D. S. Levene. *The Histories*. New York: Oxford University Press, 1997 (Oxford, England: Clarendon Press, 1912).

Theissen, Gerd. *The Gospels in Context: Social and Political History in the Synoptic Tradition*. Edinburgh: T. & T. Clark, 1992.

Thiede, Carsten Peter. *The Cosmopolitan World of Jesus: New Findings from Archaeology*. London: SPCK, 2004.

————. *The Earliest Gospel Manuscript? The Qumran Papyrus 7Q5 and Its Significance for New Testament Studies*. Carlisle, England: Paternoster Press, 1992.

van Biema, David. "Is This Jesus's Tomb?" *Time*, February 26, 2007.

Vermes, Geza. *The Dead Sea Scrolls in English*. Revised edition. London: Pelican, 1987 (first edition 1962).

————. *Jesus the Jew: A Historian's Reading of the Gospels*. London: William Collins, 1973.

————. *The Religion of Jesus the Jew*. London: S. C. M. Press, 1993.

————. *Scrolls, Scriptures, and Early Christianity*. New York: T. & T. Clark International, 2005.

Webb, Robert L. *John the Baptizer and Prophet: A Socio-Historical Study*. Sheffield, England: JSOT Press, 1991.

Wilson, A. N. *Jesus*. London: Sinclair-Stevenson, 1992.

————. *Paul: The Mind of the Apostle*. London: Sinclair-Stevenson, 1997.

Wilson, Ian. *Are These the Words of Jesus?: Dramatic Evidence from Beyond the New Testament*. Oxford: Lennard Publishing, 1990.

————. *Jesus: The Evidence*. London: Weidenfeld and Nicolson, 1984.

Wink, Walter. *John the Baptist in the Gospel Tradition*. London: Cambridge University Press, 1968.

Witherington III, Ben. *The Jesus Quest: The Third Search for the Jew of Nazareth.* Carlisle, England: Paternoster Press, 1995.

————. *Women in the Ministry of Jesus: A Study of Jesus' Attitudes to Women and Their Roles as Reflected in His Earthly Life.* New York: Cambridge University Press, 1984.

Yamauchi, Edwin M. *Gnostic Ethics and Mandaean Origins.* Cambridge, MA: Harvard University Press, 1970.

————. *Pre-Christian Gnosticism: A Survey of the Proposed Evidences.* London: Tyndale Press, 1973.

INDEX